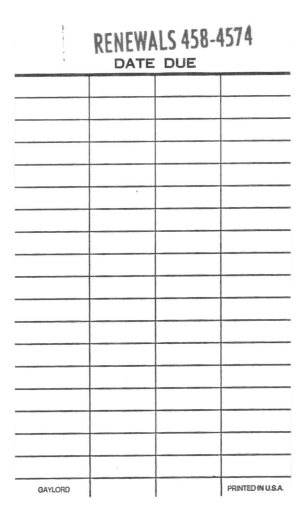

Charting Caribbean Development

Florida A&M University, Tallahassee
Florida Atlantic University, Boca Raton
Florida Gulf Coast University, Ft. Myers
Florida International University, Miami
Florida State University, Tallahassee
University of Central Florida, Orlando
University of Florida, Gainesville
University of North Florida, Jacksonville
University of South Florida,Tampa
University of West Florida, Pensacola

Charting Caribbean Development

Anthony Payne and Paul Sutton

University Press of Florida

Gainesville / Tallahassee / Tampa / Boca Raton
Pensacola / Orlando / Miami / Jacksonville / Ft. Myers

Published in the United Kingdom as part of the Warwick University
Caribbean Studies Series by Macmillan Education Ltd.

Published simultaneously in the United States of America by the
University Press of Florida

Printed in China

06   05   04   03   02   01   6   5   4   3   2   1

Library of Congress Cataloging-in-Publication Data
Payne, Anthony, 1952–.
Charting Caribbean development/Anthony Payne and Paul Sutton.
p. cm.
Includes bibliographical references and index.
ISBN 0-8130-2092-1 (alk. paper)
1. Caribbean Area—Economic policy. 2. Caribbean Area—Economic
conditions—1945–. 3. Caribbean Area—Economic integration. 4. Caribbean
Area—Foreign economic relations. I. Sutton, Paul K. II. Title.
UC151. P39 2001
338.9729 dc21   00-051116

The University Press of Florida is the scholarly publishing agency
for the State University System of Florida, comprising Florida A&M
University, Florida Atlantic University, Florida Gulf Coast University,
Florida International University, Florida State University, University
of Central Florida, University of Florida, University of North
Florida, University of South Florida, and University of
West Florida.

University Press of Florida
15 Northwest 15th Street
Gainesville, FL 32611-2079
http://www.upf.com

Map by TechType

To Jill and Lorraine

Contents

Preface

This book seeks to live up to its title. It charts the shifting politics of development within the countries of the Commonwealth Caribbean over the past forty years – the era of independence for most of these countries. It begins by identifying the main phases in the region's post-independence development strategy and relating them to the various theoretical traditions which have shaped development thinking. The main part of the book then proceeds to focus on the key episodes, strategies and themes which have arisen in the Caribbean's persistent search for a viable development strategy. Different models of development are examined, including liberal, statist, radical and open dependent approaches; different visions of regional integration are assessed, varying in the definition of the Caribbean used and the types of issues incorporated; and different patterns of association with the wider international political economy are explored, highlighting alternative European and North American destinies for the region. As indicated, the analysis focuses principally on the countries of the Commonwealth Caribbean (with particular reference to Jamaica, Trinidad and Tobago, Grenada and the other territories of the Eastern Caribbean), but increasing attention is paid to the wider Caribbean and Latin America as a whole as the changing circumstances of the 1980s and 1990s forced the Commonwealth core of the region to widen both its thinking and sphere of action.

We hope that the book contributes in its own right to the development debate about and within the Caribbean, but we have also been motivated to put it together by our own experience of the lack of a suitable overarching account of Caribbean development with which to introduce students to this region. With that purpose in mind we have deliberately designed the book to suit the now familiar semester system. Accordingly, the introduction and the subsequent ten chapters of the book are designed to act as core readings for the first eleven weeks of the standard twelve-week semester. The last week is left to the tutor and can obviously be used either as revision or as a commentary on events which postdate the writing of this book. At any rate, we hope that new students alighting upon the Caribbean for the first time will appreciate something of the intellectual interest that we have experienced over many years in visiting and studying this part of the world.

We must acknowledge here where some of the following chapters were published in their original versions. Chapters 1 (Sutton) and 2 (Payne) appeared in *Dependency under Challenge: The Political Economy of the Commonwealth Caribbean*, edited by ourselves and published by Manchester University Press in 1984; Chapter 4 (Payne) derives from his book, *Politics in Jamaica*, published by Ian Randle in 1994; Chapter 7 (Payne) was published in an earlier form in *The Political Economy of Regional Cooperation*, edited by Andrew Axline and published by Pinter Publishers in 1994; and Chapter 10 (Sutton) appeared first in the *Journal of Interamerican Studies and World Affairs*, 39, 2, 1997. We have edited the original versions of these arguments wherever necessary, but we must still thank all the editors and publishers cited above for the permission they gave us to use the substance of the material already published under their imprint. As regards the rest, the Introduction (Payne) and Chapters 3 (Payne), 5, 6 and 8 (Sutton) and 9 (Payne) were written specifically for this book.

Finally, we would like once more to thank all of those who over the years have made the publication of this book possible. They include Alistair Hennessy for his support for the project through several missed deadlines; the British Council for funding the Higher Education Links Scheme between the Universities of Hull, Sheffield, Guyana and the West Indies, of which this book forms a part; our many friends and acquaintances all over the Commonwealth Caribbean for allowing us insight and entry into their absorbing culture and society; and our families in Holmfirth and Kirk Ella who have borne the cost of many weekend telephone calls and lost holiday days as the book has taken shape. We dedicate the book to them all, especially Jill and Lorraine.

Anthony Payne
Paul Sutton
Sheffield and Hull

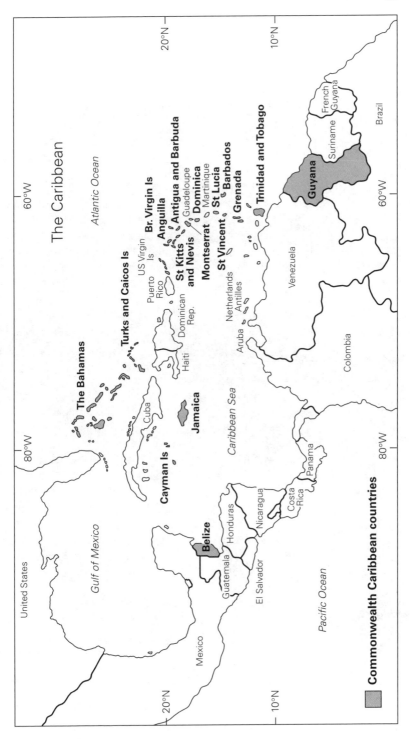

The Caribbean

■ **Commonwealth Caribbean countries**

Introduction
The rise and fall of Caribbean development

The Caribbean has often been said to be one of the richest of laboratories for social scientists. It owes this reputation to a combination of the sheer intensity of its experience of so many of the forces that have made the modern era, on the one hand, and the extraordinary, subtle diversity of its many constituent states and societies, on the other hand. For students of development, the importance of the Caribbean is increased still further by the fact that it is unique in the developing world in belonging to two of the great North-South systems of the twentieth century – the American hemispheric system with the US as metropolis and Latin America and the Caribbean as periphery, and the European imperial system with Britain, France and the Netherlands, and now the European Union (EU), as metropolis and Africa, the Caribbean and the Pacific as periphery. Within the Caribbean the historically English-speaking, or so-called Commonwealth Caribbean territories, sit right at the centre of this matrix of relationships – closely linked to the US by geography, language and increasingly culture, yet deeply tied to Europe by history and sentiment. Such an insight is no more than a starting point, but it does begin to give some sense of the complexity and intractability of the development dilemmas that these particular states and societies have had to grapple with over the past forty years.

The story of Caribbean development over this period has largely consisted of a series of bouts of optimistic endeavour followed by disillusion, although, of late, much of the hope has disappeared. This introduction seeks to provide a map by which the reader can navigate his or her way through the various stages which marked the rise and fall of Caribbean development and thereby locate analytically the specific studies which follow in the succeeding chapters. It discerns four broad phases in Caribbean development, each indicative too of more widespread trends in the unfolding Western debate about development. The first phase was characterised by the confident espousal of the modernising potential of industrialisation and economic diversification in general. The second was marked by the emergence of dependency analysis and the attempted escape from dependency which this mode of thinking almost inevitably generated. The third witnessed the counter-offensive of neo-liberal political economy and the enforced embrace of the market as the dominant philosophy of development. The fourth, and current, phase is overwhelmingly shaped by the forces driving forward globalisation and promoting regionalism in response and poses questions about the continuing capacity of national states and societies to chart their own development course (of whatever nature). Each of these phases is now examined in greater detail before a final section reflects briefly on the Caribbean development debate at the end of the century.

The panacea of modernisation

The concept of development only became a preoccupying concern of Caribbean governments after the end of the Second World War. Although all of the Commonwealth Caribbean states were then still colonies and remained so until the more populous territories became independent in the 1960s, they were led step-by-step through the late 1940s and 1950s towards greater self-government. This process inevitably created expectations on the part of the various peoples that economic improvements would also follow. The result across the region was broadly the same – to seek to develop by diversifying the national economy and by overcoming the traditional Caribbean problem of dependence on agriculture, especially sugar monoculture. In some territories the emergence of more modern export industries located in the mineral sector was the first sign of this new developmental thrust. Trinidad began to take advantage of its position as the only Caribbean country to possess significant reserves of oil, and the Bahamas became a substantial refiner of imported oil. In this period, too, Jamaica and Guyana started to increase their production of bauxite, the ore from which aluminium is made. However, these industries were all initially developed by foreign corporations, which limited their contribution to the economic development of the region. For example, as a consequence of foreign ownership, the lucrative processing of bauxite was undertaken only on a fairly limited scale. All these industries tended also to be highly capital intensive and, although they often came to dominate a country's exports, they generally made little contribution to job creation.

In these circumstances the panacea most widely adopted in the Caribbean in the post-war period as a means of providing the necessary new employment was the promotion of manufacturing industry. The theoretical insights underpinning this strategy were provided by W. Arthur Lewis, the St Lucian economist, in two articles published in

The Caribbean Economic Review in December 1949 and May 1950, and subsequently reprinted in pamphlet form in 1951.[1] His thesis began with a consideration of the region's longstanding role as a producer of primary commodities, but immediately departed from the traditional colonial perspective by demonstrating that agriculture was already unable to support the growing population of the islands and indeed could be made more efficient only if the numbers engaged in it were drastically reduced. Contrary to common belief, he did not see industrialisation as an alternative to agriculture, but rather as 'an essential part of a programme for agricultural improvement'[2] which, by providing new jobs, would take surplus labour off the land. From this point of departure he set out a policy of industrialisation for the Commonwealth Caribbean designed to overcome the dual problems of resources and markets. The region was short of capital, industrial power was expensive and the available raw material base limited, but wage rates were low by the standards of the developed world. Many of the 'most favourable industries' which the islands could establish fairly cheaply were thus based not on the use of local raw materials but on the processing of imported inputs.[3] As for markets for these products, the fact that the territories individually were too poor and too small necessitated the establishment of a regional customs union as an essential prelude to any vigorous policy of industrialisation.

But in Lewis's mind this was not enough and was certainly not central: regional import substitution would account for only a small part of the industrial output necessary to generate full employment. Export-oriented industrialisation was the main requirement. The final part of his argument therefore addressed the difficulties faced by the Commonwealth Caribbean in breaking into established export markets. Here the key was not to attempt to establish new external trade channels, but rather to persuade manufacturers who were already selling in overseas markets actually to locate their plants in the Caribbean. This in turn required a number of governmental initiatives in direct contravention of the inherited *laissez-faire* economic philosophy of the region. For Lewis, industrialisation was like 'a snowball': once started, it would move of its own momentum and get bigger and bigger as it went along. To attract foreign manufacturers and thus get the snowball rolling, he recommended the implementation of a package of investment incentives modelled upon recent Puerto Rican experience – the provision of basic infrastructural services, the establishment of special Industrial Development Corporations and Development Banks, the enactment of appropriate policies of protection via tariffs and quotas and the proclamation of 'tax holidays' for newly-established industries, including, in particular, the remission of taxes on imported raw materials and machinery.[4] Eventually, in Lewis's view, the inflow of foreign investment would produce sufficient profits, generate sufficient local savings and transmit sufficient skills to local people to set in motion self-sustaining growth.

This prescription for industrial development had an immediate impact on newly-emerging Commonwealth Caribbean governments. A period of what Lewis himself referred to as 'wooing and fawning upon'[5] foreign capitalists followed the publication and dissemination of his analysis. With the appropriate institutional and legal apparatus in place, foreign capital responded to the entreaties of the region's governments and flowed into the area in substantial amounts, bringing in its wake several highly visible manufacturing industries. By 1967 manufacturing contributed 15 per cent of the gross domestic product of Jamaica and 16 per cent in the case of Trinidad, whilst the figures for Guyana and Barbados were 13 per cent and 9 per cent respectively.[6] However, the reality was that the industries established were largely 'final-touch' enterprises, based on the assembly of imported inputs, which had relatively little value added and generally failed to penetrate export markets, in part because governments frequently made it too easy for local manufacturers to live off their domestic markets by instituting extensive 'negative lists' of imports. There certainly did not emerge as extensively as Lewis had originally hoped a thriving export sector geared to overseas markets. Moreover, the industries that were set up produced few jobs and were often itinerant in their commitment to the Caribbean, finding it profitable, once the incentive plan had expired, to move their operations to other locales offering a new package of inducements. Some of the smaller islands in the Leewards and Windwards benefited from this on occasion, but the Caribbean economy as a whole lost.

The other new enterprise into which the Caribbean moved in a major way in the 1950s and 1960s was tourism. In some territories this was heralded, even more than manufacturing, as the road to prosperity, especially after the Cuban revolution in 1959 took out of the market one hitherto favoured tourist destination. Jamaica, Barbados and the Bahamas all moved to develop the necessary infrastructure and policies to widen their tourist appeal, to the point where tourist income soon became critical to their economic stability. However, the trouble with tourist development was that it was extremely vulnerable to recession in the developed economies and to bad publicity at any time. In the particular case of the Caribbean, where the industry was geared from the outset to a particularly affluent sector of North American and European society, it was able to compete only by maintaining the highest standards of accommodation and hospitality. This meant that foreign capital and foreign imports, especially of food, underwrote the tourist industry, producing the diseconomies of inflated import bills and extensive profit repatriation. To a considerable extent, therefore, the industry became an enclave within the Caribbean economy, having few linkages with, and contributing little to, the development of other sectors.

These various attempts to diversify the economies of the Commonwealth Caribbean countries were generally quite successful in the 1950s and 1960s in the single matter of engendering economic growth. Several territories, notably Jamaica and Trinidad and Tobago but also the Bahamas, grew at an annual rate of about 5 per cent during this period, which is, conventionally speaking, a good economic performance. What was less certain was whether the regional economy had been shifted to a new level of development as a result. In an original and highly influential analysis of the condition of the Caribbean economy published in 1965, William Demas, then the head of the Economic Planning Division of the Trinidad government, pointed to two important weaknesses in the post-war pattern of economic growth in the Commonwealth Caribbean region.[7] First, the level of unemployment and underemployment, which had been the main motive force behind Lewis's thinking, was thought actually to have grown; second, the use made of local resources in the process of growth had been negligible. Demas argued that the critical constraint upon the development prospects of the Caribbean economies was their small size, defined in terms of both land area and population.[8] The smallness of the domestic market, he reasoned, imposed sharp limits on the process of import-substitution industrialisation and thus removed the option of balanced growth, incorporating a roughly equal mixture of export promotion and import substitution. For the small Caribbean territories this path of development could most satisfactorily be secured by regional economic integration, which would not only eliminate excess capacity in existing manufacturing industry but also stimulate investment in new industries which would become economically feasible for the first time in the Commonwealth Caribbean on the basis of the expanded market. He did stress that 'integration may often not remove the necessity to seek export markets outside the region',[9] but no one was in any doubt that, in Demas's mind, the key to the strategy of economic integration was the pursuit of import substitution on a regional basis.

The Caribbean Free Trade Association (CARIFTA), when it was established in 1968 between all the territories of the Commonwealth Caribbean, was modelled directly on Demas's thinking. From the outset the new regime liberalised the great bulk of intra-regional trade, thereby extending the size of the 'home' market for the region's various light industries. Intra-CARIFTA trade in manufactures increased as planned, to the point where, by 1972, Trinidad was consigning 34 per cent of its exports of manufactured goods to other CARIFTA countries, Jamaica 49 per cent, Barbados 40 per cent and Guyana 66 per cent – all very sizeable proportions.[10] The weakness underlying these figures was that the 'value added' in the production of manufactured goods in the Caribbean was relatively small. In consequence, as Demas himself was eventually forced to admit, a great deal of intra-Caribbean trade 'from a strictly economic point of view may not be all that beneficial to the member countries who are exporting.'[11] Indeed, by the beginning of the 1970s a growing awareness of the limitations of CARIFTA was beginning to develop, even among the officials of the integration movement of whom Demas was by then the chief. This gave rise, in turn, to a deeper questioning of the whole postwar Caribbean modernisation strategy, of which regional free trade was, after all, no more than a neat extension. Indeed, it was the Commonwealth Caribbean Regional Secretariat, the administrative agency of the integration movement, which in 1972 admitted that, in many essential respects, the post-war era of fast growth represented:

> a continuation of the centuries-old pattern of West Indian economy – growth without development; growth accompanied by imbalances and distortions; growth generated from outside rather than within; growth without the fullest possible use of West Indian manpower, entrepreneurial, capital and natural resources; growth resting on a foreign rather than indigenous technological base; and growth accompanied by imported consumption patterns.[12]

It was also increasingly recognised in these official circles that the structure of post-war development strategy had actually served to exacerbate, rather than ameliorate, divisions within the region. Caribbean economies had in effect become competitor economies in this period: they produced broadly the same commodities, they wanted to attract the same foreign investors, and they appealed to the same would-be tourists. There was thus no easy route to development to be found simply by making a regional connection.

Dependency under challenge

Even as these weaknesses of the modernisation approach were being exposed and debated by the region's governments and their advisers, an alternative analysis of the development predicament of the

Commonwealth Caribbean was being forged within the University of the West Indies (UWI), whose campuses were located in Jamaica, Trinidad and Barbados. In a seminal review of Demas's contribution to the Caribbean development debate, Lloyd Best, then a lecturer in economics at the St Augustine campus in Trinidad, argued that the basic fallacy of his theory was its almost exclusive emphasis on 'natural' variables, such as size, as opposed to 'societal', and therefore 'manipulable', policy variables.[13] In his view, Demas had failed to demonstrate that 'smallness necessarily places economies at a disadvantage in the exploitation of their own "endowment" of resources'.[14] The bulk of the explanation had instead to come from 'systematic examination of the instruments that control' economies.[15] In this vision the concept of dependency was seen to be the key. Thus New World Associates[16] in describing the Guyanese economy, Clive Thomas[17] in analysing the monetary and financial arrangements of the Caribbean, and Alister McIntyre[18] in assessing the trade policy of the region all felt it necessary to begin by stressing the dependence of the Caribbean economy on the rest of the world: for markets and supplies, transfers of income and capital, banking and financial services, business and technical skills and 'even for ideas about themselves'.[19] These early insights grew into a whole school of thought characterised by the theory of plantation economy. Developed initially by Best, in collaboration with the Canadian economist Kari Levitt, the theory consisted of an historical and structural analysis of the development of plantation economy in the Caribbean from the seventeenth century to the post-1945 era.[20] Whilst conceding the achievement of economic growth during the 1950s and 1960s, Best nevertheless argued that many of the classic features of a pure plantation economy were replicated in this modern period. Like other Latin American dependency writers, he took the view that the transnational corporations, which had come to play a growing role in the Caribbean economy since the end of the Second World War, served just as effectively to integrate the region into the metropolitan economic system as had the joint-stock trading companies of a former era.

Other members of the so-called New World Group formed within the University around Best took up these arguments and proceeded to refine the intellectual basis of what was to become a new left politics for the Commonwealth Caribbean. Among them, Brewster set out perhaps the most rigorous definition of economic dependence, describing it as 'a lack of capacity to manipulate the operative elements of an economic system'.[21] For their part, Beckford drew further attention to the multiple 'underdevelopment biases' of plantation agriculture,[22] Girvan analysed the emergence of mineral-export enclave economies in the Caribbean, with particular emphasis on the bauxite industry,[23] and Jefferson contributed a wide-ranging survey of the post-war Jamaican economy.[24] A series of UWI studies of regional integration also set out a more radical view of regional economic integration based upon the notion of 'production integration'.[25] These various arguments collectively constituted a powerful critique of the condition of economic dependency within the Commonwealth Caribbean, undermining to a very considerable degree the intellectual credibility of the conventional modernisation strategy hitherto pursued by regional governments. Indeed, their vivid excoriation of this strategy as 'industrialisation by invitation' is a memorable aphorism in its own right.[26] Yet the New World approach was not without its own limitations, which related mainly to its structuralist methodology. Part of the problem was its exaggeration of the extent of the 'exceptionalism' enjoyed by the Caribbean from the social and political characteristics of other developing societies;[27] part derived from an over-economistic bias which obscured the changing political interests and patterns of collaboration which permitted the essence of plantation economy to survive without radical transformation;[28] and part reflected the Group's failure to go on to develop 'an *operational* model of economic development ... [and] ... by operational, I mean "likely to succeed in real world conditions" '.[29]

This last point was particularly important. The criticism was made by Courtney Blackman, a former junior member of the New World Group, when he was grappling with 'real world' dependency as Governor of the Central Bank of Barbados in 1980. It highlighted the fact that the central, and highly passionate, argument in the politics of the Commonwealth Caribbean throughout the decade of the 1970s was focused upon the appropriate political economy of development to be pursued by the governments of the independent states in the light of the perceived deficiencies of the Puerto Rican model. This debate was shaped by the ideas of the Caribbean dependency school, but it drew its political urgency from the severe economic difficulties created across the region by the massive oil price rises generated in 1973–4 by the action of the Organization of Petroleum Exporting Countries (OPEC). With the exception of Trinidad, every other country was faced with hugely increased import bills, which they were unable to meet with their earnings from commodity exports, light manufacturing industries and tourism. In this situation, the validity of the orthodox model of development came increasingly under question in political discussion and, in a number of countries, including Trinidad, the state was pushed into a position of greater involvement in the management of the economy. The thinking generally, born as much of desperation as ideology, was that the various countries of the region had to negotiate better terms for themselves in their dealings with the international economy and that the state, rather than the local business class, had to assume primary responsibility for executing that task. In short, dependency was now under challenge.

Accordingly, several countries began to search around for new strategies of development. No clear pattern and no precise direction of change emerged, although the broad trend was to reject the traditional order. For example, in Guyana in 1970 the government of Forbes Burnham declared its commitment to 'co-operative socialism'; in Jamaica in 1974 the Michael Manley administration announced its attachment to the principles of 'democratic socialism'; and, most dramatically of all, in March 1979 in Grenada the existing corrupt regime was overthrown by force and the People's Revolutionary Government (PRG), led by Maurice Bishop, was set up to popular acclaim. Burnham, Manley and Bishop also marched the Caribbean into the Third World coalition and the active embrace of organisations like the Group of 77 and the Non-Aligned Movement. Regional integration was 'deepened' with the conversion of CARIFTA into the Caribbean Community and Common Market (CARICOM); clear positions of support were enunciated for the concept of a 'New International Economic Order'; and effective negotiations were undertaken with the European Community on a new form of association agreement which culminated in the signing of the Lomé Convention in 1975. Contrary to the many simplistic interpretations advanced at the time in the US and elsewhere, these changes did not represent the victory, real or prospective, of communist or socialist politics in the Caribbean. New and radical ideas were abroad, and some governments were prepared to listen and be persuaded. Several leading New World economists took up positions as technocrats, either in the government of their own countries or in international development agencies. New friends, such as the Castro regime in Cuba, were also making their entreaties and achieving some inroads. But, in the end, rather less was changed than perhaps many had expected and some had hoped. Guyanese 'co-operative socialism' degenerated into a programme to entrench in power by ever more unpleasant means the ruling party elite and Jamaican 'democratic socialism' stepped back when it reached the bounds of reformism. In general, the much vaunted ideological pluralism of the Commonwealth Caribbean in the 1970s concealed only different techniques for 'living with dependency'.[30]

The one exception to this was the Grenadian revolution which turned out to be genuine, if ultimately misguided, in its endeavour to break with the capitalist liberal-democratic model of development. By comparison with the structuralist strand, the other major element within Latin American (and Western) dependency theory, the so-called neo-Marxist approach, developed relatively late in the Commonwealth Caribbean. Part of the problem was that Marxism, more generally, had no historical roots in the region, either as the basis of intellectual commitment or of political praxis. The study of Marxism had no place within the British colonial education tradition and was slow to take off even within the University of the West Indies, itself by origin an overseas college of the University of London. This meant that Caribbean intellectuals who espoused Marxism, such as C. L. R. James and George Padmore, had tended to feel it preferable to leave the region in order to find wider opportunities to practise their political beliefs. Similarly, Marxist political parties were historically unsuccessful in the region in the colonial era and the rare politician who did embrace Marxism, such as Cheddi Jagan in colonial British Guiana, was swiftly isolated by a combination of internal and external opposition. Yet, in the turbulent years of the 1970s, some strands of neo-Marxist theorising did flow into the region from other parts of the world. The most able West Indian political economist to move in this direction was Clive Thomas. He had been a founder member of the New World Group but, following a period working outside the region in Tanzania, he acquired a wider vision of the internationalisation of capitalism and a greater awareness of class and politics in the construction of underdevelopment. Above all, he drew attention in his writing to the failure of an indigenous capitalist class to create its own material base for selfreproduction in small societies with limited markets like those of the Caribbean, and to the corresponding existence of dominant social classes who stood to benefit from the maintenance of existing patterns of underdevelopment. 'That is why', Thomas concluded, 'we have argued time and again that the historical options of these economies are limited either to a comprehensive socialist strategy for transforming the productive forces and liberating the political and social order, or to the continuation of the present neo-colonial mode'.[31] In this respect Thomas was, of course, reiterating in the Caribbean context the 'stagnation or socialism' thesis of André Gunder Frank and the neoMarxist development of underdevelopment school as a whole.

However, other neo-Marxists within the Caribbean did not build creatively on Thomas's analysis. Rather than focusing upon theoretical and academic work, they tended to move more into active political opposition to their respective governments and, in so doing, they often found themselves discovering traditional Marxism-Leninism. Several – though not Clive Thomas – came to espouse the 'non-capitalist path of development', or the 'path of socialist orientation' as it was sometimes called.[32] This theory posited that the construction of socialism was not dependent on the prior emergence and full development of capitalism: the task could be begun before the material and productive prerequisites for socialist transition were available and the capitalist phase thereby effectively bypassed or interrupted. The key requirement was a period of socialist orientation, built upon a broad class alliance involving the proletariat, the semi-proletarian masses, the peasants, the revolutionary or democratic strata of the petty bourgeoisie and even the progressive patriotic elements of the emerging national bourgeoisie. During the 1970s this doctrine became the official philosophy of left-wing opposition groups such as the Workers' Party of Jamaica and assorted small radical parties in other parts of the region and it came also to shape the thinking and actions of the leading elements of the PRG in Grenada after their seizure of power in 1979. In this latter context, and amidst an external environment marked by cumulative pressure, even destabilisation, the strategy proved to be too rigid and it disintegrated in 1983 into bitter internal conflict which eventually led to a tragic and bloody *dénouement*. The collapse of the Grenadian revolution brought to an end the radical phase in Caribbean development and consigned to the unthinkable all forms of Marxism, of whatever type, across the whole of the Commonwealth Caribbean region.

The neo-liberal revolution

The 1970s were thus not only 'crisis years' for the Caribbean political economy: they were years of failure too. It could fairly be said that the radical experiments initiated in Guyana, Jamaica and Grenada were each in different ways checked and ultimately brought to book by the hostility to their ambitions shown by US-based multinational corporations and the various agencies of the US state. Dependency theory had identified correctly the core elements of the international capitalist system which would respond to challenge, but it had not thought through the politics by which such challenges were to be sustained. As a result, as far as the ordinary people of Guyana, Jamaica and Grenada were concerned, the most tangible results of the turn to the left in their countries were economic decline and political violence. In these circumstances it is not easy to assess how Caribbean development would have been reconfigured during the 1980s if the region could have been somehow left to its own devices. No strong 'model' of development remained, other than that of the national development state in Trinidad and Tobago. But this was manifestly a special case and even in its own terms it had yet to lay the basis of stable economic growth and indeed ran into real problems of its own by the middle of that decade. In retrospect, the beginnings of a vacuum in the Caribbean development debate can be discerned. It was not noticed at the time because any options seemingly open to Caribbean states were quickly overlaid, indeed overwhelmed, by the interests and actions of the US.

The context was the ending of that unquestioned hegemony over the world order, the *Pax Americana*, enjoyed by the US since the end of the Second World War. The reaction against this in the US came in the form of an attempt to reassert control of the system during the course of the 1980s by means of the political economy of Reaganism. Feeding upon a popular emotional rejection of the new realities of US power, or 'weaknesses', which President Jimmy Carter had asked the US people to confront, President Ronald Reagan, coming into office at the beginning of 1981, offered the twin prospects of 'militarism' and 'monetarism'. The former involved a major re-arming of the US military machine designed to allow the US once again to 'walk tall' on the world stage. The latter was premised upon increasing profit margins, weakening trade unions, eliminating inflation through the adoption of monetarist macro-economic management and boosting growth by means of supply-side economics. It also sought to impose the same neo-liberal economic doctrine within the multilateral financial institutions in which the US voice was still critical. In other words, the thinking behind the Reagan strategy, which was a good deal more clever than was initially realised, sought to re-create behind the rhetoric of the 'Second Cold War' a new mixture of consent and coercion comparable in effect to that which had characterised the original establishment of *Pax Americana* after 1945.[33]

In the final analysis, the US was not able fully to reconstitute its control of the world order. But, as far as the Caribbean was concerned, the US did succeed during the 1980s in reshaping the agenda of politics and political economy to the point where it was able to lay down the parameters of what could be done and even what could be articulated. In accordance with the broad tenets of the new neo-liberalism, its main goal in respect of development was to create in the region a growing number of market-based economies capable of competing successfully in international export markets. This was deemed to require less reliance on statism, market intervention and import substitution than had been the norm in the development strategies deployed in the Commonwealth Caribbean, in particular during the 1960s and 1970s. The tools to be deployed by the US to bring about this economic revolution were the traditional ones of the carrot and the stick. The carrot was announced by Reagan when he unveiled the Caribbean Basin Initiative (CBI) in a speech before the Organization of American States (OAS) in early 1982; the stick was wielded in the various structural adjustment packages imposed on several Caribbean governments during the decade by the actions of the International Monetary Fund (IMF), the World Bank and the US Agency for International Development (USAID).

The two aspects of the policy might have had a developmental impact if they had genuinely operated in tandem. In practice, the CBI was crippled from the start. As set out in Reagan's OAS speech, it offered considerable inducements to virtually all states in the Caribbean Basin (the US-favoured definition of the Caribbean), including one-way free trade for most exports, increased economic aid, tax incentives to encourage US entrepreneurs to invest in the region and technical assistance to the private sector. As eventually passed by Congress following intensive lobbying by special interests in the US, it was described even by *Business Week* as 'more a symbolic gesture than the ambitious program for economic stimulus' originally signalled.[34] In particular, a wide range of items, including textiles and garments, petroleum products, frozen citrus juices and leather goods, were excluded from preferential treatment. Yet, despite the fact that the US market had not been significantly opened up in a way likely to stimulate Caribbean production and exports, the IMF/World Bank/USAID nexus still adhered rigidly to the need for structural adjustment. In essence, these institutions offered financial assistance to help with balance of payments difficulties, but insisted on the implementation of policies designed to adjust economies in such a way as to bring them back into financial balance. The favoured measures, which derived directly from fashionable neo-liberal doctrine, were always the same: the liberalisation of foreign exchange and import controls, the devaluation of the currency and the deflation of domestic demand. After absorbing this medicine, the economy in question was then to be returned to the international market-place, supposedly ready and able to export its way back to solvency.

Commonwealth Caribbean states widely followed this prescription during the 1980s. Indeed, the CARICOM heads of government went so far, at their summit in the Bahamas in 1984, as to issue the so-called Nassau Understanding, in which they endorsed structural adjustment as 'a conscious shift to a new development path'.[35] Why? The reality is that there was little alternative. The international recession of 1980–2 severely reduced demand for a number of the region's main exports – particularly bauxite, petroleum products and sugar – and lowered the number of tourists visiting the islands. It created, in effect, three crises in one in nearly all Caribbean economies: a balance of payments crisis, a fiscal crisis and a debt crisis. Desperate for emergency financial support, governments of all political hues turned to the IMF and its associated bodies. The conservative government of Edward Seaga in Jamaica (1980–9) espoused the ethic of structural adjustment with enthusiasm. Others were driven more reluctantly into the hands of the international financial institutions. Even the PRG in Grenada turned to the Fund for support in its final months. In another case, that of Guyana, the successor regime following Burnham's death in 1985 was forced to implement its own programme of structural adjustment, having, as it were, to prove its credentials to the financial institutions before IMF funds were released. Even oil-rich Trinidad and Tobago was not immune. The new National Alliance for Reconstruction (NAR) government which came into office in 1986 was faced with severe economic problems caused by collapsing oil prices and it too was forced to appeal to the IMF before the end of 1988. It is also highly significant that, on his re-election to office in Jamaica in February 1989, Michael Manley, renowned in the 1970s for his commitment to social democratic reform, endorsed and deepened the liberal market-oriented economic policies of the outgoing Seaga regime. To many observers, it was this shift of position on the part of Manley that most effectively symbolised the new consensus on economic issues that had emerged in the region during the decade.

In all these settings, the social costs of such market-friendly policies, measured in terms of unemployment, inflation and sharply declining living standards generally, were immense, provoking riots in Jamaica (for all that, under Seaga, it was the Caribbean 'showcase' of the neo-liberal revolution), underpinning widespread industrial action in Guyana, and generating a mood of popular indifference to the fate of the government in Trinidad when it was suddenly and unexpectedly faced with a 'coup' in 1990. The likelihood of these political effects was always understood by the US and other proponents of structural adjustment; the point was that the policies were supposed to engender economic growth, which would, in time, trickle down to the masses. At the end of the 1980s, it was apparent that this type of open dependent development had only been achieved at best, and then only partially, in Barbados and some of the smaller islands of the Eastern Caribbean. These were, however, achievements against the trend. The regional economy as a whole still faced fundamental structural problems associated with the character of its production base as well as with the distribution of its economic assets. As a study by Policy Alternatives for the Caribbean and Central America (PACCA) noted, 'export diversification might reduce the degree of Caribbean vulnerability to fluctuation in the international economy, but it can do little to foster a structure of production that can withstand the volatility of world markets, for decisions as to what is best to produce and at what price still remain external'.[36] The observation is a telling one. The very fact that, against the general gloomy trend, some of the smallest Caribbean economies floated their way to prosperity during the decade by expanding tourism and embracing the offshore economy generally serves only to reinforce PACCA's general *dependentista*-style argument.

In retrospect, what is striking about the Caribbean's embrace of neo-liberalism in the 1980s is that the intellectual driving force behind the region's development strategy came from outside the region for the first time in the post-1945 period. This is not to suggest that the ideas of Lewis or Demas or members of the New World Group were wholly indigenous to the Caribbean. No body of thought in political economy is ever that contained. But, whatever their external connections and sources of inspiration, they did offer a distinctively Caribbean variant of a particular developmental approach. Put another way, it is plausible to claim that there was both an authentic and a meaningful Caribbean dynamic to the strategy of development being pursued by the region up to the end of the 1970s. Thereafter the sad truth is that the script was largely being written elsewhere. Caribbean intellectuals neither sought to re-theorise the political economy of liberalisation as it applied either to their own countries or the region as a whole; nor did they take it upon themselves to try to undermine in any fundamental way the major imported neo-liberal orthodoxies. Critical analyses of the economic and social impact of structural adjustment did appear and had their impact, especially in drawing attention to the peculiarly harsh costs imposed by such programmes on women.[37] Yet they broke little, if any, new theoretical ground and certainly did not succeed in charting any sort of realistic alternative course of action for Caribbean states in the critical arena of national and regional economic management.

Globalisation and regionalism

The paradox at the heart of the many tensions generated by the US attempt to 'restructure' the Caribbean during the 1980s was that these were replaced, not by relief, but rather by a new and almost tangible sense of beleaguerment when that political interest was suddenly withdrawn right at the end of the decade. This was arguably even more alarming – for was it worse to be ignored than intimidated? The reality was that, for the US, other priorities had emerged – in eastern Europe, the Middle East and elsewhere – with the result that the Caribbean was downgraded. Perhaps in any case, the US considered that its job there. had been well enough done. Even though structural adjustment had manifestly not launched the Commonwealth Caribbean or indeed any other part of the region upon the path of self-sustaining export-led growth, most states had come to embrace Western economic and political norms. The one significant exception in the wider region, Cuba, was grappling with its own crisis of political identity, courtesy of the dramatic changes taking place in the Soviet Union, and was in no position to offer either example or resources to the rest of the Caribbean. Accordingly, the administration of George Bush, coming into office in Washington in 1989, was disinclined to give special attention to the Caribbean, preferring to take Latin America as a whole as its policy framework and initiating its Enterprise for the Americas Initiative (EAI) in mid-1990.

Yet, within the Commonwealth Caribbean itself, the political mood was far from complacent. The experience of the 1980s was seen to have brought to light several alarming prospects. First, there was the possibility that individually impoverished Caribbean states would be driven to function as little more than offshore platforms of the US economy, utterly dependent on US investment, US market opportunities and US tax and tariff regimes. Second, the Commonwealth Caribbean's traditional commitment to democratic forms of politics seemed to be increasingly vulnerable, with ever more desperate attempts to find economic growth in the international market-place inevitably bringing greater, and perhaps ultimately intolerable, pressures to bear on social and political stability. Third, the very security of a number of Caribbean states appeared at risk, with the temptations offered by collaboration with the powerful and wealthy drugs barons who wanted to use the region as a transhipment zone en route to the US presenting a constant invitation to corruption, lawlessness and even political take-over. A. N. R. Robinson, the then prime minister of Trinidad and Tobago, warned his fellow CARICOM heads of government at their summit meeting in July 1989 that, unless something was done to address the situation, 'the Caribbean could be in danger of becoming a backwater, separated from the main current of human advance into the twenty-first century'.[38] As already indicated – and as Robinson himself was made aware when he was captured and held hostage during the 'coup' attempt in Trinidad a year later – this was far from being the worst-case scenario. Nevertheless, to their credit, Caribbean leaders responded to his challenge and took a decision to set up the West Indian Commission of wise men and women, headed by Shridath Ramphal, the Guyanese former secretary-general of the Commonwealth. The Commission was charged with the momentous task of presenting a report to CARICOM governments by 1992, the year of the 500th anniversary of the arrival of Columbus, on the options facing the region in the future.[39]

The Commission's massive and impressive report, entitled *Time for Action*, was a genuinely indigenous response to changing times and generated many important debates within the region. Two in particular command attention here – one driven by external events, the other shaped by the Commission itself. The first focused on the question of the Commonwealth Caribbean's 'location' in the world order. This set the region's growing connections with the US economy and the prospect of entry at some stage into the North American Free Trade Area (NAFTA), instituted in January 1994 as an outgrowth of the EAI project initiated at the beginning of the decade by George Bush, against its longstanding link with Europe and the need to maintain the essence of the Lomé accords in the negotiations with the EU that were due before 2000. In the eyes of many, this posed the uncertainty, and risk, of forging necessary new relationships against the complacency, and risk, of trying to hold on to old ones. More controversially, it could be said to separate the region's geopolitical and geoeconomic future from its past. In the real world of negotiation, the choice was not so stark since there was manifestly a strong argument for endeavouring to delay for as long as possible the need to choose, even if ultimately relocation in the emerging transregional political economy of 'Caribbean America' seemed unavoidable. It was also the case that, by the early 1990s, both the US government and EU governments were relatively indifferent to the fate of the Caribbean. The former made a commitment at a hemispheric summit in Miami in late 1994 to bring into being a Free Trade Area of the Americas (FTAA) by 2005, but only seemed to be concerned in the first instance with opening up NAFTA to Chile, and in general was forced by Congressional suspicion to proceed slowly on the FTAA front. The latter were increasingly preoccupied during the 1990s with their dealings with eastern and central Europe and looked to end, or revise, their Lomé connections. In addition, the Caribbean found that, as over bananas in particular, it sometimes got caught up awkwardly and painfully in US–EU trade conflicts. Here the central issue was the future of the traditional preferential access enjoyed within EU markets by bananas produced in Jamaica and the tiny Windward Islands in the face of fierce pressure to bring about a fully liberalised trading regime for the commodity. The outcome was a protracted struggle in and around the new World Trades Organisation (WTO) during the course of which the prospects of the Caribbean banana industry steadily deteriorated.

The second debate concerned the nature of the Caribbean's 'sub-regionalist' response to the trend towards new regionalist centres of power in the global economy like the EU and NAFTA. The West Indian Commission sought to resolve the situation by proposing in its final report a simultaneous 'deepening' and 'widening' of CARICOM. However, its key proposal in the first regard – the establishment of a permanent Caribbean Commission of three former political leaders designed to drive forward the internal integration process – was rejected by the heads of government. They acknowledged the problem that CARICOM needed a stronger executive agency to see that decisions taken at the regular summit meetings were indeed subsequently implemented, but fell back on a feeble compromise whereby a so-called CARICOM Bureau, composed of past, present and future chairs of the heads-of-government summit, be set up and charged with filling the vacuum that had been detected. As a consequence, CARICOM of itself did not take the big step forward demanded by the West Indian Commission and, for all of its eventual embrace of the concept of a single regional market, it has certainly not become in the 1990s the decisive agency for charting the region's future development strategy that is so badly needed at the regional level in the English-speaking Caribbean. What has been set up is the Commission's solution to the 'widening' dilemma, namely a new body called the Association of Caribbean States (ACS). This came into being in July 1994 and is made up of twenty-five states of the Caribbean Basin, thereby including the Central American countries and the three big South American states whose shores are washed by the Caribbean Sea, Colombia, Mexico and Venezuela. It was a promising initiative and was consistent with an analysis which saw the need for the formation of a region-wide organisation which had the potential, in the short term, to act as a negotiating body with both the US and the EU on trade matters and, in the long term, to build a genuine framework for development across the whole of the Basin. However, as events transpired, the ACS was set up with too few resources and too weak an institutional basis and it has yet to make much of an impact in any field.[40]

The West Indian Commission report stands, nevertheless, as an honest appraisal of the situation faced by the Commonwealth Caribbean at the beginning of the 1990s and, in particular, of the difficulties involved in designing effective strategies for avoiding marginalisation within a changing world order. As one 'appreciative critic' put it, the report was 'literally a source of wisdom on everything under the sun: from currency to culture; from science to human rights; from exports to cricket; from CARICOM to gender issues'.[41] More of its many recommendations deserved to have been implemented than was the case. Perhaps the main disappointment was its treatment of the appropriate model of national development in the region. The Commission was largely uninnovative in this matter, broadly accepting neo-liberal doctrines, either out of belief or perceived necessity. Moreover, for all of its recognition of the unrelenting nature of the process of global change, it can be seen in retrospect, as Hilbourne Watson later suggested, to have been 'not sufficiently aware of the implications of the contradictions of globalization and restructuring for the world economy and the international state system as a whole and for the future development of the Caribbean in particular'.[42]

This argument is important and needs to be developed. It relates directly to the ending of US hegemony over the world order mentioned earlier in the context of the rise of Reaganism. Bush's EAI became the seminal statement of US economic policy towards the Americas during the 1990s, giving early insight into the new significance being attached to hemispheric leadership in at least some official US perceptions of that country's role in international affairs after the Cold War. Put another way, it constituted one of the first major policy responses of the US to its own global hegemonic decline and should be interpreted as evidence of a growing realisation in Washington that the US was no longer able to shape on its own the rules of a consensual world order and needed to initiate its own form of regionalist project in the Americas as one of the bases from which to organise its own future participation in the new world order. Linked to this interpretation is a wider argument about globalisation. This suggests that, with the ending of US hegemony, control of the world order has slipped beyond the capacity of any single state and perhaps even any group of states. Moving into this vacuum and then both inspiring and drawing sustenance from the ascendancy of neo-liberal ideas during the Reagan years, a 'transnational managerial class' or 'an international business civilisation' has come to the fore, based in the major private banks and global corporations.[43] Under its auspices a genuine global economy, grounded in production and finance, has been created, replacing the former Bretton Woods international economy premised upon exchange relations between national economies. This change contains within it other technological and organisational features, such as robotisation, the dematerialisation of production and post-Fordism, which are much discussed in the literature. Nevertheless, the formative aspect of the new global political economy is seen to be the structural power of internationally mobile capital.[44] States are not rendered irrelevant, as some 'hyper-globalisation' theorists suggest,[45] but they do now have to recognise the power not only of other states and inter-state organisations, on which international relations analysis has traditionally focused, but also of international capital, the banks and the foreign exchange markets, all of which constantly scrutinise what states are doing and have the means, by either bestowing or withdrawing their favour, to force them to adopt economic policies appropriate to capitalist interests.

This argument, even in its weaker form, changes the way we have to think about the political economy of all states and it certainly changes the political economy of development. The process has been described within the field of international political economy as the internationalisation or transnationalisation of the state, by which is meant, simply put, the adjustment of national political practices to the exigencies of the global economy.[46] In other words, the argument is that all states – the strong and the weak, the ex-hegemon as well as the would-be developer – now have to react to the pressures of global production, choosing broadly between an offensive strategy which takes on the challenge and usually gives some support to the competitive thrust of national industries, and a defensive strategy which enshrines protection and seeks to effect at least a partial withdrawal from world competition in some sectors. The formulation of the choice in this way has distinct echoes, of course, of old development debates. As we have seen, Caribbean development strategies have oscillated between these options for more than thirty years. In that sense, it can perhaps be claimed that globalisation theory offers little of a conceptual nature that takes the discussion beyond the core tenets of dependency theory. That would, however, be too dismissive a view. The options open to developing countries within the contemporary world order have changed since the heyday of dependency analysis in the 1970s and have generally become narrower. It matters that there no longer exists an alternative world socialist system to act as model and support; that the global links of production, trade and finance are both quantitatively and qualitatively greater; and that the emergence of major regionalist projects in all parts of the world have set up new processes of inclusion and exclusion. All in all, the development environment of the 1990s has been more forbidding than perhaps ever before, bringing significant parts of sub-Saharan Africa, for example, close to economic and political collapse.

Whither Caribbean development?

The Commonwealth Caribbean has not, as yet, been so severely undermined. But there is no doubt that over the last decade globalisation, as both emergent reality and manifest perception, has shaped both the practice and theory of Caribbean development, rendering the former largely acquiescent in the face of powerful external forces and the latter predominantly defensive and compromising in the face of similar powerful external arguments and ideologies. This introduction thus ends by asking: whither Caribbean development at the end of the twentieth century?

In practice, the 1990s were characterised by what might be called the consolidation of the neo-liberal revolution, tempered only by the realisation that more attention had to be paid to so-called 'human resources' if the new technological imperatives of a globalising economy were not to pass the region by. Otherwise, development was universally seen as a market-driven, private sector-led process. On the international front, the orthodoxy was best expressed by Owen Arthur, the prime minister of Barbados, in a lecture he gave in 1996:

> Generally, the strategy has to accept the reality of the globalisation of economic forces rather than hanker after a less complicated but impoverished past. The strategy must also recognise that the Caribbean countries, singly and as a group, must make the transition from the old age of preferences to the new age of reciprocity in its international economic relationships. In so doing, it must be designed to minimise the costs and dislocations associated with the transition, and to put in place mechanisms that can allow the region to exploit the market opportunities which are being created by the international liberalisation of trade and the formation of mega trade blocs.[47]

Such a strategy has required, in particular, that as many of the benefits of Lomé are preserved as is possible in the negotiations which began in 1998, that the option of joining the FTAA is established and kept open and that banana producers, faced with WTO opposition to their traditional preferential markets, are given enough time to shift to other activities. In essence, the policy has been to secure space and time to find an appropriate Caribbean niche within globalisation.

However, what has clearly emerged as a prospect over the last few years is that some countries within the Commonwealth Caribbean may succeed more than others in this endeavour. There is no necessary *regional* niche. Indeed, it has been noted that 'a region which had a fairly "homogenous" level of under-development in the mid-1960s, now finds itself at the end of the twentieth century with such sharp differences in development levels that Barbados (25), Bahamas (26) and Belize (29) are in the top quintile of the listing of 174 countries in the UNDP's 1995 human development index, while there are others such as … Guyana (105) close to the bottom.'[48] Trinidad and Tobago is not highlighted here, but it has lately been the relative economic success story of the Commonwealth Caribbean. Although it remains the case, of course, that its economy still depends on oil and gas and economic strategy thus focuses on exploiting these dependencies, a return to steady growth has been secured, in good part on the basis of a genuine elite consensus about development. This is perhaps the key: as Kari Levitt has observed, there has been 'an essential stability and continuity in the management of that country's affairs which has opened spaces for private enterprise in industry, agriculture and services without destroying the capacity of the government to govern'.[49] Manifestly, the same cannot be said of Jamaica, Grenada or Guyana. Even so, Trinidad stands as the exception, not the rule, and that achievement is new and fragile. The broader picture across the whole region still reveals endemically high unemployment, severe poverty amidst wealth and good living for some, social decay, growing amounts of crime and worrying levels of environmental deterioration. Within such a general context the pockets of prosperity that do exist do not generally extend to whole countries: they are based much more in certain sectors or districts set apart from, and increasingly guarded against (literally), the rest of Caribbean society.

It is a matter of concern that within the region the theoretical response to all of this has been less than inspiring, certainly by comparison with the period, no more than twenty-five years ago, when, as Kari Levitt has recalled, 'the University of the West Indies was a vibrant center [sic] of intellectual ferment'.[50] This is not to suggest that a full grasp of the significance of what had occurred was not properly established. Clive Thomas, for example, has argued in the clearest possible terms that 'the developmental state which emerged in the Caribbean after Independence has collapsed under the twin pressures of US self-defined geo-strategic national interest and the world-wide process of globalization'. It has been replaced, in his view, with a state 'recomposed' to meet the demands for 'good governance' imposed by the international financial institutions and thereby fashioned 'to serve "efficiently" the logic of deregulated competitive markets and integrated global production, led and directed by private capital'.[51] Yet, for all the insight contained within such a position, it did not constitute the charting of a new vision or a new course of action. Radical intellectuals within UWI seemed unable to think their way creatively out of the region's development impasse. Their depressed mood can be seen in their various contributions (subsequently published) to a symposium held in late 1989 to honour the work of their colleague, George Beckford, who was seriously ill.[52] In the most revealing recantation Lloyd Best, *doyen* of the former New World Group, declared that the more faithfully the strategies deriving from the former visions of radical theorists in the region had been followed, 'the more disastrous have been the consequences for the common people'.[53] But, as he openly conceded, he could not articulate a viable, preferred alternative to either of these failed nostra or the familiar claims of neo-liberalism. Asking what he deemed to be the two central questions of development theory, namely, how do people apprehend reality and how is mobilisation achieved, Best acknowledged that 'we do not know the answer to either of these questions. The only lesson you can learn from history is that there is no lesson you can learn from history'.[54]

This struck a very pessimistic note and reflects the depth to which Caribbean development thinking had sunk at the end of the 1980s. Although it would be an exaggeration to claim that a renaissance has since occurred, there can now be discerned a number of new and thoughtful strands within the contemporary debate. Three are worthy of emphasis. The first is grounded in an academic Marxism which posits the continuing necessity to place at the centre of analysis the changing processes of capital accumulation. This approach has been taken forward most actively by a number of social scientists of Caribbean origin now working within black studies programmes in US universities, of whom the most prominent is Hilbourne Watson. In his view, global restructuring is being driven forward by a 'techno-paradigm shift' marked by several concrete transitions – 'in manufacturing (from emphasis on production to *thinking*); in business dynamics (from single technologies to technological diversification); in research and development (R & D) activities (from visible competitors to invisible enemies); in technology development (from linear progression to demand articulation); in innovation patterns (from technical breakthrough to technology fusion); and in technical diffusion (from technical change to institutional inertia)'.[55] On this basis he argues that Caribbean economies lack the necessary requirements to take advantage of the new paradigm and find for themselves a viable position within the contemporary global political economy. The region's supposed traditional comparative advantages which have been based on low wages and large reserves of raw materials, such as bauxite, no longer offer any security in this new environment, which instead calls for the existence of a critical mass of trained professional and technical labour, an innovative industrial bourgeoisie and, in general, the ability to absorb and exploit large amounts of productive capital.

The second strand is constituted by an incipient school of 'anti-development' thinking. Within the Commonwealth Caribbean this derives in the main from the experiences of poor and other disaffected peoples trying to transform their lifeworlds through their own agency via new social movements, non-governmental organisations and other mechanisms of community empowerment.[56] In this view, social change is best achieved, not by seeking to transform the macrostructure of society by the capture of state power, but rather by privileging the role of human agency – in particular, in Davin Ramphall's words, by 'building on the experience of routine, everyday struggles by the poor for resources which they need to satisfy their basic needs'.[57] This kind of argument connects up directly with the groundswell of 'postmodern' development thinking which has grown up since the late 1980s and wants to reject the Western conception of development, Western rationality and indeed the whole Western modernist project.[58] However, this connection has only lately been made within the Caribbean and even now there is limited awareness of these wide-ranging debates in current social theory within Caribbean development circles. Davin Ramphall has in fact been virtually the only analyst, thus far, to try to build on this deconstruction of the modern development discourse and lay out a theoretical agenda for a new postmodern Caribbean development. The core of this, as he sees it, must be a rejection of the 'productivist epistemology' of past Caribbean development strategy, i.e. the argument that 'poverty could be eradicated, or at least ameliorated, by increasing economic production in the region'.[59] This impacted disastrously, he argues, on the Caribbean's ecological, technological and cultural resources, which are actually the necessary bases of the region's potential liberation from poverty. Postmodern development thinking in the Commonwealth Caribbean should therefore focus its attention on the preservation of indigenous agroecological knowledge, traditional crafts, local techniques of health care and the people's own inherited cultural mores.

The third position represents a compromise between the traditional concerns of radical development theory in the Caribbean and the ideological power of neo-liberalism. The two most important contributors here have been the familiar figures of Norman Girvan and Clive Thomas. During the 1990s both undertook research into poverty alleviation and reduction, often in the form of consultancies for agencies such as the Pan-American Health Organisation, and as a result they were drawn conceptually to explore more fully the relationship between economic development and social development.[60] What they realised was that certain trends in the international community, epitomised by the holding of the World Summit on Social Development in Copenhagen in March 1995, legitimised 'recognition of the linkage between poverty, persistent underdevelopment and the exclusion and marginalisation of certain social groups and classes' and provided justification for 'regional public investment programmes biased towards job creation and enhanced self-employment opportunities, as well as an expansion in the provision of social entitlements to those in dire need'.[61] In the real world of policy, post-structural adjustment, this was a door worth pushing open, but it did not add up to 'rethinking development', as Girvan certainly realised.[62] Of late, though, Thomas has at last attempted to proceed with the task, in his words, of 'reconstructing' the region's political economy. In so doing, he has explicitly sought to 'find "common ground" between the concerns of neo-liberal and mainstream political economy and radical political economy' in the region, aware that this may be interpreted as 'either opportunistic, less than revolutionary, or open to co-optation by neo-liberalism', but defending his choice as 'socially responsible'.[63] His ideas still constitute no more than points of departure (by his own admission), but they identify the household as the primary survival mechanism of Caribbean people and assert the 'priority claim of households' rights on the Region's economic production and growth'.[64] In similar fashion he also advocates the reinforcement of official initiatives in favour of regional integration with voluntary forms of cooperation grounded in areas of Caribbean life where there are strong and common cultural roots.

None of the arguments coming out of the current work of either Watson, Ramphall or Thomas are yet fully worked out. They may turn out to lead nowhere. However, what is striking is that, although each derives from a very different theoretical perspective, they concur that 'globalisation' has forced into being a new era that is far from being fully understood. In the meantime political and economic elites in the Commonwealth Caribbean still give the impression of embracing the global economy with reluctance, rather than enthusiasm. This may still come, but as and when it does it will be likely to mark the beginning of a new phase in the region's history characterised more by partial and local modes of insertion into the global economy than genuinely national strategies of development. The post-colonial period in the Caribbean has concluded and, in so doing, has brought down the curtain on a whole development era.

Notes

1   W. Arthur Lewis, 'Industrial development in Puerto Rico', *Caribbean Economic Review*, I, 1949, pp. 153–76, and 'The industrialisation of the British West Indies', *Caribbean Economic Review*, II, 1950, pp. 1–61. The pamphlet, which received much wider attention, appeared as *Industrial Development in the Caribbean*, Port of Spain, 1951.

2   Lewis, 'The industrialisation of the British West Indies', p. 7.

3   See *ibid.*, pp. 26–7.

4   For the details, see *ibid.*, pp. 37–53.

5   *Ibid.*, p. 38.

6   Commonwealth Caribbean Regional Secretariat, *CARIFTA and the New Caribbean*, Georgetown, 1971, p. 10. Manufacturing was defined to include sugar-milling operations, although they were obviously still closely connected with sugar cane production in the agricultural sector. To this degree the figures exaggerate the extent to which new non-traditional industries were established in this period.

7   William G. Demas, *The Economics of Development in Small Countries with Special Reference to the Caribbean*, Montreal, 1965.

8   See, in particular, *ibid.*, pp. 21–2.

9   *Ibid.*, p. 89.

10   Economic Commission for Latin America, 'The impact of the Caribbean Free Trade Association (CARIFTA)', *Economic Bulletin for Latin America*, XVIII, 1973, p. 144.

11   William G. Demas, 'The Caribbean Community and the Caribbean Development Bank', speech delivered at a seminar on Management in the Caribbean, Port of Spain, 2 December 1975, mimeo, p. 5.

12   Commonwealth Caribbean Regional Secretariat, *From CARIFTA to Caribbean Community*, Georgetown, 1972, p. 14.

13   Lloyd Best, 'Size and survival', in Norman Girvan and Owen Jefferson (eds), *Readings in the Political Economy of the Caribbean*, Kingston, 1971, p. 29.

14   *Ibid.*

15   *Ibid.*, p. 31.

16   New World Associates, 'The long-term economic, political and cultural programme for Guyana', in Girvan and Jefferson (eds), *Readings*, pp. 241–65.

17   Clive Y. Thomas, *Monetary and Financial Arrangements in a Dependent Monetary Economy*, Kingston, 1965.

18   Alister McIntyre, 'Some issues of trade policy in the West Indies', in Girvan and Jefferson (eds), *Readings*, pp. 165–83.

19   *Ibid.*, p. 165.

20   Lloyd Best and Kari Levitt, 'Externally Propelled Industrialization and Growth in the Caribbean', Montreal, 1969, mimeo, and 'Character of Caribbean economy', in George Beckford (ed.), *Caribbean Economy: Dependence and Backwardness*, Kingston, 1975, pp. 34–60.

21   Havelock Brewster, 'Economic dependence: a quantitative interpretation', *Social and Economic Studies*, 22, 1973, p. 90. It is worthy of note that this formulation of dependence is remarkably similar to the classic definition offered by the Latin American school, that of Dos Santos in Henry Bernstein (ed.), *Underdevelopment and Development: The Third World Today*, London, 1973, p. 76.

22   George Beckford, *Persistent Poverty: Underdevelopment in Plantation Economies of the Third World*, Oxford, 1972, pp. 183–214.

23   Norman Girvan, 'Multinational corporations and dependent underdevelopment in mineral export economies', *Social and Economic Studies*, 19, 1970, and *Foreign Capital and Economic Underdevelopment in Jamaica*, Kingston, 1971.

24   Owen Jefferson, *The Post-war Economic Development of Jamaica*, Kingston, 1972.

25   The most discussed of these studies was Havelock Brewster and Clive Y. Thomas, *The Dynamics of West Indian Economic Integration*, Kingston, 1967. The others included George Beckford, *The West Indian Banana Industry*, Kingston, 1967; George Beckford and M. H. Guscott, *Intra-Caribbean Agricultural Trade*, Kingston, 1967; and Norman Girvan, *The Caribbean Bauxite Industry*, Kingston, 1967.

26   Girvan and Jefferson (eds), 'Introduction', in *Readings*, p. 1.

27   For further discussion of this point, see Ivar Oxaal, 'The dependency economist as grassroots politician in the Caribbean', in I. Oxaal, T. Barnett and D. Booth (eds), *Beyond the Sociology of Development: Economy and Society in Latin America and Africa*, London, 1975, pp. 28–49.

28   For further discussion of this point, see Dennis Pantin, 'The plantation economy model and the Caribbean', *Institute of Development Studies Bulletin*, 12, 1980, pp. 17–23, and Marietta Morrissey, 'Imperial designs: a sociology of knowledge study of British and American dominance in the development of Caribbean social science', *Latin American Perspectives*, 3, 1976, pp. 112–14.

29   Courtney Blackman, 'Speech to the students of Chancellor Hall, University of the West Indies, 14 March 1980', *Caribbean Monthly Bulletin*, 14, 6–7, 1980, p. 45.

30   Paul Sutton, 'Living with dependency in the Commonwealth Caribbean', in Anthony Payne and Paul Sutton (eds), *Dependency under Challenge: The Political Economy of the Commonwealth Caribbean*, Manchester, 1984, p. 281.

31   Clive Y. Thomas, *Dependence and Transformation: The Economics of the Transition to Socialism*, New York, 1974, pp. 116–17.

32   For a regional exposition of this approach, see Ralph Gonsalves, *The Non-capitalist Path of Development: Africa and the Caribbean*, London, 1981, and, for a critical view from Thomas himself, see Clive Y. Thomas, ' "The non-capitalist path" as theory and practice of decolonization and socialist transformation', *Latin American Perspectives*, 5, 1978, pp. 10–36.

33   For a fuller account of the impact of US hegemony on the Caribbean as a whole, see Anthony Payne, 'US hegemony and the reconfiguration of the Caribbean', *Review of International Studies*, 20, 1994, pp. 149–68.

34   *Business Week*, 11 July 1983, p. 28.

35   *The Nassau Understanding*, a declaration issued by the heads of government of Caribbean Community countries, Nassau, 1984.

36   Carmen Diana Deere *et al.*, *In the Shadows of the Sun: Caribbean Development Alternatives and U.S. Policy*, Boulder, 1990, p. 46.

37   See *ibid.*, and Kathy McAfee, *Storm Signals: Structural Adjustment and Development Alternatives in the Caribbean*, London, 1991.

38   A. N. R. Robinson, 'The West Indies beyond 1992', paper prepared for the CARICOM Heads of Government Conference, Grand Anse, Grenada, mimeo, July 1989.

39   The West Indian Commission, *Time for Action: Report of the West Indian Commission*, Bridgetown, Barbados, 1992.

40   For further discussion of the ACS, see Jessica Byron, 'The Association of Caribbean States: growing pains of a new regionalism?', *Current Trends*, 7, May-August 1998, pp. 33–63, and Anthony Payne, 'The Association of Caribbean States', in Glenn Hook and Ian Kearns (eds), *Subregionalism and World Order*, London, 1999, pp. 117–37.

41   Havelock R. Brewster, 'The Report of the West Indian Commission, Time for Action – a critical appreciation', *Caribbean Quarterly*, 39, 1, 1993, p. 29.

42   Hilbourne A. Watson, 'Caribbean integration under global neo-liberalism: selected issues in the West Indian Commission Report', *21st Century Policy Review*, 2, 1–2, 1994, p. 63.

43   The former phrase was used by Robert Cox in R. W. Cox, 'Structural issues of global governance: implications for Europe', in Stephen Gill (ed.), *Gramsci, Historical Materialism and International Relations*, Cambridge, 1993, p. 261; the latter phrase was used by Susan Strange in S. Strange, 'The name of the

game', in N. X. Rizopoulos (ed.), *Sea-Changes: American Foreign Policy in a World Transformed*, New York, 1990, p. 260.

44   See Stephen Gill and David Law, 'Global hegemony and the structural power of capital', *International Studies Quarterly*, 33, 1989, pp. 475–99.

45   This phrase is fully explained in David Held and Anthony McGrew, David Goldblatt and Jonathan Perraton, *Global Transformations: Politics, Economics and Culture*, Cambridge, 1999, pp. 3–5.

46   These positions are set out in Robert W. Cox, 'Social forces, states and world orders: beyond international relations theory', *Millennium: Journal of International Studies*, 10, 1981, pp. 144–6, and Stephen Gill, 'American hegemony: its limits and prospects in the Reagan era', *Millennium: Journal of International Studies*, 15, 1986, pp. 311–36.

47   Owen Arthur, 'The new realities of Caribbean international economic relations', lecture in the Distinguished Lecture Series, Institute of International Relations, University of the West Indies, St Augustine, Trinidad, mimeo, 15 April 1996, pp. 47–8.

48   Clive Thomas, 'The crisis of development theory and practice: a Caribbean perspective', in Kari Levitt and Michael Witter (eds), *The Critical Tradition of Caribbean Political Economy: The Legacy of George Beckford*, Kingston, 1996, p. 227.

49   Kari Levitt, 'From decolonization to neo-liberalism: what have we learned about development?', in *ibid.*, pp. 213–14.

50   Kari Levitt, 'Preface', in *ibid.*, p. xii.

51   Clive Y. Thomas, 'Globalization, structural adjustment and security: the collapse of the post-colonial developmental state in the Caribbean', *Global Development Studies*, 1, 1–2, 1998, p. 81.

52   Beckford died on 13 November 1990.

53   Lloyd Best, 'Independence and responsibility: self-knowledge as an imperative', in Levitt and Witter (eds), *The Critical Tradition of Caribbean Political Economy*, p. 4.

54   *Ibid.*, p. 9. Attention was also drawn to these particular remarks in the review of the book by Jay R. Mandle in *New West Indian Guide*, 73, 1 and 2, 1999, p. 132.

55   Hilbourne A. Watson, 'Introduction: the Caribbean and the techno-paradigm shift in global capitalism', in Hilbourne A. Watson (ed.), *The Caribbean in the Global Political Economy*, Boulder, 1994, p. 3. His emphasis. See also Hilbourne A. Watson (ed.), *Human Resources and Institutional Requirements for Global Adjustments: Strategies for the Caribbean*, a special issue of *21st Century Policy Review*, 2, 1–2, 1994.

56   For a discussion of these activities, see Deere *et al.*, *In the Shadows of the Sun*; McAfee, *Storm Signals*; and David Lewis, 'Nongovernmental organizations and Caribbean development', *The Annals of the American Academy of Political and Social Science*, 533, 1994, pp. 125–38.

57   Davin Ramphall, 'Postmodernism and the rewriting of Caribbean radical development thinking', *Social and Economic Studies*, 46, 1, 1997, p. 21.

58   For a flavour of a vast and growing literature, see Jan Nederveen Pieterse, 'Dilemmas of development discourse: the crisis of developmentalism and comparative method', *Development and Change*, 22, 1991, pp. 5–29, and Arturo Escobar, 'Imagining a post-development era? Critical thought, development and social movements', *Social Text*, 31/32, 1994, pp. 20–56.

59   Ramphall, 'Postmodernism and the rewriting of Caribbean radical development thinking', p. 13.

60 See Norman Girvan, 'Introduction: report on the Caribbean Symposium on Social Development', and C. Y. Thomas, 'The interrelationship between economic and social development', in Norman Girvan (ed.), *Poverty, Empowerment and Social Development in the Caribbean*, Kingston, 1997, pp. 1–19 and 20–49 respectively.

61 Thomas, 'The interrelationship between economic and social development', p. 21.

62 See Norman P. Girvan, 'Rethinking development: out loud', in Judith Wedderburn (ed.), *Rethinking Development*, Kingston, 1991, pp. 11–13.

63 Clive Thomas, 'On reconstructing a political economy of the Caribbean', mimeo, Georgetown, December 1998, p. 14.

Dr Eric Williams and the national development state in Trinidad and Tobago

In 1956 the political fortunes of Trinidad and Tobago were transformed with the election of Dr Eric Williams to office as chief minister and later prime minister. He was to be the most important figure in the country for the next twenty-five years, dominating the political agenda and shaping the pattern of economic development. The vision he had throughout this period was of an independent Trinidad and Tobago drawing on its oil wealth to build a modern industrial state and a liberal democratic system. This chapter examines his attempt to do so, with a particular focus on the 1970s when the fortunes of the country were transformed with the sudden rise in oil prices and the opportunity it provided to use the state as the prime moving force for development. The 'national development state' that emerged then was in many respects unique to Trinidad and Tobago, although some of its salient features, such as the concentration of power in the hands of the prime minister and the constraints and frustrations that were encountered in laying the foundations for economic development, were shared with other countries in the Commonwealth Caribbean.

Background: the political system, 1955–73

The necessary background to an understanding of this later period is the years 1955–73, in which Williams's power was first confirmed, then consolidated, and finally corroded. While hard-and-fast dates for this process cannot be projected, it corresponds approximately to the years 1955–61, 1962–6 and 1967–73.

The confirmation of power: 1955–61

These are the most important years, 'setting a stamp on all government and politics in the country'.[1] They are the years of energetic pursuit of government-led modernisation and charismatic domination of the creole crowd. To realise the former, the machinery of government was seen as all important, which inevitably brought Williams into conflict with the Colonial Office in London and the nascent Federal Government of the West Indies, both of which had claims to a share in power. Williams's character and temperament were utterly against this, and the story of these years is largely of how he confronted and defeated both them and their allies in Trinidad and Tobago.[2] In this the other element, that of charismatic domination, was critical. Williams's ascendancy over the People's National Movement (PNM), the party he founded in January 1956, was early confirmed,[3] to be extended into society at large by the adroit appropriation of the flag of the nationalist cause by means of agitation for the return to Trinidadian patrimony of the US naval base at Chaguaramas. Williams's success here rebounded to his advantage when in the general elections of 1961 the PNM increased its share of the vote to 58 per cent, as against 39 per cent in 1956, albeit on a pronounced racial basis.[4] Independence was soon to follow, with a constitution modelled on Westminster and reflecting *de jure* what already existed in practice – the concentration of administrative power in the hands of the prime minister.[5]

The principal feature of politics in this period was the ascendancy of Dr Williams. The style was that of 'Doctor Politics' in which 'the Leader is expected to achieve for and on behalf of the population. The community is not expected to contribute much more than crowd support and applause'.[6]

The consolidation of power: 1962–6

These are essentially years of 'state-building'. Williams's main concerns were 'the development and implementation of a foreign policy; the development of a sense of national community; public service reform; and reform of the economy by way of development planning, regulation of labour and capital, and tripartite consultation'.[7] They are marked by the advance of 'technocracy' through the promotion of an administrative elite in the public service, whose prime loyalty lay with Williams and in whose service they were prepared to labour long hours.[8] The centralising tendency of the earlier period thus continued, held marginally in check only by the formal requisites of the Westminster system. Certainly, the PNM was offered no real part in policy-making, and after indifferent attempts at reform in 1963 morale and activity slumped, as Williams himself was to find out in his much publicised 'Meet the Party' tours.[9] Other groups in the country, more vocal in demands, fared no better. In particular, there was the failure of an opposition to develop within the framework of the main rival to the PNM, the Democratic Labour Party (DLP).[10] The general election of November 1966 was thus in essence 'no contest', Williams running on the not unimpressive record of government in these years. There was, however, a straw in the wind. Whilst the PNM was again returned in two-thirds of the seats, the percentage of the registered electorate actually voting fell considerably (88 per cent to 66 per cent), as did the absolute number of votes cast.[11]

The corrosion of power: 1967–73

At the end of 1966 Williams could look back on a decade of power with some satisfaction. He had led Trinidad and Tobago to independence; he had set the agenda for social and economic modernisation; and he was without a political rival in a political system which superficially could be described as 'liberal democratic'. If he now consciously thought it was time to take stock, to write the autobiography and the history of the Caribbean long promised,[12] publicly to take a 'back seat' in government, involving himself only as and when absolutely necessary, as in his assumption of the finance portfolio in 1967, following considerable agitation among business circles in Trinidad, then his reasoning was understandable, if ultimately mistaken. The one event which was to shake his confidence, and put in question his administration, was the widespread Black Power disturbances of February–April 1970.

The 'how' and 'why' of 1970 is exceedingly complex. Essentially, however, the explanation lies in the following:

1 The withdrawal of Williams from the spotlight produced first unease and then a loss of confidence among his supporters, the whole being compounded by rumours of corruption in high governing circles.
2 Concentration of executive power in the Office of the Prime Minister and administrative decisions in the Cabinet resulted in considerable overload at the centre, the result of which was inept and indifferent public administration.
3 Neither Parliament nor established political parties were meaningfully engaged in the political process or showed any likelihood they might be, with the result that political activity was projected on to other organised groups such as religious bodies, trade unions and employers' confederations.
4 The goals of economic reform and social progress were yet to yield tangible results, particularly the reduction of unemployment, which increasingly bore disproportionately upon the young blacks of Port of Spain and its environs.[13]

In its programme and actions the Black Power movement touched on all these points. It brought people (the crowd) back into politics; identified the agents of political and economic oppression (the Catholic Church, local business and the multinationals); sought the means by which they might be confronted (demonstration and debate); and finally gambled (and lost) on an overthrow of the state. Its miscalculations were Williams's gains and, following the failure of the *coup* in the army, he moved swiftly and decisively to restore lost power.

Once again, Williams put himself visibly at the centre of decision-making, taking on the portfolio for almost everything and sacking those ministers who had been the main targets of criticism. He also sought to restore confidence through, first, the launch of a programme of 'National Reconstruction' which promised, *inter alia*, an immediate reorganisation of the government machinery, to be followed by a fundamental reform of the constitution; second, a revision of the third Five Year Plan to provide more jobs through public works and enlarge the area of national decision-making in the economy; and, third, the involvement of all citizens of Trinidad and Tobago in the difficult task of nation-building. Later in the year these themes were to be expanded and developed as 'The Chaguaramas Declaration',[14] a fundamental statement of policy for the 1970s as 'The People's Charter' had been for the PNM during the 1950s and 1960s. These in turn formed the basis of the PNM's manifesto for the 1971 general election, which it again won easily, but not convincingly, owing to an effective opposition boycott of the polls.[15] Unassailably in power, the question as it unfolded in 1972 and 1973 was whether Williams had either the will or the capacity to stay there.

As it turned out, he had neither. On 28 September 1973 he announced without warning his intention to 'return to private life and take no further part in political activity'. In his 'resignation' speech he highlighted three reasons for his departure – Caribbean integration (it was not progressing); the 'state of the nation' (the economy was crumbling and there were guerrillas in the hills); and the PNM and its objectives (individualism and indiscipline were rampant).[16] These conclusions but echoed his earlier pessimistic independence anniversary message, which ended significantly with a quotation from Ralph Emerson, 'a nation never fails but by suicide'.[17] The nation was indeed failing from a combination of internal and external pressures to which the political system as fashioned by Williams could not effectively respond. He saw this clearly and, tired of office, decided to go. It was a decision not wholly in character, and thus the cause of much speculation; but it was nevertheless genuinely taken and not contrived.

A summary of the political system to this date would pinpoint strength and weakness, development and decay, which imparted to political life as a whole an element of predictability but no particular guarantee of durability. That is, while the regime could maintain itself administratively and politically without undue recourse to coercion (though there were elements of this), its legitimacy, as expressed in the satisfaction of demands and the mobilisation of support, was far from clear. In itself this was not enough to sustain a full-blown 'crisis', though it was sufficient to engender a feeling of unease and uncertainty throughout the nation to which Williams was eventually to respond with his 'resignation'.

Background: the economic system, 1955–73

Parallel to, impinging on, and in turn being influenced by political events, were developments in the economy. Attention must be drawn to four areas: the dependence on oil; the decline of agriculture; the limits to manufacturing; and the role of government.

The dependence on oil

The PNM's rise to power coincided with an upturn in the economy. From 1955 to 1961 the economy grew by some 10 per cent per annum in real terms. Thereafter growth fluctuated, being constant between 1962 and 1965; increasing from 1966 to 1968; declining in 1969–70; and recovering in 1971–2.[18] In all this there was one constant – the link with crude oil production. When this was high, the economy was buoyant; when falling, it was depressed. It could not be otherwise as long as petroleum accounted for such a high proportion of GDP (27 per cent) and central government revenues (30 per cent).[19] This dependence, of course, was of concern to the government throughout these years. It felt, however, that it could do little to alter the situation, given Trinidad's tiny crude oil production by world standards (0.5 per cent of total production) and its vulnerable position as an intermediate refiner, sustained predominantly by one dominant, vertically integrated company, Texaco. Government intervention and regulation were thus at a minimum, confined chiefly to the purchase in July 1969 of the assets of BP Trinidad Ltd for US$22 million, subsequently incorporated in a joint venture as Trinidad-Tesoro, and the passage in December that year of a Petroleum Act designed to consolidate and amend, rather than revise, existing legislation relating to petroleum.

The decline of agriculture

Between 1956 and 1968 the contribution of agriculture to GDP just about halved (15 per cent to 8 per cent).[20] The chief cause was stagnation in the sugar industry, which dominated the agricultural sector and which operated more or less indifferently throughout this period, its high costs being shielded by sales to protected markets in the UK and USA. External dependence was matched for the government by internal dependence on the industry as an employer of labour. Throughout the 1960s an average of 25,000 persons were directly employed in the industry, the majority of whom were unskilled and middle-aged and therefore without prospects elsewhere. Maintaining the industry was thus an essential aspect of government policy, to which political and ethnic factors further contributed, over 90 per cent of sugar workers being of East Indian descent, organised politically in the DLP. In 1968 and 1970 the government therefore moved to participate directly in the sugar industry when jobs were threatened or it otherwise appeared politically expedient to do so, through outright purchase in one case and 51 per cent ownership in another (Caroni Ltd, a subsidiary of Tate & Lyle). Efforts elsewhere to stimulate agriculture, notably the distribution of Crown lands, met with little success.

The limits to manufacturing

Faced with excessive dependence on two commodities, governments in Trinidad and Tobago since 1950 have sought diversification in the development of manufacturing. For most of the period under review the PNM enthusiastically endorsed this, closely following the prescriptions of the 'Puerto Rican model' of development. By the end of the 1960s, however, the returns were meagre, particularly in the generation of employment. From 1955 to 1969 the labour force increased from 267,400 to 368,400 (by 38 per cent).[21] 'Pioneer' manufacturing absorbed only a small proportion of this – one estimate being that at the end of 1972 only 18,627 persons were employed in 'assisted' establishments.[22] For this the government had to forgo a loss of revenues estimated by Frank Rampersad at between 1 per cent and 2 per cent of GDP, i.e. 7–14 per cent of revenues collected.[23] Additionally, the programme directly raised the level of foreign ownership in the economy (local participation in such ventures being minimal), thereby further emphasising dependence, marked not only by remittances of profits abroad but also by the fact that few local raw materials were used.

The role of government

Government action in this period largely took two forms. One was to set the framework for economic development as a whole through the medium of indicative development planning. The other was to regulate the system in whole or in part through the establishment of a number of pragmatic *ad hoc* institutional devices, the rationale of which was either the fact of independence itself or an immediate reaction to pressing problems.

Four major development plans were drafted and three implemented. The first Five Year Plan (1958–62) concentrated on improving infrastructure to support industrialisation; the second (1964–8) emphasised diversification and community development; the third (1969–73), diversification and the freeing of the economy from dependence on external decision-making. A fourth plan was prepared but not adopted when it became clear that the fortunes of Trinidad and Tobago were being rapidly transformed by the 'oil boom'. It also corresponded to a belief by Williams, expressed as early as 1969, that planning was failing:

> In Trinidad and Tobago results so far do not give much grounds for optimism about the effectiveness of indicative planning ... Unless satisfactory solutions are found, either attempts at indicative planning will have to be abandoned in favour of more direct measures, or the planning process in many of the developing countries will remain less than fully effective.[24]

The attempt to regulate the system as a whole, other than through the budget, focused on financial institutions, labour and capital. In 1964 Acts established a central bank and licensed commercial banks. In 1966 an Insurance Act was passed. Attempts at regulating labour, by way of the Industrial Stabilisation Act, 1965, raised a storm of protest,[25] as also did the passage of the Finance Act in 1966, with its alleged 'controls' of capital. The fact that the latter was subsequently modified whereas the former was not became a contentious issue in politics in the late 1960s and early 1970s, leading to a degree of alienation of trade union support (notably among the Oilfield Workers' Trade Union, the best organised and strategically most powerful union in the country).

Regulation in part increasingly took the form of direct government participation in the economy. This derived largely from *ad hoc* responses to private-sector retrenchment of labour and more generally from the weak performance of the private sector as a whole. By mid 1972 the government employed more than 100,000 people, making it the biggest and most diversified employer in the country. Some 80,000 of them were employed in the public service and 20,000 others in commercial and industrial activities through government participation in some twenty-one companies with a book-value shareholding of around TT$60 million.[26] In this way the government of Trinidad and Tobago was to obtain the largest stake in the economy of any Caribbean country, except Cuba.

All the above, however, failed to alter the essence of the economy. It remained, in 1973 as in 1955, small, dependent and very open. This made it extremely difficult to manage, as Havelock Brewster, among others, noted. In a quantitative analysis based on 'personal observation and close contact with political leaders and civil servants over the past fifteen years',[27] he demonstrated that over two decades no significant co-variation between the major economic functions in the Trinidad economy – employment, wage rates, exports, import ratio, output, consumption, prices and investment – had occurred in the manner prescribed by orthodox economists. A consequence of this was that 'the standard range of institutions – the Plan, the Planning Department, the Central Bank, the Industrial Court' – which had been established in Trinidad and worked elsewhere, did not operate effectively in this instance. Given, however, that such institutions 'flourish but do not function', Brewster could only conclude that their rationale was not economic but symbolic – their 'very physical presence is projected as the living symbols that governments govern'.[28] That the hollowness of this should finally have dawned on Williams in the third quarter of 1973 when foreign exchange reserves were the equivalent of less than two weeks of the country's imports is, of course, far from coincidental.

'Resignation' and 'renewal': 1973

In 1973 the new offshore oil fields developed by the US transnational company, Amoco, came substantially on stream, offsetting the serious decline in crude oil production of the previous few years and returning the level of production to that recorded in 1968.[29] In January 1973 Amoco paid approximately US$0.50 tax and royalty per barrel of oil; in December 1973 it was paying US$4.69 and, as new prices and taxes posted by Trinidad and Tobago took effect from 1 January 1974, this was practically to double again. With this the central government revenues of Trinidad were transformed. In 1973 the total was TT$591.2 million, the following year TT$1,397.7 million, and by 1978 it was TT$3,226 million.[30] 'Money is no problem' was how Williams was to explain the new situation in 1976. More than other factors it was the desire to exploit it fully that prompted him to remain in office at the end of 1973, thereby ushering in a new phase in Trinidad and Tobago's development.

This, of course, is not to discount political factors as operative in his decision to remain. They undoubtedly played a part – particularly in respect of the confusion and dissension caused within the PNM by his 'resignation'.[31] However, there is no reason to believe that politics alone would have prompted a change of heart, though Williams was later to capitalise on the situation which his 'resignation' had caused. Indeed, it is precisely such 'opportunism' that was most characteristic of him in respect of his actions then and earlier. If it could be firmly grounded on an economic base, which from his earliest days he had recognised as 'ultimately determinant' of political action,[32] then so much the better. The 'oil crisis' of late 1973 promised precisely this, and it was towards defining policy in this area that he first turned.

Oil capitalism and national development: 1974–6

The changed fortunes of the nation in 1974 as compared to 1973 were evident in many government pronouncements, but nowhere did they have greater contrast than in the independence messages delivered in these years by Williams. Whereas that of 1973, as cited earlier, had ended with an ominous warning, the conclusion in 1974 was positively euphoric: 'let us say, with pride but yet with humility, we are going well, and may God bless our Nation'.[33] More than this, however, the speech was noteworthy for spelling out how the oil 'windfall' was to be used for the development of the country:

> In our case oil means (a) a large number of additional permanent jobs through downstream petroleum operations or new industries based on petroleum, (b) greater national ownership of our national resources meaning specifically greater national decision-making and the local utilisation and diversification of products which we formerly exported, (c) larger allocations for our domestic services, (d) more rapid progress towards Caribbean integration, to supplement our own domestic efforts at greater self sufficiency.[34]

In the furtherance of the second of these goals the speech also marked the purchase of the holdings of Shell Trinidad for TT$93.6 million, a price regarded as inflated by some but of incalculable symbolic significance for the government.

Taking in turn the four headings spelled out by Williams, the following observations on the economy in the period 1974–6 can be made.

Energy-based industrialisation

The government's response to the 'oil crisis' was the establishment of an Energy Secretariat to co-ordinate all matters relating to petroleum and the despatch overseas of three separate high-powered diplomatic missions to examine the ramifications of the 'oil crisis' and the way in which it was likely to affect Trinidad and Tobago. Simultaneously Williams, in a series of 'addresses to the nation' in the first half of 1974, reported that Trinidad and Tobago was being courted by a number of large transnational corporations intent on using the country's abundant natural gas reserves to establish a manufacturing presence on a joint venture basis with the government. In October 1974 he listed this activity as follows: agreement with Texaco in respect of two petrochemical plants (51 per cent government holding); work in progress on a second ammonia plant as a joint venture with W. R. Grace (51 per cent government holding); discussion of an aluminium smelter to be located in Trinidad, based on alumina from Jamaica and Guyana (34 per cent government holding); discussion on a sponge iron plant to be located in Trinidad, based on iron ore from Brazil; and examination of proposals from Amoco, Hoechst, Beker, Kaiser, Mississippi Corporation and Tenneco for additional fertiliser plants (all 51 per cent government holdings). Additionally, the government was to embark on a major electricity expansion programme and to lay a natural gas pipeline to a new purpose-built industrial estate at Point Lisas.[35] While not all these ventures were eventually to get off the ground, the majority did so. Evident within them was not only an expansion of the Trinidad state but also the directing hand of Dr Williams, eventually made explicit with his resumption of the finance portfolio in 1975.

National ownership

It is important to remember that the goal of greater national ownership came before the 'oil crisis' and was the object of a comprehensive White Paper in 1972. It was to be realised alongside new foreign investment, to which it was seen as complementary rather than substitutive, i.e. the mixed economy was to remain as before: all that had changed was that the government was now expected to play the role of a prime mover in its development. Nationalist, rather than socialist, objectives were the motivating forces, for which more

than any other figure Williams was responsible. Accordingly, pragmatic considerations decided the national interest in each case. This
is well illustrated by the example of Texaco. In May 1974 Williams
indicated that the government was interested in acquiring a stake in
its activities in Trinidad. Thereafter he proceeded to make haste
slowly. 'Serious' negotiations did not begin until nearly a year later,
by which time the indications were that he was changing his mind.
In two speeches in April 1975 the whole question of national ownership was raised rhetorically and the answer given that it was not
always expedient to proceed, especially at that moment in the oil
industry.[36] Thereafter Texaco slipped from view. This did not mean,
however, that the government was not proceeding on other fronts. In
1975 a second White Paper on public-sector participation in industry
was published which noted that government holdings had increased
to approximately TT$209 million, covering a wide range of activi-
ties. The most notable additions in that year were the purchase of the
remaining shares in Caroni to make it a wholly government-owned
company.

Domestic relief

The 'oil crisis' coincided with the onset of recession and double-digit
inflation in the Western economies. Trinidad and Tobago, with its
very open economy, was particularly vulnerable and the government
quickly moved to cushion the effects through the deployment of
various devices to raise standards of living, which elsewhere in the
Commonwealth Caribbean were being seriously eroded. Its action
took three principal forms. The first, affecting everyone, was the
implementation of a comprehensive system of subsidies. From 1974
to 1976 they amounted to some TT$492 million, allocated under the
following heads: basic food (17.8 per cent, agriculture and fishery
(1.8 per cent), welfare (13.0 per cent), utilities (37.2 per cent), petroleum products (29.6 per cent), other (0.6 per cent).[37] The second was
a series of measures to reduce taxes, hence primarily affecting the
employed. The areas covered were income tax (relief and rebates);
motor vehicles and motoring; purchase tax (refrigerators, freezers,
stoves and garments); and stamp duty (land transfers). The amounts
of revenue estimated as foregone were, in 1974, TT$36.8 million;
1975, TT$41.6 million; and 1976, TT$26.4 million.[38] Finally, action
was taken to expand the various programmes designed specifically to
relieve unemployment. The problem here, as Williams frankly recognised in 1975, was that jobs were traded for votes, with the PNM and
its representatives, not surprisingly, being the principal beneficiaries.

This he condemned.[39] However, little was subsequently done to remedy the situation, and the question must be asked as to how different in intent this was to the other measures outlined above, especially given the well-known consumerist ethos of West Indian society.

Caribbean integration

Williams's 'addresses' on the 'oil crisis' in the first half of 1974 were peppered with references to how oil could be the fuel for advancing Caribbean integration. As it turned out, his hopes were not to be realised, and the forward momentum of 1972, already slowing in 1973, came to a full stop by 1977, the year which, in his words, 'witnessed the near total collapse of the Caribbean Community Treaty'.[40] All that need be said is that, whatever transpired afterwards, Trinidad and Tobago was not to blame up to that date.

The combined effect of the above measures was to widen the role and scope of the state. By 1976 the public sector, directly and indirectly, was employing over half the labour force and there was scarcely any area of economic activity in which its remit did not run. Williams was not unaware of the problems this posed, but naturally enough solutions were not easy to find. In the event, two appear to have been adopted. One – less a solution than a postponement – was the medium of Special Funds. Every budget since 1974 set aside considerable revenues in a number of such funds, each earmarked for a specific purpose and designed to effect long-term development. At the end of 1976 twenty-three such funds had been established and appropriations totalling TT$1,420 million had been made.[41] The other was the promise of future divestment of government holdings. This was in accord with a philosophy which saw state ownership largely as a temporary form of trusteeship pending the emergence within the economy of the 'small man'. Since the latter had still to be realised, caution was to be exercised – especially given the checkered record of the business class in Trinidad and Tobago.[42] Here, starkly laid out, was Williams's personal preference and strategy for development. Simply put, it saw the future economic development of Trinidad and Tobago as lying in the hands of a national middle class then in formation but not yet independently formed. The task of the PNM, through control of the state, was to preside over its creation.

Political reconstruction: 1974–6

The system of specifically political power that Williams had built to 1973 rested on three foundations: the Westminster system, the PNM and the public service. In all three Williams dominated by virtue of office and example, and in all three the habit of concentrating the power of decision in his own hands was very evident. As he himself said in the 1971 general election campaign, 'I'm the one who has power here. When I say "come" you "cometh", and when I say "go" you "goeth" '.[43] What, then, is most extraordinary about the period 1974–6 is that Williams believed he did not have enough power, or perhaps more exactly, given the experiences of 1970–3, that his power was insecurely based. He therefore systematically set about breaking all three 'foundations', reconstructing them in a way designed to give him absolute personal power by the time the general election was fought in September 1976. The way in which he did so is examined below.

Constitutional reform

On 18 June 1971 the establishment of a Constitution Commission was announced in the Speech from the Throne and in January 1974 the Commission duly presented its report and draft constitution. Its main recommendation was that 'the Westminster model in its purest form as set out in our present Constitution is not suitable to the Trinidad and Tobago society'.[44] Consequently, in its draft constitution, it proposed a number of changes, some of which were significant departures from the existing constitution, though none was cumulatively enough to question in any fundamental way the Westminster system as formally established.[45] Thereafter the issue was put to the public in a largely inconsequential debate until Williams pronounced on it in a massive seven-hour speech to the House of Representatives in December 1974.

A speech of such length obviously covered much ground. However, in the light of later developments one aspect appears fundamental – his accusation that the Constitution Commission had 'an illogical obsession proceeded with logically to reduce the powers of Parliament, to create confusion and to break up the centralisation of Parliament, Cabinet and the political party',[46] i.e. a belief by Williams that the Commission's motivation was partisan and that by design it sought no less than the destruction of the system he had created, to the immediate disadvantage of himself and the PNM. He therefore refuted almost in their entirety its investigations and recommendations, paying particular attention to the question of proportional representation, the adoption of which he utterly opposed, either in whole or in part, on the grounds that it would 'dissolve the present PNM majorities'.[47] Not stated, though obviously derived from it, was the concomitant proposition that it could also lead to an end to Williams's sole leadership in Parliament (i.e. coalition government or, even worse, opposition). Needless to say, and on his past record, this was something Williams would not easily have been able to accommodate. He therefore proposed that note only be taken of the reports of the Commission and that Parliament itself proceed to draft a constitution more acceptable to the country as a whole.

This exercise took up the whole of 1975 and finally, on 12 March 1976, Williams moved the adoption of the new constitution in the House of Representatives. It contained a number of novel features. Trinidad and Tobago was to become a republic with a President as head of state; the Senate was to remain, but whereas the previous constitution had limited the number of ministers that could be drawn from the Senate, no such limitation was now to be imposed; eighteen was to be the age of majority, and voting was to be by ballot box, not by voting machine; an Ombudsman was to be appointed; and an Integrity Commission to be provided for, its exact powers to be determined in future legislation.[48] Much of this was uncontroversial, the measure which raised the greatest comment being that related to the Senate. The Constitution Commission had recommended the abolition of the Senate. Williams rejected this out of hand, favouring instead an enhanced role for the Senate in Parliament and in government. The stated reason for this, in so far as one was discernible, was to cast the net for talent as wide as possible. At the same time, however, it must be noted that a consequential effect was a substantial increase in prime ministerial power. That is, while members of the House of Representatives retained a measure of independence from the government by virtue of their seat, senators were removable at will. In such a situation, pressures to conform, it might be adduced, were more likely to prevail than vociferous dissent.

The public service

In his address to the sixteenth Annual Convention of the PNM, Williams hinted that all was not well in the public service. It was still imbued with 'the techniques and procedures of colonialism, as well as the mental outlook associated with it ... [and] with the exception of a very few public servants is just not geared to the execution of the responsibilities which the scope and pace of present development are imposing on it'. He went on:

If all the advice tendered to us recently had been accepted, we would have found ourselves leaning over backwards to support some group's political line; we would have crawled on our belly to achieve a subordinate role in one particular organisation; we would have broken off diplomatic relations with this country or that; we would have gone out of our way to show our support for this leader or that; and all of you would have awakened one morning to find that overnight you had become the Protectorate of some country outside on the basis of demands stated with brutal precision.[49]

A year later this was expanded to form the substance of a considerable attack on what he termed 'a small ambitious minority of senior civil servants',[50] among whom were included D. Alleyne, then Head of the Civil Service and Permanent Secretary to the Prime Minister.

The choice of 'target' here was far from fortuitous. If Alleyne was not safe from public censure and disgrace, then who was? Equally, the thrust of Williams's attack was well chosen – it was on the activities of the Energy Secretariat in the early part of 1974. This body, he charged, had illegally by-passed the Tenders Board; transferred individuals from substantive positions in various ministries without approval; offered partisan and unsound advice in the interests of foreign companies and governments; and, finally, sought to involve the Prime Minister himself in its nefarious activities.[51] In other words, a government within a government was in the making and Trinidad and Tobago 'stood close to take-over by a technocracy, only wanting someone to convey an aura of respectability by chairing its committee'.[52]

If so, then Williams's own part in this cannot be ignored. He early courted technocracy and his initial decision to establish an Energy Secretariat was in no way surprising or in any sense an unusual departure from existing practice. What was new, of course, was the context. The 'oil boom' necessarily placed a premium on technical advice and the 'independence' that went with it. Hitherto, Williams had been able to manage the latter either by direct oversight (location of such advice principally within the Office of the Prime Minister); or by political control at one remove (the device of the minister of state); or simply by adroit personnel management (which included 'banishment' from the prime minister's favour). Now the very scale of operations envisaged threatened this. Temporarily, Williams was disarmed. Once the future pattern of the development of hydrocarbon resources had been decided, however, he was able to act decisively. One means, disciplinary vigilance, signalled that, if his reliance on technocracy had increased, it was not to be unconditional. The other, later developed extensively, was the institution of multiple portfolio-holding by subordinate ministers. This led to a situation which, if not exactly analogous to the politics of a Renaissance court, was not far removed from it either. With everyone watching everyone else and everyone entitled to make a decision even if they chose not to do so, administrative efficiency was clearly discouraged at the same time as central political control was effectively exerted.

Party control

The PNM had been built and developed under the unquestioned leadership of Williams. His association with the party was its guarantee of success and little was done to develop it either organisationally or ideologically. When, therefore, he 'resigned' in 1973 'confusion glorified' reigned, only finally to be dispelled by his 'return'. This, initially, was not explicitly on any understanding of change in party procedure or organisation. That emerged only later, and specifically in the context of the 1976 general election.

In a speech to an 'elections preparations' meeting of the PNM's General Council on 23 May 1976, and to the astonishment of those present, Williams announced:

> The electorate wish no part whatsoever of the majority of the PNM incumbents and nominees, no matter who else is satisfied with them ... Let it be understood now – once and for all, by all and sundry – the Political Leader has not the slightest intention of encumbering himself, yet again, with these traditional party millstones, unable to speak properly, knowing nothing of basic issues facing country and world; incompetent for higher responsibilities which ultimately fall on the Political Leader's shoulders, unable – unbelievable though it sounds – even to seek to assist their constituents in difficulty who further turn to the Political Leader and interfere with his attention to his formal, public, national responsibilities ... Either the nominees remain and you get a more appropriate Political Leader, or the Political Leader remains and you get more appropriate candidates for whom no apology need be made. There is no other alternative.[53]

As in 1973, the initial reaction within the PNM was confusion and dissension. But Williams was eventually to have his way and fifteen new nominees were presented (along with five of the 'millstones' for whom he subsequently refused to campaign). More to the point, all had accepted the new conditions for candidates which Williams had long advocated[54] but previously been unable to impose on the party. These required, *inter alia*, the declaration of assets and liabilities; a cast iron commitment to pay a percentage of salary to the PNM; and, most important, the provision of an undated signed letter of resignation to the Speaker of the House of Representatives, to be held personally by Williams. This last condition, of course, was the disciplinary measure *par excellence*. Williams's own justification of it was couched in such terms – past practice had shown it to be absolutely necessary in such an essentially undisciplined society as Trinidad and Tobago.[55] His main opponent within the PNM, Karl Hudson-Phillips, saw it differently, however. He declared he would not sign such a letter (and hence not contest the election), declaring that it 'could lead to the subjugation of the will of Parliament to a single individual and to a frustration and indeed subjugation of the will of the electorate'. It was, he went on, 'a sure recipe for dictatorship'.[56] On this question Williams wisely kept his counsel; after all, he had achieved what he intended. Not only was he leader of the PNM but, when occasion demanded, he could also be above it.

In the late 1960s, as we have seen, Lloyd Best coined the phrase 'Doctor Politics' to describe the political system in Trinidad and Tobago. His description of the evolving situation as it emerged in 1976 is equally apt:

> We have returned to Crown Colony Government with a vengeance. A Governor (masquerading as a Prime Minister) as the only responsible official; a Legislature as decoration pure and simple; an Executive Council of hand-picked officials, some from the Lower, some from the Upper House but all at the mercy of the Chief Executive. It is the Trinidad and Tobago variant of Latin American Presidential power.[57]

All that was lacking was a new mandate from the people. This Williams now sought and won. He did so in an extraordinary campaign which saw him launching attacks on all around him, friend and foe alike.[58] He did so because he knew that, whatever else had transpired, he retained the faith of a significant percentage of the electorate. This was mapped at the time in a national opinion survey. Asked 'Do you on the whole approve of Dr Williams's performance as prime minister?', 62 per cent of respondents said 'yes', 22 per cent 'no', with 16 per cent having no opinion. More pointedly, asked 'Who would you like to see as the next prime minister?', 35 per cent of respondents expressed a preference for Williams – a level of support greater than that of all of his opponents combined.[58] The PNM, not surprisingly, won the election easily, being returned in twenty-four of the thirty-six seats contested, with the support of 54 per cent of those who voted. Again the turn-out was low, only some 56 per cent of registered electors voting.

'Presidential power' and the national development state: 1976–81

In his final administration Williams sought to harness the political gains of the previous three years to the task of rapid economic development. As in 1962–6, this was an attempt at consolidation of power through the medium of 'state-building', but whereas then the task had been essentially politico-administrative in character, now it was overwhelmingly economic, shown most forcefully in Williams's retention of the finance portfolio throughout this time. This permitted him, by virtue of office, not only to give general direction to economic transformation, but also to establish the priorities, notably the creation of a petroleum-based and energy-intensive industrial sector and the use of Special Funds as instruments of development. To carry this out a considerable concentration of political and administrative 'talent' was gathered together. At all times, though, Williams was careful to retain formal authority, further manipulating the political system to this end and appealing direct to the people as 'father' of the nation when occasion arose. A presidential style thus evolved against which opposition often appeared futile. However, it was not entirely absent and, much as power was being consolidated, it was also being eroded, especially in the very last years of his administration. Indeed, at the time of his death these contrary tendencies were finely balanced, imparting to the political process as a whole that same degree of uncertainty which had characterised Trinidad and Tobago in 1970 and 1973.

Industrialisation

Williams's first commitment was to industrialisation. The basis for this was natural gas, which Trinidad and Tobago possessed in abundance, being 'one of no more than ten countries in the entire world to have this precious commodity surplus to needs'.[60] The export of gas via the construction of a liquefied natural gas facility was thus a distinct possibility, and feasibility studies and investment arrangements to this end continued throughout the period. However, of far greater importance was the utilisation of gas locally to link the petroleum sector directly with industry, and during Williams's administration three major projects were realised in this area – a fertiliser joint venture with W. R. Grace (TRINGEN), a fertiliser joint venture with Amoco (FERTRIN) and the establishment of a wholly government-owned iron and steel plant (ISCOTT). The estimated cost of all three, at the end of 1979, was some TT$1,700 million,[61] to which should be added substantial infrastructure costs relating to the development of the Point Lisas industrial estate of not less than TT$200 million directly and millions more indirectly.

Such massive investments were unprecedented in Trinidad and it was only to be expected that difficulties would arise. To meet them, a Co-ordinating Task Force under the chairmanship of a long-standing associate of Dr Williams, Professor K. Julien, was appointed in 1975. This agency soon assumed the central direction of the industralisation effort and, despite setback and delay, retained Williams's confidence throughout, being reorganised as the National Energy Corporation in 1979. Williams's role was thus not one of day-to-day direction (this falling to Errol Mahabir as minister in the Ministry of Finance and Minister of Energy and Energy-based Industries) but of 'propagandist at large' for the entire effort and final arbiter of difficult decisions. Among the most controversial of these were the introduction of government-to-government arrangements in the 1979 budget speech. The background to this was weak performance by local contractors in fulfilling the tenders awarded to them. The solution proposed, in a novel twist on the 'industrialisation by invitation' theme, was for the government to approach selected foreign governments and ask them to sponsor a particular project by (a) designating competent national firms (public and private) with which the government of Trinidad and Tobago would enter into agreements; and (b) guaranteeing or assuming responsibility in some explicit and practical way for the satisfactory completion of projects undertaken by the designated firms. Eventually, some forty-one projects were identified under these arrangements, and inevitably those involved were drawn overwhelmingly from transnational corporate interests in North America and Western Europe. The paradox of energy-based industrialisation in Trinidad and Tobago was thus revealed as acute dependence in the short run in the hope of independence in the long run, a cost amply illustrated by Williams at the end of 1978 when he noted:

> United States firms and institutions dominate our energy-based industries. We have joint ventures with United States

firms for fertiliser and liquefied natural gas, and are negotiating in respect of methanol, aluminium, petrochemicals. The United States Export-Import Bank has loaned us over US$200 million in respect of FERTRIN, ISCOTT and the new Point Lisas power plant. US commercial banks are heavily involved in the financing of FERTRIN, TRINGEN, ISCOTT and the power plant. US firms have won in the international bidding for such contracts as the power plant and major water projects.[62]

Needless to say, such developments met with considerable criticism inside Trinidad, where it was argued that for all the costs involved the returns might turn out to be slight, with risks outweighing certainties, particularly in securing adequate foreign markets for which production was necessarily geared. It was also noted that only limited employment opportunities would arise from such industries and that 51 per cent control in joint ventures with transnational corporations was in essence no control at all. Against this, Williams simply counterposed the alternatives – leave the gas in the ground, flare it or, more realistically, export it, in which case he gave a warning:

Some ten years ago the Government, with the knowledge that extensive hydrocarbon resources were discovered off the East coast, was presented with a deal signed and sealed in foreign boardrooms, a deal which effectively said to us: Company X was going to sell Company Y our Trinidad gas which Company X had discovered. It was going to sell it at 25 cents per thousand cubic feet, liquefy it, and ship it to a country where the President had committed himself to provide cheap gas for the population. A deal signed and sealed, ready for execution. We almost did execute it in the moment of our exhilaration: we had gas and there were people interested in buying it from us. What account of our stewardship would we have provided today if following the advice and recommendations of many, we had proceeded along that path of 25 cents for gas which can now sell across the Mexican border at US$4.00 per thousand cubic feet. Millions of cubic feet of gas leaving our shore every day while we have deficiencies in the gas supplies for our electricity. No iron and steel, no more fertilisers, no methanol, no urea, no possibility of aluminium.[63]

In other words, the arguments for energy-based industrialisation were irrefutable and the programme would proceed come what may.

Special funds

In 1974, as noted earlier, the government set aside quinquennial development planning for a system of annual review. In practice, this had two elements: expenditure incurred in what continued to be referred to as a Development Programme under which head some TT$1,818.9 million was spent to the end of 1980; and appropriations to Special Funds for long-term development amounting to some TT$7,503.3 million in the same period.[64] This latter figure, in both absolute and relative terms (37 per cent of government revenues 1974–80), was by any account a considerable commitment to future growth in Trinidad and Tobago. What form it initially took may in part be gauged from a sectoral breakdown of fund allocation and expenditure in the first few years.

Of the total appropriations, 26.2 per cent were made to the 'economic' sectors, 22.4 per cent to the 'social' sectors, 43.4 per cent to 'infrastructure' and 8 per cent to 'other' sectors.[65] In the economic group, agriculture's share was 2.7 per cent, compared to petroleum's 16 per cent, manufacturing's 0.7 per cent and that for commerce and finance of 7 per cent. On this basis, 'petroleum', in its widest sense, was not only to carry within it significant government participation but was also to continue to be a prime motor for growth. In the 'social' category, education received 7.4 per cent, health 1.7 per cent and housing 10.4 per cent. The high figure for housing here represented the government's response to spiralling costs which had put home ownership beyond the reach of even the moderately well-to-do. With respect to the appropriations for infrastructure, approximately half was intended for transport (air, land and sea), while the provisions for water and sewerage amounted to 9.7 per cent of total appropriations. The intention here was clearly to make available in Trinidad and Tobago all the necessary trappings of a modern, namely Western, society at its most advanced. Finally, in the category 'Other Funds', two funds relating to building projects and land acquisition made for nearly 40 per cent of total appropriations under this head.

Expenditure from the funds amounted to TT$3,482.3 million to the end of 1979.[66] It was allocated as follows: 'economic' sector, 35.2 per cent, the two highest-spending funds being the Petroleum Development Fund (25.6 per cent) and the Participation in Commercial Enterprises Fund (6.5 per cent); 'social' sectors, 16.3 per cent, the two highest-spending funds being the Education Fund (6.7 per cent) and the Housing Fund (6.5 per cent); infrastructure, 45.7 per cent, the principal expenditures being the Water Resources Fund (12.2 per cent), the Air Transport Fund (7.3 per cent), the Roads Fund (7.2 per cent) and

the Point Lisas Infrastructure Development Fund (6.5 per cent); and
'Other Funds', 2.8 per cent. Patterns of expenditure, as might be
expected, were thus similar to patterns of appropriation, and the combined effect of both was to increase considerably the share of GDP
accruing to the construction and financial sectors. Alongside this, of
course, was the deepening and widening of the government's role in
the economy, to the extent that one observer of events at the time suggested that 'government's current and capital expenditure taken
together may now be well in excess of 50 per cent of Gross Domestic
Expenditure as compared to 15 per cent in 1959'.[67] The very real
power that this gave the Minister of Finance needs no emphasis.
Williams, of course, was well aware of it and he used it as the principal
foundation upon which he further elaborated his presidential style.

Presidential style

In the flush of victory after the 1976 general election Williams told the
PNM: 'As your Political Leader, I remain at your service for as long as
I may be needed or available. I have helped in twenty years to make
PNM great. I shall do all I can to assist PNM in continuing to
prevail'.[68] Three years later, he revealed to the party how he was
fulfilling this pledge:

> I have in effect taken the back seat – taking care particularly
> not even to appear to compete with our new head of state,
> the President of our Republic ... and taking equal care to
> allow my Cabinet colleagues to occupy the centre of the
> stage so that the public can judge between them... I have
> taken care also to avoid even the semblance of foreign inter-
> ference or local lobbying ... avoiding like the plague all that
> wining and dining which has traditionally been associated
> with West Indian society and politics. The Government, the
> Cabinet, speaks on this, that or the other as its duty to the
> country, the Prime Minister's utterances are reduced to the
> irreducible minimum... So I reserve my statement and activ-
> ities for general issues and fundamental national objectives
> and for re-affirming the basic philosophy of the PNM.[69]

Withdrawal, not engagement, was the essence of the Williams presidential style, leading him to live the life of a recluse in the last few
years before his death. Administration and government were carried
out by others – authority, however, remained vested in William's
hands, and he took care to ensure that it should stay that way.

First and foremost, this meant control of the party, and the principal stratagem here was a steadfast refusal to designate a successor. This, of course, capitalised on the experience of 1973 and proved an effective whip, keeping all but the most recalcitrant in line. Leadership issues thus did not emerge publicly in this period and the party made do with the 'temporary' arrangement of 1970 – the provision of three Deputy Political Leaders, namely Mahabir, George Chambers and K. Mohammed. At the next level, that of the legislature, discipline was effected through the medium of the undated letter of resignation coupled with the passage of the Constitutional (Amendment) Act of 1978. This provided that 'a member of the House of Representatives shall vacate his seat in the House where, having been elected with the support of a party, he resigns from or is expelled by that party'.[70] The introduction of this legislation followed immediately upon the 'defection' from the Cabinet and the PNM of the former Minister of Works, Hector McClean, and was clearly intended to give 'teeth' to the 'letter of resignation' held by the Prime Minister. Its effect overall is difficult to judge, since it did not deter two 'millstones' – Carlton Gomes and Brensley Barrow – from writing to Williams to ask for the return of their letters; and the legislation itself was later declared unconstitutional by the Appeal Court of Trinidad and Tobago. At the same time, however, it did give force to Williams's assertion that 'when a constituency chooses its member of Parliament, he is not just a Member of Parliament, he is a PNM Member of Parliament'[71] and the record shows no others following McClean's example. If only negatively, then, it might be concluded that the measure acted as some form of constraint. Finally, at the level of the individual party member, disciplinary procedures could be invoked. This was the course followed most emphatically in the cases of Karl Hudson-Phillips and Ferdi Ferreira, both senior members of the PNM and both suspended in March 1980 for publicly criticising Williams's address to the 1979 Annual Convention of the PNM as 'totally irrelevant'.[72]

Beyond the PNM, Williams could, of course, appeal to the country direct. In these last years he chose to do so largely through the medium of live broadcasts, favouring especially the set pieces of the annual address to the PNM convention and the annual budget speech. These typically became occasions for wide-ranging reviews over the whole spectrum of government and the economy. In them, Williams not only revealed his erudition but underlined and emphasised his unrivalled claim to authority as visionary and technical expert rolled into one. An image of the statesman in action – remote, omnipresent, but above all benevolent – was thus assiduously fostered, the benevolence stemming directly from his position as trustee for the nation in his dual capacity as

'Corporation Sole'[73] and Minister of Finance. The rhetoric employed here was an identification with the interests of 'the small man', whom Williams claimed constantly to represent and defend. At one level, this meant promotion of the policy of divestment of government holdings, with its promise of shareholding for all, either directly or indirectly. At another, it implied continuation of the policy of subsidies and tax concessions. The extent of these to 1976 has already been indicated. Thereafter they continued to escalate, with subsidies reaching a staggering level of TT$2,420 million for the period 1977–80 inclusive. Allocations under this head were as follows: basic food (14.7 per cent), agriculture and fisheries (2.6 per cent), welfare (10.7 per cent), utilities (39.6 per cent), petroleum products (27.3 per cent), and others (3.8 per cent).[74] Income tax concessions were also granted in each budget, with the amount of revenue foregone estimated as TT$24.8 million in 1978; TT$16 million in 1979; TT$13.1 million in 1980; and TT$32 million in 1981.[75] From 1978 onwards the wisdom of such measures came to be questioned, both inside and outside Trinidad and Tobago; the government responding with the appointment of a Committee to Review Government Expenditure which reported in October 1978. Its major recommendations were that no new welfare programmes be implemented and that there should be a moratorium on further tax reductions. While in subsequent budget pronouncements Williams was to pay tribute to the work of the committee, there is little evidence of any real attempt to implement its recommendations or grapple seriously with the problem posed. 'Giveaways' thus continued to characterise government fiscal policy, and it was finally left to Williams's successor to call a halt with his sober presentation of the 1982 budget, which ended ominously with the words, 'the fête is over and the country must go back to work'.[76]

The erosion of power

In the 1976 general election campaign Williams invited those who did not like the PNM's policy to 'emigrate to the Bronx and clean toilets'.[77] This contemporary update of an early 1960s remark that those who did not like what he was doing 'can get the hell out of here' was to find an immediate test case in Tobago, where the electorate had just rejected the two PNM incumbents and returned to the House of Representatives Williams's former deputy, A. N. R. Robinson. His vigorous presentation of the case for internal self-government for Tobago constituted a vexatious problem for the government over the next five years. The question of whether internal self-government should be conceded was not itself an issue, the government agreeing to it early in 1977.[78] The form it should take, however, was, and led to inordinate delay and tortuous proceedings, so that the bill granting internal self-government did not reach the House of Representatives for debate until 12 September 1980. As enacted, it provided for a fifteen-member Tobago House of Assembly (twelve elected and three appointed) charged with implementing in Tobago government policy in respect of finance, economic planning and development, as well as the provision of various local services. These were powers considerably greater than any local government in Trinidad, yet at the same time they were less than the self-government originally envisaged. Moreover, the legislation carried a sting in its tail. This was the provision, ostensibly under-lining the unique powers of the Assembly, that members of the Senate and House of Representatives were barred from belonging to it. For Robinson, for whom no doubt this bar was intended, it left a particu-larly cruel choice of alternatives with which he was faced almost immediately when elections were held for the Assembly on 24 November. Robinson chose to contest, resigning his seat in the House of Representatives to do so. His Democratic Action Congress (DAC) was returned in eight of the twelve seats in what was regarded as a high poll (63 per cent). Williams took no part in the campaigning and, all things considered, the PNM retained a substantial foothold, winning 45 per cent of the votes as against the DAC's 53 per cent.[79] This served to underline the fact that, while Tobago had been an irri-tant and running sore for the government, it had never led to a haemor-rhage of support. What was questionable, however, was whether the same could be said by then of other issues, of which corruption and accountability were to receive prominent coverage.

The belief that 'corruption is rife among those who hold high political office'[80] has been a staple of Trinidadian politics both before and after the PNM came to power. It has fed largely on rumour and gossip, with the added spice of the odd uncovered instance of adminis-trative impropriety, usually at lower levels.[81] Williams, and other high officials in the PNM and public service, did not escape accusation, although proof that would lead to a conviction in a court of law proved difficult to obtain. In 1980, however, a number of scandals surfaced and it appeared that at last evidence might be found to implicate, if not Williams himself, then a number of those around him. Easily the most embarrassing were the so-called 'DC9 scandal' and the 'race track scandal'. In each case it was later shown that questionable payments had been made to former high officials of the Trinidad government by US-based transnational companies to obtain lucrative government con-tracts, and in both instances the matter was thoroughly aired in the

Trinidad and Tobago press, to the delight of the opposition. Williams's reaction was to attempt to distance himself from any controversy, seeking to avoid making any specific comments and reserving his interventions to general statements on the themes of accountability and integrity. On this front, however, far more was promised than was ever achieved, raising doubts as to his desire to prosecute the matter vigorously. Two examples may be cited. One concerns the Integrity Commission, provided for in the 1976 constitution. By 1981 it had still not appeared, and in that year all he was promising party and nation was that more would be said 'in due course'.[82] The other was to show that, if Trinidad and Tobago was not entirely above reproach on this matter, then nor were others. In 1979 he thus warned:

> We must be on our guard against the agents and promoters, international and local, who seek to peddle their services and create by their very presence an environment which is a congenial breeding ground for corruption. We must guard against those who would seek to have us smeared and set about in a very deliberate and subtle manner to achieve that end. We must guard against the impression that the mere fact we are a young and developing country automatically qualifies us for a handout over or under the table. I am aware of this growing breed of agents and promoters. What are the services they offer and to whom? I may not know all the answers but I have knowledge of some.[83]

In other words, corruption could not be condoned, though it might be understandable in the circumstances. A constant temptation to many, it was 'a sword of Damocles' hanging over their heads giving Williams an advantage in the short term, with effects clearly corrosive to the body politic in the long run. That the reckoning itself might be sooner rather than later was indicated sharply with the emergence of a new party on the political scene.

On 19 April 1980 K. Hudson-Phillips, the designated successor to Williams at the time of the 1973 resignation crisis,[84] launched the Organisation for National Reconstruction (ONR) in Woodford Square, Trinidad. The timing was significant. It was but two days before the local government elections in Trinidad, which were widely expected to confirm, and indeed did, the collapse of the United Labour Front (ULF) as a credible opposition within the country.[85] It also anticipated, by a matter of weeks, Hudson-Phillips's expulsion from the PNM for criticisms of Williams, the party and the government. The ONR was thus conceived simultaneously as a response to a political vacuum and as a vehicle for the ambition of its leader. Over the coming months it attracted widespread publicity and generated significant support, so creating difficulties within the PNM camp. Of these, the most important was the acknowledged fact that the ONR was in many respects a 'clone' of the PNM, advocating the same policies and seeking to represent the same social constituency.[86] It thus constituted a serious potential inroad into PNM power and a genuine threat, the magnitude of which was shown in a poll conducted by St Augustine Research Associates early in 1981. Asked 'If an election were to be held in Trinidad and Tobago in the next two months, which party would you vote for?, 29 per cent of a sample of 561 opted for the ONR, 28 per cent for the PNM, and 14 per cent for other parties, with the remainder indifferent or uncommitted.[87] Equally promising for the ONR were replies to two other questions. The first, 'Do you think Dr Williams should resign as Prime Minister to make room for a successor?, saw 50 per cent answering 'yes' and 35 per cent 'no'. The second took this further, asking 'If the Prime Minister did in fact resign, whom would you like to see become the next Prime Minister of Trinidad and Tobago?'. The replies here were 33 per cent for Hudson-Phillips, 33 per cent 'don't know' and 34 per cent for other candidates or no one.[88] True enough, this poll did not predict victory for the ONR – but then, neither did it for the PNM, and that in itself was a considerable change from the situation only nine months earlier.

As the election year of 1981 loomed, Williams, paradoxically, was both stronger than ever before and also weaker. His strengths were his hold on power at the centre – the authoritative command of the decision-making processes of a government growing ever larger as it sought, with some success, to manage the consequences of dependency. His weaknesses were those associated with the performance of this government as it affected the citizenry in their daily lives – bestowing a favour here or apportioning blame there in ways so arbitrary they could be interpreted as either capricious or pernicious according to context and observer. How this situation might be translated into votes on the day no one, not even the most experienced commentator, was prepared to say. What was only now apparent, though, and not before, was that Williams himself was preparing to run for office for a sixth consecutive term.

Death, succession and evaluation

On 25 January 1981 Williams ended his address to the Silver Jubilee convention of the PNM as follows:

> So, my dear friends and party colleagues, here we stand
> after 25 years, to report on our stewardship, to establish

our readiness and fitness to continue the struggle on which we embarked 25 years ago, then as now against the rest, then as now with powerful vested interests against us, then as now with the mightiest force in the country in our support, ready to go at the word of command, keeping our powder dry till we see the whites of their eyes, confident in the support of the Lord God of Hosts who will rule, as he has ruled so often in our 25 years. Great is the PNM and it will continue to prevail.[89]

Nine weeks later President Ellis Clarke was to inform the nation he was dead of undiagnosed diabetic coma. The immediate reaction, as reported in the press, was one of loss and sorrow at the passing of a great man.[90] But, if his death constituted a shock for the country, it did not create a trauma. Contrary to expectations, the succession was accomplished with a minimum of fuss, President Clarke naming George Chambers, one of the deputy leaders of the PNM, as Prime Minister. He was not the obvious choice, although his confirmation in office proceeded without opposition. How this was achieved thus invites consideration of the complex of factors involved. It also points out the nature of the political system Williams left behind.

Most important was the government. In his final speech Williams reiterated a theme he had emphasised earlier when he noted:

The prime minister has remained as virtually chairman of the Cabinet, co-ordinating, establishing priorities, working through committees, the work of which is done by the ministers without even the presence of the prime minister. The result is that, something of which few countries can boast, Trinidad and Tobago now has a team of eight or so top flight speakers and negotiators, ready to deal with any subject in any part of the world, presenting the point of view of the Cabinet as a whole. Pride of place herein is the number of ministers in the Ministry of Finance, all given increasing insight into our financial problems and ramifications.[91]

Chambers was one of these – and, indeed, had perhaps the greatest experience within the Cabinet of matters directly relating to finance. This, however, was not enough without recognising the system of power Williams had established. As noted earlier (and above), it was one where Williams retained ultimate authority while permitting delegated decision-making and limited initiative in important and sometimes sensitive areas. This was supplemented at a second level,

outside the Cabinet, by what Parris accurately described the following year as 'rule through interlocking directorates'.[92] The reference
here was to the existence of some 300 persons of ability running the
public sector, all of whom were 'political appointees' of the prime
minister and whose role was 'to communicate the political line which
is dominant at the particular time'. At the apex of this small and
select constituency, according to Parris, were twenty-two individuals,
all men, chiefly of African descent, whose average age was fifty-one.
Chambers, of African descent and then aged fifty-two, though not
one of them, fitted the profile perfectly. He did so by giving legitimacy to technocracy in the form of the party. The PNM thus constituted an indispensable and necessary base for power. Chambers could
deliver this, not only because he was close to the party stalwart in the
sense of being a self-educated man of lower middle-class origins, but
also because he was thought to be loyal to Williams's memory, the
recollection being that he was the man who in 1973 had not sought
power but, on the contrary, had led a movement to persuade Williams
to stay on.[93] Chambers thus represented continuity, as opposed to
change for change's sake. As he told the PNM special convention
which nominated him unopposed on 9 May, 'what is wrong must be
put right, and what is right must stay right',[94] with the emphasis, as
his first few months in office showed, on the latter without compromising in any fundamental sense his commitment to the former.
Obviously important here were the imperatives of the impending
election and a desire not to rock the boat in troubled waters. They
were the third factor which facilitated a smooth succession and one
in which 'chance', as Machiavelli would have it, played as much a
part as judgement in determining the final outcome. Without changing very much, Chambers performed the miracle of transforming the
PNM's fortunes at the polls. In one taken in June and published in
the *Trinidad Express* in July, he emerged as clear favourite for the
national leadership, with 35 per cent as compared to 14 per cent for
his nearest rival, Hudson Phillips. Of those polled, 29.2 per cent said
they would vote for the PNM and only 10.9 per cent for the ONR.[95]
Chambers, it appeared, had not only learnt from the departed master,
but was actually in the process of surpassing him – a feat confirmed
in the resounding win achieved by the PNM in the general election of
9 November, subsequent analysis of which by an experienced
observer drew the comment that 'Trinidad is inexorably moving
toward a dominant one-party state'.[96]

   Any pronouncement of political stability as Williams's major
legacy must be qualified, however, by a frank recognition of the economic foundation on which it rested. From 1974 to 1980 he presided

over a boom in the economy in which real output grew at an average annual rate of 7 per cent and government revenues at an average annual rate of 44 per cent.[97] Much of this, of course, can be ascribed to one factor alone – the continued domination in the economy of the petroleum sector, which in 1980 contributed some 35 per cent of GDP, nearly three times the contribution of the next highest sector (transport, storage and communications), nearly five times that of manufacturing excluding petroleum and eighteen times that of agriculture.[98] Acute dependence on this area had, however, been recognised and government-directed policies of diversification had been vigorously promoted to attempt to change it. Pride of place had gone to the establishment of the energy-based industries, to which massive commitments were made. This was not without considerable risks, which Williams presumably knew and weighed carefully before taking. 'I understand what Nasser meant, when he showed me proudly his steel plant, by saying, since you have hydrocarbons, go for steel. I understand now what Luxembourg meant, a tiny country in the EEC, with an incredible steel complex, when it told me years ago, go for steel,'[99] was how Williams attempted to rationalise his decision to the people of Trinidad and Tobago. His vision was sound, but the immediate legacy was a programme which the country found difficult to sustain in the harsh economic climate of the 1980s and which ultimately it had to review and revamp as it weathered the storms of recession and structural adjustment.

Notes

1   P. K. Sutton, 'Dr Eric Williams and politics in Trinidad', in *Caribbean Societies*, Vol. I, Collected Seminar Papers, No. 29, Institute of Commonwealth Studies, University of London, 1982, p. 54.

2   See, in particular, Selwyn Ryan, *Race and Nationalism in Trinidad and Tobago*, Toronto, 1972.

3   See Ivar Oxaal, *Black Intellectuals Come to Power*, Cambridge, Mass., 1968.

4   See K. Bahadoorsingh, *Trinidad Electoral Politics: The Persistence of the Race Factor*, London, 1968.

5   'Insider' accounts confirm this. See C. L. R. James, *Party Politics in the West Indies* (formerly PNM Go Forward), San Juan, n.d.; W. Mahabir, *In and Out of Politics*, Port of Spain, 1978; and P. Solomon, *Solomon: An Autobiography*, Port of Spain, 1981.

6   Lloyd Best, 'Options facing Williams, the ruling party and the country, *Trinidad Express*, 31 May 1969.

7   Sutton, 'Dr Eric Williams and politics in Trinidad', in *Caribbean Societies*, p. 56.

8   See, in particular, M. Kroll, 'Political leadership and administrative communications in new nation states: the case study of Trinidad and Tobago', *Social and Economic Studies*, 16, 1, 1967.

9   See Eric Williams, *Inward Hunger: The Education of a Prime Minister*, London, 1969, p. 322, and PNM, General Council – Research Committee, *The Party in Independence*, Port of Spain, 1964.

10 See, in particular, Y. K. Malik, *East Indians in Trinidad: A Study in Minority Politics*, London, 1971.

11 Ryan, *Race and Nationalism in Trinidad and Tobago*, pp. 285–7.

12 See his *Inward Hunger* and *From Columbus to Castro: The History of the Caribbean 1492–1969*, London, 1970.

13 See P. K. Sutton, 'Black Power in Trinidad and Tobago: the crisis of 1970', *Journal of Commonwealth and Comparative Politics*, 21, 2, 1983.

14 People's National Movement, *The Chaguaramas Declaration: Perspectives for the New Society* (Approved at a Special Convention, 27–29 November 1970), Port of Spain, n.d.

15 Of those registered to vote, only 33 per cent did so. As virtually the sole significant party the PNM won all the seats.

16 See People's National Movement, *Address by the Political Leader Dr Eric Williams* (Fifteenth Annual Convention, September 1973), Port of Spain, n.d.

17 *Prime Minister's Eleventh Independence Anniversary Message 1973*, Press Release No. 520, 30 August 1973.

18 Figures from Trinidad and Tobago, *Third Five-Year Plan, 1969–1973*; and Trinidad and Tobago, *Review of the Economy, 1972*, Port of Spain.

19 Figures from V. Mulchansingh, 'The oil industry in the economy of Trinidad', *Caribbean Studies*, 11, 1, 1971.

20 Figures from *Third Five-Year Plan*.

21 Trinidad and Tobago, Ministry of Planning and Development, *Causes of Unemployment in Trinidad and Tobago and some Remedial Measures*, mimeo, Port of Spain, 1970.

22 1. Jainarain, *Trade and Underdevelopment: A Study of the Small Caribbean Countries and Large Multinational Corporations*, Georgetown, 1976, pp. 332–3.

23 Frank Rampersad, 'Overseas investment and fiscal policy in Puerto Rico, Jamaica and Trinidad and Tobago', in P. Ady (ed.), *Private Foreign Investment and the Developing World*, New York, 1971.

24 Dr E. Williams, 'The purpose of planning', in M. Faber and D. Seers (eds), *The Crisis in Planning*, Vol. 1, London, 1972, pp. 46–7.

25 See Carl Parris, *Capital or Labour? The Decision to Introduce the Industrial Stabilization Act in Trinidad and Tobago*, Working Paper No. 11, Institute of Social and Economic Research, UWI, Jamaica, 1976.

26 Trinidad and Tobago, *White Paper on Public Participation in Industrial and Commercial Activities*, Port of Spain, 1972.

27 Havelock Brewster, 'Economic dependence: a quantitative interpretation', *Social and Economic Studies*, 22, 1, 1973.

28 *Ibid.*, p. 94.

29 Production was at the following levels: 1968, 67 million barrels; 1971, 47.2 million barrels; 1973, 68.2 million barrels. Figures from Organisation of American States, *The Economic and Social Development of Trinidad and Tobago: Characteristics, Policies and Perspectives*, OEA/Ser. 4/XIV, CEPCIES/99, October 1975.

30 Trinidad and Tobago, Central Statistical Office, *Annual Statistical Digest*, 1978, Port of Spain.

31   For details, see Selwyn Ryan, *The Politics of Succession: A Study of Parties and Politics in Trinidad and Tobago*, mimeo, St Augustine, chapter 1.

32   See Sutton, 'Dr Eric Williams and politics in Trinidad', in *Caribbean Societies*.

33   'Prime Minister's Independence Day Message 1974', in Dr Eric Williams, *Forged from the Love of Liberty* (selected speeches of Dr Williams compiled by P. K. Sutton), Port of Spain, 1981, p. 80.

34   *Ibid.*, p. 76.

35   'Economic Transformation and the Role of the PNM', *Address* by the Political Leader, Dr Eric Williams, to the sixteenth Annual Convention of the PNM, October 1974, mimeo, Port of Spain.

36   See 'The Energy Crisis – 1975', *An Address to the Nation*, at Point Fortin, 11 April 1975, Trinidad and Tobago, 1975, and 'Speech by Dr Eric Williams' at Harris Promenade, San Fernando, 13 April 1975, mimeo, Port of Spain.

37   Figures calculated from Trinidad and Tobago, *Accounting for the Petrodollar*, 1980, Table 31.

38   *Ibid.*, pp. 46–8.

39   See '1976 and 1956', *Address* by the Political Leader, Dr Eric Williams, to the seventeenth Annual Convention of the PNM, October 1975, mimeo, Port of Spain.

40   House of Representatives of the Republic of Trinidad and Tobago, *Budget Speech 1978* (Dr E. Williams, 2 December 1977), p. 10.

41   Calculated from Trinidad and Tobago, *Review of Fiscal Measures in the 1980 Budget*, Port of Spain.

42   The perils of careless divestment are set out in Williams, 'Address at the Opening of the First Branch of the National Insurance Board, 19 May 1977' in *Forged from the Love of Liberty*, pp. 55–61.

43   Cited in Ryan, *Race and Nationalism in Trinidad and Tobago*.

44   Constitution Commission of Trinidad and Tobago, *Report of the Constitution Commission*, para. 51.

45   See, in particular, D. Moore, 'The Westminister model under attack: the report of the Constitution Commission of Trinidad and Tobago', *Journal of Constitutional and Parliamentary Studies*, 8, 3, 1974.

46   'Constitution Reform', Speech by the Prime Minister in the House of Representatives, 13 and 17 December 1974, Port of Spain, 1975, p. 82.

47   'PR: To Dissolve the Present PNM Majorities', *Address* by Dr Williams to the Sixteen Southern Constituencies Rally, 1 April 1973, Port of Spain, n.d.

48   See 'Constitution (Republic) Bill', Second Reading, House of Representatives of Trinidad and Tobago, *Hansard*, Speech by Dr Williams, cols. 677–734.

49   'Economic Transformation and the Role of the PNM', mimeo, pp. 29–30.

50   '1976 and 1956', in Williams, *Forged from the Love of Liberty*, Part 2, Section 4, p. 185.

51   *Ibid.*; see also Speech on the Constitution (Republic) Bill, cols. 685–730.

52   '1976 and 1956', in Williams, *Forged from the Love of Liberty*, p. 191.

53   *Trinidad Guardian*, 26 May 1976.

54   See his 'Address to the Fourteenth Annual Convention of the PNM, September 1972', in Williams, *Forged from the Love of Liberty*, Part 2, Section 1; and his 'Address to the Fifteenth Annual Convention of the PNM', September 1973.

55   *Ibid.*

56   Letter from Karl Hudson-Phillips to the Prime Minister in *Trinidad Guardian*, 30 May 1976.

57   *Tapia*, 3 October 1976.

58   See Ryan, *The Politics of Succession*, chapter 5.

59   S. Ryan, E. Greene and J. Harewood, *The Confused Electorate – A Study of Political Attitudes and Opinions in Trinidad and Tobago*, St Augustine, 1979, Table 1.37, p. 23, and Table 1.40, p. 25. The figures for others were: Panday, 7 per cent; Robinson, 6 per cent; Best, 5 per cent; others, 10 per cent. Significantly, 37 per cent said they didn't know.

60   'Problems of Industrialization', *Address* by Dr E. Williams to the twentieth Annual Convention of the PNM, 29 September-1 October 1978, mimeo, p. 10.

61   House of Representatives of the Republic of Trinidad and Tobago, *Budget Speech 1980* (Dr E. Williams, 30 November 1979), pp. 3–4.

62   House of Representatives of the Republic of Trinidad and Tobago, *Budget Speech 1979* (Dr E. Williams, 1 December 1978), p. 8.

63   'Twenty-fifth Anniversary', Political Leader's *Address* to the Special Convention of the PNM, 25 January 1981, mimeo, paras. 75–6.

64   Calculated from *Review of Fiscal Measures in the 1980 Budget*, pp. 11–12.

65   *Ibid.*

66   Calculated from *Accounting for the Petrodollar*, Table V.

67   Ramesh Ramsaran, *The Growth and Pattern of Public Expenditure in Trinidad and Tobago 1959–1979*, St Augustine, mimeo, p. 103.

68   'The PNM in the Next Five Years, 1976–1981', *Address* by Dr E. Williams to the eighteenth Annual Convention of the PNM, 3 December 1976, mimeo, Port of Spain, p. 63.

69   'The Caribbean Man', *Address* by Dr E. Williams to the twenty-first Annual Convention of the PNM, 29 September 1979, mimeo, Port of Spain, pp. 3–4.

70   See *Caribbean Contact*, June 1978.

71   'The Party's Stewardship, 1956 to 1980', Speech to the twenty-second Annual Convention of the PNM, 26 September 1980, in Williams, *Forged from the Love of Liberty*, p. 425.

72   *Latin America Newsletters*, Caribbean Regional Report, 28 March 1980, p. 6.

73   'Corporation Sole' was designated in 1973 as the device by which the Minister of Finance held all government shareholdings by virtue of his office.

74   Calculated from Trinidad and Tobago, *Accounting for the Petrodollar*, Table 31.

75   *Ibid.*, pp. 48–50; *Budget Speech 1978*, p. 61; and House of Representatives of the Republic of Trinidad and Tobago, *Budget Speech 1981* (Dr E. Williams, 5 December 1980), p. 49.

76   George Chambers, *Budget Speech 1982*, mimeo, Port of Spain, p. 64.

77   Ryan, *The Politics of Succession*, p. 204.

78   See, in particular, the speeches of Robinson and Selwyn Richardson in J. G. Davidson (ed.), *Tobago versus PNM*, Port of Spain, 1979, pp. 11–67.

79   *Caribbean Contact*, December 1980.

80   *Report of the Constitution Commission*, para. 235.

81   For details, see W. Richard Jacobs, 'Patterns of Political Corruption in Caribbean Society: A Comparative Study of Grenada, Jamaica and Trinidad and Tobago', *Occasional Papers*, ISER, UWI, St Augustine, December 1978, pp. 49–91.

82   *Budget Speech 1981*, p. 35; 'Twenty-fifth Anniversary' *Address* (PNM), para, 137.

83   'The Caribbean Man', pp. 82–3.

84   Of the 250 PNM party groups which made valid nominations, 224 endorsed Hudson-Phillips as against twenty-six for K. Mohammed. See Ryan, *The Politics of Succession*, p. 20.

85   In the elections the PNM won control over every county and municipal council in Trinidad, conceding only eleven of the 113 seats available, and winning thirty-one of them unopposed. See *Caribbean Contact*, May 1980.

86   See, in particular, Selwyn Ryan, 'The church that Williams built – electoral possibilities in Trinidad and Tobago', *Caribbean Review*, 10, 2, 1981.

87   *Ibid.*, Table 4, p. 45.

88   *Ibid.*, Tables 1 and 2, p. 45.

89   'Twenty-fifth Anniversary' *Address* (PNM), para. 139.

90   See, in particular, the commemorative issue of *Caribbean Contact*, May 1981.

91   'Twenty-fifth Anniversary' *Address* (PNM), para. 138.

92   Carl Parris, 'Power and rule under Williams', *Trinidad and Tobago Review*, 5, 12, 1982. This is not the first reference to interlocking directorships. A. N. R. Robinson in his *The Mechanics of Independence: Patterns of Political and Economic Transformation in Trinidad and Tobago*, Cambridge, Mass., 1971, notes in respect of difficulties surrounding the passage of the 1966 Finance Act: 'The defects of the corporate structure had other fiscal implications; the social and political consequences were tight control of the economy of the country by an oligarchy made all the more limited through interlocking directorships,' p. 92. Is the situation Parris refers to one of private economy absorbing public polity, or public economy absorbing private polity? Or is it just state capitalism?

93   Of the forty PNM party groups who refused to nominate a candidate to succeed Dr Williams, twenty were from the St Ann's constituency represented by Chambers.

94   *The Advocate-News* (Barbados), 11 August 1981.

95   See *Caribbean Contact*, September 1981.

96   John LaGuerre, 'The General Elections of 1981 in Trinidad and Tobago', Department of Government, UWI, St Augustine, February 1982, mimeo, p. 1.

97   Figures from Chambers, *Budget Speech 1982*, pp. 9 and 11.

98   Figures from 'Trinidad and Tobago Country Notes' in United Nations, Economic Commission for Latin America, *Economic Activity in 1980 in Caribbean Countries*, CEPAL/CARIB 81/10, Appendix, Table 2.

99   'The Caribbean Man', p. 78.

2 | The 'democratic socialist' experiment of Michael Manley in Jamaica

During the 1970s Jamaica aroused more interest in the eyes of the world than any other country in the Commonwealth Caribbean. It owed this attention to the election of a government publicly committed to the ideology of 'democratic socialism' and determined to reshape Jamaican society, economy and external relations accordingly. The government, formed by members of the People's National Party (PNP) and led by Michael Manley, held office for some eight and a half years between 1972 and 1980 and was witness, in Manley's own estimation, to 'some of the more controversial events'[1] of Jamaica's colourful history. It came to power on a tide of hope buoyed up by the support of Jamaica's underprivileged classes for its wide-ranging programme of reform, but ultimately fell from grace following one of the heaviest electoral defeats ever suffered by a leading political party in modern Jamaica.

The whole Manley experiment thus constitutes dramatic evidence of the problems and possibilities that attach to 'democratic socialist' strategies of reform in trying to overcome dependency in the Third World. This chapter examines the early Manley years in Jamaica, assesses the PNP government's particular achievements and failures and sets out some of the lessons that can be learnt from the attempt to bring about radical change in a context of underdevelopment and dependency. It begins by describing the main features of the political economy with which Manley and the PNP had to grapple.

The political economy of Jamaica

At the beginning of the 1970s, when the Manley government first came to office, the political economy of Jamaica was more complex and diverse than ever before in the island's history. The days of sugar monoculture and the resulting ascendancy of foreign plantation owners were past. Even the prevailing pre-independence pattern of an economy consisting mainly of traders importing finished goods in exchange for the export of primary products (extended beyond sugar to include bananas, coffee, citrus and, most important, bauxite, production of which began in 1952 and grew swiftly to an output of one million tons by 1953 and six million by 1958) had been substantially altered. As in other parts of the region, successive Jamaican governments during the 1950s and 1960s pursued policies of industrialisation aimed at encouraging the establishment of both import-substitution and export-oriented manufacturing enterprises. In addition, tourism was assiduously promoted as a further valuable earner of foreign exchange. By these various means the economy was able to grow throughout the 1960s by an average of nearly 6 per cent per annum.[2]

Despite this apparently creditable achievement, Jamaica retained at the end of the decade a weak and dependent economy suffering from many serious defects. Domestic agriculture had remained stagnant and was the source of continuing poverty in rural areas. Income distribution was more uneven than ever, the share of the poorest 40 per cent of the population in personal earned income declining from 7.2 per cent in 1958 to 5.4 per cent in 1968. Illiteracy, poor housing and unemployment remained the lot of large numbers of Jamaicans. Indeed, the level of unemployment and underemployment had increased hugely, doubling from 12 per cent to 24 per cent during the very period of fast economic growth. The higher wage rates paid in the new mineral and manufacturing sectors encouraged people to forsake low-paid agricultural employment in the hope of finding work in these industries, even though the capital-intensive character of most of the imported technology meant that few jobs were created. The expanding sectors of the economy generally forged very limited linkages with other parts of the economy. A substantial amount of sugar was shipped in a raw state, although it was technically and commercially feasible to refine it on the island; the bulk of the bauxite mined was exported as ore despite the advantages to Jamaica of processing it locally; the manufacturing sector consisted largely of 'screwdriver' operations, heavily dependent on imports of raw materials and partly finished components; and the tourist industry was notorious for its failure to create a web of linkages with local agriculture and was thus partly responsible for Jamaica's growing imports of foodstuffs. The effect overall was accurately described as 'a form of perverse growth'.[3]

Much of the explanation lay with the extent and nature of the foreign control to which the Jamaican economy was still subject at the beginning of the 1970s. The island's leading sugar estates were owned by a large British company, whilst the bauxite industry was in the hands of four American and Canadian corporations; many hotels were part of foreign businesses. Banks and insurance companies, a large part of the communications network and even a number of basic public utilities (including the electricity and telephone services) were also in foreign ownership. Only in the manufacturing sector were most firms in majority local ownership, although the distinction between a family firm and the branch plant of a foreign company was difficult to draw in practice. As a New World economist pointed out, 'a family firm may manufacture a metropolitan product under a franchise, the clauses of which are so detailed that the metropolitan enterprise is determining almost all the major managerial decisions – raw and intermediate materials procurement, capital equipment, marketing methods, accounting formats and even employment policy'.[4] What is certain is that economic growth was dependent on private foreign capital transmitted to the island by one mechanism or another but then lost to the local economy by means of profit repatriation and intra-company transfer pricing. Jefferson has calculated that between 1959 and 1969 the funds flowing out of the Jamaican economy actually exceeded all the incoming investments attracted by official incentive policies.[5] By 1972 the bulk of this exchange of capital was with the US, effectively inserting Jamaica into the domain of US hemispheric power.

The continuing external domination of the economy had a powerful influence on the structure of the class system. In particular, it fostered the emergence of a weak local capitalism. The Jamaican capitalist class was initially based on its ownership of land and its control of the colonial distributive trade through import/export agencies and commission houses; in the 1960s it succeeded in adjusting its role in the economy by moving, albeit reluctantly, into local manufacturing. It was very tightly knit, not extending much beyond twenty-one family groupings, and focused upon just five interrelated 'super-groups', the Ashenheims, the Desnoes-Geddes, the Harts, the Henriques and the Matalons, who between them occupied over a third of available directorships in the corporate economy, and enjoyed an additional sense of unity derived from the absence of blacks and the predominance of Jews, local whites, Syrians and Chinese in its ranks.[6] The visibility and assertiveness of this class should not, however, be allowed to give an exaggerated impression of its power. As we have seen, it maintained its position in the local economy only by securing subordinate agency relationships with foreign firms and by generally effecting a deferential alliance with foreign capital. It had become dependent for further growth on state patronage in the form of subsidies, incentives, import protection, tax holidays and the like. Increasingly, therefore, it was forced to cultivate the local political elite which since independence had come to control the state. As Stone noted, however, 'the alliance between members or sectors of the capitalist class and ruling politicians is one that grows out of the weakness of that class rather than its strength'.[7]

The unformed character of the capitalist class at the beginning of the 1970s also extended to the working class, the peasantry and the unemployed. The latter typically lived at subsistence level and devoted their energies to the search for individualistic solutions to their dilemma, ranging from crime to 'hustling' and political gangsterism. The urban working class grew in size during the economic expansion of the 1960s, but remained only partially organised. The small size of many of the industrial plants established under the import-substitution programme led to a low level of unionisation and the prevalence of paternalistic labour relations. The unionised sector of the working class did possess a capacity for collective action, but limited its activities to narrowly-defined goals, such as industrial disputes and wage bargaining. Similarly, the various agricultural associations which represented the interests of small peasants devoted their efforts mainly to extension work, the improvement of marketing facilities and the distribution of state subsidies. In short, there existed few channels by which ordinary Jamaicans could influence national economic policy-making.

As in other dependent societies in the Third World, the fact of external domination and the underdeveloped nature of local class relations placed heavy demands on the state. It was in a position of economic subordination to powerful overseas interests, but nevertheless could direct the domestic political system. What emerged in Jamaica in the 1950s and 1960s, despite superficial similarities to the political norms of Western liberal democracy, was a clientelist style of politics, whereby the political elite functioned as brokers, channelling state patronage both to the depressed masses and to the capitalist class.[8] The first aspect of this system is easy to understand. The low level of stable employment afforded by the particular pattern of economic growth meant that employment through the state and its various departments, boards and agencies became crucial as a source of livelihood. A tradition developed in which political support was exchanged for the material benefits of a job, even a home. The second aspect relates to the ambiguous position of local capitalists within the power structure. They played a significant role in the funding of the political parties which competed for control of the state and they sat in important positions on many of the statutory agencies, like the Industrial Development Corporation, by which the policy of the state was implemented. All of which meant that their political influence was considerable. Nevertheless, the fact remains that since independence they had been forced to act more and more as subordinate clients of the professional educated elites which dominated both the main political parties. To this extent, the state possessed a degree of autonomy which was at one and the same time both real and qualified, a point nicely made by

Stone's sardonic observation that 'the hegemony of international corporate capital presents the only constraint to the petty bourgeois party
leadership from consolidating into an independent ruling class'.[9]

Manley's strategy of change

From the moment in 1969 when he became leader of the PNP in succession to his father, Michael Manley demonstrated a clear understanding of the nature of the political economy produced in Jamaica by the
post-war era of expansion. As a former trade union leader, he was
aware that the social benefits of economic growth had been spread
thinly and that there were pockets of alienation within the urban environment of Kingston which on more than one occasion during the
1960s had exploded into violence.[10] By addressing himself to this dis-
content, and adopting a dynamic approach to such issues as unemployment, poverty and political participation, Manley was able to lead the
PNP to victory in the 1972 elections. The result reflected the broad
range of support which Manley received from the young, the unemployed, large sections of the working class and peasantry, most of the
professional and administrative middle class and intelligentsia and
even some newer members of the capitalist class disaffected by the
economic failures of the previous Jamaica Labour Party government,[11]
and could only be interpreted as a decisive mandate for change.

By this time Manley had also developed a coherent vision of the
changes he wished to introduce in domestic and foreign policy. In the
former sphere, they consisted of three basic commitments. The first
was the creation of an economy that would be more independent of
foreign control and more responsive to the needs of the majority of the
people. This required a wide range of initiatives, including land
reform, the creation of co-operative farms, the promotion of worker
participation and measures to achieve a more equitable distribution of
wealth, but it revolved at heart around the extension of state control
into the 'commanding heights' of the economy. In the various public
utilities Manley envisaged the swift implementation of complete government ownership, but admitted that, 'as a matter of common sense
and reality, public ownership will have to work together with foreign
and private capital'[12] for the foreseeable future in such areas as
bauxite, sugar, tourism and banking. He rejected expropriation and
asserted that 'the question is not whether to use foreign capital in
development planning', but how to bring it into 'harmony with
national aspirations'.[13] He also accepted the permanent existence of a
mixed economy. In his own words, 'once certain priorities have been

overtaken in the field of human resources, infrastructure and certain strategic areas of the economy, private enterprise is the method best suited to the production of all the other goods and services which are necessary to the functioning of an economy'.[14]

The second feature of the strategy was the development of a more egalitarian society not only in terms of opportunity, but also in the deeper sense of mutual respect and appreciation. To this end, Manley sought to use the state to ensure that certain basic rights were enjoyed by all Jamaicans. Education facilities, previously narrow and elitist, were to be expanded and opened to all classes; resources in the health service were to be concentrated upon preventive medicine in the countryside, rather than sophisticated hospital care in the capital; certain laws were to be amended to improve the legal position of employees and women, especially mothers; and, significantly, the government was to accept responsibility for organising massive work programmes of unemployment relief as a positive social duty. A common theme in all these proposals was a commitment to the use of public expenditure to increase the level of egalitarianism in society.

The third aspect of Manley's programme was political. Manley was critical of the remoteness of traditional multi-party democracy in Jamaica, in particular its tendency to reduce itself to the act of choosing a party to form a government every five years. To this he posed the alternative, not of the single-party state, but what he described as 'the politics of participation'. This called for basic political engineering to 'create the institutions through which people feel continuously involved in the decision-making processes'[15] even as governments faced the need to make compromises or take unpopular decisions. Accordingly, Manley proposed the revitalisation of Jamaican local government, the establishment of community councils, the involvement of the public in economic planning, the deployment of the political party as an instrument of mass political education and communication, and a host of other measures designed to intensify the level of popular political mobilisation.

The various elements of this strategy of change were conceived by Manley as 'a third path'[16] for Jamaica and the rest of the Caribbean, signifying a rejection of both the Puerto Rican and the Cuban models of development. In his view the former was, to all intents and purposes, the policy pursued in Jamaica in the 1950s and 1960s, emphasising economic growth and foreign investment but neglecting social welfare. By contrast, the latter was a model of revolution with impressive social achievements but based on the Marxist-Leninist view of democracy which did not allow political rights outside the concept of the dictatorship of the proletariat. For Manley, both models also stood condemned by their respective dependence on the two super-powers, the US and the USSR. It was, as he put it, 'self-evident to us that we want to be pawns neither of East nor West, economically or politically'.[17] Only the third path offered Jamaica and the Caribbean the option of real independence.

This last point is of real importance because it highlights the fact that Manley's programme of change possessed a clearly articulated international dimension. He understood from the outset that domestic reform could be secured only if his government was able to negotiate better terms for Jamaica in all its dealings with the international economy. To some extent this was met by the proposal to bring such industries as bauxite and sugar into partial public ownership, but it was also deemed to require a radical revision of the direction of post-independence foreign policy. Manley worked from the perception that Jamaica was a part of the Third World: he attached considerable weight to the development of a global Third World economic strategy designed to increase collective self-reliance, and he favoured the creation of an organisation of bauxite-exporting countries on the lines of OPEC. More generally, he proposed the adoption of an open foreign policy which envisaged relations with a variety of countries beyond Jamaica's traditional partners, including those with communist ideologies and political systems. Notice was also given of Jamaica's readiness to support wars of liberation on the African continent. In short, Manley sought to establish the fact, hitherto largely unacknowledged in Jamaican foreign policy, that 'the entire world is the stage upon which a country, however small, pursues this perception of self-interest'.[18]

Manley's thinking contained, therefore, a number of diverse elements which made it difficult to categorise. In this respect, the ideological label he himself adopted, that of 'democratic socialism', does not necessarily help. Manley has recorded that when the PNP came to choose a name around which to mobilise support for its programme of change it considered three possibilities:

> Christian socialist was rejected on the grounds that it might sound like a political ploy. We decided not to use the word socialist alone because it seemed to invite too much speculation. Quite apart from communism, there were a number of African socialist states organised on a one-party basis. Then again, the local communists were at that time in semi-hiding under the term 'scientific socialist'. Since we were neither communist nor seeking to establish a one-party state, it seemed to invite unnecessary risk to use the term socialist without qualification. In the end, we settled on democratic

> socialist. The democratic was to be given equal emphasis
> with the socialist, because we were committed to the mainte-
> nance of Jamaica's traditional and constitutional plural
> democracy; and more importantly, because we intended to do
> everything in our power to deepen and broaden the democra-
> tic process of our party and in the society at large.[19]

One notes the care with which Manley and his party tried to establish
the particular nature of the ideas that were to guide their attempt to
reshape the political economy, and one can appreciate the reasons for
their choice. Respect for democracy was both genuine and the *sine qua
non* of securing popular support in Jamaica, where the concept is well
embedded in the political culture, whilst there was an obvious attrac-
tion to the idea of reaffirming the PNP's original socialist appeal which
had lain dormant since the expulsion of a small Marxist faction from
the party in 1952. From the analytical point of view, however, 'democratic socialism' is hardly the most precise term in the political vocab-
ulary, the content of the socialism as well as the reality of the
democracy begging all sorts of questions, quite apart from the manner
and mode of their attainment.

It is more accurate to view Manley's approach to politics as a
complex, but not inconsistent, combination of several strands of
thought. First, he was a nationalist, committed to the service of
Jamaica, the assertion of its place in the world and the achievement
of a greater degree of economic independence for it within the international capitalist system. Second, he was a populist, hostile to class politics, attracted by the idea of wide mass involvement in decision-making
and determined to bring the benefits of reform to all sectors of society.
Third, he was a social democrat, holding typically Fabian views on the
key questions of social and economic organisation. He learnt his political economy at the London School of Economics in the late 1940s,
studying under Harold Laski and admiring the reformist policies of the
post-war British Labour government. In sum, all Manley's thinking
disavowed, either explicitly or by implication, Marxist-Leninist
notions of class struggle and proletarian dictatorship. It rested instead
on what he called the 'single touchstone of right and wrong',[20] the
notion of equality, which he made the foundation of his strategy of
change for Jamaica in both its internal and external dimensions.
'Social organisation,' he wrote, 'exists to serve everybody or it has no
moral foundation . . . the fact that society cannot function effectively
without differentials in rewards, together with the fact that men are
manifestly not equal in talent, must not be allowed to obscure the
central purpose of social organisation. That is, and must always be, the

promotion of the welfare of every member of the human race.'[21] Armed with this package of ideas and possessed of the power of the state, Manley set about the business of reform.

Reform and re-election: March 1972 – December 1976

The first two years of the PNP government brought a number of significant social reforms but no decisive break with the previous direction of economic policy. The reforms included the release of some land to farmers under the Land Lease project, the inauguration of 'crash programmes' of job creation to relieve unemployment and the introduction of a number of new welfare commitments, most notably the announcement of free secondary education for all. Foreign-owned electricity, telephone and omnibus companies were nationalised, but with compensation, and there was a reorganisation of the various statutory corporations in the state sector which, however, served to ensconce some of the PNP's supporters among the capitalist class in important management positions.[22] In all, it was an even-handed start entirely in keeping with the government's multi-class electoral base.

The year 1974 was a turning point for the Manley administration. The fact of dependency rendered Jamaica more than usually vulnerable to the economic crisis which came to a head all over the world. Its economy simply could not cope with the effects of the sudden rise in the price of oil and the generalised economic recession that followed. In one year, from 1973 to 1974, the island's oil import bill rose from J$65 million to J$177 million.[23] Other import prices rose in consequence, especially food and manufactured goods, putting further pressure on the cost of living and the balance of payments. Foreign capital inflows declined, as did income from tourism, and, although the price of sugar reached high levels towards the end of 1974, it plummeted the year after. In addition, the government's own measures of welfare reform had considerably increased state expenditure, which, in an economy lacking the resources to sustain such a sudden expansion, meant that the public sector debt also increased dangerously. Between 1972 and 1974 it rose by 56.7 per cent from J$332.6 million to J$520.8 million; more significantly, the foreign component of the debt went up by even more, from J$117.3 million to J$206.3 million over the same period, an increase of 75.6 per cent.[24] It was the cumulative impact of this severe economic situation, rather than political commitment *per se*, which forced the Manley government to press ahead with the more radical of its proposed reforms.

The first sign of this change of gear came in January 1974 when the government announced its intention of renegotiating the tax agreements signed with the American and Canadian-owned bauxite and alumina companies. These agreements had not been altered since the early 1950s, when the industry was first set up in Jamaica, and produced only a token tax yield for the government. After four months of inconclusive talks Manley abrogated the agreements and imposed a novel method of raising revenue, a production 'levy' on all bauxite mined or processed in Jamaica set at 7.5 per cent of the selling price of the aluminium ingot instead of a tax assessed according to an artificial profit level negotiated between the companies and the government. It was an extremely effective mechanism from the Jamaican point of view, raising the revenue from the industry from a meagre J\$22.71 million in 1972 to no less than J\$170.34 million two years later.[25] Interestingly, the new policy was supported by, and indeed derived a good deal of impetus from, the Jamaican capitalist class, whose economic well-being, dependent on substantial imports of goods not only for personal consumption but as inputs for their 'final touch' manufacturing industries, was being threatened by a shortage of foreign exchange.[26] Their role was recognised by the appointment of two leading members of the class, Meyer Matalon and Patrick Rousseau, as chairman and vice-chairman respectively of the National Bauxite Commission, which presided over the negotiations with the companies. Many of the benefits of the increased revenue also went to these industrialists. To handle the additional money the government created a so-called Capital Development Fund, whose official purpose was to bolster the productive capacity of the economy. Management was again placed in the hands of Meyer Matalon, who instead proceeded to direct the bulk of its budget into the construction industry to the particular advantage of companies owned by his fellow capitalists.[27]

As far as the government was concerned, the institution of the levy marked only the beginning of a 'bauxite offensive'. It initiated talks with the companies aimed at the purchase of majority control in their local operations, set up the Jamaica Bauxite Institute to provide it with independent data on the technical side of the industry and played the leading part in the formation of the International Bauxite Association (IBA), a producers' cartel inspired by OPEC. The aluminium corporations responded to these moves aggressively at first: they filed a suit with the World Bank's International Centre for the Settlement of Investment Disputes contesting the legality of the levy, pressed the US government to intervene on their behalf with the Jamaican government, and began to transfer bauxite and alumina production from Jamaica to other parts of the world. The Jamaican share of the world bauxite market fell from 19 per cent to less than 14 per cent between 1973 and 1976, whilst that of countries like Australia and Guinea increased markedly.[28] Yet, ultimately, an accommodation was reached between the companies and the Manley government.[29] The companies realised that new tactics were needed to guarantee continued access to the Jamaican ore for which many of their alumina plants were specifically geared and so resolved to accept the production levy and the government's joint venture proposals. Under these, the government purchased all the land the companies owned in Jamaica and 51 per cent of their mining operations, whilst the companies kept their refining plants and retained management control for the next ten years at least. In the unspoken part of the agreements they also maintained their superiority in technology, control of the market and access to capital. In this light the government's challenge to the position of the bauxite companies appears rather more muted.

Perhaps the longer-term significance of the new bauxite policy was that it brought the Manley government directly to the attention of the US administration. Bauxite is a mineral of strategic importance and in the mid-1970s the US drew approximately half its supplies from Jamaica.[30] It seems, however, as if the US government was initially prepared to tolerate Jamaica's actions. Manley later reported that he had an affable meeting with US Secretary of State Henry Kissinger on the subject in 1974, in which, he believed, he had forestalled any US hostility to the levy.[31] Accordingly, the part of the government's bauxite strategy most likely to have aroused Kissinger's opposition was the formation of the IBA. Potentially, at least, this touched a raw US nerve in that it purported to promote a wider Third World resistance to Western economic interests. Such a commitment was, of course, an integral part of Manley's programme of change and was to contribute to the hostility which he quickly came to arouse within the US government.

The main cause of this was Cuba. Not long after assuming office Manley had incurred the displeasure of the US ambassador, who considered him particularly responsible for the decision of the independent Commonweath Caribbean countries to announce their full diplomatic recognition of Cuba. In September 1973 he attracted further suspicion by flying to the Non-aligned summit meeting in Algiers on board Fidel Castro's private plane. Manley's attendance at the conference indicated the prominence of the role that he and his government intended to play in the Third World movement and, in particular, in the diplomacy attached to the call for the enactment of a 'New International Economic Order'. It also marked the beginning of a friendly relationship between the PNP government and the Cuban regime, which agreed to provide Jamaica with technical assistance in school construction and fishing. In the middle of 1975 Manley paid a state visit to Cuba to give his thanks and, at Castro's side, made an impassioned anti-imperialist speech before cheering crowds. These moves raised real, if unfounded, doubts in Washington about the extent of Jamaica's commitment to the West. In US eyes the doubts were more than confirmed by Manley's reaction to the Cuban decision to send an army to assist the Marxist regime in Angola. Manley has described a very different meeting with Kissinger during a short vacation the Secretary of State spent in Jamaica towards the end of 1975. 'Suddenly he raised the question of Angola and said he would appreciate it if Jamaica would at least remain neutral on the subject of the Cuban army presence in Angola. I told him that I could make no promises but would pay the utmost attention to his request.'[32] Kissinger then apparently brought up the separate matter of a Jamaican request for a US$100 million trade credit. 'He said they were looking at it, and let the comment hang in the room for a moment. I had the feeling he was sending me a message.'[33] In Manley's mind the linkage was clear, but nevertheless five days later he publicly announced Jamaica's support for Cuban involvement in Angola. This declaration, made out of a sense of morality typical of Manley's approach to international relations, ensured that US economic aid to Jamaica was embargoed until the end of the Ford administration.

These geopolitical considerations were no doubt the primary cause of the deterioration of US-Jamaican relations, but the situation cannot have been helped by one further important initiative of the Manley government in the aftermath of the economic crisis of 1973–4, namely the PNP's dramatic reaffirmation of its commitment to 'democratic socialism' in September 1974. The launch was widely and deliberately publicised,[34] but the manifesto, when it appeared, contained little that was new, defining 'democratic socialism' as a commitment to four principles already fundamental to Manley's approach to politics: the democratic political process, the Christian principles of brotherhood and equality, the ideals of equal opportunity and equal rights, and a determination to prevent the exploitation of the people.[35] Certainly, the direction of the government's policy was not noticeably changed by the declaration of support for socialism. The intention was rather to mobilise the people more actively behind the PNP's strategy of change. Following a loss of popularity in the face of spiralling living costs and persistently high unemployment since he came to power, Manley felt it necessary to revive the populist fervour of his 1972 election campaign. In this sense the reaffirmation of socialism was conceived primarily as a piece of mid-term electioneering.

The campaign did, however, have one important unintended consequence. It marked the limit of the PNP's acceptability to members of the local capitalist class. Until this point they had been content to let Manley deal in the rhetoric of the masses and indulge in any symbolic manipulation that helped to placate the evolving consciousness of the oppressed in Jamaica. They were unhappy about the government's developing friendship with Cuba, yet knew, or thought they knew, what Manley was about. But socialism! That broke all the rules. It seemed to constitute the introduction of ideology into the neutered Jamaican political arena and thus risk the development of a kind of politics that articulated, rather than masked, class interests.

From this point onwards, domestic and international opposition to Manley's programme of change came together and worked in tandem. Politically, the local capitalist class turned their energies towards a resuscitation of the opposition Jamaica Labour Party; economically, they contracted their investments in Jamaica, exported foreign currency illegally and migrated in large numbers to North America. Those who stayed created such a mood of panic in the private sector that the corporate economy was slowly drained of activity. From outside Jamaica there appeared to emanate all the signs of what has become known as 'destabilisation': inaccurate foreign press reports calculated to undermine the tourist industry,[36] unexplained violence and arson in the ghettoes of Kingston, a barrage of vituperation against the Manley government in the columns of the main newspaper, the *Daily Gleaner*, owned by the Ashenheim family, and allegations of a strong CIA presence among US embassy personnel in Jamaica.[37] Most damaging of all was the credit squeeze to which the country was subjected. The US Agency for International Development turned down a request for a food grant, the US Export-Import Bank dropped Jamaica's credit rating from the top to the bottom category and commercial banks ceased all lending to the island. In combination with the decline in the production of bauxite immediately following the imposition of the levy, these measures served to bring about a catastrophic deterioration in the foreign exchange position.

In response, Manley allowed the process of socialist mobilisation to take off more intensively than the terms of his original strategy dictated. Whilst the economy was temporarily shored up by means of bilateral loans from friendly governments, such as those of Trinidad and Canada, the attack on the country by imperialist forces was made the theme of the PNP's 1976 election campaign. Until then Manley had endeavoured to preserve a balance between the left and the right in the party, but now he gave his support to the left and allowed the party secretariat, under the leadership of Dr D. K. Duncan, to organise a heavily ideological campaign. Even the communist Workers' Liberation League offered him 'critical support'. In a sense it was hugely successful, because, despite the desperate condition of the economy, the PNP was re-elected in December 1976 with a massive majority, winning forty-seven out of the sixty seats. In fact, although nobody realised it at the time, the victory represented the failure of Manley's initial conception of the politics of change. The PNP no longer represented the majority of people of all classes. Its support among the capitalists and the middle class had all but disappeared and been displaced by gains among the working class and the unemployed.[38] The overall effect was to polarise class voting patterns and rob Manley of his chance of leading a genuinely populist movement of reform.

The IMF and retreat: January 1977 – October 1980

In the heady atmosphere that followed the election, the extent to which the nature of Manley's victory had undermined his original strategy of change was not realised. Instead, the result was interpreted by many in the PNP as an endorsement of the socialist mobilisation of the preceding year. Before the election Jamaica's dire economic situation had been thought by the government to necessitate an appeal for assistance from the IMF. A provisional set of measures had been worked out and the foreign exchange markets closed as a prelude to their implementation. After the election, however, this policy was cast aside in the face of intense opposition from members of the party's left-wing. They were doubtful of the efficacy of the monetarist approach of the IMF when applied to Third World economies and argued that, in the short run, Jamaica could survive the foreign exchange crisis by careful rationing of earnings, supplemented by loans and other kinds of material support from socialist bloc and progressive OPEC countries. Manley's personal position is not known, but he powerfully articulated the government's defiance of the IMF in a speech to the nation on 5 January 1977:

> The International Monetary Fund, which is the central lending agency for the international capitalist system, has a history of laying down conditions for countries seeking loans . . . this government, on behalf of our people, will not accept anybody anywhere in the world telling us what to do in our country. We are the master in our house and in our house there shall be no other master but ourselves. Above all, we are not for sale.[39]

Accordingly, the government announced a very different programme of economic measures to the deflationary package implicit in
the proposed IMF agreement. To be sure, certain moves were perhaps
intended to keep that latter option open, such as the imposition of a pay
moratorium and a higher tax on petrol, but they could not disguise the
dominant influence of the left on the government's post-election thinking. There was to be no devaluation, which was the main demand of
the IMF. Several left-wing economists from the University of the West
Indies, under the leadership of Norman Girvan, were brought in to
strengthen the national planning apparatus. Radio Jamaica was to be
purchased as part of a political education programme led by the newly-
formed Ministry of National Mobilisation, whose first head was D. K.
Duncan, the PNP's left-wing General Secretary. Negotiations were also
announced for the take-over of three foreign banks, including Barclays,
and the island's only cement factory, owned by the Ashenheim family.
Finally, preparation of a 'production plan' was set in motion, to be
based on suggestions made by the ordinary people. The strategy as a
whole envisaged the mobilisation of Jamaica's exploited classes
against local and foreign capitalist control.

It turned out to be only a brief interlude in the political economy
of the Manley years. As Fitzroy Ambursley has observed, these initiatives brought the PNP to 'the Rubicon of retreat or social revolution'.[40]
At this point Manley could have embarked fully upon the committed
socialism of class confrontation, a road he had tentatively set out upon,
albeit under pressure of external events, during the mobilisation of
1976 and in the immediate aftermath of the election. The goal of a
populist programme of change supported by all classes in society
would have had to be abandoned and a different sort of politics erected
in its place. There can be no doubt that this was the aim of the left,
both inside and outside the PNP. There were, however, still those in the
party who shied away from this prospect and, as Manley put it, 'looked
askance at all these young Turks of the left, often sporting beards, tams
and jeans, playing so prominent a part in affairs'.[41] The left themselves
have subsequently argued that, in the final analysis, Manley himself
was to be found in this category, betrayed by 'his lack of confidence in
the capacity of the masses of black Jamaican people to assert their productive creativity', a view that derived from 'a brown Jamaican petit-
bourgeois perspective'.[42] Certainly, nothing in the evolution of
Manley's political thought predisposed him to accept the ideology of
class politics which was being urged upon him. As noted earlier, his
thinking had developed along entirely different lines. At any rate, he
retreated. The announcement that negotiations would resume with the
IMF was made in April 1977, from which moment onwards the story

of the Manley government became, to all intents and purposes, the story of its relationship with the Fund.

Manley subsequently claimed that he had 'no choice at that time'[43] but to do as he did. Within the limits of his own politics, that may well have been right. At home, the call for 'people's planning' produced a massive response, but of half-baked, unrelated and often trivial ideas, and ultimately foundered on the harsh reality of the lack of technical and economic knowledge at the mass level. Nor was there ever very wide support for the anti-imperialist implications of the left's strategy. A national poll conducted by Carl Stone in May 1977 showed, by contrast, that 76 per cent of the population favoured the receipt of US aid[44] – hardly the ideal political base from which to challenge the hegemony of international capitalism. Abroad, the constraints were even tighter and, from the left's point of view, not short of irony. As part of the post-election plan, tentative efforts were made to seek financial aid from the socialist world, including an unpublicised approach to the Soviet Union. They proved unsuccessful: Jamaica had not prepared the ground in any way for forging the connection and was not otherwise of sufficient political or military significance to attract large-scale Soviet support.[45] At the same time as this rejection was becoming manifest, signals were emanating from Washington that the new Carter administration, which had replaced the Ford-Kissinger team at the beginning of 1977, was desirous of a more friendly relationship with the Caribbean, beginning with Jamaica. Prompted by Carter's ambassador to the United Nations, Andrew Young, an old friend of Manley, the aim of US policy seemed to be to coax Jamaica back into the Western camp. The opening was seized upon by the moderates in the Manley government, who included P. J. Patterson, the foreign minister, to argue for a return to the traditional focus of foreign relations. The conjuncture of these two pieces of diplomacy was critical and, in so far as the US made it known that the resumption of aid would be easier if Jamaica repaired its relations with the IMF, paved the way for the decision to resume talks.

Initially, Jamaica was able to wield a good deal of bargaining power in its negotiations with officials of the Fund.[46] In the early rounds the main sticking point was the scale of the devaluation required. The government proposed a dual exchange rate: a 37.5 per cent devalued 'special rate' applicable to traditional exports and inessential imports, but a 'basic rate' at the old level for government transactions, essential imports of food and medicines and, most important, bauxite exports, the value of which would thereby be maintained. The Fund opposed this and the government's slight easing of its wage guidelines, but Manley was able to utilise his personal friendship with

Prime Ministers Callaghan of Britain and Trudeau of Canada to bring some leverage to bear on the board of the IMF. In the end, however, it was probably the readiness of the Carter administration to 'lean' on the IMF on Jamaica's behalf that forced the Fund to settle largely on Jamaica's terms. The amount to be provided was US$74.6 million over the two years to June 1979, subject to the economy meeting the well-known IMF performance tests. In the circumstances, the agreement was relatively satisfactory from Manley's point of view. Additional foreign exchange would become available, the basic imported goods on which the island's poor depended would be spared a huge increase in price, and the government's general programme of extending public ownership could even be slowly advanced. In 1977 the National Sugar Company took over several more of the island's sugar estates and a State Trading Corporation was established with a view to eventually handling all imports.

However, the embrace of the IMF was not to prove so tolerant for long. In a development utterly unexpected by Manley, at least, the economy failed the first performance test in December 1977. On the day in question the net domestic assets of the Bank of Jamaica exceeded the required ceiling of J$355 million by a mere J$9 million, or 2.6 per cent. The Fund seized on this as evidence of irresponsible domestic economic management, suspended the next tranche of the loan and returned for further talks to be conducted in an altogether harsher manner. There is no need to follow every aspect of the negotiations, for there was little that the government could do but agree to a virtually total overturn of its previous economic policies. A new agreement was finally concluded in May 1978, providing US$240 million over three years, but depending upon the introduction of, in Manley's words, 'one of the most savage packages ever imposed on any client government by the IMF'.[47] It contained as its centrepiece the reunification of the exchange rate, along with a further immediate general devaluation of 15 per cent, to be followed by a 'crawling peg' arrangement under which there would be further mini-devaluations every two months (which amounted to 15 per cent over the first year of the programme). There were also to be drastic cuts in the size of the public sector, a cutback in the operations of the State Trading Corporation, sharp tax increases, price liberalisation to guarantee a 20 per cent rate of return on capital invested by the private sector, and finally a mandatory limit on wage settlements of 15 per cent a year, in comparison with the predicted increase in the cost of living of some 40 per cent.

By this stage, what else could the Manley government do? In terms of domestic politics, the PNP left was a defeated force in the struggle within the party, its decline symbolised by Duncan's resignation as Minister of National Mobilisation in September 1977, whilst the moderates and conservatives who dominated the cabinet could neither prevail on the IMF to soften its position nor think of any alternative source of foreign exchange. As the tone of his speeches and public appearances at the beginning of 1978 indicated, Manley himself was subdued. Internationally, the Jamaican government had lost even the qualified support of the Carter administration, partly as a result of internal changes within that government, notably the declining influence and eventual resignation of Young, but also because Manley insisted throughout Jamaica's economic traumas on maintaining a radical and pro-Cuban foreign policy. He entertained Castro on a state visit to Jamaica in October 1977 and repeatedly praised the social and economic achievements of the Cuban revolution. He also continued to assert aggressively Jamaica's commitment to a 'New International Economic Order'. In the light of his experience of the IMF one can appreciate his reasons for doing so, but in the short term – and that was by 1978 the only consideration relevant to the Jamaican economy – it was not the most effective way of improving his country's bargaining position with Fund officials.

For Manley, the tragedy of all this is that the IMF recipe could not work for a structurally dependent economy like Jamaica's, so lacking in productive capacity. It is now a commonplace of political economy analysis to say this,[48] in good part as a result of Jamaica's experience. The fact is that, although the Manley government proceeded to carry out every single aspect of the new agreement, in both letter and spirit, the economy never recovered. The harsh economic medicine did not generate additional inflows of foreign capital or halt the outflow of Jamaican capital, with the result that the economy became locked into a vicious deflationary spiral, with predictable consequences for employment and living standards. Even the bauxite levy was lowered slightly in an attempt to induce the companies to increase production and expand their investment in the industry. Yet in December 1979 the economy once more failed a performance test, again largely because of factors outside governmental control, in particular further increases in the price of oil. The Fund demanded huge public expenditure cuts as the price of continuing the assistance programme, only to find that opinion had hardened in the PNP and in the government during the course of the long and difficult relationship with the IMF. In a clear sign of the changing mood, Dr Duncan had been re-elected to the post of General Secretary in September 1979 and had set in train a detailed discussion within the party of the government's economic policies. The impact was catalytic: a special delegates' conference in January 1980 gave enthusiastic support to proposals that the government should find a 'non-IMF' path and urged it to resist the full extent of the budget cuts being demanded. Eventually, in March 1980, the National Executive Committee of the party voted by a two-to-one majority to break with the IMF and start implementing an alternative programme. The cabinet accepted this and Manley announced that elections would be held before the end of the year to enable the people to decide what economic strategy the country should follow.

This was to be the final lurch in what has been referred to as 'the zig-zag politics'[49] of the Manley regime over the course of the 1970s. A new left-wing finance minister was appointed and some attempt made to renegotiate the country's commercial debts, but little emerged by way of concrete policy.[50] Once his original strategy had been upset, paradoxically by the great electoral success of 1976, Manley was never again able to develop a coherent approach to the management of the political economy. The pattern was indeed one of endless vacillation in which he danced uncomfortably in turn with the domestic left and the international right. As he did so, the economy deteriorated and destroyed whatever chance he and his party had of being re-elected. In elections finally held on 31 October 1980 the PNP was massively defeated by the conservative Jamaica Labour Party, winning only nine out of sixty seats in Parliament, the party's lowest-ever representation.[51] In the view of Norman Girvan, the UWI economist and head of the National Planning Agency under Manley, the IMF had at last 'succeeded in manipulating the Jamaican political process to re-establish the political conditions in which the previous model of dependent, unequal capitalist development may function'.[52]

Conclusion

The heavy electoral defeat suffered by the PNP was hardly surprising in the light of the overall record of the Manley government over the preceding eight and a half years. It had promised so much and in the end achieved so little. The economic statistics alone are revealing: between 1974 and 1980 there was a cumulative fall of 16 per cent in gross domestic product, whilst unemployment rose from 24 per cent to 31 per cent and the cost of living by an enormous 320 per cent. The exchange rate against the US dollar moved from approximately J$0.88. to J$1.76. and, as we have seen, foreign exchange reserves and foreign capital inflows fell dramatically over the period.[53] One could continue the catalogue of figures, but it would not brighten the picture. As far as ordinary Jamaicans were concerned, the reforms of the

Manley government had produced a severe decline in living standards, lower levels of employment, acute shortages of basic goods in the shops and a mood of depression pervading the whole economy and society. Against this dismal background the government's few achievements in the social field and in foreign affairs could not be said to count for much.

What went wrong? Manley's own retrospective analysis emphasised the question of 'destabilisation',[54] instigated by the US government, implemented ultimately by the IMF and abetted by treacherous opposition forces in Jamaica. It is part of the explanation, of course, but it does not say everything and too easily becomes a misleading shorthand expression of the fact that the world which Manley took on was often hostile to his aims. Obviously international factors bore heavily, and at times oppressively, upon his regime, but their impact can be properly understood only in relation to the type of politics which he was trying to pursue.

To go back to the beginning, Manley's initial strategy of change was sensibly conceived. It was not likely to be easy to implement, but there was no reason to think it impossible either.[55] The post-colonial state in Jamaica enjoyed a significant degree of autonomy and, if led with sufficient political skill and sense of *realpolitik*, ought to have been able to restructure the political economy along the lines Manley proposed without arousing the implacable opposition of either the indigenous capitalist class or international capitalist interests as a whole. The former had a good deal to expect from such a strategy, both economically as businessmen and politically as leading citizens; the latter had not too much to lose from schemes of joint ownership in terms of real economic control and something of distinct value to gain if social tensions were thereby reduced and the country's politics stabilised accordingly. In short, an accommodation was possible. The international economic crisis which came to a head in 1973–4 made the task of achieving it more difficult because it forced Manley to increase the pace of change, but again it is doubtful whether it rendered it inherently unattainable. After all, the bauxite levy was supported by the local capitalist class and was eventually accepted with more or less good grace by the US government and the corporations themselves, leaving Manley still balanced on his tightrope.

Two other initiatives, however, tipped him off, both of which could have been avoided. The first mistake concerned the direction of foreign policy, in particular the developing friendship with Cuba and the support, ostentatiously offered, for the latter's involvement in the Angolan civil war. Manley subsequently defended these policies as non-negotiable matters of principle. However, his excessively romantic view of the world underestimated the reality of Jamaica's strategic location in the US sphere of interest. In the last analysis the relationship with Cuba (which in concrete terms produced only minor technical assistance) was not worth the opposition it engendered from the US. It was not integral to the government's domestic reforms or even the wider pursuit of changes in the international economic order, and in the context of US paranoia about the role of Cuba in the Caribbean would have been better avoided. The second mistake concerned the PNP's readoption of 'democratic socialism' as the ideological framework for reviving populist support for its policies. The choice of label proved to be counterproductive: it alarmed even those local capitalists who had till then supported Manley, further perturbed the government of the US and appeared to give official approval to the activities of the small left-wing element in Jamaican politics inside and outside the PNP. Other ways of mobilising the Jamaican people existed which need not have incurred such heavy costs.

These two mistakes were critical. Both served to over-politicise what Manley was trying to do and make his policies appear more radical and threatening to established interests than they really were. They aroused unnecessary opposition at home and abroad which not only badly damaged the country's economy but undermined Manley's intended strategy of change. He was unable to rebuild the class alliance on which he had come to power and, although for a time he seemed to toy with the idea of embarking upon a complete disengagement from the capitalist world economy, sustained domestically by the adoption of the politics of class confrontation and internationally by Soviet support, his government was largely devoid of strategy from the moment it became embroiled with the IMF. Manley thus got caught in that no man's land between rhetoric and reality in which so many reformist politicians of the Third World have found themselves in the post-colonial era. His failure teaches the need for consistency of purpose in the pursuit of development. If the strategy is to be fully socialist, it must be followed all the way. This means that the state must be capable of maintaining the productive level of the economy, sufficient outside support must be available, the party must be committed and tightly organised, and a certain level of class mobilisation must be present to sustain the regime through the transition period. Manley never intended to lead Jamaica down this path, knowing how unrealistic an option it was in the circumstances in which he had to work, but some of his language and some of his policies nevertheless suggested that this was his goal, thereby bringing upon his government the wave of opposition one would expect. Equally, if the strategy is to be populist and social democratic in character, as it was in Manley's case in the 1970s, it must be so not only in implementation but in style and presentation. Manley had no need to lose the support of either his local capitalists or the government of the US, yet he sacrificed both and found that, without the former, he could not run the economy and, without the latter, he could not manage the external environment in the way his programme of domestic change required. In the face of the antagonism of these two powerful interests, the degree of manoeuvre left to the Jamaican state was minimal.

In summary, Manley's 'democratic socialist' experiment offers important lessons for the pursuit of Caribbean development. The task of overcoming, or even adjusting, dependency is never going to be easily accomplished, least of all in the difficult economic circumstances of the mid- and late 1970s, but success cannot even be approached unless policy is as consistently implemented and articulated as it is conceived. Manley failed at the end of the day because he got himself into a muddle.

Notes

1 Michael Manley, *Jamaica: Struggle in the Periphery*, London, 1982, p. ix.
2 For a full discussion, see Owen Jefferson, *The Post-war Economic Development of Jamaica*, Kingston, 1972.
3 *Ibid.*, p. 285.
4 Steve De Castro, *Tax Holidays for Industry: Why we have to Abolish them and How to do it*, New World Pamphlet No. 8, Kingston, 1973, p. 6.
5 Jefferson, *Economic Development of Jamaica*, p. 285.
6 See Stanley Reid, 'An introductory approach to the concentration of power in the Jamaican corporate economy and notes on its origin', in Carl Stone and Aggrey Brown (eds), *Essays on Power and Change in Jamaica*, Kingston, 1977, pp. 15–44.
7 Carl Stone, *Class, Race and Political Behaviour in Urban Jamaica*, Kingston, 1973, p. 50.
8 For an elaboration of this model, see Carl Stone, *Democracy and Clientelism in Jamaica*, New Brunswick, 1980, especially pp. 91–110.
9 *Ibid.*, pp. 94–5.
10 See Terry Lacey, *Violence and Politics in Jamaica 1960–70*, Manchester, 1977.
11 See Carl Stone, *Electoral Behaviour and Public Opinion in Jamaica*, Kingston, 1974.
12 Michael Manley, *The Politics of Change: A Jamaican Testament*, London, 1974, p. 118.
13 *Ibid.*, p. 106.
14 *Ibid.*, p. 215.
15 *Ibid.*, p. 68.
16 Manley, *Jamaica*, p. 38.
17 *Ibid.*, p. 221.
18 Manley, *Politics of Change*, p. 130.
19 Manley, *Jamaica*, p. 123.

20   Manley, *Politics of Change*, p. 17.

21   *Ibid.*, p. 18.

22   To take a single example, K. Hendrickson, chairman and largest shareholder in the National Continental Conglomerate and Caribbean Communications, was made chairman of the island's new electricity utility, Jamaica Public Service, majority-owned by the state. See Reid, 'An introductory approach to the concentration of power in the Jamaican corporate economy', p. 29.

23   National Planning Agency, *Economic and Social Survey: Jamaica 1979*, Kingston, 1980.

24   Claremont Kirton, 'A preliminary analysis of imperialist penetration and control via the foreign debt: a study of Jamaica', in Stone and Brown, *Essays*, pp. 80–1.

25   National Planning Agency, *Economic and Social Survey: Jamaica 1976*, Kingston, 1977.

26   See 'Bauxite: how the PNP liberals satisfy the local capitalists and betray the masses', *Socialism* (a Marxist-Leninist journal), 1, 1974, pp. 5–14.

27   See Sherry Keith and Robert Girling, 'Caribbean conflict: Jamaica and the US', *NACLA Report on the Americas*, XII, 1978, p. 21.

28   *Ibid.*, p. 24, table 7.

29   *Ibid.*, pp. 23–4.

30   *Ibid.*, p. 19, table 5.

31   Manley, *Jamaica*, pp. 100–1.

32   *Ibid.*, p. 116.

33   *Ibid.*

34   For a full discussion, see Anthony Payne, 'From Michael with love: the nature of socialism in Jamaica', *Journal of Commonwealth and Comparative Politics*, XIV, 1976, pp. 82–100.

35   People's National Party, *Democratic Socialism: The Jamaican Model*, Kingston, 1974.

36   See Marlene Cuthbert and Vernone Sparkes, 'Coverage of Jamaica in United States and Canadian press in 1976', *Social and Economic Studies*, XXVII, 1978, pp. 204–20.

37   Made by the former CIA agent, Philip Agee, on a visit to Jamaica in 1976.

38   See Carl Stone, 'The 1976 parliamentary election in Jamaica', *Journal of Commonwealth and Comparative Politics*, XV, 1977, pp. 250–65.

39   Michael Manley, Speech to the Nation, 5 January 1977, Kingston, mimeo, 1977.

40   Fitzroy Ambursley, 'Jamaica: the demise of "Democratic Socialism" ', *New Left Review*, 128, 1981, p. 82.

41   Manley, *Jamaica*, p. 155.

42   George Beckford and Michael Witter, *Small Garden . . . Bitter Weed: The Political Economy of Struggle and Change in Jamaica*, Morant Bay, 1980, p. 93.

43   Manley, *Jamaica*, p. 155.

44   Stone, *Democracy and Clientelism*, p. 176.

45   According to one account, 'the Soviets were so unenthusiastic about acquiring another ward in the Caribbean that they laid down prerequisites for aid that bore a striking resemblance to the standard IMF regimen for a country in Jamaica's position'. J. Daniel O'Flaherty, 'Finding Jamaica's way', *Foreign Policy*, XXXI, 1978, p. 148.

46   The subsequent discussion of Jamaica's relationship with the IMF relies heavily on the following: Norman Girvan, Richard Bernal and Wesley Hughes, 'The IMF and the Third World: the case of Jamaica, 1974–80', *Development Dialogue*, 11, 1980, pp. 113–55.

47 Manley, *Jamaica*, p. 160.
48 For a review of these arguments, see John Rapley, *Understanding Development: Theory and Practice in the Third World*, Boulder, 1996.
49 Beckford and Witter, *Small Garden*, p. 99.
50 See the interview with Hugh Small, the new Minister of Finance, published in the *Guardian Third World Review*, 1 October 1980.
51 For a fuller discussion, see Carl Stone, 'Jamaica's 1980 elections', *Caribbean Review*, X, 1981, pp. 4–7 and 40–3.
52 Girvan *et al.*, 'The IMF and the Third World', p. 155.
53 For these and other statistics, see National Planning Agency, *Economic and Social Survey: Jamaica 1979*, Kingston, 1980.
54 In his account of this period Manley entitled the chapter describing the fall of his government 'Destabilisation triumphs'. Manley, *Jamaica*, p. 193.
55 For a similar argument, see Evelyne Huber Stephens and John D. Stephens, *Democratic Socialism in Jamaica: The Political Movement and Social Transformation in Dependent Capitalism*, London, 1986.

3 | The Grenadian revolution

The Grenadian revolution has almost been forgotten. Outside the Caribbean it is remembered, if at all, for the bloody way in which it imploded when in October 1983 the murder of its leader, Maurice Bishop, by some of his own soldiers prompted an invasion by US troops. Inside the region, it is generally seen as an aberration, a brief episode during which longstanding Commonwealth Caribbean norms in respect of economics and politics were broken, with predictably unfortunate consequences. Even amongst those on the left, so searing was the experience of the end of the revolution that there has since been a marked unwillingness to explore in any depth what the political economy of the revolutionary period in Grenada between 1979 and 1983 might have meant for Caribbean development more generally. Notwithstanding the undoubted ultimate failure of the revolution, there are development lessons which can be culled from the experience and this chapter seeks to do just that by reviewing the theory of so-called non-capitalist development which inspired Bishop and the other leading Grenadian revolutionaries and the different elements of the development strategy which the People's Revolutionary Government (PRG) followed during its short period in power.

One point which needs to be raised at the outset is the question, much asked and debated at the time, of whether the Grenadian revolution was 'exception or vanguard'.[1] In retrospect, it is easy to see that it was the former – for a variety of reasons, partly because the authoritarianism, corruption and incompetence of the preceding regime in Grenada, that of Eric Gairy, had so widely discredited conventional politics in the island, partly because some of the international trends of the 1970s had seemed to sustain the argument that the 'correlation of forces' between capitalism and socialism was moving in the direction of the Soviet Union, thereby adding hugely to the appeal of Soviet ideology, and partly too because few small island societies in the Commonwealth Caribbean or elsewhere can be expected to generate in one short historical period two political leaders of the drive of Maurice Bishop and his one-time ally and eventual rival, Bernard Coard, Minister of Finance in the PRG and chief executor of its development strategy during its four and a half years in office. Yet the exceptional nature of the Grenadian revolution should not be taken to imply that it does not at the same time fit into the broader story of post-colonial Caribbean development. A good deal of what the PRG tried to do with the Grenadian economy resonates with the experience of other Commonwealth Caribbean territories both before and since the 1979–83 period. As we shall see, the real failure of the revolution in Grenada lay in its politics, not its economics.

The theory of 'non-capitalist development'

The theory of non-capitalist development was first advanced by Soviet scholars during the 1960s. Its principal exponent, Professor R. Ulyanovsky, was a noted Soviet academician and influential adviser on Soviet foreign policy towards the Third World.[2] As initially formulated, the theory had a tendency to be associated exclusively with the prospects of socialist transformation in the newly-independent states of Africa and Asia. However, in June 1975 important aspects of it were incorporated into the Declaration of Havana, the final document unanimously approved at the Conference of Communist and Workers' Parties of Latin America held in Cuba. A transition to the Caribbean was thereby effected and the theory was taken up with particular vigour by a number of Commonwealth Caribbean intellectuals who saw in it a plausible route to power.

As explained by one of them, Ralph Gonsalves, the theory had 'its roots in the science of historical materialism as creatively applied to countries where capitalism is either non-existent or underdeveloped, as in Africa and the Caribbean' and posited that 'capitalism can be by-passed or interrupted on the route to the construction of socialism'.[3] Critically necessary for the realisation of this was 'a broad class alliance involving the proletariat, the semi-proletarian masses, the revolutionary or democratic strata of the petty-bourgeoisie (including the peasantry) and even the progressive patriotic elements of the emerging national bourgeoisie', governing through 'a revolutionary democratic or national democratic state which links up itself increasingly with the forces of world socialism'.[4] It is clear from the writings of Gonsalves and others that the decisive aspect of non-capitalist development was deemed to reside in the realm of politics, deriving its effect from a 'relative autonomy' of the state evident in many post-colonial countries. It followed that the policies pursued by such states were crucial in determining whether or not they were following the path of non-capitalist development, or 'socialist orientation', as it came to be called.

Gonsalves listed nine main features of the non-capitalist path as follows: (1) the abolition of imperialism's political domination; (2) the reduction and eventual abolition of imperialism's economic control; (3) the consolidation of the mixed structure of the economy and its development into one in which the state and cooperative sectors become dominant; (4) the transformation of the political culture towards socialist values; (5) the engendering of new attitudes towards work and production; (6) the expansion of mass participation in and control of the state administration and state economic enterprises; (7) the removal of plantocratic national bourgeois and imperialist elements from the supreme command of government and the transfer of power to revolutionary democrats and scientific socialists; (8) the development of appropriate planning techniques and organisational methods to raise productive forces; and (9) a raising of the cultural, scientific and material level of living for the mass of the people.[5] The non-capitalist road, therefore, involved both analysis and programme, theory and practice, of 'one possible path' to socialism. If fully implemented, it would not have constituted socialism itself, but rather a political, material, social and cultural preparation for the transition to socialism.

A grasp of these arguments is important, because from the outset some theoreticians from within Grenada argued that the revolution was guided by just such a perspective. For example, the Jacobs brothers, in a kind of semi-official exposition of the philosophy of the revolution, claimed that this commitment went back to the emergence of the New Jewel Movement (NJM) at the beginning of the 1970s. The 1973 NJM manifesto is cited as evidence of a 'non-capitalist ideological perspective' and the NJM party structure is seen as possessing 'distinctly scientific socialist characteristics'. Additional considerations were the pre-eminence within the NJM's leadership of 'the progressive young middle-class intelligentsia'; the class character of the emerging political forces opposed to Gairy; 'the need to maintain the neutrality, if not the support, of the middle strata'; and, finally, the frank recognition, given the circumstances in Grenada in the 1970s, that 'to adopt an overtly Marxist-Leninist path . . . is to court alienation and take a deliberately long route to national liberation'.[6] Accordingly, the non-capitalist way emerged as 'the most appropriate intermediate option' – a strategy that permitted 'the mobilisation of diverse social elements in the movement towards national liberation and revolutionary change'.[7] Although there is much that is revealed by this line of commentary, it reconstructs the NJM's ideological development too neatly. The party's original 1973 manifesto in fact drew more closely on the thinking of the New World Group at the University of the West Indies, in particular its rejection of the notion that small size was a constraint on

Grenada's development and its awareness of the need for development to be based on domestic resource endowment, a theme emphasised in the later writings of Clive Thomas, one of the founders of New World, and inspired by his knowledge, not of the Soviet Union, but of Tanzania under Julius Nyerere. It is the case, however, as the Jacobs brothers themselves note, that the NJM moved strongly thereafter in a Marxist-Leninist direction, especially following the return to Grenada of Bernard Coard in September 1976 and his subsequent emergence as a major influence within the party.

Certainly, after the revolution had been made in March 1979, amidst genuine popular relief at Gairy's overthrow, little was said in public about the theory of non-capitalist development. The PRG was composed in the first instance predominantly of non-NJM members and included two or three local capitalists. As Bishop later explained to party members, 'we need the alliance to hold power in the first few days and weeks ... to consolidate and build the revolution and to ensure the defeat of imperialism ... because we don't have enough managers, because we don't have enough international contacts, because we don't have enough markets'.[8] Over time, however, party cadres came to control the government and confirmation that the imperatives of non-capitalist development were always in the minds of the leadership was occasionally provided. In an interview in July 1979 Bernard Coard thus stated:

> So fundamentally, at this time, we see our task not as one of building socialism. It is one of restructuring and rebuilding the economy, of getting production going and trying to develop genuine grassroots democracy, trying to involve the people in every village and every workplace in the process of the reconstruction of the country. In that sense we are in a national democratic revolution involving the broad masses and many strata of the population.[9]

Bishop reiterated this in an interview in July 1981. The Grenadian revolution was at 'the national democratic stage, the anti-imperialist stage of the process we are trying to build'. In the sphere of economics, this involved policies such as building a strong state sector, stimulating the private sector to boost production and disengaging rapidly from imperialism; and in the sphere of politics, the promotion of measures such as the reform of the state apparatus and the development of 'revolutionary democracy'.[10] The class character of this democracy was all important. Those for the revolution were seen as 'the broad masses of our working people' (the urban and rural working class, the small and middle farmers, revolutionary youth and students, and patriotic women) and those against 'a very small minority clique' (the biggest and most unpatriotic landowners and businessmen, corrupt trade union leaders and bureaucrats, and the *lumpen* and criminal elements).[11] The essence of the national democratic state as so established, and that aspect wherein lay its decisive and historic importance within this body of theory, was that the minority was politically subject to the majority. In Ulyanovsky's words, power lay with 'the broad social bloc of the working people' within which 'the national-bourgeois elements ... are deprived of monopoly political power'.[12]

The PRG's development strategy

It is important to understand the distinctive class politics that under-pinned the theory of non-capitalist development. Otherwise, the PRG's decision to retain a mixed economy, albeit with a dominant state sector and a newly-established cooperative sector, can be misunderstood. For example, some critics of the PRG, notably Fitzroy Ambursley and Hilbourne Watson, have construed this pattern of ownership as evidence of the regime's commitment to the capitalist ethic.[13] This reading is erro-neous, as Courtney Smith has noted, since it fails to appraise realisti-cally the impracticality of a totally statist model of development in the context of Grenada's objective conditions in 1979.[14] As Bishop's 'Line of March' speech revealed, the PRG opted for a mixed economy model for tactical reasons in the hope that it could continue to draw on the skills, experience, resources and connections of patriotic elements within the Grenadian private sector. It was recognised, as Bishop put it, that 'the capitalist prefers to deal with the capitalist, and capitalist gov-ernments allow other capitalists to come in, even when their government is a socialist-oriented government like our government in Grenada'.[15] In short, the strategy was that the state would assuredly lead the develop-ment process and plan the economy, but would enlist the cooperation of the private sector, at least in the short term, in order to boost production and offset the limitations of the inevitably undercapitalised state sector. As regards key sectors of the economy, as far back as the 1973 NJM manifesto three were identified: agriculture, tourism and manufacturing.

Agriculture

Agriculture was described by Bernard Coard as 'the base, the bedrock of everything we do'.[16] It was planned that it would generate foreign exchange, provide inputs for industrial development, create employ-ment, supply food and increase Grenada's general self-reliance by utilising all agricultural land to its fullest.[17] Implicit in all these objectives was a predominant emphasis on export promotion. Accordingly, the PRG established the Grenada Farms Corporation to manage the thirty state farms it had inherited from the Gairy regime, set up a National Cooperative Development Agency whose work was to be symbolised by the slogan 'Idle Hands plus Idle Lands = End to Unemployment', and both enacted and sought to implement the Land Utilisation Act, which gave it the power to acquire ten-year leases on estates over 100 acres deemed to be underutilised. Many measures were also introduced to assist the existing private sector, including the building of roads, the provision of more electricity, water and other services to the country-side, the establishment of the Productive Farmers' Union to represent small farmers, the creation of new agricultural schools, the expansion of extension services to farmers and much more besides. Efforts were further made to link the agricultural sector closely with the Marketing and National Importing Board (MNIB) as the main state agency for marketing agricultural produce and Grenada Agro-Industries Ltd (GAI) as a means to produce new processed agricultural products, such as juices, nectars and jams, from local fruit.

All in all, the energy and creativity devoted to agricultural development under the PRG was impressive. But it failed to deliver increased growth. Indeed, the performance of Grenada's traditional agricultural crops deteriorated during the revolutionary period, total foreign exchange earned from bananas, cocoa, nutmeg and mace falling from US$19.26 million in 1979 to US$11.31 million in 1983.[18] These problems have been unfairly blamed by Joefield-Napier on 'half-hearted attempts to introduce major policy initiatives' by the PRG.[19] The reality is that natural disasters, market shortages and, above all, declining prices experienced by all producers of these crops in the context of global economic recession were the more significant causes. It was admittedly the case that many of the products made by GAI, although of excellent quality, languished and ultimately perished on the shelves of MNIB storerooms because of the latter's managerial inadequacies. But that is no more than typical of all attempts to build new enterprises in the context of underdevelopment and could have been addressed with time and experience. The overriding reason why Grenada's farmers were reluctant to invest more resources in agriculture during the PRG period was the absence of the necessary external price incentives.

Tourism

Courtney Smith has observed that 'had Grenada been better endowed with natural resources (especially valuable minerals) the revolutionary government would probably not have assigned so prominent a role to tourism'.[20] But the sheer paucity of development resources available in 1979 forced the PRG to promote tourism. Bishop set out the dilemma as follows:

> In terms of the development of the economy . . . over the next 10–15 years, as we see it, the next 5 years – emphasis will undoubtedly be on tourism. That is not to say that we like tourism, that is because we have no choice. Tourism is the sector that has the greatest potential for giving us the profits to invest in the areas we really want to invest in – agriculture, agro-industries, fisheries and non-agro industrialization generally. That is really where we would like to go, but those cannot produce the money at this time, while tourism can.[21]

To maximise these benefits but at the same time to alleviate some of the undesirable social, cultural and environmental outcomes often associated with tourism, the government proposed a policy of 'new tourism', conceived as the antithesis of the traditional tourism prevalent in the Caribbean.[22] New tourism would thus seek to diversify Grenada's tourist base to include non-white visitors from the Caribbean and the wider Third World, establish intersectoral linkages with the rest of the economy, promote indigenous culture, foster regional integration and eliminate prostitution, gambling, drugs and other socially deleterious practices conventionally associated with tourism.

However, apart from some modest efforts to promote the handicraft sector, virtually nothing was actually done by the PRG to implement the new tourism. In practice, the centrepiece of the government's tourist strategy became the project to build a new international airport at Point Salines, much nearer to St George's and the island's main beaches than the existing, inadequate facility at Pearls airport near Grenville. Long recognised, even in the colonial era, as a pressing development need, the airport came to be seen by the regime as the talisman of the whole revolutionary project. Coard argued that its potential was the equivalent for Grenada of the development by other countries of railroads or electrification or a seaport, and predicted that the opening of the airport would mark 'the beginning of a whole new economic era for our country'.[23] In an extraordinary gesture of revolutionary solidarity, the Cuban government agreed to provide more than half the cost of the project, some US$40 million in the form of manpower and machinery, which still left the PRG with the considerable task of raising the remainder of the funds, either from internal sources or further external support. Given the numerous other calls upon the regime's limited resources, this was perhaps too demanding a task, certainly once fierce US opposition to the building of the airport came to the fore on the grounds, largely spurious, that it could have been used by the Soviet Union to project power into Latin America.

More generally, Grenada's emergence as a *cause célèbre* in the renewed Cold War of the early 1980s, something that was brought about much more by security than development considerations,[24] rendered the prospect of maintaining, let alone substantially increasing, the island's number of tourist arrivals distinctly unlikely. In fact, the sector performed dismally between 1979 and 1983, notwithstanding the fact that the PRG established a Ministry of Tourism and took several other sensible measures to boost arrivals. From an impressive figure of 32,000 when the PRG assumed power, the number of overnight visitors fell to 30,100 in 1980, 25,000 in 1981 and 23,200 in 1982. Decline was especially pronounced in the US market, the number of American overnight visitors dropping from 9,100 in 1979 to only 5,000 in 1982.[25] The virtual dislocation of the tourist industry had a disastrous impact on the wider economy, badly hitting foreign exchange earnings and reducing employment and tax revenue. What is more, it seemed to take the government by surprise. This exposed a serious flaw in the PRG's whole development strategy: quite simply, the pursuit of tourism was incompatible with the anti-imperialist, pro-Soviet and pro-Cuban character of the regime's foreign policy. In the Caribbean context, the US is always going to be the major potential source of tourists and most Americans were scarcely likely to be attracted by the image of an island whose government had, rightly or wrongly, been branded by the US as a tool of the Soviet Union.

Manufacturing

The PRG recognised the untapped potential of the manufacturing sector and designed several policies to integrate this sector into its national development strategy. Its particular aims were to use indigenous natural and human resources, develop low energy-intensive products, manufacture items either not produced or underproduced in the Caribbean and focus on areas where there was strong local demand.[26] Studies therefore identified a range of products which could be made in Grenada and, in accordance with the wider tactical imperative to work with the private sector, it was hoped that foreign and local investors would be found to work with the state in the exploitation of these opportunities. Accordingly, discussions were initiated with the local private sector on the promulgation of an investment code designed to set out the PRG's distinctive approach to relations with all forms of private capital. The task proved to be controversial and the code, although initially drafted in mid-1981, was not published until 1983. Its major preoccupation was the needs of the Grenadian national economy. Investment proposals from foreigners were required to do one of the following: facilitate the transfer of appropriate technology, utilise domestic raw materials and labour, boost government revenue and foreign exchange earnings, provide new market outlets overseas, stabilise the cost of living or augment the supply of capital in the local economy. In addition, foreign capital was explicitly forbidden from certain activities deemed by the state to be central to the national interest.[27]

In the end, the guidelines were not that radical in themselves, but they did depart from the supplicant stance towards foreign investment that had long been the norm in the Commonwealth Caribbean. They were also based on an exaggerated sense of the potential attractiveness of Grenada as an investment site. This would have been the case even in the best of times. The additional problem was that, by the time the guide was eventually published, relations between the PRG and the local private sector had moved beyond tactical accommodation to bitterness and outright opposition. Some of the reasons for this related to the economy, in particular the growth in the state sector which had been much more extensive than local business people had anticipated; others, however, related more to politics and the growing distaste, even fear, felt by members of the private sector for the PRG's so-called 'revolutionary manners' in dealing with dissent. Here the closure of the *Torchlight* newspaper and the subsequent banning of another paper, *The Grenadian Voice*, both of them private-sector ventures, caused particular anxiety. At any rate, aggregate private investment fell dramatically over the PRG's period in office – from a high of US$5.4 million in 1980 to US$2.6 million in 1983[28] – and more and more capital began to leak, legally and illegally, out of the country. Unlike the situation in Jamaica in the 1970s, foreign capital was not a major hostile force, because, apart from a limited presence in the financial sector, it was virtually non-existent in Grenada.

Economic performance and the IMF

In his review of the PRG's management of the Grenadian economy between 1979 and 1983, Courtney Smith has been able to draw upon, and arbitrate between, what he has referred to as 'inside' and 'outside' accounts of economic performance; the former are constituted by the PRG's own extensive presentation of its record, the latter by a series of World Bank and IMF reports and memoranda. They agree that the

Grenadian economy certainly grew in these years, although there is disagreement about the magnitude of that growth. According to the PRG, real gross domestic product increased by 2.1 per cent in 1979, 3.0 per cent in 1980, 3.1 per cent in 1981 and 5.5 per cent in 1982.[29] The IMF, on the other hand, reported a slightly lower growth rate: 2.1 per cent in 1979, 1.8 per cent in 1980, 1.9 per cent in 1981 and 4.7 per cent in 1982.[30] The construction sector accounted for the bulk of this growth, given the extent of the infrastructural projects undertaken by the state. However, as we have seen, both traditional agriculture and tourism experienced sharp downturns and manufacturing did not take off, starved of investment as the local business class turned against the regime. Growth was therefore being built upon a fragile base.

Critically, from 1981 onwards, the government's own impressive investment programme, which until that point had been sustained by foreign aid and concessionary loans, also began to falter, largely as a consequence of the poor performance of its traditional foreign exchange earners, allied with difficulties in mobilising further external resources in the face of the country's growing diplomatic isolation. The airport was the only major project that was kept going since the PRG, for symbolic reasons, was determined to have it completed for the fifth anniversary of the revolution in March 1984. The 'social wage', which was the phrase used to refer to the benefits of better education, improved health facilities and so on which the PRG had genuinely brought about in the first two years of the revolution,[31] was effectively frozen in the face of these budgetary pressures and unemployment began again to rise. Notwithstanding some scepticism expressed on this matter by both the IMF and the World Bank,[32] the PRG had for a while succeeded in considerably reducing unemployment, albeit largely by means of its own spending. With the interruption of the public investment programme, many workers were forced to rejoin the ranks of the unemployed. The government also had to resort to measures which further incurred the wrath of the private sector, in particular new taxes and a law which made it mandatory for commercial banks to deposit 20 per cent of their funds with the government.

In August 1983, in the midst of enormous cash-flow problems, the PRG turned to the IMF for assistance. Even though the government had received small stand-by loans from the IMF in 1979 and 1981 and had not experienced any problems in complying with the associated performance targets, its recourse to the Fund at this moment in its history was a measure of its increasing desperation. Claremont Kirton, a consultant on economic planning with the PRG between 1980 and 1983, has argued that the PRG had other motives for turning to the IMF at this point, including the belief that 'once an IMF "seal of

approval" was granted to Grenada . . . a much more favourable economic climate would exist allowing for increased levels of participation of both domestic and foreign capital in the country's development
efforts'.[33] The government was also of the view, according to Kirton,
that its bargaining power would be the greater if it approached the IMF
before the liquidity crisis manifested itself fully.

The 1983 package was both substantially larger and more interventionist than anything the PRG had had to handle before. As Smith
put it, 'the lion's share of the EC$39.7 million ... was to be used to
address what the IMF diagnosed as the main problem-areas of the
economy ... the parlous state of the resources of the commercial
banks, the growing indebtedness of the government, and the stifling of
the private sector'.[34] Only EC$9.7 million was allocated to the govern-
ment's investment programme. A number of conditions also ran
counter to PRG development strategy. Among the most detrimental
were the curtailment of the role of the state in foreign trade (particularly the activities of the MNIB), the imposition of ceilings on the contraction of further commercial loans, wage restraints for public sector
workers, the trimming of public expenditure on social works and the
further introduction of new taxes.

These conditions, as they unfolded, would have alienated the
PRG's popular class base and put further political pressure on the
revolution. Yet it should also be noted that the conditionalities imposed
were relatively lenient in relation to exchange rate adjustments, the
size of the public sector deficit and foreign exchange restrictions, all of
which have been standard areas of rigorous IMF intervention in other
Caribbean economies. Bartilow's comparative study of IMF dealings
with Jamaica, Guyana and Grenada in the 1970s and 1980s in fact
shows a good deal of tolerance towards the PRG on the part of IMF
managers, as opposed to the IMF executive board, reflecting what he
described as their 'general attitude of consolidating the Grenadian revolution politically and giving the PRG "the benefit of the doubt"'.[35]
This at least demonstrates how much more severe the IMF regime
could, and probably would, have become if the revolution had not
entered its own terminal crisis shortly after consummating the loan.

The revolutionary crisis

Although it was not known at the time, throughout the period when the
PRG's shortage of money was becoming most apparent and talks with
the IMF were taking place, the ruling NJM was engulfed in an extraordinary series of bitter internal debates between the leading figures in the

party, notably Bishop and Coard. The details of this fierce struggle subsequently emerged in the pages of the party documents confiscated and later published by the US following its invasion in October 1983. They show that there was a connection between the difficulties into which the PRG's development strategy had run and the deeper political problems that were beginning to confront the entire revolutionary process.

For example, at the July 1983 plenary session of the NJM Central Committee, which lasted no less than $6\frac{1}{2}$ days, the parlous state of the Grenadian economy was in the forefront of discussion. Attention was drawn in particular to the effects of faltering cash flow on investment projects, the continuing poor performance of key productive sectors and the difficulties being faced in mobilising external funds and even obtaining sums which had been promised. It was formally noted that '1983/1984 will be difficult years ... requiring maximum efforts of the party on the economic front, hence the ideological work has to be stepped up to combat the consequent difficulties that these two years will pose for us'.[36] Indicative of the growing loss of self-confidence, and indeed of the intellectual confusion, at the heart of the revolution's policy-making was the series of recommendations that were thrown up. They ranged between establishing a new Ministry of State Enterprises to generate greater efficiency in the operation of state economic activities, continuing the land acquisition policy, dispatching a ministerial delegation to Libya to plead for funds, and encouraging the private sector to explore investment opportunities under the US-led Caribbean Basin Initiative.

Economic problems received further elaboration at another three-day Central Committee meeting held in mid-September 1983. One member summed up the situation in the following words: 'The honeymoon period of the revolution [is] over. In the past $4\frac{1}{2}$ years progress was seen in many areas and the masses were on a high; now the work is becoming more difficult and complex. A striking feature in this period is the absence of the masses in the activities of the revolution because of the deep frustrations which exist ... The serious economic situation we face is affecting the people'.[37] This was typical of the arguments mounted and it was significant that, although the meeting concluded that the main reason for the revolutionary crisis was 'the functioning of the Central Commitee', it acknowledged that it had been 'compounded by the weakness in the material base, electrical black outs, bad roads, retrenchments and jobs as an issue'.[38] The tragedy was that, rather than devoting its remaining energy to the solution of these development difficulties, the party immersed itself in obsessive debate of its own leadership structures, which led inexorably to the arrest of Bishop, his subsequent murder and the US invasion.

These events have been much discussed, with Gordon Lewis taking the lead in advancing the view that Coard and an ultra-left faction within the party had been seeking for some time to oust Bishop and, therefore, in reviewing the state of the revolution had necessarily 'to paint a dismal diagnosis of the patient in order that they, as the doctor, could move to undertake radical surgery'.[39] Be that as it may, his evaluation of the state of the economy was manifestly too sanguine in the light of all the evidence that now exists. He wrote:

> The prognostications about the economic collapse of the revolution seem unbelievable when compared with the available statistical evidence for the economic record of 1982–3. Coard . . . had brought in comprehensive economic planning and had claimed that in 1982 the gross national product had grown by 5.5 per cent, corroborated by the World Bank report of that year. Statistics for 1983 on particular sectors were equally encouraging . . . It is true that foreign exchange assets accruing from exports declined in the vital traditional areas such as cocoa, nutmegs, and bananas, but . . . all of the small island economies had achieved only minimal growth in 1982, due mainly to the general worldwide fall in prices of primary commodities, certainly not the fault of any one island government. None of these indicators prove that the Grenada economy was on the verge of collapse. What is more, the relationship between the public and private sectors remained buoyant, with both sectors enthusiastically working together, especially in tourist promotion.[40]

As already suggested, the economic problems facing the PRG were much more deep-seated than Lewis was prepared to admit. He was right that some of them were not the fault of the Grenadian government; he was wrong to think that the undoubted economic achievements of the first two heady years of the revolution had been sustained and carried forward into a viable development strategy for the medium-term future. Even if the NJM leadership had stayed united and focused on the development of their country, they would have been hard put to deliver on their original goals.

Conclusion

Nevertheless, Gordon Lewis did correctly argue that 'no examination of the Grenada revolution of 1979 to 1983 should end on a pessimistic note'.[41] Many of the economic and social achievements of the PRG have already been delineated, including, not least, the (virtual) completion of the new international airport. Its management of its finances, even as they dwindled, was proper and professional and its conduct of negotiations with the IMF won the plaudits of the Fund's own technocrats. There was much, too, that was meritorious in its overall development strategy. The PRG's plans for the agricultural, tourist and manufacturing sectors, with their emphasis on inter-sectoral linkages, were often laudable and, as indicated, failures were far from always being its responsibility.

What went wrong was the politics. It was not that attachment to the theory of non-capitalist development locked the PRG into a doomed set of development policies, at least not in the initial tactical phase during which a working alliance was being pursued with the private sector. For the truth is that, viewed from a solely development perspective, the dominant themes of Grenadian economic policy during the revolution were social democratic, not Marxist-Leninist, in conception. Indeed, much of what the revolution wanted to do inside Grenada could have been done within a social democratic political framework without incurring so many of the external costs otherwise generated. There is every likelihood, too, given the widespread hostility to the preceding Gairy regime, that this would have generated a more cooperative response from local business people. In short, the great failing of non-capitalist development in Grenada was the way it tied the regime to a rigid, imported political model based on Marxist-Leninist norms and, as such, totally out of line with the political culture of a society which remained stubbornly attached to the values and practices of Westminster-style democracy. In the final analysis, Grenada's revolutionary politicians had themselves mostly to blame for the fact that they were not able to create and sustain the political conditions in which their own economic development strategy could have had a realistic chance of succeeding.

Notes

1   Anthony Payne, Paul Sutton and Tony Thorndike, *Grenada: Revolution and Invasion*, London and New York, 1984, p. 221.
2   See R. A. Ulyanovsky, *Socialism and the Newly Independent Nations*, Moscow, 1974.
3   Ralph Gonsalves, *The Non-Capitalist Path of Development: Africa and the Caribbean*, London, 1981, p. 2.
4   *Ibid.*, pp. 2–3.
5   See *ibid.*, pp. 8–14.
6   W. R. and R. I. Jacobs, *Grenada: The Route to Revolution*, Havana, 1980, pp. 80, 78, 82, 35 and ff.

7   *Ibid.*, pp. 35–6.
8   Maurice Bishop, 'Line of March for the Party', address to the General Meeting of the Party, 13 September 1982, in US State Department and Department of Defense, *Grenada Documents: An Overview and Selection*, Washington DC, 1984.
9   Bernard Coard, *Grenada: Let Those who Labour Hold the Reins*, London, 1981, p. 12.
10 Interview with Bishop, July 1981, in Maurice Bishop, *Forward Ever! Three Years of the Grenadian Revolution*, Sydney, 1982, pp. 35–8.
11 'Freedom of the press versus CIA destabilisation', in *ibid.*, p. 181.
12 Ulyanovsky, *Socialism and the Newly Independent Nations*, p. 82.
13 Fitzroy Ambursley, 'Grenada: the New Jewel revolution', in Fitzroy Ambursley and Robin Cohen (eds), *Crisis in the Caribbean*, London, 1983, pp. 191–222, and Hilbourne Watson, 'Grenada: non-capitalist path and the derailment of a populist revolution', unpublished paper presented to the Caribbean Studies Association, St Kitts, May 1985.
14 Courtney Smith, *Socialist Transformation in Peripheral Economies: Lessons from Grenada*, Aldershot, 1995, p. 63.
15 Bishop, 'Line of March for the Party'.
16 Bernard Coard, 'National reconstruction and development in the Grenadian revolutionary process', in People's Revolutionary Government, *Grenada is Not Alone*, St George's, 1982, p. 45.
17 For a discussion of the development role assigned to the agricultural sector, see George Louison, 'The role of agriculture in the revolution', in *ibid.*, p. 95.
18 Figures from the Central Statistical Office, Ministry of Finance, St George's, cited in Smith, *Socialist Transformation in Peripheral Economies*, pp. 114–5.
19 Wallace Joefield-Napier, 'Macroeconomic growth under the People's Revolutionary Government: an assessment', in Jorge Heine (ed.), *A Revolution Aborted: The Lessons of Grenada*, Pittsburgh, 1990, p. 97.
20 Smith, *Socialist Transformation in Peripheral Economies*, p. 131.
21 Bishop, 'Line of March for the Party'.
22 The main features of the 'old tourism' were articulated in the party's 1973 Manifesto and reiterated in an address by Bishop delivered in December 1979, 'The new tourism', in Maurice Bishop, *Selected Speeches 1979–1981*, Havana, 1982, p. 68.
23 Bernard Coard, *Report on the National Economy for 1981 and Prospects for 1982*, St George's, 1982, p. 44.
24 For an account of US-Grenadian relations during the PRG era, see Anthony Payne, 'The foreign policy of the People's Revolutionary Government', in Heine (ed.), *A Revolution Aborted*, pp. 137–42.
25 Grenada Department of Tourism, 'Annual statistical overview', St George's, various years, cited in Smith, *Socialist Transformation in Peripheral Economies*, p. 151.
26 Two studies were of crucial importance in shaping this strategy. They were Jiri Cerhonek, 'A project for Grenada's economic development in the period 1983–1985', mimeo, St George's, 1982, and Anthony Boatswain, 'The development of the manufacturing sector in Grenada, 1980–2000', mimeo, St George's, 1984. For further discussion, see Smith, *Socialist Transformation in Peripheral Economies*, pp. 186–8.
27 See People's Revolutionary Government, 'The Grenada Investment Code (Draft)', mimeo, St George's, 1981. The final document was published by the Overseas Private Investment Corporation as *The Grenada Investment Guide*, St George's, 1983; the title was designed to avoid the legal connotation of the term *code*.

28 World Bank, 'Economic memorandum on Grenada, 1984', mimeo, Washington DC, 1984, p. 42, cited in Smith, *Socialist Transformation in Peripheral Economies*, pp. 189–90.

29 See People's Revolutionary Government, *Report on the National Economy for 1982*, St George's, 1983.

30 International Monetary Fund, *Grenada: Recent Economic Developments*, Washington DC, 1984, p. 2.

31 See People's Revolutionary Government, *Report on the National Economy for 1982*, p. 9.

32 The World Bank noted that 'the available data on the Grenadian labour force is inadequate for analysing trends in employment and unemployment over the period 1975 through 1982'. See 'Economic memorandum on Grenada, 1984', p. 17. In a similar vein, the IMF noted that 'no comprehensive labour survey has been undertaken to back the PRG's estimate'. See IMF, *Grenada*, p. 19.

33 Claremont Kirton, 'Grenada and the IMF: the People's Revolutionary Government's EFF programme', mimeo, no place, no date, p. 2.

34 Smith, *Socialist Transformation in Peripheral Economies*, p. 225.

35 Horace A. Bartilow, *The Debt Dilemma: IMF Negotiations in Jamaica, Grenada and Guyana*, London, 1997, p. 97.

36 'Central Committee Report on First Plenary Session, 13–19 July 1983', in US State Department and Department of Defense, *Grenada Documents*.

37 'Extraordinary Meeting of the Central Committee of the New Jewel Movement, 14–16 September 1983', in *ibid.*

38 *Ibid.*

39 Gordon K. Lewis, *Grenada: The Jewel Despoiled*, Baltimore, 1987, p. 44.

40 *Ibid.*, pp. 42–3.

41 *Ibid.*, p. 10.

4 | Liberal economics vs. electoral politics in Seaga's Jamaica

The period of Jamaica Labour Party (JLP) government which began in November 1980 and eventually ended in February 1989 merits consideration as another distinct era in the management of the Jamaican political economy. Edward Seaga's time in power was certainly characterised, as he had amply promised, by a rejection of the 'democratic socialist' aspirations of the Manley years. Yet, somewhat unexpectedly, it acquired ideological shape in its own right. The key to Seaga's successful appeal to the Jamaican electorate in 1980 had been his reputation as a manager and fixer. With his Harvard education and his smart business suits, he appeared as the experienced technocrat who understood the international economic system and had the necessary connections outside the country to promote sustained economic growth. By contrast, Manley had been presented in JLP propaganda as a dangerous ideologue who had unwisely allowed his personal political philosophy to dictate policy at the expense of pragmatic common sense. In the light of these claims, the surprise was the extent to which the JLP government itself quickly became associated with a model of economic development derived from ideological considerations.

The ideas which influenced the JLP's handling of the Jamaican economy during the 1980s were broadly those of neo-liberalism, as refined over the course of the decade by such leading international financial institutions as the IMF and the World Bank. Indeed, the relationship which the Seaga government established with the IMF was so central to its existence that the government's overall management of the economy, and indeed its entire political record, can advantageously be analysed by reference to the changing nature of this relationship. This chapter examines the politics of the whole Seaga period and sets out in detail the phases of policy through which the pursuit of economic revival and the maintenance of political power passed. It starts by explaining the notion of structural adjustment which became the centrepiece of neo-liberal theories of economic management in the 1980s and which was rhetorically embraced from the very outset by the Seaga government.

Structural adjustment

The concept of structural adjustment can only be understood in the context of the debate about the working of the international economy, and the role of the IMF within it, which had gone on during much of the post-war period. Between 1945 and 1973 large US balance of payments deficits financed the whole international trading system which meant that there existed no fundamental payments disequilibrium for developing countries as a group. During these years it was generally accepted that those countries which did get into balance of payments trouble, and had consequently to turn to the IMF for help, had done so because they had in some way mismanaged their economic affairs, rather than because there was a general lack of liquidity in the global economy. In a world of growth it was also usually the case that the IMF remedy of a temporary deflation of demand, combined with the provision of credit, quickly restored external balance and recreated the basis for economic expansion. Relatively little controversy attached to the IMF's approach. After 1973, however, all that changed. Developing countries had to cope with major rises in the price of oil, a general deterioration in their terms of trade and sharp increases in the rates of interest determining debt service repayments. Indeed, the decline in their general balance of payments position was described by one political economist as 'so continuous and so serious that there can be little doubt that it can only be described as "structural" or "fundamental" in its nature'.[1]

In such conditions, IMF prescriptions were no longer capable of generating an automatic economic recovery and the harshness of their terms attracted growing political opposition within the Third World. Jamaica's experience with the Fund under the Manley government, although far from unique in its time, was a key part of the emerging critique. The argument came to a head in 1980 at a major conference on the international monetary system jointly organised by Jamaica and Tanzania, another state whose 'democratic socialist' programme of reform had been effectively broken on the back of an IMF intervention. The conference drew up the 'Arusha Initiative', which *inter alia* condemned IMF policies as 'a form of political intervention' designed to subordinate states to 'the free play of national and international market forces' to the advantage of the 'traditional centres of power' in the world.[2] It called instead for a major shift of resources from the richer to the poorer parts of the world in order to enable deficit economies to produce their way out of balance of payments problems. The legitimacy of the Fund was damaged by such criticisms and a response was soon forthcoming – the concept of structural adjustment.

The thinking underlying this new approach was well set out by Manuel Guitian, one of the Fund's theorists, in an IMF publication in 1982. He accepted the argument that the payments imbalances existing in the world economy in the 1980s were structural in kind and could therefore only be dealt with on the basis of longer adjustment periods than had been deployed in IMF programmes in the past. A new recognition was also given to the need for production – to be achieved, it was said, by means of 'foreign borrowing strategies that directly enlarge the amount of resources to the member', thus allowing 'higher levels of expenditure ... as well as higher growth rates over the medium term'.[3] Having incorporated this extra emphasis on the transfer of resources to developing countries, Guitian then felt able to defend the IMF against the charge that its preoccupation with deflation served primarily to retard, rather than promote, growth. Yet, as Brett for one pointed out, this concession did 'not leave orthodoxy far behind'.[4]

As it turned out, the domestic adjustment policies subsequently favoured by the IMF were little changed from those of the 1970s. According to Guitian, they included:

> public sector policies on prices, taxes, and subsidies that can contribute to eliminate financial imbalances and to promote efficiency in public sector activities; interest rate policies that foster the generation of domestic savings and improve inter-temporal resources allocation; exchange rate policy that helps to control absorption and the external accounts but is also a powerful tool for development; and incomes policies that keep claims on resources from out-stepping their availability.[5]

The technicality of the language did not obscure the hostility towards all forms of state intervention in economic management, the attachment of merit to low wages, the rejection of protection as a trade policy or the disregard for the impact the programme would have on domestic prices. Indeed, devaluation was recommended as the best means to control the inflow of imports. In short, there was little real change in the IMF's approach: its new prescriptions were more sensitive to the timing and pace of the adjustment being demanded but were still firmly based on orthodox liberal economics.

The logic on which such neo-liberal thinking depended was simple. If a country suffered from a balance of payments deficit, it meant that its currency (in effect, its externally-traded goods and services) was less in demand than the foreign currencies which it used to make purchases. The country should correct its payments deficit by allowing its currency to float until it found its correct level or by devaluing sufficiently to eliminate the distortion. This would discourage imports and promote exports. It was also presumed that the country would attract enough extra foreign investment to generate more production in the medium-to-long run to offset short-run inflation. It did not need to impose any controls on imports or exports as the market mechanism would do the job perfectly well. The market, in turn, would dictate all other required fiscal measures, such as regulation of the money supply to control public expenditure, the removal of subsidies and the privatisation of state enterprises. In this way, the whole society would be returned to the environment of the free market, debts could be repaid and the integrity of an open international trading system would be preserved.

Such an ideology was as crude as it was simple, which was one of the main reasons why Seaga, who had to operate within the competitive Jamaican electoral system, never articulated it as clearly as the IMF technocrats. Nevertheless, in the period leading up to the 1980 election, he made no secret of his attachment to free enterprise, his awareness that Jamaica had to operate in an international market-place and his desire to shift the country's economy away from import-substitution towards export promotion.[6] It certainly was assumed in Washington that it was precisely a process of structural adjustment, as understood by the IMF, which the JLP government was seeking to effect after October 1980. Seaga, at the very least, did not deny it; indeed, it may have been an important part of his political strategy to give this impression. The debate about Edward Seaga's motivation and politics is considered later; it is necessary now to examine the performance and policies of his government from beginning to end.

IMF management

Phase I: November 1980 – October 1983

The JLP administration set about its mission with style and confidence. Within months, Jamaica had emerged as probably the most committed client state of the US government in the Caribbean area, a status neatly symbolised by Seaga's invitation to become the first foreign head of state to visit President Reagan in the White House after the latter took office at the beginning of 1981. Seaga played up to his host, extolling the virtues of capitalism and calling upon the US and its allies to rescue the Caribbean Basin from left-wing influence by putting together a programme along the lines of the Marshall Plan, prepared for Europe after 1945. Although the latter proposal took shape in much weaker form as the Caribbean Basin Initiative (CBI), the plea on behalf of Jamaica worked. Reagan instructed the State Department to set up a special office to coordinate US governmental aid to Jamaica and asked David Rockefeller, the chairman of Chase Manhattan Bank, to mobilise the US private sector to take an interest in the island. By March 1981, a US business committee on Jamaica, composed of leading corporate executives, had been established and had begun meeting with a local counterpart, set up by Seaga, to find ways of promoting new inward investment in Jamaica.[7]

A commitment to begin negotiations with the IMF at the earliest opportunity had been given by the new Seaga government immediately on assuming office, and in the prevailing cordial atmosphere being signalled by Washington, the talks were quickly brought to a successful conclusion. An extended fund facility (EFF) agreement was signed in April 1981, providing for a loan of US$650 million over three years. In addition, the government received a further US$48 million from the compensatory financing facility set up specifically to offset temporary shortfalls in traditional export earnings. The EFF agreement was also (in the language of the IMF) 'front-loaded', which meant that 40 per cent of the loan could be drawn in the first year of the agreement's term. To ensure payment of subsequent tranches, the government had to meet certain targets. Limits were set on the net amount of domestic bank credit distributed to the public sector and on the extent of the domestic and international reserves held by the Bank of Jamaica. The government further agreed not to introduce multiple currency practices (as the Manley regime had done) and not to place new restrictions on payments and transfers for current international transactions. Finally, a ceiling was placed on new external borrowing by the government.[8]

What was interesting were the conditions the IMF did not see fit to impose on the Seaga government compared to those it had demanded of the PNP government in the 1970s. Crucially, there was no demand for a devaluation of the Jamaican currency, although this was called for by the tenets of structural adjustment. Nor were the restrictions on domestic public sector borrowing made to apply to the private sector. The ceiling on government borrowing abroad excluded loans to refinance existing debts and loans from foreign governments and their agencies or multilateral lending organisations. Seaga certainly made a virtue of the absence of 'negative features' in the deal when he explained it to the Jamaican people[9] and indeed, it does seem that he was able to negotiate much more favourable terms with the IMF than did his predecessor.[10] He already had cleverly advertised his anti-communist, pro-Western credentials in such moves as his expulsion of the Cuban ambassador from Kingston immediately on assuming office, and they now won him due financial reward.

The whole episode also offered a textbook illustration of how a loan from the IMF could put a stamp of financial respectability on a country that had been effectively frozen out of the international money markets for several years. Following the signing of the agreement, the way was cleared for the Seaga government to mount a massive borrowing and refinancing operation over the next two years. Although the World Bank was the single most important contributor, the sources of the loans on which it was able to draw were so diverse that they implied nothing less than the existence of a coordinated international rescue of the Jamaican economy. The immediate gain was the ample provision of foreign exchange with which to rehabilitate traditional industries and stimulate new ones; the long-term price was a substantial rise in foreign debt, which increased from an estimated US$1.2 billion at the end of 1980 to US$3.1 billion by the end of 1983.[11]

On the basis of this financial support and the increased foreign investment that the government expected to start flowing again soon, ambitious growth and production targets were set in virtually all sectors, none more so than in the crucial bauxite and alumina industry. Speaking in June 1981, Seaga revealed plans to increase the annual production of bauxite from the 1980 figure of 12 million tons to 26 million tons within three years. Alumina production was to be similarly expanded, from 2.4 million tons to 8.6 million tons, primarily through a proposed joint investment by the government, several Norwegian firms, and the US company Alcoa, which would double the size of the latter's refinery in Jamaica.[12] The trouble was that, just as the government was promoting this future expansion, Alcoa announced a cutback in existing production levels because of decreasing world demand for alumina. Despite warnings from local experts and opposition politicians, the government was unprepared for the recession that occurred in the bauxite market. The other companies operating in Jamaica followed Alcoa's lead, with the result that bauxite production, far from expanding hugely as anticipated, fell disastrously to only 7.3 million tons in 1983. Government revenue from the industry fell accordingly, from US$206 million in 1980 to US$137 million in 1982.[13]

This was a severe setback – and one against which the Seaga regime could not have protected itself other than by a more accurate prediction of market trends. It appealed for immediate assistance to its main overseas ally, the Reagan administration, which responded in December 1981 by ordering 1.6 million tons of Jamaican bauxite for its strategic defence stockpile. Although the purchase helped to maintain activity in the industry for a while, its contribution to the balance of payments was limited by US insistence on paying for the bauxite, in part, in agricultural products. The emerging balance of payments problem caused by the reduction in bauxite production was further worsened by the poor performance of other traditional agricultural exports. Sugar production declined by 50,000 tons between 1980 and 1982 and banana production by 11,000 tons over the same period.[14] Only tourism offered consolation, the number of visitors increasing from 1980 levels in response to a vigorous publicity drive and the favourable impression that Seaga made on North American audiences. The difficulties experienced by these long-standing foreign exchange earners inevitably placed responsibility for the generation of economic growth on non-traditional exports at a much earlier stage in the process of structural adjustment than had been anticipated.

However, despite all the paraphernalia surrounding the establishment of joint US-Jamaican business committees, foreign investors were slow and, ultimately, timid in their response to the new opportunities being offered. The reasons for this were several: apart from a general disinclination to invest in new activity at a time when international interest rates were at record levels, there was the residual legacy of Jamaica's reputation in the 1970s as a place of violence and extremism, the continuing problem of bureaucratic inefficiency and new concern over the adequacy of the country's basic infrastructure. The Seaga team initially thought that the CBI was likely to be a great source of future investment, but its delayed passage through Congress (it was not passed into law until mid-1983), the dropping of proposed tax credits on new US investments in the Caribbean, and the exclusion of textiles, apparel and a number of other categories of goods markedly reduced its impact on the Jamaican economy. As a result, although the government could point to the many inquiries handled by Jamaica National Investment Promotion Ltd (JNIP), the new agency set up in 1981 to facilitate the inflow of foreign investment, the number of projects actually initiated in the first year or two was very few. Moreover, even when foreign businessmen were persuaded to set up new operations, they often borrowed on the local market rather than bring in foreign funds. As for the response of the Jamaican capitalist sector, that was accurately encapsulated in the Stephens's wry observation that it persisted in its 'preference for quick and easy profits over entrepreneurial risk-taking, new investments and a search for new markets.'[15] In consequence, the figures show that 'non-traditional exports' grew from J$197 million in 1980 to J$235 million in 1982 – not enough by any means to offset the poor performance of the traditional commodity sector.[16]

The Seaga government's development strategy was itself partly responsible for the unwillingness of Jamaican businessmen to take chances in export markets. To put it simply, they could make money more easily at home in conventional import-export activities. The policy of liberalising the flow of imports fuelled an enormous consumer boom during 1981 and 1982 as the rich and the middle class enjoyed imported luxury items forbidden to them during the foreign exchange squeeze at the end of the 1970s. There was launched what a local gibe referred to as the era of the three Vs – Volvos, videos and venereal disease, the latter associated with the revival of the tourist industry. Although politically attractive (and thus to some extent necessary) as a way of pleasing the government's more affluent supporters, the import boom created serious difficulties. In the first place, it raised expectations about improvements in the standard of living to new and unattainable heights; second, it made it impossible for local manufacturers to preserve their hold on the domestic market, let alone launch into the export battle; third, it put out of business many small farmers who could not compete with cheap food imports once restrictions had been lifted; and, last, it worsened the already shaky prospects for the balance of payments. The latter was especially critical.

By the middle of 1982, the Jamaican dollar, officially valued at J$1.78 to the US dollar, was trading on the black or 'parallel' market at nearly twice that figure. In what amounted to an offer of legitimacy to this system, the government initially tried to draw some of the parallel market dollars, many of which had been earned illegally from trading in marijuana (*ganja*), into specified imports intended to help local manufacturing. It issued so-called 'no-funds licenses', which permitted businessmen to pay for certain goods without recourse to the Bank of Jamaica. By January 1983, however, it was forced to go a step further and openly institute a two-tier exchange rate. Seaga's aim was to encourage exports by making imported materials for manufactured goods less expensive than imported goods for consumption. The former would continue to be costed at the official rate, the latter at a rate expected to level out around J$2.70.[17] The move was thus a hidden devaluation of the currency, an issue of particular political sensitivity because of the JLP's earlier attacks on the Manley government's policies in this area in the 1970s. The most immediate effect of the introduction of the dual exchange rate was, of course, on prices, thereby threatening the reduction in inflation that had accompanied the liberalisation of imports and the capture of the local market by the cheapest available foreign goods.[18]

The deepening balance of payments crisis was bound to make its presence felt in the quarterly tests the economy had to undergo as part of the 1981 IMF agreement. The moment of failure came in March 1983, by which time the deficit had reached US$150 million. The Fund promptly suspended further disbursements and Seaga had no alternative but to plead for a waiver. To maintain IMF support, he introduced austerity measures, including new taxes, public spending cuts, reduced foreign exchange allocations for imports and the shift of many more items to the more expensive parallel market rate. The idea was to curb the use of precious foreign exchange on non-essential imports by pricing them out of the reach of most people. As such, the move was an extension of the previous devaluation, having the same inflationary consequences over an even wider range of goods, including many items of basic utility like gasoline. Jamaicans felt the impact of the squeeze, but the reaction of Seaga's external backers was favourable. The IMF granted the waiver, the World Bank produced two more small loans, and the US government offered US$25 million in emergency balance of payments assistance as well as agreeing to make a further purchase of bauxite for its strategic reserve. It was, to say the least, an impressive demonstration of continuing support for Seaga by the dominant forces of the international liberal economy.

What is striking is that it was to no avail. Production in the Jamaican economy had reached a depth that could not be corrected simply by devaluation. In October 1983 the IMF again suspended payments following a further protracted dispute with the government over figures relating to the failure of the September test.[19] It was announced that the agreement was to be terminated six months early and negotiations were started on a new package of assistance, with Seaga and his colleagues in a much weaker bargaining position than in 1980–1.

Phase II: November 1983 – March 1985

The talks with the IMF took place in the context of deteriorating political support for the JLP government. Its initial honeymoon with the Jamaican electorate ended with the increases in inflation and unemployment and the renewal of hard times for the poor, especially after the liberal consumption of goods in the preceding couple of years by business people and the middle classes. The political consequences were charted in the regular opinion polls taken by Carl Stone. A commanding 28 per cent lead in May 1981 fell to 7 per cent a year later. Then, for the first time, in October 1982, the PNP pulled ahead of the JLP – by 43 per cent to 38 per cent – and maintained that ascendancy into 1983.[20] It was not so much that the PNP had been able to arouse a renewed faith in its capacity to govern so soon after the debacle of the late 1970s but, rather, that its traditional association with the poor, with public expenditure and with the expansion of welfare policies, regained it some support as the issue of economic weakness again took precedence in the public mind. Thus, by the autumn of 1983, the prospect of being the first Jamaican government since independence to lose office after just one term loomed before the JLP.

The crisis was further exacerbated because pressure on the exchange rate built up as the new IMF talks got under way. The government had seriously miscalculated the balance of supply and demand for foreign exchange: the decision to push extra imports on to the parallel market caused a rapid bidding up of the price to over J$3 by the end of October. The Fund focused on this as a sign of the continuing uncompetitiveness of Jamaican exports and made a unification (i.e., another devaluation) of the exchange rate its main demand in return for a new standby credit. The original intention was that this new arrangement would run for fifteen months from the beginning of January 1984, but it soon became evident that the IMF had other demands too and wanted to see them implemented before it agreed to the loan, not after it had been approved and disbursed. Its approach can be aptly described in sporting parlance as one of 'getting your retaliation in first'. In this connection, the key announcement came at the end of November 1983: the Jamaican dollar would henceforth be fixed at a single rate, initially set at J$3.15, but adjustable every two weeks by the Bank of Jamaica in a kind of 'managed float'. This signified a devaluation of no less than 43 per cent for any item hitherto traded at the former official rate and was the beginning of a series of harsh economic measures introduced at the insistence of the IMF.

Politically, it was highly significant that the announcement of the devaluation came only after the murderous self-destruction of the Grenadian revolution and the ensuing US invasion, in which Jamaican troops were actively involved, albeit in a minor supporting role, had served to create a surge of domestic support for the JLP. In fact, the Stone poll taken immediately after the killings in Grenada, which showed the JLP converting a 3 per cent deficit *vis-à-vis* the PNP into a 5 per cent lead, altered the course of Jamaican politics. It revealed the extent of the latent suspicion of left-wing ideology in Jamaica and led Seaga 'to deepen the Jamaicanisation of the Grenada issue'[21] by seeking to tarnish local PNP figures by association with Cuba, the Soviet Union and the Grenadian revolutionaries.

Given the tenor of the talks that were simultaneously taking place with the IMF, the temptation to call a snap election before the effects of a devaluation worked through the economy and before the Grenada issue was forgotten was plainly compelling. The only obstacle was an agreement between the two major parties that an election would not be called until a new voters' list being worked on by the electoral commission was ready. This was, however, overridden by Seaga, who announced the date for an election just two days after revealing the government's austere new economic package. The PNP chose to boycott the poll on the grounds that the inter-party agreement on electoral reform had been unilaterally abrogated by Seaga and thus, by default, the JLP won all sixty seats when voting took place in mid-December 1983. The ploy was highly controversial, even among some JLP activists, but it bought the JLP five more years in office and in that sense cleared the decks politically for the austerity that was to come.[22]

The IMF thus achieved its goal of a substantial devaluation; its other major demand related to the size of the government's budget deficit, which it wanted to see reduced from 15.6 per cent of gross domestic product to a single figure in the space of just one year. Yet, even before the task of meeting this requirement could be properly confronted, its achievement was made considerably more difficult by another damaging development within the bauxite industry. In March 1984, apparently without any prior warning to the government, another of the major North American multinational companies, Reynolds, announced that it was shutting down its bauxite operation. It blamed the international recession, although some felt that an argument with the government, a year or so earlier, about the distribution of the US stockpile contract between the companies operating in Jamaica was at least a partial cause. Seaga expressed anger that a company that had worked in Jamaica for over forty years should behave in such a way and admitted, in a state of some shock, that the loss to the fiscal budget being planned for 1984–5 could be as much as J\$100 million and the shortfall in the foreign exchange budget some US\$30 million.[23]

If, therefore, the IMF target was to be met, the level of deflation had to be even more severe than had been projected. For political reasons, Seaga took two bites at it: he raised taxes by J\$138 million in a 'mini-package' in April 1984 and then extended the process by a further J\$45 million in the regular budget in May. In addition, public expenditure was reduced and many civil servants and other public sector workers were laid off, adding to the already high unemployment rate. Food subsidies were also cut, although a minimum level of support for basic commodities was maintained. Other measures designed to appease the IMF included restrictions on domestic credit, the promise of accelerated divestment of state enterprises, and a more intensive policing of the leakage of foreign exchange from the tourist sector, which was notorious for the way it was able to siphon money to Miami. It should be noted too that, while these measures were being put into place in the first half of 1984, the Jamaican dollar continued to slide downward on the floating exchange, reaching J\$4.15 by June. Eventually, enough was enough. Jamaica's second major IMF loan in the Seaga era came five months late in June 1984: it provided US$143 million – well below the US$180 million the government had been hoping for since the end of 1983 – divided between standby credit and compensatory finance, and was scheduled to last only until the end of March 1985. With the loan in place, debt rescheduling was again possible and shortly afterwards the Paris Club of international creditors agreed to roll forward US$135 million of external debts due for repayment before March 1985.

The idea behind this loan was to give the Jamaican economy some breathing space in which the prescribed free-market remedy, as insisted upon more firmly by the IMF on this occasion, could at last begin to work. The Fund itself issued a statement declaring optimistically that the various measures that had been introduced would 'place fiscal and credit policies on a sounder footing in order to improve the balance of payments and restore conditions for the implementation of structural reform'.[24] The reaction, both inside and outside the country, can be imagined, therefore, when the economy almost immediately failed the regular quarterly test at the end of September. Seaga had to travel to Washington in person to seek the familiar waiver. On this occasion the Fund chose to accept his argument that the failure was more technical than real – foreign loans had not been paid on time – and the only price exacted for the continuation of the credit was the removal of any attempt to manage the Jamaican dollar and to allow it to float freely from the beginning of December. Yet, by the time the end-of-year test came around, the position of the reserves was no better, and two loans from the US government, which still loyally supported the Seaga regime, were hurried through. Despite government denials, it was obvious that another IMF agreement was coming to an ignominious end.

Seaga's problem was that not only did he have to satisfy the IMF's demands, but he had to manage the domestic political situation in Jamaica, which by the beginning of 1985 was becoming more and more tense. The economic boom of 1981 had long since disappeared; inflation stood at 30 per cent; the currency had floated downwards to J$5.00; and unemployment (notwithstanding the continuation under JLP auspices of a number of former PNP job training programmes) was estimated at 25.6 per cent of the labour force. In this last respect, the unpalatable fact was that the creation of 6,705 jobs, which the JNIP proudly announced in mid-1984 as the result of almost four years of trying to promote new investment in manufacturing industry, barely exceeded the 6,200 jobs the government itself had agreed to cut from the public sector to secure the second IMF loan.[25] In the circumstances, the two days of riots and protests that followed the announcement of gas price increases in January 1985 were not unexpected.[26] Even so, the government was shaken by the extent of the anger obviously felt by ordinary working-class Jamaicans at its economic policies, and was further taken aback by the announcement shortly afterwards that Alcoa was to follow in the footsteps of Reynolds and close its alumina refinery on the island, pending a revival of market conditions. The conclusion the government drew, however, was not that the adjustment programme needed to be abandoned, but that the people would have to be told more openly of the harsh choices facing the country as a result of the economy's plight – especially as the next round of IMF talks was about to begin.

Phase III: April 1985–April 1986

The new policy of candour was initiated in a nationwide television address delivered by Seaga in April 1985. He spoke of the need to secure a further IMF deal but warned there would have to be sacrifices in the form of more public sector job losses, higher interest rates and still heavier taxation. The sole ray of hope he could offer was the news that the Alcoa plant would open again in July under a leasing arrangement whereby production and marketing would be undertaken by a new government company, Clarendon Alumina Production Ltd., although operational responsibility would be retained by Alcoa. Seaga claimed that buyers had already been found for virtually all of the plant's capacity, albeit initially at loss-making prices. The government's willingness to intervene in this way was highly revealing: it showed how desperate it had become to preserve the basis of the bauxite industry for the future and to prevent any further redundancies in the meantime. It also revealed that, despite its free-enterprise rhetoric, the Seaga administration was prepared to use the powers of the state to defend key national economic interests. In this sense, its approach to the bauxite industry – when really put to the test – was more in keeping with the interventionist policies of the Manley government of the 1970s than with the neo-liberal theories of economic management, which it generally espoused.[27]

As promised, the next IMF agreement was soon announced. It represented a twenty-month EFF of US$120 million, to run from August 1985 to March 1987, and was deemed to require a further reduction in the size of the government's budget deficit. Apart from threatening more jobs, this permitted a wage rise of only 10 per cent for public employees at a time when inflation was more than three times higher. The political reaction was both swift and fierce: within two weeks of the announcement Jamaica was immersed in the first general strike in its post-independence history. For several days at the end of June 1985 essential services all over the island were either closed down or maintained at only skeleton levels, and a call from Seaga for an immediate return to work was rejected. Yet the action stemmed from despair rather than calculated planning, and the initial solidarity of the strikers was fairly quickly undermined by the government's uncompromising insistence that there really was no more money available for pay if the lifeblood of IMF credit was to be kept flowing. For all that, the strike indicated in a more tangible way than opinion polls the extent to which Seaga's programme had lost the support of the bulk of the country. The fact that the Bustamante Industrial Trade Union (BITU) took part was particularly damaging, not just because it was affiliated with the JLP but because it was the very organisation from which the party had been born in the 1940s.

Although the strike's collapse undoubtedly weakened the union movement and generally was seen as a victory for Seaga, it had a significant impact on his political tactics. The period following the strike brought no sign that investment and enterprise were responding to the cheap labour economy created by the massive devaluation of the currency over the preceding two years. The Rockefeller Committee had been disbanded a year earlier, and indeed, the economy in general continued to worsen. Alpart suspended production at its alumina refinery in August 1985, with more loss of jobs and revenue; official forecasts warned of a decline in gross domestic product of as much as 6 per cent in the year; tourism declined in the aftermath of the gas price disturbances; and the exchange rate almost reached J$6 to the US dollar at the end of September. There was nothing new in these further manifestations of economic difficulty, except for the evidence of growing political opposition – not just from the unions, but from a more active PNP, which had been revitalised by what was seen as the deceit underlying the 1983 election and was again well in the lead in the opinion polls. These political pressures seemed to persuade Seaga of the need to adopt a softer stance to improve his domestic political position. The IMF annual meeting in the South Korean capital of Seoul, which Seaga attended in October, was thus treated to a description of the 'huge toll in human suffering' experienced as a result of the 'over-hasty' reform programme demanded by the Fund in countries like Jamaica. It was not the substance of the programme that he challenged, but its pace; seven years, rather than three, was advanced as a more appropriate adjustment period.[28]

The political thinking that lay behind this plea was quick to emerge. The economy had failed the September 1985 quarterly test, several loans had been delayed, and once again the government required a waiver. In the face of restiveness among leading figures in his own party and a further fall in the currency to J$6.40 (at which point the Bank of Jamaica did intervene financially to arrest what had become an almost uncontrollable slide), Seaga knew that he could mollify the Fund only by, in effect, arguing the opposition's case – that the Jamaican people could not take any more deflation of the economy. Accordingly, he used his contacts in the Reagan administration to engineer a visit to Jamaica in the first few months of 1986 by a joint team from the IMF, the World Bank and the US Agency for International Development (USAID). The visit was designed to enable the mission to witness the 'progress' that had already been made towards structural adjustment and to hear the arguments for easing future terms. In the meantime, as a token of good faith, the government took a step towards the further reduction of its budget deficit by introducing another emergency tax package in January 1986. The measures included an annual licence fee for television satellite antennae, the 'dishes', which had become symbols of prosperity during the 1981 import boom.

The Fund, however, was unimpressed. Although a waiver was given to enable more credit to be drawn while negotiations continued, the visiting Tripartite Mission roundly criticised the Seaga government for failing to carry out its promised programme of structural reforms, particularly the divestment of public enterprises and adequate currency devaluation. It noted that, five years after the JLP took office, 'there remains substantial government involvement in, and control of, economic activity, and the structure of incentives is still complex and even haphazard'.[29] Seaga, by all accounts, was furious and tried to suppress distribution in Jamaica of the critical parts of the report. At the same time, pay disputes with teachers, police and junior doctors, as well as protests from students at the UWI about the introduction of tuition fees, kept up the domestic political pressure and virtually eliminated scope for concessions to the IMF orthodoxy being demanded by the Tripartite report. In short, an impasse had been reached.

Phase IV: May 1986 – March 1988

The first move to end the stalemate was made by Seaga when in May 1986, in an extraordinary reversal of the deflationary approach of the preceding two years, he introduced an expansionary budget designed to regenerate growth in the economy. Its main features were a reduction in interest rates, a pledge to peg the exchange rate at J$5.50, the use of temporary controls to reduce the price of basic foods, animal feed and cement, and an increase in capital expenditure from

J$1.4 billion in the previous fiscal year to J$2.1 billion in the forthcoming year. In contradiction of earlier warnings, there were no new taxes. The change of approach was evident, but what it meant was unclear. The budget had been delayed a week following arguments about strategy with the Tripartite Mission and, on the surface at least, appeared to reflect a decisive rejection of IMF policy. Seaga also observed enigmatically that the government had prepared, but would not disclose, 'a contingency programme in the event that there is any insistence by the institutions on returning this time to further devaluations, budget cuts, reduction of services, redundancies and no growth' – for all of which he now disclaimed responsibility.[30] Against this, the government did accept orthodox IMF/World Bank/USAID policy to the extent that it also announced the divestment of the government-owned National Commercial Bank and significant reductions of import tariffs.

The most likely interpretation of Seaga's behaviour is that he was, in effect, playing poker with the IMF and its allies. The crucial background factor was the fall in the international market price of oil in early 1986. Given the Jamaican economy's considerable dependence on oil imports, this gave the balance of payments an unexpected boost, thus providing the government with more room to manoeuvre economically than had been anticipated. It quickly took advantage of the situation by buying three years' supply of oil when the price was US$10 per barrel. The probability is, therefore, that Seaga saw the oil windfall as the best chance to bargain with the IMF for the softening of its terms which he had first asked for in Seoul. Certainly, the May budget did not indicate the adoption of a non-IMF strategy of any kind, although Seaga did endeavour to use the dispute with the Fund to regenerate public support in Jamaica.

Local elections had originally been due to be held in June 1984; they had been postponed once by agreement between the parties to allow new voter registration to be completed, and a second time as a result of a proposed reform of local government, subsequently withdrawn by the government. Eventually called for July 1986, elections were fought as a national campaign (thereby constituting the first major electoral assessment of the JLP record since 1980) and were resoundingly won by the PNP, which took 57 per cent of the vote and 126 of the 187 available local authority seats. Although Michael Manley repeated the demand for an early general election, which he had made many times since the non-election of 1983, Seaga was predictably unresponsive.[31] The rebuff the voters dealt him had at least revealed that the symbolism of conflict with the IMF was insufficient to impress ordinary Jamaicans: they wanted a tangible amelioration of their economic circumstances.

In September Seaga went to Washington for more talks, having revealed that repayments to the IMF had been deliberately delayed as part of his tactics. These were high stakes, since the debt to the IMF (some US$70 million by late 1986) unquestionably meant a moratorium on new loans or debt rescheduling agreements. Indeed, it was debt and the threat of default that Seaga was trying to bargain with. According to Timothy Ashby's account, Seaga's meeting with the US Assistant Secretary of State for Inter-American Affairs, Elliott Abrams, was especially blunt. Abrams apparently told Seaga to initiate a proper privatisation process and to devalue the Jamaican dollar still further to its true market level.[32] The latter was certainly the key issue in dispute with the IMF. Attempts to rescue the stalled third agreement, which technically ran until the end of March 1987, were abandoned in favour of discussion of a completely new three-year programme. As a prerequisite for this, the Fund wanted another devaluation to take the rate from J$5.50 to J$6.06, Seaga countered with a proposal to move to J$5.91 in fiscal year 1987–8 and then to J$6.43 a year later. He defended this position by claiming that it maintained the rate in real terms and was not, therefore, a means to further restructuring, yet this was precisely why the Fund's officials were reluctant to accept it. As an alternative, Seaga proposed a wage freeze, only to find that as soon as that possibility emerged into the open all the major trade unions on the island, including the BITU, rejected it emphatically.

The bargaining between the government and the Fund was undoubtedly genuine and very hard, and for a long while no accommodation could be reached. The warmth had also clearly gone out of US-Jamaican relations in general. Seaga's former easy access to the Reagan administration had been considerably curtailed by this time and towards the end of 1986 a substantial cut in US aid to Jamaica and a reduction in the country's sugar import quota into the US market were announced in Washington. Fearful that his main means of external support were disappearing, Seaga pressed ahead with some privatisation measures, finally offering 51 per cent of the shares in the National Commercial Bank for public sale in December. However, on the substance of his difference of opinion with the IMF, namely the currency, he had no political alternative but to stand firm. In the end, the Fund relented, with the result that, in January 1987, the JLP government's fourth major agreement with the IMF was concluded. It was for a loan of US$132.8 million for fifteen months, running until 31 March 1988.

Seaga presented the deal as 'a major breakthrough'. 'The negotiations were long and tough', he declared, 'but they were worth it. We were determined to avoid any up-front devaluation of the Jamaican dollar. We did so! But we must maintain this with a low inflation level'.[33] This last was a reference to the main condition of the agreement, which was a government commitment to reduce inflation in 1987–8 to only 7 per cent, about half the existing level. With this objective in mind, the list of price controls on basic foods imposed the previous May was retained and new controls instituted on fertilisers, animal feed, herbicides, pesticides, medicines and educational textbooks. Pay guidelines were also announced limiting increases to 10 per cent a year, compared with the previous year's average settlement of 12.5 per cent. Import duties were to be further reduced, giving extra-regional goods even easier access to the Jamaican market and acting as a downward pressure on prices, albeit to the disadvantage, as before, of local manufacturing interests embedded in traditional import-substitution enterprise. In fact, Douglas Vaz, who had been Minister of Industry and Commerce until the previous October, resigned from the government on this issue, revealing something of the internal conflicts going on within the JLP.

On balance, it appeared Seaga's relief was justified. The IMF had retreated from its demand for an immediate devaluation and had given him more time – both economically and politically. Once more too, debt rescheduling within the framework of the Paris Club was made possible by the signing of the IMF deal. Even so, the new agreement also had its dangers for the government. Under questioning, Seaga was forced to admit that a devaluation was likely to take place at the end of the fifteen-month period if the inflation target was not met and, with the trade unions reacting angrily to the proposed pay guidelines, problems were only to be expected, especially with public sector workers such as nurses, doctors, teachers, civil servants and the police. The reductions in import duties also threatened to set in motion another consumer boom led by those who were well-off; this was likely to widen the trade deficit and force the government into new borrowing as the only means of taking pressure off the exchange rate but could be expected to win back middle-class political support for the JLP, which was still a long way behind the PNP in the polls. In short, Seaga's claim that 'we have now left behind us the bitter part of these programmes'[34] of structural adjustment was premature: his plea to the IMF had won him a temporary easing of terms but still left him and his government firmly tied to the dictates of the Fund.

In the event, this fourth IMF agreement was the most successful of the Seaga era. Introducing the 1987–8 budget in April, Seaga was able to announce real GDP growth in the previous fiscal year of 3–4 per cent, which he claimed was the best figure since 1972. The main factors responsible were the fall in the price of oil, a slight rise in bauxite production, the growth of exports of apparel to the US under the terms of advantageous tariff concessions like the so-called 807 and Super 807 programmes[35] and, above all, the substantial expansion in tourist earnings (to US$503 million in the year ending March 1987, an increase of 21 per cent over the previous year). Although there was a tourist boom in many parts of the Caribbean in the 1980s, it was the one unequivocal economic achievement of the JLP period in government and was attributable largely to the restoration of Jamaica's image as an attractive holiday destination in the minds of the American public, following the bad publicity of the 1970s. Although the balance of trade deficit grew as the economy continued to expand throughout 1987, it was financed and all the IMF's performance tests were satisfactorily passed. As regards wages, the unions had no stomach for a fight with the government after their defeat in the general strike of 1985 and inflation was successfully contained to around 8–9 per cent at the end of March 1988. Although higher than the 7 per cent ceiling set under the IMF agreement, it caused no difficulties and was obviously within the margin of error permitted in the unspoken part of the deal.

Phase V: April 1988 – February 1989

The final phase of the Seaga government's intricate dealings with the IMF was overlaid politically by the impending election, which was due, in the normal sense of a five-year parliamentary term, by December 1988. But the precise wording of the Jamaican constitution requires that parliament be dissolved within five years of its first sitting after an election and another poll be called within three months of this dissolution. Since the first sitting of the post-1983 parliament had been on 10 January 1984, technically, Seaga had until 10 April 1989 to go to the country – although most commentators assumed he would be reluctant to enter the period of grace for fear of being thought frightened to face the people's verdict. Either way, the April 1988 budget was likely to be the last before an election had to be held. Even a year earlier, the government had significantly increased public expenditure, especially on road building, a classic form of political patronage in Jamaica. On this occasion Seaga announced a 'social well-being programme', designed to rebuild the country's social services over a five-year period. Spending on health and education was to be increased by 123 per cent and 67 per cent respectively over the forthcoming year. In addition, expenditure on relief of the poor, school meals and food subsidies was also to be increased and no new taxes were proposed. The political message was evident: the social costs of adjustment could now be tackled but only because the country's finances had been put in order by a disciplined and diligent administration.

On the financial side Seaga signalled in his budget speech that further assistance from the IMF was to be sought under a fifth programme which he expected to be negotiated without any problems by the end of the summer.[36] By this stage in the relationship, the IMF was as much tied to Seaga as he was to the Fund. The election was the dominant consideration. Although the PNP, and Michael Manley in particular, had worked hard in the second half of the 1980s to convince the international financial community that the party's re-election would pose no threat to Jamaica's capitalist orientation, and although Seaga was regarded with nothing like the favour in Washington that he once enjoyed, the JLP remained much the safer prospect from the point of view of most external interests, certainly those of the IMF. Its officials were pleased to see further privatisations taking place in respect of the Caribbean Cement Company and Telecommunications of Jamaica, but they knew that Seaga was willing to use the state to defend what he saw as key national interests – as when in March 1988 the government resolved its long-running dispute with Alcoa over the Clarendon refinery by agreeing to buy a 50 per cent equity share (up from 6 per cent) in the company's operation in Jamaica. In short, by late 1988 Seaga was a familiar customer, well known to the Fund, warts and all. In all these circumstances, the negotiation of another agreement was indeed unproblematic: access to US$114 million was offered over fourteen months from September 1988 on terms that did nothing to restrain the expansionary approach, which the JLP government had adopted over the preceding two years, to the management of the Jamaican economy.

These various reflationary measures did little, however, to improve the JLP's poll ratings. An election had still not been called when, on 12 September 1988, Hurricane Gilbert struck Jamaica with devastating force. Agricultural production was badly damaged. Even though mining, manufacturing and tourism were quickly restored, substantial emergency financial assistance was required and the JLP briefly gained in political support as it presided over the recovery of a traumatised population.[37] The IMF agreed to readjust some of the targets in the agreement that had just been signed and the Paris Club agreed to rescheduling. However, disputes over the distribution of aid to give one party an advantage damaged the JLP, and it was not long before the PNP's lead in the polls reasserted itself. Seaga had in effect run out of time politically. The economy had been slowing down in 1988 – even before Gilbert – largely because of a downturn in bauxite production after the brief rise in 1986–7. The abolition of the controversial bauxite levy (introduced by the PNP in 1974) and the reinstatement of conventional corporate taxation were negotiated with each of the multinationals from mid-1988 onwards, but came too late for the government to benefit from the expected stimulation to production. Elections were eventually called for February 1989 and, following a generally peaceful campaign by local standards, were triumphantly won by the PNP, which took forty-five of the sixty seats, with 57 per cent of the popular vote.[38]

Conclusion

What emerges, above all, from this account of the Seaga government's management of the economy of Jamaica during the 1980s are the twists and turns by which it sought to stay afloat, both economically and politically. One discussion of the preceding PNP administration drew attention to 'the zig-zag politics'[39] it followed; the same can be said of the JLP regime. Conventionally, the two governments have been differentiated by commentators: the PNP era was associated with the pursuit of democratic socialism and the JLP era with the pursuit of orthodox liberal development. In the same way, Manley as a man of the left has been contrasted with Seaga as a man of the right. The analysis offered here suggests that this line of argument is misleading and that it is the structural constraints on the freedom of manoeuvre of both governments that ought to be emphasised rather than the differing ideological predispositions or styles of their leaders.

In a nutshell, these constraints are of two kinds. The first is represented by Jamaica's geopolitical and geoeconomic location in the US sphere of influence. This gives substantial power over the Jamaican political directorate to a range of external forces, from US political leadership in the White House and various US departments of state, to the officials of the IMF, the World Bank and other US-dominated international financial agencies, to the managers of major multinational corporations with investments and interests in Jamaica. The second constraint is represented by Jamaica's commitment to its particular form of electoral democracy. In a broad sense the legacy of British colonialism, this ethic has been substantially internalised by the Jamaican people over the last fifty years. In other words, Jamaican leaders have two sets of masters, two constituencies that they must please: one external, the other internal. Put like this, many of the shifts of policy of the Seaga government become more explicable. Seaga was endeavouring to find and follow a path between conflicting pressures: from without, the pressure of 'liberal economics' imposed by the IMF and the Reagan administration, and from within, the pressure of 'electoral politics' imposed by the exigencies of winning votes and holding on to office.

This interpretation of Jamaican politics makes discussion of the real Seaga somewhat redundant. Admittedly, an accurate reading of Seaga's political outlook is not easy to arrive at. He has not written books or published collections of his speeches or given many revealing interviews. The clues that litter his political career are also contradictory. Born of Syrian stock and by training a sociologist, he early acquired a radical reputation in Jamaica by making a speech in the old Legislative Council in 1961 contrasting the lot of the 'haves' and the 'have-nots' in local society.[40] When Jamaica achieved independence, he was elected to (and continued to represent) a constituency in one of the poorest parts of West Kingston, his majority built up over the years by deliberate patronage. He later emerged as one of the key modernisers in the 1962–72 JLP government, first as Minister of Development and Welfare and later of Finance and Planning, acquiring in the latter post a new reputation for his toughness in collecting taxes from the business community. As leader of the opposition from 1974 onwards, he cultivated an appeal based on rabid anti-communism and a close association with the private sector, locally, and big business, internationally. In government in the 1980s, as we have seen, he both pandered to the IMF and bitterly criticised the institution; fawned over the US administration and let his dissatisfaction with its support be known; and followed policies that reduced state control of the economy in some areas and promoted it in others. This led some writers from the right to condemn him as 'a Caribbean conman'[41] who led a government that was every bit as statist, indeed socialist, as that of Manley in the 1970s, and others from the left to characterise his beliefs at the end of the day as 'a combination of populism and state capitalism'.[42]

In the circumstances, it is sensible to view Seaga simply as a pragmatist or, more pejoratively, an opportunist. He is not a politician for whom a package of guiding ideas is particularly important. He saw in 1980 that the global trend in economic management favoured the return of neo-liberal premises; he knew that the Jamaican economy could not manage without the financial support of the IMF and that the idea of structural adjustment was dominant in the Fund's thinking; and, above all, he saw an opportunity for Jamaica to cultivate a reputation in Washington for free-market beliefs. On this basis he won for the country massive amounts of US assistance in the early years of his government (Jamaica becoming one of the five highest per capita US aid recipients in the world), and he clearly expected that innovations like the Rockefeller Committee would lead to a much greater flow of new inward investment than actually occurred. He also knew that the Jamaican capitalist class was weak and, having been nurtured on import-substitution industrialisation, lacked the capacity to initiate and sustain export-led growth as an indigenous bourgeoisie. The state thus had to be used to protect the Jamaican economy – especially in moments of crisis – for no better reason than that there was no alternative agency available. In fact, state intervention kept bauxite alive in the midst of a major recession in the world aluminium industry for which neither Seaga nor Jamaica could be held responsible.

In sum, Seaga is best understood as a political manager who tried to reconcile external economic pressures with domestic electoral imperatives. In this effort, he showed a cunning and resourcefulness typical of the Caribbean political tradition. As Carl Stone put it in one of his newspaper columns, 'those critics who are trying to make out Mr Seaga as simply a clerk administering IMF policies are being mischievous. The international agency input is great in helping to define the overall framework. But the game plan, the tactics and the strategies are entirely Eddie's doing'.[43] In the final analysis, of course, Seaga failed in his balancing act. On the economic front, this can be seen in the average rate of economic growth generated over his eight years in office – 1.2 per cent per annum, scarcely the stuff of economic miracles; in the continuing high levels of unemployment in the country; in its deteriorating social and economic infrastructure; and in the accumulated external debt of US$4.5 billion by the end of his term. On the political front, it can be seen in the crushing defeat he suffered in the February 1989 election. He failed because he was never able to gain control of events and chart a coherent development strategy for the country. He was constantly forced to be reactive, rather than proactive; he was pulled and pushed in different directions by different pressures at different times. Notwithstanding his reputation for personal authoritarianism, Seaga's role in Jamaican politics in the 1980s highlights more than anything else the weak position in which Caribbean leaders habitually find themselves in the present structure of the world system.

Notes

1   E. A. Brett, *The World Economy since the War: The Politics of Uneven Development*, London, 1985, p. 219.

2   'The Arusha initiative', *Development Dialogue*, 2, 1982, pp. 14–16.

3   Manuel Guitian, 'Economic management and IMF conditionality', in Tony Killick (ed.), *Adjustment and Financing in the Developing World*, Washington DC, 1982, p. 88.

4   Brett, *World Economy*, p. 223.

5   Guitian, 'Economic management and IMF conditionality', p. 88.

6   See the Jamaica Labour Party manifesto for the 1980 election, *Change without Chaos: A National Programme for Reconstruction*, Kingston, 1980.

7   For further discussion, see Anthony Payne, *Politics in Jamaica*, London and New York, 1988, pp. 83–91.

8   For the details, see *Government Ministry Paper No. 9*, Kingston, 1981.

9   See Timothy Ashby, *Missed Opportunities: The Rise and Fall of Jamaica's Edward Seaga*, Indianapolis, 1989, p. 12. Ashby, in fact, suggests that the agreement also stipulated a reduction of 6,000 persons in the government work force, but no other source confirms this.

10 This judgement is confirmed by Jennifer Sharpley, 'Jamaica 1972–80', in Tony Killick (ed.), *The IMF and Stabilisation: Developing Country Experiences*, London and New York, 1984, pp. 115–17.

11 *Daily Gleaner*, 1 June 1981.

12 *Ibid.*

13 National Planning Agency, *Economic and Social Survey – Jamaica 1982*, Kingston, 1983, pp. 9.3–9.5.

14 *Ibid.*, p. 8.1.

15 Evelyne Huber Stephens and John D. Stephens, *Democratic Socialism in Jamaica: The Political Movement and Social Transformation in Dependent Capitalism*, London, 1986, p. 255.

16 National Planning Agency, *Economic and Social Survey*, p. 8.1.

17 For the details of the system's operation, see Michael Witter, 'Exchange rate policy in Jamaica: a critical assessment', *Social and Economic Studies*, 32, 4, 1983, pp. 27–9.

18 See Derick Boyd and Everton Pryce, 'Jamaica's devaluation spree', *Caribbean Contact*, October 1984, p. 6.

19 For further discussion, see Colin Bullock, 'IMF conditionality and Jamaica's economic policy in the 1980s', *Social and Economic Studies*, 35, 4, 1986, p. 146.

20 See Carl Stone, *The Political Opinions of the Jamaican People*, Kingston, 1982.

21 Anthony Payne, Paul Sutton and Tony Thorndike, *Grenada: Revolution and Invasion*, London and New York, 1984, p. 211.

22 For further discussion, see Payne, *Politics in Jamaica*, pp. 92–102.

23 *Caribbean Insight*, April 1984.

24 IMF press release, Washington DC, June 1984.

25 *Caribbean Insight*, August 1984.

26 For further discussion, see Payne, *Politics in Jamaica*, pp. 103–10.

27 See Evelyne Huber Stephens and John D. Stephens, 'The political economy of Jamaican development: from Manley to Seaga to Manley', unpublished paper presented to the Latin American Studies Association, Miami, December 1989.

28 *Caribbean Insight*, November 1985.

29 *Jamaica: A Medium-Term Assessment, Report of the Tripartite Mission*, Washington DC, 1986, p. 32, cited in Ashby, *Missed Opportunities*, p. 14.

30 *Caribbean Insight*, May 1986.

31 See *ibid.*, August 1986.

32 See Ashby, *Missed Opportunities*, p. 35.

33 Edward Seaga, 'Statement to Parliament on the International Monetary Fund agreement, January 13 1987', press release, Kingston, 1987, pp. 7–8.

34 *Ibid.*, p. 11.

35 For further details, see Gregory K. Schoepfle, 'US – Caribbean trade relations over the last decade: from CBI to ACS,' in Ransford W. Palmer (ed.), *The Repositioning of US – Caribbean Relations in the New World Order*, Westport, 1997, pp. 101–50.

36 See *Caribbean Insight*, May 1988.

37 A 9 per cent swing to the JLP took place between the poll taken by Stone at the beginning of September and his poll at the end of September, even though the PNP

remained in the lead by 2 per cent even in the immediate post-Gilbert poll. See Carl Stone, ' "Gilbert" swings public opinion towards Seaga', *Jamaica Weekly Gleaner*, 25 October 1988.

38   For an analysis of the 1989 election, see Carl Stone, *Politics versus Economics: The 1989 Elections in Jamaica*, Kingston, 1989.

39   George Beckford and Michael Witter, *Small Garden . . . Bitter Weed: The Political Economy of Struggle and Change in Jamaica*, Morant Bay, 1980, p. 99.

40   See Rex M. Nettleford, *Mirror Mirror: Identity, Race and Protest in Jamaica*, Kingston, 1970, p. 131.

41   Ashby, *Missed Opportunities*, p. 25.

42   Stephens and Stephens, 'The political economy of Jamaican development', p. 14.

43   Carl Stone, 'Mr Seaga's correct priorities', in Carl Stone, *On Jamaican Politics, Economics and Society* (columns from the *Gleaner* 1987–8), Kingston, 1989, p. 12.

5 | Open dependent development in the Eastern Caribbean

The seven small countries of the Eastern Caribbean – Antigua and Barbuda, Barbados, Dominica, Grenada, St Kitts-Nevis, St Lucia and St Vincent and the Grenadines – have for many years constituted a special developmental problem. All of them are small in population and land size and all have a long history as agricultural mono-economies relying on the export of one or, at best, a few agricultural commodities. The standard of living was generally low and the economic and social infrastructure deficient everywhere except Barbados. In comparison to the larger countries of the Commonwealth Caribbean, and again with the exception of Barbados, they were considered as relatively backward and in need of special assistance. For this reason, all but Barbados were classified within CARICOM as 'less developed countries' (LDCs) to which special preferential measures would apply.

What went for economic development also went for politics. Again, with the exception of Barbados, independence was delayed by Britain on account of their vulnerability as small states and a presumption that none of them could sustain viability as independent countries. In 1974 this was successfully challenged by Grenada which proceeded to independence that year, but its unhappy experience provided a cautionary tale to others and it was not until the late 1970s that independence was sought and granted to Dominica, St Lucia and St Vincent, with Antigua and St Kitts-Nevis eventually also gaining independence in the early 1980s. At this point the British government had effectively discharged most, but not all, of its colonial responsibilities in the Caribbean,[1] although it was to remain closely in touch with affairs in the Eastern Caribbean.

The small islands of the Eastern Caribbean were now on their own. Fears of economic stagnation and political instability have, however, largely proved unfounded. In fact the opposite occurred: the 1980s proved to be a 'decade of development' for all of them with only Grenada experiencing some economic difficulties at the beginning of the decade and Barbados towards the end. The six independent members of the Organisation of the Eastern Caribbean States (OECS)[2] achieved annual growth rates of around 5 per cent, and by the end of the decade per capita incomes had increased dramatically everywhere. Westminster-style democracy was restored in Grenada in 1984 and democracy in most countries was further entrenched through protection of civil liberties and regular free and fair elections, leading in some instances to changes of government. More to the point, this continued into the 1990s, with continuing high rates of economic growth and flourishing democratic practice nearly everywhere, raising the possibility that the Eastern Caribbean had at last found a model of development capable of delivering increasing standards of living to its previously impoverished peoples.

This chapter explores this singular success. The first part examines the economic performance of the seven countries and explains their success as deriving from both luck and judgement, the latter expressed in the adoption of an 'open' model of development pioneered by Barbados. The key factors in this model are then examined in relation to tourism and offshore finance which were the 'boom' sectors of the 1980s and remained buoyant in the 1990s. The next part examines the political experience of the Eastern Caribbean. It sets out some reasons for the adoption and entrenchment of Westminster-style democracy and provides examples of its adaptability in the face of economic change. Finally, the last part examines the sustainability of the development experience in the light of pressures and threats emerging from rapid tourist development, money laundering and the phasing out of the generous development assistance on which the region has relied.

Economic development

Economic structure and economic performance

Although most of the islands are similar in size there are important differences among them which account for their specific individuality. The most important distinction is between Barbados and the others. Barbados is not only the largest in population but also by far the most developed. Since the 1960s a steady process of diversification has taken place away from sugar, such that by the 1980s the leading sectors of the economy were services and manufacturing. Tourism has proved to be particularly important and Barbados has an established industry catering for a range of markets. It has also set up a relatively sophisticated offshore financial sector which is well regulated and growing in importance. Its well-developed infrastructure, including efficient health and education systems, in combination with its reputation for public sector efficiency, have made it an attractive hub for international and regional organisations, which base their personnel in Barbados and from where they service other islands in the Eastern Caribbean.

The other major distinction is between the Leeward Islands (comprising Antigua and St Kitts-Nevis) and the Windward Islands (Dominica, Grenada, St Lucia and St Vincent). The Leeward Islands were classical sugar mono-economies dominated by large expatriate-owned plantations. In St Kitts sugar remains a major economic activity and sugar exports still provide valuable foreign exchange, largely on account of access under preferential terms to markets in the EU and the US. In Antigua the sugar industry went into terminal decline and finally collapsed in the early 1980s, leaving the country dominated by the tourist industry on which it is now almost wholly reliant for its prosperity. St Kitts also moved into tourism in the 1980s and its sister island of Nevis is especially dependent on 'up-market' tourism in which it has been able to present itself as a privileged destination. The manufacturing sector remains important to St Kitts but has an uncertain future due to high wage costs. Antigua has sought to capitalise on offshore finance and has set up various facilities, although poor regulation has led to their abuse by criminal elements.

For their part, the Windward Islands remain highly dependent on agriculture for employment. The banana industry dominates in Dominica, St Lucia and St Vincent and was important in Grenada until the mid-1990s. Banana production expanded in the 1980s and by the end of the decade was an important source of foreign exchange (in Dominica the most important source). In the 1990s the industry experienced serious difficulties arising from hurricane damage and uncertainties as to its continued preferential access to the EU market. This gave an added impetus to the search for diversification. St Lucia has gone furthest, having established first a small but growing manufacturing sector in the late 1970s and then developing its tourist industry in the 1980s, such that it is now the mainstay of the economy. Grenada and St Vincent have also promoted their tourist industries, the latter seeking to capture 'up-market' tourism in the exclusive and idyllic Grenadines. Dominica only began tourist development in the early 1990s, aiming to capitalise on the growing market for eco-tourism. Manufacturing in the Windwards is limited, accounting for only a small fraction of employment and growth. There have also been moves in several countries to develop an offshore sector, although this is very much a feature of the mid- to late-1990s.

The similarity of development in all the islands is therefore quite marked, notwithstanding their differences which have been historically based. They have gone for comparable strategies and this in part explains comparable performance. This is summarised in Table 1. The figures for Gross National Product per capita show Antigua overtaking Barbados in the period 1985–96. Among the OECS per capita figures have doubled or tripled; annual growth rates between 1985–95 have been very high and have bettered figures for the 1980s as a whole. The service sector (which includes tourism and finance) is everywhere dominant, although government services are a major component and provider of employment. Agriculture everywhere is stagnant or in relative decline and, while the contribution of manufacturing appears high, it includes construction and public utilities (water, gas and electricity) which have seen high growth rates as a result of the tourist boom. All the countries can be classified as 'middle income developing countries' and, as measured by the UN Human Development Index, the prospect of a tolerable and rising standard of living for a majority of the population has greatly improved, in spite of pockets of real poverty.

The open dependent economy

How may this be explained? In his 'Foreword' to the *Annual Report of the Eastern Caribbean Central Bank 1991*, the Governor, Dwight Venner, acknowledged the growth of the previous decade and noted: 'the economies have been dependent on the success of the banana and tourist industries, concessional flows, remittances and foreign investment for their growth'[3] – in short, on favourable external circumstances.

Tourism and bananas in particular benefited from spectacular growth. Most OECS countries were relatively new entrants to the tourist market and were able to exploit undeveloped potential. Even where this was not the case, Barbados and, to a lesser extent Antigua, were still able to ride on growing tourist markets in the US and EU. Earnings from tourism in 1980 for the Eastern Caribbean were valued at US\$381 million and in 1988 at US\$984 million.[4] Banana producers also expanded production and exports and benefited from 'windfall' gains due to the change in relative prices between the pound sterling, in which banana earnings were denominated, and the US dollar, in which many imports were paid. In 1980 banana exports from the Windward Islands were worth US\$24 million; in 1988 they reached US\$139 million.[5]

Also important was a massive increase in external resource flows, public and private. The Eastern Caribbean benefited from the revolution and invasion of Grenada and its immediate aftermath. The US and other aid donors poured money into the region in the early 1980s in an attempt to ensure political stability. In the period 1981–5 the

Table 1: *Eastern Caribbean: Basic statistics*

	Population 1985 (thousands)	GNP US$ per capita 1985	GNP US$ per capita 1996	GNP growth rate 1985/95 (per cent per year)	Sectoral distribution of GDP 1990 per cent		
					Agriculture	Industry	Services
Barbados	252	4480	6439	3.5	5	18	76
Antigua and Barbuda	79	3440	7330	11.7	4	20	77
Dominica	78	1160	3090	8.6	26	18	56
Grenada	96	970	2880	8.6	15	19	64
St Kitts and Nevis	43	1520	5870	10.7	6	29	64
St Lucia	136	1210	3500	9.1	13	18	68
St Vincent and the Grenadines	119	840	2370	8.1	19	23	58

Sources: Commonwealth Secretariat, *Small States: Economic Review and Basic Statistics*, Vol. 3, 1997 (Columns 5–8) and Vol. 4, 1998 (Columns 2–4).

US disbursed some US$307.5 million in assistance to the Eastern Caribbean, including special assistance to Grenada, and the UK some US$22.6 million.[6] Relatively large sums were also given by multilateral donors like the Caribbean Development Bank, the European Development Fund and the World Bank, with commitments to the Eastern Caribbean (excluding Grenada but including Barbados) of some US$57.9 million in 1983 alone.[7] Although the US began reducing its aid to the Caribbean in the late 1980s, overall concessional flows remained high with an official development assistance (ODA) commitment from all sources (bilateral and multilateral) of US$70.9 million in 1990.[8] Most foreign direct investment (FDI) has been directed toward the tourist industry and, in particular, hotel construction. In the period 1988–90, the OECS countries received US$390.8 million in FDI, with Antigua securing the most and Dominica and St Vincent the least.[9] The figures for Barbados were much higher with US investment alone standing at US$304 million in 1988 and US$502 million in 1992.[10] Finally, in some countries such as Dominica and St Vincent, remittances were important sources for consumption and savings.

However, it has not only been a matter of fortuitous circumstances. The countries of the Eastern Caribbean, with the exception of Grenada during the revolution, have adopted an essentially conservative approach to economic development. In part, this has been presented as a matter of necessity premised on the small size of the economies and their dependence on external markets. But it has also been a matter of choice. The exemplar here has been Barbados, which has followed a generally open and highly pragmatic economic policy since independence in 1966. Barbados has welcomed foreign capital and sought to provide it with the conditions in which it can flourish. In the 1960s and 1970s these policies led to modest sustained growth which was sufficiently robust for it to weather brief recessions in 1973–4 and 1982–3. In the later 1980s the economy began to experience difficulties and in 1991–3 it entered a deeper and longer recession than the previous two as it undertook a programme of structural adjustment overseen by the World Bank and the IMF. The return to growth since then has confirmed its reputation for success, even though many economic problems remain, rooted in the very absence of fundamental change which is in itself the foundation of the model.

In essence, Barbados has followed the W. Arthur Lewis model of capital import, supplemented by local investment and public sector support.[11] The government established a range of institutions to promote economic development, including a Central Bank, the Barbados Development Bank, an Industrial Development Corporation and in 1987 a Securities Exchange. It invested in infrastructure, such as the port and airport, as well as roads, hospitals, schools, public housing and public buildings. Modest funds were committed to agriculture, food processing, broadcasting, banking, oil production, hotels, airlines and cement. Its efforts were supplemented by a long-established local merchant class and a growing middle class which invested in public utilities, manufacturing and housing and provided a range of services for the economy as professionals, managers and businessmen. However, it was foreign investment that was most significant and was the country's 'engine of growth'. Foreign investment was concentrated in tourism and in manufacturing for export to extra-regional markets. Along with sugar and government borrowing overseas, these provided the crucial foreign exchange to modernise Barbados and to support its rising living standards. Its development was therefore ultimately externally propelled, not locally propelled, underlining the fact that the strategy of successive governments in Barbados has been the successful management of dependence, rather than any challenge to it.

In spite of this limitation the model remains attractive to the OECS. The experience of Barbados is seen as instructive and appropriate and its consistent high living standards a matter for emulation. However, in seeking to operationalise the model the OECS countries are at a disadvantage since they possess neither the strong state nor the well-developed middle class which have been essential features of economic growth in Barbados. On the other hand, they can and have sought to replicate its openness to foreign capital and readiness to exploit opportunities in the two sectors in which openness is an essential feature of success – tourism and offshore finance.

Tourism

In 1993 a Special Report of the Economist Intelligence Unit noted that, for the Caribbean, 'tourism is the only sector of regional GDP that has consistently increased its share of total income during the 1980s. In some places tourism accounts for up to 70 per cent of national income directly and indirectly'.[12] As we have seen, in many countries it has been the fastest growing sector of the economy and in 1994 the Caribbean Tourism Organisation (CTO) estimated that the Caribbean as a whole earned US$12 billion from tourism. It also claimed that tourism provided direct employment for 216,000 people in the region and indirect employment for another 580,000.[13] All Caribbean governments now seek to promote tourism and many see it as their best hope for future prosperity.

This is certainly the case in the Eastern Caribbean where there has been a massive effort to attract tourists and a growing reliance on the earnings from them. Since 1980 there has been a steady growth of stop-over tourists (defined as those who stay more than 24 hours) from 657,000 in that year to 1,193,000 in 1995; a steady increase in earnings from tourism over the same period from US$381 million to US$1,490 million; and a steady increase in the proportion of export earnings attributable to tourism, with Antigua being the most dependent and Dominica the least (see Table 2). Supplementing the number of stop-over tourists has been the recent growth of the cruise-ship industry from 515,000 visitors in 1980 to 828,000 in 1988.[14] In 1992 some 848,000 cruise passengers were reported to have visited the OECS countries.[15]

The impact of tourism varies from country to country depending on the degree of integration of the industry into the economy. The most frequently used measure of this is the 'multiplier effect', i.e. the degree to which tourist expenditure is retained within the economy contributing to income and employment, rather than being repatriated as profit to foreign investors. An early figure (1969) for the Eastern Caribbean suggested a multiplier of 2.3 (for every one dollar spent 2.3 dollars would be added to the national income). Research reported for 1988, however, suggested much lower figures, with multipliers for Jamaica at 1.23, the Dominican Republic at 1.20, Antigua at 0.88, the Cayman Islands at 0.65 and the British Virgin Islands at 0.58.[16] What is clear is that in established destinations like Barbados, where the local middle class has invested in the industry, the multiplier is relatively higher than in more recent destinations, such as St Kitts-Nevis or St Lucia, where foreign capital dominates the industry.

Some of the fiercest debates in this regard have taken place around the contribution of the cruise-ship industry to the Caribbean economy. A survey prepared by the Florida Caribbean Cruise Association in 1995 estimated that each passenger spent on average US$124 and each crew member US$66. Additionally, it claimed some supplies were bought locally, making a total contribution to the Caribbean region, direct and indirect, of US$2.3 billion.[17] However, these and earlier figures released by the cruise lines have been seen as inflated and more modest figures have been put forward by regional organisations, such as the CTO, and by the largest cruise-ship host, the Bahamas (2 million cruise-ship visitors a year), which claims an overall contribution to the tourism industry of 10 per cent or less.[18] Wherever the truth lies, what is not in doubt is the growing importance of cruise-ship tourism to the Caribbean. It grew faster than land-based tourism throughout the 1980s and has expanded even more in the 1990s as massive new cruise-ships have come into service. The smaller islands of the Eastern Caribbean are an increasingly favoured

Table 2: Eastern Caribbean: Tourist arrivals and earnings

	1980			1995		
	Tourist arrivals (thousands)	Tourist earnings (US$ millions)	Tourist earnings as % total export earnings	Tourist arrivals (thousands)	Tourist earnings (US$ millions)	Tourist earnings as % total export earnings
Barbados	370	252	46	442	680	54
Antigua and Barbuda	87	43	72	212	329	82
Dominica	19*	4*	12	60	33	28
Grenada	29	15	37	108	58	46†
St Kitts and Nevis	35*	17*	52*	79	65	49
St Lucia	80	34	39	232	268	67
St Vincent and the Grenadines	37*	16*	33*	60	57	35†

* 1982 figures
† 1994 figures

Sources: Commonwealth Secretariat, *Small States: Economic Review and Basic Statistics*, Vol. 1, 1995 (Table 15); and Vol. 4, 1998 (Table 26).

destination and expensive new facilities have lately been built in Dominica and St Kitts and commissioned in St Vincent.

In all, although difficult to estimate, the overall contribution of tourism to GDP is considerable, reaching a high of 80 per cent for Antigua. In addition to employment and foreign exchange, Caribbean governments earn revenues from airport departure and hotel occupancy taxes, aircraft and cruise ship landing fees, and indirect taxation on services supplied, such as sales taxes on tourist purchases. The tourist market stimulates infrastructural development and opens opportunities. In some countries it has led to improved government services and measures to preserve the environment. But it also carries costs. In the past these have been more stressed than at present. In particular, the social costs of tourism were highlighted. Tourism was said to stimulate prostitution, drug trafficking and casino gambling and to perpetuate servitude and racial discrimination in so far as most of the visitors and managers in the tourist complexes were white and from Europe and North America while the waiters, maids and entertainers were coloured and black. Although such charges remain true, they are now rarely discussed. Tourism has become acceptable everywhere. As Polly Pattullo notes: 'there are now no organised voices raised in protest against tourism. It has been accepted; it is assumed that it is here to stay'.[19] This is certainly true for the Eastern Caribbean. The politicians and the international development agencies preach only the virtues of tourism and profess a belief in 'the more the better'. Although understandable in the present circumstances, this can, as noted later, be short-sighted and, if left unsupervised, will lead to increased dependence and future unpredictabilities.

Offshore finance

The 1980s also witnessed the development and marketing of a range of offshore services and related activities in the Caribbean. In essence, these can be defined as services and activities that are provided within the territory of one state but which are almost wholly or exclusively oriented to foreign markets or clients in other states. At one level they can be extensions of existing policy. This has been the case in the growth and spread of export processing zones throughout the Caribbean as a variant of the 'industrialisation by invitation' strategy. In these zones, products (typically garments and electrical items) are imported from one country and then assembled or finished using local labour (usually female) before being sent back to the supplier for sale in that country. The products imported, processed and then re-exported usually benefit from low or no taxes on the processing operation in the host country and special tariff provisions in the supplier country, as in the CBI and the later Super 807 tax regime offered by the US. In the Eastern Caribbean such zones, or their equivalent, have been established in Antigua, Barbados, St Kitts and St Lucia. The main benefit in each case has been the employment of semi-skilled labour in a situation of relative labour abundance, although a critical literature has arisen which has emphasised costs in terms of low wages, poor working conditions and 'foot loose' industries that leave if conditions change to their disadvantage.[20] This has already happened in Barbados, which through its high wage policy had priced itself out of the garments and electronics sectors by the mid-1990s.

However, the most innovative offshore growth has been in the provision of services. These include offshore medical schools, as in Grenada, which provide a medical education for those unable to gain places in medical schools in the US; offshore gambling, as in Antigua, in casinos and now the Internet; and offshore finance, embracing a variety of financial services for those living outside the country. These include offshore banking, offshore insurance and the provision of offshore trusts and companies. Various Caribbean countries have chosen to specialise in one or the other, although they usually offer all three services. The Bahamas and the Cayman Islands have become major international banking centres, ranked respectively eleventh and sixth in the world in 1982. The British Virgin Islands is a major centre for international business companies and trusts, with over 50,000 companies incorporated at the end of 1991. And Bermuda has emerged as the most important offshore insurance market in the world. The 'services' offered in most centres include either no profits tax for companies or low tax based on tax treaties with other countries; tax exemption; provisions for the incorporation of holding companies, offshore companies and management companies in which regulation is minimal; offshore banking facilities; and captive insurance (a tax-efficient way of insuring a company). Parallel to these corporate services, services for individuals were developed in the 1980s and include no income or low income tax; tax exemption; no estate duty; provision of trusts; bearer shares (used to disguise the ownership of a company); and bank secrecy. Although the exact size of the offshore market is, by definition, difficult to determine, one estimate for the Caribbean suggested a total of US$10 billion at the end of the 1980s.[21]

To date, the major offshore players in the Eastern Caribbean have been Barbados and Antigua. The former established itself as a low tax jurisdiction in 1985 and has steadily expanded its range of services to include banking, insurance and company registration. By early 1993 there were approximately 800 international business companies, more than 700 foreign sales corporations, 220 captive insurance companies and 16 offshore banks operating in the country, with the offshore sector as a whole earning some US$100 million in 1991.[22] In promoting itself as an offshore centre, Barbados has sought to publicise as assets its relatively sophisticated infrastructure, including high class hotels and excellent international air connections; its large pool of accountants and lawyers; and its image as a 'law abiding' country.[23] Its continuing growth suggests these have worked to its advantage. By contrast, Antigua has sold itself as a tax haven with virtually no regulation. The offshore centre was established in 1982 and in 1996 there were forty-two offshore banks registered. There is also provision for insurance and company registration. However, growth has been slow due to the reputation the country has gained for operating at the margin of the law. The US especially has been concerned with the possibility of money laundering in what it has described as 'one of the more vulnerable financial centers in the Caribbean'.[24] The loosely regulated offshore environment and strict bank secrecy laws have protected the confidentiality of investors, including those laundering gains from drug trafficking in which Antigua has also been involved. Those benefiting in the past have included government ministers and senior officials in Antigua, as well as the Italian mafia, the Colombian cartels and criminal groups based in Russia. The need for Antigua to 'clean up its act' was acknowledged by the government in the mid-1990s and legislation designed to bring that about was passed in 1996. However, the wider point remains. The offshore financial centres in the Caribbean offer services that are open to abuse and the record of such abuse has been well documented over the years, with few countries entirely escaping investigation and censure. Among them have been the largest centres, such as the Bahamas and the Cayman Islands, as well as the smallest, such as Anguilla and Montserrat.

Despite this record, the offshore strategy remains attractive, especially for the smaller islands. Nevis has now established an offshore financial sector and Dominica, St Lucia and St Vincent have recently passed legislation to establish offshore financial zones (in the latter case an offshore zone was established in the early 1980s but collapsed due to poor regulation and financial instability). Proposals to establish offshore financial facilities are also underway in Grenada and St Kitts. The rationale is clearly the benefits such zones are said to bring. They include government revenues through fees and licences and some very limited employment prospects. Offshore financial sectors are also said to be complementary to the tourist industry in so far as the facilities offered to the wealthy tourist are also attractive to the highly-paid executive seeking to minimise company liability. In some cases, such as the Cayman Islands, the combination of tourism and offshore financial activity has provided a real impetus to development, but elsewhere the benefits have proved to be exaggerated. The Bahamas is one well-documented example where the returns have been small compared to tourism.[25] The costs of regulation are also climbing as offshore finance faces increasing international scrutiny by the developed countries of the Organisation for Economic Cooperation and Development (OECD) concerned about their use as centres for tax evasion and money laundering. While such centres thus retain important advantages at the moment, their long-term future is more uncertain as pressures for the international regulation of international finance increase.

Political development

Democracy in the Eastern Caribbean

The economic model in the Eastern Caribbean has both contributed to and benefited from the political model adopted in the region since independence. With the exception of Grenada during the revolutionary period, this has been a variant of the Westminster system adapted to the region from the British experience. The 'core elements' of this system are the convention of constitutionalism; the doctrine of civilian supremacy; the presumption of bureaucratic and police neutrality; the habit of competitive elections; and the practice of pluralist representation.[26] Collectively, these have served as the institutional underpinning to a remarkable record of democratic politics and accompanying political stability throughout the Commonwealth Caribbean which has found favour and support from both political elites within the region and important external actors.[27] Among the benefits provided by the latter have been enhanced donor assistance and a positive attitude by foreign investors to service industries such as tourism, where the social and political values of the host society are judged to be important.

The foundation of the Westminster system in the Caribbean is a deeply conservative political culture. This derives in part from size (small states tend to have conservative regimes) but more so from a history of slavery and assimilation. These factors have combined to leave legacies throughout the region which, once emancipation was achieved, have valued private property, the free expression of opinion and social mobility, all previously denied to chattel slaves. Social mobility, in particular, assumed significant historical proportions as 'free people of colour' emerged as elements of a middle class. Their rising agitation for political representation, and its gradual concession through election to increasingly representative institutions modelled on Westminster, became the basis for a protracted political decolonisation which did not challenge fundamentals but rather sought their reform. The result was that political independence, when finally achieved, was consensual and constitutionalist, the political elite simultaneously subscribing to the Westminster model and to mercantile capitalism, both of which they had inherited and from which they increasingly benefited.

Barbados has been a particularly good example of this process at work. Its parliamentary system is one of the oldest in the world (first established in 1639) and its planter-merchant elite one of the most cohesive and well-entrenched in the Caribbean. Once change became inevitable this elite sought to accommodate to it through strategies which have been remarkably successful in preserving its power and then influence. These have included the encouragement of a black middle class, which has emerged as the modern political elite, and the incorporation of a well-organised trade union movement through a variety of welfare policies. The two main political parties which have emerged to contest for power, the Barbados Labour Party (BLP) and the Democratic Labour Party (DLP), have both subscribed to similar philosophies of pragmatic government intervention for economic development and social justice, with the major differences among them being ones of political personality expressed in the varying political styles and diverse networks of their leaders. The electorate has given its support fairly evenly to the two parties since independence, with the DLP winning elections in 1966 and 1971 and again in 1986 and 1991; and the BLP in 1976 and 1981 and again in 1994 and 1999. In consequence, each has been in power for approximately the same period of time and throughout the political process has been decidedly democratic and essentially measured, providing Barbados with the strongest record of political stability in the Commonwealth Caribbean.[28]

By contrast, the pre-independence economic and political history of the OECS countries was more turbulent. The ruling planter elites proved more intransigent and the struggle with labour more confrontational. The middle class was slower to emerge and played a less important role in politics. Nevertheless, eventual outcomes have not been too dissimilar to Barbados, although qualification is always needed in respect of the individual circumstances of each country. The trade union leaders, who mostly led the struggles for greater political representation and social improvement in these islands, eventually opted for an accommodation with established capitalist interests. The political parties they formed and led and through which they won political office were essentially pragmatic coalitions designed to further the interests of the political leader of the moment. The spoils of political office were used for personal enrichment (usually modest but occasionally extravagant) and political patronage, which became the principal means of retaining future power. While this could, and did, lead to abuse, it was mostly proportional and, outside of Grenada, did not lead to any fundamental challenge to the essential elements of the Westminster system. In particular, regular democratic elections remained important in determining who won power. In the period since independence this has led to changes in government in all the countries of the Eastern Caribbean except Antigua, with an emerging pattern in which established parties alternate in power. The consistently high levels of turnout in such elections show widespread support for democratic values and a continued expectation that government performance will deliver economic growth. In sum, as one of the few studies of the contemporary politics of the region suggests, 'the Eastern Caribbean democratic model is not the perfect democratic system, but in the light of failures of other democratic models across the globe, the model emerges as a strong system that is stable and functional, and above all meets the political needs of its people'.[29]

Some recent trends

Although there is a high degree of political stability in the Eastern Caribbean, one of the strengths of the political model is its ability to accommodate to change.[30] In recent years political accommodation to the economic imperatives of the model of 'open dependent development' has been evident in three areas. The first has been the rise to prominence of a more technocratic leadership. As noted above, political leadership and political personality is all important in the Eastern Caribbean. In the past such leadership has been drawn from the trade unions and latterly the professional sector (overwhelmingly male lawyers). While such figures remain in politics and continue to occupy positions of leadership, the demands of government in the region in the last decade have taken a decidedly economistic tinge. The modern prime minister has to be aware of the complexities of political economy, national and international, in a way his or her predecessors were not. Government in other areas has also become subject to greater professionalism as public sector reform has become an important issue pressed on several of the countries by influential foreign donors. The net result is the emergence of a new type of political leader. He or she may be a lawyer by training, but the main qualification for high political office has come to rest on a presumed or real reputation for managerial efficiency, with the electorate and with international donors and investors. Some recent (and current) prime ministerial examples in the region are Erskine Sandiford and Owen Arthur in Barbados; Kennedy Simmonds and Denzil Douglas in St Kitts; Keith Mitchell in Grenada; and Vaughan Lewis and Kenny Anthony in St Lucia.

The second has been an even greater emphasis in economic policy in favour of the private sector as 'the engine of growth'. This was introduced in Barbados in the 1986 budget and became an issue in the subsequent elections of that year. The governing BLP proposed substantial income tax reductions in an effort to increase the level of effective demand among the middle and upper income groups, in the belief that this would stimulate the private sector. The opposition DLP countered by offering even greater income tax cuts and was in part rewarded by being returned with a massive parliamentary majority in the general election. However, in the face of a mounting fiscal crisis it was later obliged to claw back some of the concessions. The performance of the private sector also proved disappointing, with consumption rather than investment being stimulated. Nevertheless, the presumption in favour of the private sector remained and was reinforced by selective privatisation of state enterprises and the espousal of 'economic democracy' in the 1991 general elections.[31] The BLP, on taking office in 1994, continued in a similar vein, introducing a value-added tax system on consumer goods and services in 1997 and further opening the economy to foreign competition following agreements with the IMF which dated back to 1992.

Elsewhere in the Eastern Caribbean similar developments have taken place, although significant constraints exist in terms of the smaller size of the private sector and the lower level of infrastructural development. This was made clear early on by the example of Grenada. In the wake of the invasion, the United States Agency for International Development produced a report urging a reversal of the previous policies of state control introduced by the People's Revolutionary Government and their replacement by a private-sector-led development strategy. This included widespread deregulation, the privatisation of many state-owned businesses, new tax and industrial relations provisions and the replacement of centralised price and import controls by private competition.[32] In 1986 a controversial budget was introduced, on the advice of USAID officials, which abolished income tax and replaced it with value-added tax, in the belief that this would act as an incentive to private enterprise. The results were not as expected. Tax revenues fell and the Grenada government found itself contracting loans to cover the costs of government. The private sector did not respond dynamically and the expected foreign investment did not materialise. By 1990 the programme was in serious difficulties and elections that year saw the defeat of the government which had introduced it. In spite of this example, the other OECS countries have themselves in the 1990s sought to provide greater incentives to the private sector, local and foreign, through tax reforms and have also undertaken limited privatisation of government assets. As yet, it is too early to judge the success of these policies, but their ubiquity, along with their endorsement by all the major political parties, suggests a fundamental shift in thinking which is unlikely to be reversed, whatever difficulties may be encountered.[33]

Thirdly, there has been a greater sensitivity to international affairs. Although their economies have long been open, their politics for the most part have been parochial and insular. Small size has played a part (small countries tend to be inward-looking in their politics) as has the colonial past, which filtered exposure to world affairs through the controlling hand of colonial officials. Independence and recent developments in the international system have now forced a change of attitude. Major aid donors have become more interventionist, insisting on political dialogue and imposing strict conditionalities on their grants and loans. Trade issues have become more salient, and their effects more far-reaching, as the appearance of regional blocs in Europe and the Americas, along with a general liberalisation of world trade through the WTO, are in the process of displacing the preferential trade on which the Eastern Caribbean has depended. FDI too has become more difficult to attract and retain as international competition has increased and capital world-wide has become more mobile. The consequences are that issues to do with international economic relations have become major items on the domestic agendas of Eastern Caribbean states and a matter of political survival for the various political directorates. They now necessarily devote much greater time to them than they did in the period immediately following independence and their engagement in various international and regional fora is now more prominent, and remarked upon, than it was in the past.[34]

Sustainable economic development

The policy of open dependent development appears, then, to have served the region well. Barbados ranked twenty-fifth in the Human Development Index in 1997 (the highest among the developing countries), with Antigua and Barbuda ranking twenty-ninth, Dominica forty-first, St Kitts-Nevis forty-ninth, Grenada fifty-fourth, St Lucia fifty-sixth and St Vincent fifty-seventh (out of 175 countries).[35]

However, there are important qualifications, in both the general and the particular, which pose questions about the quality and economic sustainability of the development experience in the Eastern Caribbean. The latter, in particular, has emerged as a real challenge as the external economic environment has become more competitive and threatening to the future of small states.

Barbados

Barbados provides an example of the general. In June 1991 Erskine Sandiford, the DLP prime minister, announced that Barbados was entering into discussions with the IMF to establish a stabilisation programme with the aim of saving foreign exchange and reducing the fiscal deficit. In October he announced a 'supplementary budget' which included an 8 per cent cut in the wages of public employees, additional income and consumption taxes and a massive cut in subsidies to public sector enterprises. This was followed by the lay-off of temporary government workers and the sale of government shares in several companies. The trade unions and the BLP organised marches, which demonstrated widespread opposition to the proposals. However, the announced measures were implemented and a loan was eventually agreed in February 1992, albeit subject to some changes brought about by the protests.[36]

The episode was a shock to the country and a dent to its confidence. The much praised Barbados example was exposed as less secure than was thought. There were several problems. One was a growing lack of competitiveness in goods and services as a result of poor productivity and increasing wages. The manufacturing sector, which had been dynamic in the 1970s, stagnated in the 1980s. Another was overspending by government. The root cause of this was the reluctance of successive governments to tax the domestic sector sufficiently to pay for infrastructural development and social services. In the period 1975–85 foreign debt increased ten-fold. Finally, there was the effect of continuing reliance on FDI. While this continued to be attracted to Barbados, investment ratios fell significantly in the 1980s and overall they had little impact in diversifying the economy.

Various elements of the model of open dependent development were thus coming apart. The government, however, could contemplate no other strategy and therefore sought only changes which would restore economic growth but not lead in a new direction. For example, in return for structured consultation, via a prices and incomes protocol, it persuaded the trade union movement to accept labour market flexibility. But it could not undo 'the statist bargain' which lay at the heart of the Barbadian state[37] nor command the private sector to perform at levels which would make the country internationally competitive. It remained a prisoner of pragmatic conservatism and a hostage to the strategy of deepening the service economy – tourism, offshore finance and export processing zones. This has returned Barbados to growth in the short and medium term, but in the long term the country remains locked into a strategy which, while comparatively successful, has increased dependence and heightened vulnerability.

The OECS

The OECS provides examples of the particular. One of the most significant is the future of tourism. As noted earlier, there is now considerable emphasis on tourism, but also serious concerns. One such is the effect on the coastal environment and local services in small countries. The OECS countries have seen their tourism density ratios (the number of tourists per square kilometre on any day) and tourism penetration ratios (the number of tourists per thousand local inhabitants at any one time) double in the period 1982–94.[38] In some countries like Antigua there is now tourist congestion at certain favoured locations and the growth of mass tourism through the cruise-ship business can disrupt and distort eco-based tourism in countries like Dominica. Another worry is the issue of linkages. In many countries little has been done to create backward linkages with local agriculture and much of the food consumed by tourists is imported. An associated concern is the growth of the all-inclusive resort where everything is bought and paid for in the holiday package and where contact with local restaurants and local shops outside the holiday complex is limited. In 1994, eight out of St Lucia's twelve major hotels were all-inclusive.[39] In short, there are signs that point to the growing need for a more considered policy of tourist development if the benefits are to be properly captured for development. This is recognised by many in the tourist business, but so far little has been done to implement such policies in the OECS.

Regulation, or rather the lack of it, is also a key element in offshore finance. The *International Narcotics Control Strategy Report*, produced each year by the US government, claimed in 1997:

> In the Eastern Caribbean . . . few jurisdictions have been able to develop adequate mechanisms for regulation and oversight which would help prevent money laundering in the offshore financial services industry. Many jurisdictions lack strict licensing and supervisory procedures for offshore

financial institutions. These shortcomings are often compounded by local law enforcement authorities' lack of
resources, expertise and technical capacity. In addition, laundering techniques are becoming increasingly varied, with
growing use of non-bank financial institutions, commercial
businesses and lotteries. All of these factors together have
made the Caribbean an attractive place for money launderers
and criminal elements to do business.[40]

Top of the list for the OECS is Antigua, which is labelled a medium-
high risk country in the report, followed by St Vincent (medium risk),
St Kitts-Nevis (medium-low), Dominica and St Lucia (low), and
Grenada (no risk).[41] Antigua apart, there is therefore no urgent
problem. However, the fact that all the OECS countries have now
embraced offshore finance necessarily increases risk, especially as the
associated incidence of drug trafficking has increased rapidly in the
region in the 1990s. In turn, this has attracted the attention of the US,
the EU and its member states, which are most at risk. They have put
their weight behind the development of a raft of countermeasures,
some of which are aimed at combating money launderering in the
region, and others at reducing the wider benefits to be gained from the
legal use of loosely regulated offshore financial facilities as a whole. A
question mark therefore hangs over the future of offshore finance in its
present form and the small latecomers of the OECS may find themselves disadvantaged compared to the established larger players in the
field which are likely to be better able to adapt their product to
changed market conditions.

Lastly, there is the question of external finance. In a study seeking
to understand why the OECS countries had a better economic performance than the larger Caribbean states throughout the 1980s, two World
Bank economists came to the conclusion that concessionary finance,
used in a productive manner, played an important part.[42] The OECS
countries, in common with other small states, have benefited from high
levels of per capita concessionary finance (i.e. ODA) which has boosted
their developmental efforts. In 1989, for example, the US$ per capita
figures for ODA from all sources were: for Antigua – 57.9; Dominica –
261; Grenada – 172.9; St Kitts-Nevis – 300; St Lucia – 123.6; and St
Vincent – 131.6, well above the sums for developing countries as a
whole.[43] This has meant that most debt is official debt (above 90 per
cent of total debt for all countries except Antigua) and contracted on
relatively generous terms, leaving all countries, again except Antigua,
with modest and serviceable levels of debt. It follows that any threat to
this relatively benign situation is worrying. Such a threat did arise in the

1990s as levels of ODA from major donors fell and as they came to concentrate their aid on the poorest countries. The small states of the OECS, as 'middle income developing countries', saw their relatively privileged position eroded. They have also faced 'graduation' (non-eligibility for concessional finance or eligibility on less favourable terms than before) from the lending windows of the major multilateral financial institutions, such as the World Bank and the Inter-American Development Bank. The sum effect is that they are now more vulnerable and more dependent than before on private flows (FDI and commercial loans) to finance development, in a situation in which private capital markets generally discriminate against small states through charging higher interest rates or setting more onerous terms.[44]

Conclusion

In conclusion, the future is uncertain for the Eastern Caribbean. The strategy of open dependent development leaves these countries exposed to the pattern of growth and contraction in the OECD countries, and their own economic rhythms follow these patterns closely. This does not mean that countries in the Eastern Caribbean cannot fashion their own policies to capture impulses to growth and minimise risk; indeed the model specifies it is essential to do so. But it is to recognise that their economic development is ultimately conditioned by others and in large part is shaped by a recent past in which colonial connections played a decisive part.

In this context, the policy of closer economic and political cooperation becomes attractive. In spite of their differences the OECS countries have more in common than they are often prepared to admit, and the record of recent years underlines the benefits to be gained from integration. The Eastern Caribbean Central Bank, to which all but Barbados belong, has been instrumental in preserving the value of the Eastern Caribbean dollar, which has been fixed at EC$2.7 to US$1 since 1976, making it one of the strongest currencies in the Caribbean. Their cooperation with each other in the Eastern Caribbean Common Market, of which Barbados is not a member, has underpinned integration in CARICOM as a whole and has been both more dynamic and successful than in the latter. The OECS, as noted earlier, has provided for functional integration and political consultation and since 1982 all, including Barbados, have been members of a Regional Security System that has provided external defence and emergency assistance. In a phrase, they have gained 'strength in unity' and have collectively managed to offset some of the individual vulnerabilities that beset them as small states.

Political cooperation is again on the agenda in the Eastern Caribbean. In February 1998 the OECS and Barbados agreed to set up a task force to draft a plan of action to prepare for the eventual membership of Barbados in the organisation. It included proposals for cooperation in external representation and the cost of government and followed on from an agreement between Barbados and the OECS in 1995 which aimed to improve economic cooperation.[45] In the past, the circumstances have never been right and the progress that has been made on political cooperation has been more limited than in the economic and security fields. Nevertheless, the case for political integration in the OECS is compelling[46] and the prospective membership of Barbados gives it an impetus and additional weight that it has not had before. Indeed, the fact that Barbados is actively canvassing the support of others is itself a telling commentary on its confidence to proceed alone and reinforces a conclusion that for open dependent development to work in the future new thinking, new vision and new tactics will be required.

Notes

1   In the Eastern Caribbean the UK retains responsibility for Anguilla, the British Virgin Islands and Montserrat. Other British overseas territories in the region are the Cayman Islands, the Turks and Caicos Islands and, more distant, Bermuda.

2   The OECS was established in 1981 as an intergovernmental organisation designed to promote closer cooperation among the member states. It comprises the independent states of Antigua and Barbuda, Dominica, Grenada, St Kitts-Nevis, St Lucia, St Vincent and the Grenadines and the UK overseas territory of Montserrat. In this chapter reference to the OECS is used as a shorthand reference for the six independent states only.

3   *Eastern Caribbean Central Bank: Report and Statement of Accounts 1991*, Basseterre, 1991, p. 2.

4   Figures calculated from Trevor Harker, 'The impact of external sector developments on Caribbean economic performance 1983–1988', *Caribbean Studies*, 24, 1–2, 1991, Table 7.

5   *Ibid.*, Table 5.

6   There is a problem in getting individual data for small countries in the Eastern Caribbean. The US often only reports data for the region as a whole, which may or may not include Barbados. Figures calculated from Jacqueline Anne Braveboy-Wagner, *The Caribbean in World Affairs: The Foreign Policies of the English-Speaking States*, Boulder, 1989, Table 4.4.

7   Figures calculated from Commonwealth Secretariat, *Small States: Economic Review and Basic Statistics*, Vol. 1, London, 1995, Table 23.

8   The figure is for all seven countries and calculated from Commonwealth Secretariat, *Small States: Economic Review and Basic Statistics*, Vol. 3, London, 1997, Table 33.

9   Figures calculated from *Eastern Caribbean Central Bank: Report and Statement of Accounts 1991*, various tables.

10 Figure for 1988 from Carmen Diana Deere *et al.*, *In the Shadows of the Sun: Caribbean Development Alternatives and US Policy*, Boulder, 1990, Table 2.7 and for 1992 from West India Committee, *Caribbean Basin Commercial Profile 1994*, Washington DC, 1994, p. 14.

11 See DeLisle Worrell, 'Barbados at thirty: the economy', in Trevor A. Carmichael (ed.), *Barbados: Thirty Years of Independence*, Kingston, 1996, pp. 3–28.

12 Cited in Polly Pattullo, *Last Resorts: The Cost of Tourism in the Caribbean*, London, 1996, p. 12.

13 *Ibid*, pp. 6, 53.

14 Figures calculated from Harker, 'The impact of external sector developments on Caribbean economic performance 1983–1988', Table X.

15 Figures calculated from Eastern Caribbean Central Bank, Research Department, *Economic and Financial Review*, 10, 4, 1992, various tables.

16 Patullo, *Last Resorts*, p. 46.

17 John Warren, 'The cruise industry in the Eastern Caribbean', in Lindsay Maxwell (ed.), *The Caribbean Handbook 1997/98*, British Virgin Islands, 1997, p. 15.

18 See, in particular, the discussion in Patullo, *Last Resorts*, pp. 164–7.

19 *Ibid.*, p. 202.

20 See Thomas Klak and Garth Myers, 'How states sell their countries and their people', in Thomas Klak (ed.), *Globalization and Neoliberalism: The Caribbean Context*, Lanham, 1998, pp. 87–109.

21 Tony Thorndike, 'Offshore finance in the Caribbean', in Jeremy Taylor (ed.), *The Caribbean Handbook 1990*, St John's, 1990, p. 34.

22 West India Committee, *Caribbean Basin Commercial Profile 1994*, p. 56.

23 See John Chown, 'Offshore finance: the future for money management', in *The Caribbean Handbook 1997/98*, pp. 30–1.

24 Bureau for International Narcotics and Law Enforcement Affairs, *International Narcotics Control Strategy Report 1997*, US Department of State, Washington DC, 1997.

25 See, in particular, the discussion in Ramesh Ramsaran, *The Commonwealth Caribbean in the World Economy*, London, 1989, chapter 4.

26 See Anthony Payne, 'Westminster adapted: the political order of the Commonwealth Caribbean', in Jorgé I. Dominguez *et al.*, (eds), *Democracy in the Caribbean*, Baltimore, 1993, pp. 57–73.

27 See Paul Sutton, 'Democracy in the Commonwealth Caribbean', *Democratization*, 6, 1, 1999, pp. 67–86.

28 Two good contemporary overviews of politics in Barbados since independence are Neville Duncan, 'Barbados: democracy at the crossroads', in Carlene J. Edie (ed.), *Democracy in the Caribbean: Myths and Realities*, Westport, 1994, pp. 75–91, and Peter Wickham, 'An overview of post independence political issues in Barbados', in John Gaffar LaGuerre (ed.), *Issues in the Government and Politics of the West Indies*, St Augustine, 1997, pp. 167–204.

29 Donald C. Peters, *The Democratic System in the Eastern Caribbean*, New York, 1992, p. 216. See also Tony Thorndike, 'Politics and society in the south-eastern Caribbean', in Colin Clarke (ed.), *Society and Politics in the Caribbean*, London, 1991, pp. 110–30.

30 For further details, see Paul Sutton, 'Constancy, change and accommodation: the distinct tradition of the Commonwealth Caribbean', in James Mayall and Anthony Payne (eds), *The Fallacies of Hope: The Post-colonial Record of the Commonwealth Third World*, Manchester, 1991, pp. 106–28.

31 This is akin to the concept of 'popular capitalism'. See Wickham, 'An overview of post independence political issues in Barbados', pp. 178 ff.

32   See James Ferguson, *Grenada: Revolution in Reverse*, London, 1990 for an excellent detailed account of this period.

33   Again Grenada provides the example. The incoming government in 1990 did not seek to terminate the programme. Instead, adjustments were made and the new government 'muddled through' as best it could until it in turn was replaced in 1996. Even then, not much was to change. Indeed, the new government of Keith Mitchell abolished income tax yet again in 1996!

34   See, in particular, Vaughan A. Lewis, 'The Eastern Caribbean states: fledgling sovereignties in the global environment', in Dominguez *et al.*, *Democracy in the Caribbean*, pp. 99–121.

35   United Nations Development Programme, *Human Development Report 1997*, New York, 1997, Table 1.

36   See Neville Duncan, 'Barbados and the IMF – a case study', in John LaGuerre (ed.), *Structural Adjustment: Public Policy and Administration in the Caribbean*, St Augustine, 1994, pp. 54–87. Barbados also had brief recourse to the IMF in 1981.

37   The term is used by Jorgé Dominguez to describe the 'welfare state' in the Caribbean and refers to the bargain struck between trade unions, the private sector and the state in which each acknowledge they need the other to ensure peace, prosperity and political democracy. In the case of Barbados this proved remarkably durable. See his 'The Caribbean question: why has liberal democracy (surprisingly) flourished?', in Dominguez *et al.*, *Democracy in the Caribbean*, pp. 11–20.

38   See Janet Momsen, 'Caribbean tourism and agriculture: new linkages in the global era?', in Klak (ed.), *Globalization and Neoliberalism*, Table 6.1.

39   Patullo, *Last Resorts*, p. 84.

40   'Eastern Caribbean Regional Summary' in Bureau for International Narcotics and Law Enforcement Affairs, *International Narcotics Control Strategy Report 1997*.

41   *Ibid.*

42   See F. Desmond McCarthy and Giovanni Zanalda, *Economic Performance in Small Open Economies: The Caribbean Experience, 1980–92*, World Bank Policy Research Working Paper 1544, Washington DC, 1995.

43   Figures from UNCTAD Secretariat, *Specific Problems of Island Developing Countries*, UNCTAD/LDC/Misc.2, Geneva, 26 June 1992, Table 5. The average for all small island developing countries under one million was US$131.6 and for all developing countries US$16.

44   For a discussion on capital markets and small states, see 'An overview of vulnerability issues', in Commonwealth Secretariat, *Small States: Economic Review and Basic Statistics*, Vol. 4, London, 1998.

45   See *Caribbean Insight*, February 1998.

46   See, in particular, the persuasive exposition by William Demas, *Seize the Time: Towards OECS Political Union*, Caribbean Development Bank, Barbados, 26 August 1987. William Demas was then President of the Caribbean Development Bank.

From boom to bust to buoyancy in Trinidad and Tobago

At the beginning of 1982 George Chambers, the Prime Minister and Minister of Finance of Trinidad and Tobago, announced in his budget speech, 'the fête is over and the country must go back to work'.[1] The pronouncement was prophetic and made at the cusp as the country turned from boom to bust. The previous nine years had been marked by continuous high growth that saw per capita incomes double in real terms as living standards and consumption levels rose dramatically throughout the country. In 1982 the economy reached its peak with a GDP of TT$9.176 billion in current prices (US$7.99 billion).[2] Thereafter the economy went into decline with falling income for seven consecutive years until growth was restored in 1990. The story since then has been one of gradual restoration of economic fortune with the late 1990s marking a return to the 'good times' of the late 1970s, although not at the same level of individual prosperity or with the same measure of unbridled optimism that characterised the earlier years.

This chapter will examines this boom-bust-boom cycle in three parts. The first part examines the gathering crisis of the early 1980s that ended with the defeat of the People's National Movement (PNM) government of George Chambers in elections in 1986. The second part focuses on the difficult years of the middle to late 1980s and the attempts of the government of the National Alliance for Reconstruction (NAR) to manage the economic crisis and define a new politics for the country. Its defeat in elections in 1991, and the return of the PNM to government, were a reflection of the economic difficulties the NAR faced, as well as political problems largely of its own making. Finally, the third part examines the economic policies followed by the PNM government, and since 1995 by the United National Congress (UNC) government, which have put Trinidad and Tobago on a radically different development path to that introduced in the boom years of the 1970s.

The gathering crisis

In 1983 the World Bank released a report on the situation in Trinidad and Tobago in which it concluded that 'structural adjustment, which will be difficult for all parts of the Trinidad and Tobago economy, must be initiated in the near future'.[3] The following year the government in Trinidad and Tobago issued its own substantial study significantly entitled *The Imperatives of Adjustment – Draft Development Plan 1983–1986*. In it, the government argued that 'the economy now faces a new long-term structural situation which requires profound adjustments by everybody in the country – the public sector, workers at all levels, private sector employers, housewives, farmers and indeed consumers in general' and warned that 'the next four years will be a period of transition during which lower standards of living will have to be accepted by all persons in the community'.[4] In short, the boom was over and a new harsh reality was about to be visited on the country.

The immediate cause was the decline in oil production and price on which the economic wealth of the country had been dependent for many years. In 1978 oil production peaked at just under 84 million barrels, thereafter declining year on year to 1983 when it was just over 58 million barrels.[5] The effect of this fall was at first disguised by rising prices, but in 1981 they also began to fall in real terms which resulted in the real price of oil deteriorating by 40 per cent in the three years 1981–3.[6] The effect of this on the economy was a slowing of growth and then in 1983 a negative growth rate of –8.1 per cent was recorded.[7] Although oil production levelled off over the next few years, oil prices continued to fall, reaching a low of US$14 per barrel in 1986 (compared to US$33 per barrel in 1981). In 1986 GDP at current prices was 10 per cent below that of 1982 with negative growth rates being recorded in each of the three preceding years.

There was also growing recognition that the approach taken towards economic development during the 1970s had been wrong. This had seen the abandonment of comprehensive development planning in favour of a sectoral strategy that had sought to promote accelerated development in key strategic sectors such as energy-based industrialisation. The intention was sound, but the effect was to encourage uneven development and overheating of the economy, with some sectors, such as construction, booming and others, such as agriculture, going into sharp decline. In his 1982 budget speech Chambers signalled a return to comprehensive multi-sectoral planning and announced the formation of a National Economic Planning Commission to include representatives from the public and private sectors, the banking and financial institutions, the small business sector and the labour movement. Their detailed proposals were set out in the *Imperatives of Adjustment*.

The report, running to two volumes, is too massive to summarise in a few words. However, it essentially argued for a slow change of direction to be implemented in a phased incremental manner. It highlighted the need to develop new economic activities such as export-oriented industrialisation, as well as to rationalise and modernise agriculture and the petroleum sector. It sought to improve the fiscal and balance of payments situation through measures such as increased taxation and reduced subsidies. An incomes policy was proposed, including a freeze on wages and control of prices. The state sector, including state enterprises, was to be held more accountable and the private sector and foreign direct investment was to be encouraged. The 'public sector investment programme' was to be cut back and the public sector was to be reformed. Although such measures were bound to result in increased unemployment, the report argued the effect could be cushioned through new opportunities that would be opened up along with continuing government support. Finally, the report underlined the familiar view that regional integration could help promote national development. It therefore argued for greater support for meaningful Caribbean integration in all three areas of the Caribbean Community: the common market; functional co-operation and common services; and co-ordination of foreign policies.[8]

The policies proposed were similar to those that would be advocated in a mild programme of structural adjustment. Indeed, in his budget speech commissioning the report, Chambers indicated that a joint economic mission from the IMF and the World Bank would be visiting Trinidad and Tobago and that it would be invited to liaise and consult with the task force preparing the report.[9] However, what was different from an externally imposed structural adjustment policy was the fact that this one was locally inspired and sought what Selwyn Ryan has described as 'a soft landing'.[10] It therefore proposed that there should be attempts to maintain employment levels and to improve the housing situation among the poorer elements of the community. It also claimed that, while it was inevitable there would be a lower standard of living, this 'would not mean deprivation of basic needs or, indeed, of many of the comforts which we take for granted'.[11] In other words, the adjustment was to be proportionate and would avoid the 'draconian measures' taken in many other Caribbean and Latin American countries.

The clearest example of this policy in action is to be found in the continuing investment by the government in the energy sector. This took two forms. One was the established policy of government buying into important local industries to save jobs. Accordingly, in 1985 it purchased the local assets of Texaco, which at one time had dominated oil production and refining in the country, when faced with its withdrawal from Trinidad. In that year it also acquired the remaining 49.9 per cent holding in the Trinidad-Tesoro Petroleum Company. The other was the completion of major investment projects in support of energy-based industrialisation. The initial proposal to establish an industrial estate using the natural gas that Trinidad possessed in abundance had been made by Dr Williams, the then Prime Minister and Minister of Finance, in the 1975 budget speech. Between 1977 and 1984 five natural gas-based plants were commissioned, two of which produced ammonia, a third urea, a fourth methanol and the fifth sponge iron, billets and wire rods. The government investment in these plants, which it either wholly owned or held a majority share, totalled some TT$3 billion, much of it scheduled between 1981–4.[12] The result was that in 1985 the contribution of state enterprises to GDP was double what it had been in 1982 at TT$2.9 billion, some 16 per cent of the national total. In all, in that year the government held equity in 66 enterprises, which between them provided direct employment for 53,700 people and accounted for more than 50 per cent of exports.[13]

While the government was able to protect its involvement in the state sector it nevertheless found itself presiding over cuts in expenditure and increases in the cost of living. Some large capital projects not yet begun were abandoned and others reviewed. The 1984 and 1985 budgets froze the wages and salaries bill at 1982 levels (at which time a large increase over previous years had been agreed) and the public utilities (electricity, water, telephones, public transportation and port services) were given permission to increase prices. Subsidies on petroleum and basic foodstuffs were reduced or removed. Purchase taxes and consumption taxes on a wide variety of local and imported goods and services were increased and measures taken eventually to introduce a value-added tax.[14] The knock-on effect was felt by local businesses and impacted especially on employment. Some major companies in the retail, assembly and construction sectors went out of business and many others were forced to reduce the size of their workforce. The government halved its expenditure on its own programme of special unemployment relief between 1981–6 and further reduced expenditure on infrastructure, adding still more to the unemployment total. The net effect was an increase in unemployment from 7 per cent in 1981 to 17 per cent in 1986.[15]

The overall downturn came to a head in 1986. The *Review of the Economy 1986* painted a sombre picture.[16] The collapse of oil prices that year to their lowest level since the early 1970s indicated major problems on the horizon. The domestic economy's contraction continued and was likely to be further compounded in the near future by a fall in the amount of loans and advances by banks to the production and services sector of the economy. The recurrent account went into deficit for the first time since 1973 as a consequence of reduced revenues and increased expenditure over the previous year. Debt service payments increased by 73 per cent over 1985, largely on account of the decision to devalue the Trinidad and Tobago dollar by 50 per cent in December 1985. This signalled future problems in servicing a mounting external debt that had been largely incurred by the government in support of its energy-based industrialisation programme (state enterprises were responsible for some 60 per cent of total external debt in 1985). The balance of payments deficit in 1986 was the largest since 1970 and had increased from 1.3 per cent of GDP in 1985 to 13.6 per cent of GDP in 1986. In short, by 1986 Trinidad and Tobago had moved from recession to economic crisis in which the medium-term outlook was bleak.

The Chambers government, despite the *Imperatives of Adjustment*, had not achieved the 'soft landing' for which it had hoped. It was to prove fateful as 1986 was also an election year. Even earlier dissatisfaction had begun to set in on the government's record. In an opinion poll conducted by Selwyn Ryan in mid-1985, 70 per cent of those polled expressed themselves as 'dissatisfied' or 'very dissatisfied' with Chambers's performance, as opposed to only 21 per cent who were satisfied. More tellingly, in the same poll he was seen as less competent to deal with economic problems and to run an honest and efficient government than his three major opposition rivals.[17] He was also facing stiffer political opposition than he had in 1981. In the intervening years the previously divided opposition had first reached an 'accommodation' amongst themselves, under which they fought and won the local government elections in 1983, and then entered into unity talks which led to the creation of the NAR from four distinct political parties in early 1986.[18] Lastly, the PNM itself was in poor shape to fight the elections. An internal report commissioned after its defeat in the 1983 elections pointed to inertia and decay, and acknowledgement that little had been done to redress the deteriorating situation was made by its general secretary in a memorandum in 1985 where he lamented that the PNM was 'for all practical purposes dead'.[19]

The above factors, when combined with a lack-lustre campaign in which the Chambers government was on the defensive, led to the first defeat of the PNM in thirty years. The NAR won thirty-three seats and 67 per cent of the vote, compared to three seats and 31 per cent for the PNM. The poor economic situation was undoubtedly a major factor in explaining the defeat. In opinion polls taken during the last days of the elections, Ryan found that young blacks of thirty years and under, who would normally have supported the PNM, had swung decisively to the NAR. They were also the most likely to be unemployed, with rates of 51 per cent for those aged fifteen to twenty-four.[20] At the opposite end of the income scale, those on higher incomes were vocal in support of the NAR and contributed money and effort to the campaign. Major business companies, such as Neal and Massey, were also known NAR supporters and had done much to bring about the unity between the parties that led to the foundation of the NAR. Most crucially of all, given the history of political divide between the two major ethnic groups at election times, many of those of African and East Indian descent had come together to campaign under the slogan of 'one love', thereby promising an end to ethnic and racial politicking and the emergence of a genuinely inclusive national government. A great deal of hope and expectation thus rested on the new government and it was clear that its highest priority would be given to restoring the economic fortunes of the country.

The NAR under siege

The first budget of the NAR was delivered by A. N. R. Robinson, the Prime Minister and Minister of Finance, within weeks of taking office. It was essentially a holding operation since the state of government finances was unclear, the true size of the external debt, for example, not being known. However, what was very obvious was that government expenditure was going to be well in excess of government revenue (a shortfall of TT$1.5 billion) and that immediate action was necessary to limit costs and increase taxes. The latter was achieved by increases in purchase taxes and taxes on petrol and airline tickets, the former by suspending the merit increases and cost of living allowance (COLA) paid to all public sector employees, then fixed at TT$205.80 per month. The government also abolished the two-tier exchange rate, which had allowed food and drugs to be imported at cheaper costs, and increased income and corporation taxes. Needless to say, this was not popular and the trade unions challenged the suspension of COLA, but with no effect. Indeed, subsequent budgets confirmed it, along with a 10 per cent cut in the salaries of public servants. The government justified this on the grounds that the alternative was massive retrenchment (almost 50 per cent of recurrent expenditure was accounted for by personnel costs). In all, through these and associated measures public employees suffered losses in real income of nearly 28 per cent by 1990.[21]

They were not alone. The situation for everyone deteriorated in the late 1980s. GDP fell year on year through to 1989 and unemployment stabilised at around 22 per cent of the population, half of whom were under the age of twenty-five. In the private sector businesses continued to fail at an alarming rate and workers were routinely retrenched without the severance pay to which they were entitled. Figures given by the Minister of Labour in early 1991 indicated that some TT$68 million was owing to workers from some 76 firms and that in the period 1986–90 more than 8,000 persons had officially been recorded as losing their jobs in the private sector.[22]

In August 1988 the government enacted a mini-budget which included additional increases in the price of petrol, public utility tariffs and property taxes; further reductions in public sector finance, including the salaries of non-unionised management in the state enterprises; the introduction of an early retirement and voluntary severance scheme in the public service, along with measures to contract some services to the private sector; and proposals to close, sell or restructure some state enterprises in addition to major cuts in capital expenditure.[23] The Trinidad and Tobago dollar was also further devalued from $3.6 to $4.25 to the US dollar. Finally, and perhaps most critically of all, Robinson announced that the government would enter into negotiations with the IMF for assistance with investment and balance of payment support for the remainder of the year.

The decision to approach the IMF was a major reversal of policy. In the 1986 elections the NAR had said it would not do so (indeed, it had accused the PNM of secretly reaching an understanding with the IMF to be imposed on the country should it be returned). The Prime Minister rationalised the decision in his budget address at the end of the year on the grounds that there was 'no better alternative':

> Given the falling price of oil in 1988 and the squeeze being imposed by the commercial banks, a failure to go to the IMF would have resulted in a curtailment of the population's consumption and welfare that would have been intolerable. The entire society would have ground to a halt. One could have sought to reschedule the foreign debt, but that was impossible without the co-operation of the IMF. The implications of not going to the Fund were serious . . . it would have been necessary to cut our wages and salaries bill by some 50 per cent or, alternatively, make similar draconian cuts in our welfare appropriations, capital programme and goods and services. However hard people think things are now, please be assured they would be far, far harder if we did not obtain the inflows of foreign resources we have now managed to obtain.[24]

Two agreements were signed with the IMF: one for SDR85 million (TT$470 million) in November 1988 and the second for SDR99 million (TT$547 million) in January 1989. These were the trigger for re-scheduling debts with the commercial banks and for additional loans from the Inter-American Development Bank (IADB) (US$500 million) and from the World Bank. The latter, in particular, was contentious. The case against it was made forcefully by Denis Pantin, an economist at the UWI in Trinidad. In a pamphlet published in September 1989 he argued that the country was not yet in a debt crisis but soon would be, should debts additional to those of the IMF be incurred. These would not only mortgage the future foreign exchange earnings of the country but would also lead to inappropriate and ultimately harmful development policies. In support of this thesis he pointed to the failure of structural adjustment programmes elsewhere, notably Jamaica, and concluded that the US$40 million World Bank loan on offer (with a matching sum from the Japanese Export-Import Bank) would come with conditionalities that would lead to further economic decline and increased hardship.[25]

The trade union movement was also worried about the direction the government had taken. They concurred with the arguments of Pantin that a 'debt trap' was being sprung and pointed out that measures in the budget, such as the 10 per cent cut in the wages of public service employees, showed that 'the burden of adjustment was not being shared equally by all groups and that income was being transferred from the working class to the middle and capitalist classes'.[26] There was certainly evidence of increasing poverty. In 1989 research by another economist at the UWI reported 22 per cent of the population living below the poverty line of US$68 per month for a single person.[27] More tellingly, those who did so now included unemployed workers with skills and people who ran small businesses that had failed. The inevitable result was escalating conflict with the labour movement and its various supporters. In March 1989 they initiated a 'day of resistance', which enjoyed widespread support among public service employees, to demonstrate opposition to the government and its proposals for structural adjustment. In response, the government entered into discussions with the two main trade union groupings in the country, although differences among them eventually led to the talks failing. The trade union movement, however, came together again over the 1990 budget. This introduced a value added tax (VAT) at 15 per cent for many basic but 'non-essential' goods. It was widely condemned and led to the trade unions joining with religious and cultural organisations, feminist groups and various political activists (including elements of the PNM) to form the Summit of People's Organisation in

February 1990, with the explicit aim of reversing many of the austerity measures introduced by the government since taking office.[28]

The government was also beginning to lose support among the business community. It, too, had begun to criticise government strategy, if from a somewhat different perspective. Groups such as the Trinidad and Tobago Manufacturers' Association and the Chamber of Commerce argued that the government had been too cautious in cutting the public sector and too slow in promoting the private sector. The devaluation in 1988 was instanced as a case in which the opportunities for improvements to the balance of payments were unlikely to materialise as a result of government measures restricting the flow of foreign exchange essential for business to import inputs to produce for the local and export market.[29] As a result, business confidence remained low with consistently fewer companies newly registered in the late 1980s as compared to the early 1980s and outstanding loans by the commercial banks to the private sector falling year on year 1987–90.[30]

The high level of dissatisfaction of the country as a whole with the NAR and with Robinson as Prime Minister and Minister of Finance was charted in a series of opinion polls from 1988 through 1990. The first, which took place in May/June 1988, reported that only 16 per cent of those interviewed were 'satisfied' with the performance of the NAR since the election while 62 per cent were 'dissatisfied' (18 per cent were of the opinion it had done 'as well as could be expected'). In respect of Robinson himself, 20 per cent found his performance 'satisfactory' compared to 60 per cent who did not (14 per cent reported he had done 'as well as could be expected').[31] The poll conducted in March 1989 showed a worsening situation with 63 per cent 'dissatisfied' with the Prime Minister's performance as against 28 per cent who were 'satisfied' (as compared to 34 per cent the previous year who were 'satisfied' or who felt he had done 'as well as expected'). Of note is that, while these views were shared by all ethnic groups and social classes, those of African descent were more likely to be dissatisfied than those of East Indian descent and the unemployed and blue collar workers were more dissatisfied than those with professional and managerial jobs. 46 per cent were also of the view that Robinson should be replaced as leader of the NAR, compared to 39 per cent who felt he should be retained (15 per cent had no view on the issue).[32] In June 1990 a third poll revealed the likelihood of defeat for the NAR in elections which would have to take place within nine months. Only 15 per cent of respondents believed that the performance of the NAR had been 'good' while 56 per cent believed it had been 'poor' or 'very poor' (22 per cent believed it had been 'fair'). The performance of the

Prime Minister was rated as 'good' or 'very good' by 17 per cent, 'fair' by 21 per cent and 'poor' or 'very poor' by 48 per cent. While this appears to demonstrate an improved rating for Robinson over the previous year, more people wanted to see him replaced as leader of the NAR and, most telling of all, 56 per cent were of the opinion that the government should be changed, as against 27 per cent who felt it should be given another term. In terms of class, the numerical majority in the lower and middle classes were most resolutely opposed to the NAR, while those in the upper-middle class were the most supportive (giving credence to the view that NAR policies had indeed favoured the most prosperous). Finally, the preference of political party by ethnic group demonstrated a return to the ethnic voting of the past with those of African descent overwhelmingly supporting the PNM and those of East Indian descent the newly-formed UNC headed by Basdeo Panday.[33]

The picture that emerged in early 1990 was thus one of an ongoing economic and social crisis that spelt the future demise of the government. But it was not yet in any meaningful sense of the term a political crisis. The 'coup' of 27 July altered that and posed the most serious threat to the country since the Black Power revolution of 1970. On that day, 114 members of a fundamentalist black Muslim sect, the Jamaat-al-Muslimeen, stormed the parliament building and national television station in Port of Spain, taking as hostage around forty people, including the Prime Minister and seven of his ministers. The violence of their action was unprecedented in Trinidad, with twenty-five people killed and nearly 250 injured in the assault and subsequent looting of the business district in the capital and neighbouring towns in north Trinidad, with the losses for property estimated at between TT$300–500 million. The 'coup' itself, however, was quickly contained by the army which immediately deployed in strength to surround the Muslimeen and disperse the looters. The situation was eventually brought to an end after six days when the rebel leader, Abu Bakr, secured an amnesty for himself and his followers in exchange for the release of the hostages. Notwithstanding this outcome, on their surrender to the armed forces all were arrested and charged with a variety of offences including treason, murder, arson and unlawful imprisonment, though subsequently all were released on appeal in July 1992 on the grounds that the 'amnesty' granted was indeed legal.

The 'coup' has been the subject of a number of studies.[34] Common to most of them is the argument that the deteriorating economic and social situation formed the backdrop to the action. Abu Bakr certainly cited this factor as explanation for the 'coup' in his television appearance on the evening of 27 July with his reference to the country reaching 'the abyss of no return [with] poverty and destitution where people can't find jobs, where there is no work, where children are reduced to crime in order to live, where there is [sic] no jobs in the hospital'.[35] But more important were other motives, including his own, those of his movement, and the perceived political illegitimacy of the NAR government. It was this latter perception that led him, falsely as it turned out, to premise his action on a spontaneous outburst of support from the country. Instead, the country was largely indifferent or actively hostile to him. This was mapped out in yet another of the many opinion polls directed by Selwyn Ryan. In a national poll of nearly 1000 persons in September/October 1990, 75 per cent of respondents said that Abu Bakr was wrong to attempt to overthrow a legally established government by force, even though 60 per cent said they sympathised with his social goals as expounded on his broadcasts over Trinidad and Tobago Television.[36] In other words, the political system in Trinidad was not an issue and if government policy was wrong the way to change it was at the polls.

Nevertheless, the political system was under strain at the time as a consequence of the 'coup'. Significantly, 16 per cent of those questioned by Ryan believed Abu Bakr was right to attempt the overthrow and 24 per cent believed he and his men should be pardoned and set free. A majority, despite the trauma of the 'coup', also continued to hold negative views of Robinson and the NAR government. Indeed, their unpopularity had increased, with 32 per cent stating they had become less sympathetic to Robinson since the 'coup' and 34 per cent less sympathetic to the NAR. A final telling statistic was that support for the NAR had fallen even further, with only 15 per cent prepared to support it in an election as against 25 per cent for the PNM and 8 per cent for the UNC (31 per cent were of the view that none of the three main parties would govern effectively, while 23 per cent had no opinion). As Ryan was to summarise his own results, 'the survey revealed widespread disaffection with the Prime Minister and the NAR, majority support for early elections, and a significant level of disenchantment with the existing political parties. The population was also quite ambivalent about the Abu Bakr phenomenon'.[37]

The elections held in December 1991 confirmed the demise of the NAR. It won 24 per cent of the vote, but secured only two seats in Tobago. The PNM, which won 45 per cent of the vote, secured twenty-one seats and formed the government. Ultimately, the failure of the NAR was both economic and political. The economic crisis eroded support among those who had switched from the PNM to the NAR in 1986, while poor political leadership by Robinson led to division and faction in his government. The most damaging instance of this was his dismissal of Panday and several of his political colleagues who held ministerial posts in February 1988, which led to wholesale desertion by the now numerically preponderant East Indian electorate. They went on to provide the core support for the opposition UNC formed the following year. However, in retrospect there was one lasting achievement by the government: the elaboration of a new development strategy for Trinidad and Tobago. Building on the *Imperatives of Adjustment*, and with the support of the IMF and the World Bank, the NAR published the *Draft Medium Term Macro Planning Framework 1989–95* in July 1988. As amended and adopted in 1990, this provided the blueprint for the radical change in direction which Robinson had proposed in his 1989 budget. The emphasis in development was to shift from inward-looking strategies to export-oriented strategies, while measures were to be adopted to foster a climate conducive to investment, local and foreign. In 1990 long-standing restrictions on foreign investment were removed with the passage of the Foreign Investment Act and in 1991 a raft of measures were introduced to further liberalise trade, including sweeping reform of the Import Negative List (which imposed quantitative restrictions on competitive imports) and the implementation of tariff reductions through the adoption of CARICOM's Common External Tariff. Divestment of state enterprises was also to be encouraged, e.g. the loss-making Iron and Steel Company of Trinidad and Tobago was leased to an Indian entrepreneur in 1989 for ten years. The PNM government, on taking office, was to deepen and expand this programme, adding flesh to the bones of the nascent enterprise state.

Towards the enterprise state

The decision to continue in the same direction as that mapped out by the NAR was made clear in the first budget presented by the PNM within weeks of victory. The new Minister of Finance, Wendell Motley, stated that the economic stabilisation programme implemented with the IMF from 1988 appeared to have worked and reported that the economy had registered 2.7 per cent growth in 1991, even though overall the economy remained 'fragile'. The medium-term strategy was thus to strengthen the shoots of recovery with 'a substantial increase in investment and in exports', along with a programme of divestment of 'those assets which have no strategic or public purpose value'. In the long run, however, he argued that the country could only raise its standard of living by becoming competitive in the wider world and this required 'diligence, discipline, thrift and a spirit of enterprise'.[38]

In essence, the PNM strategy involved a threefold task. The first, and to some extent the most radical, was an acceleration of the restructuring and divestment programme in the public sector. In spite of some rationalisation carried out by the NAR, government holdings remained substantial, indeed had increased in number from sixty-six enterprises in 1985 to eighty-seven in 1992. Their value in the latter year was put at TT$6.5 billion and the contribution of the state enterprise sector to the economy at just under TT$3.8 billion (23 per cent of GDP).[39] At the same time, however, the reforms introduced by the NAR had improved performance and losses of TT$1.8 billion in 1985 (including public utilities) had been reduced substantially, so that by 1993 they were a relatively manageable TT$172 million.[40] This made the state enterprises more commercially attractive and, following a substantial review, the government eventually resolved in 1994 to sell or liquidate all but two. Its rationale for doing so was set out in detail in its *Report on Public Sector Participation in Industrial and Commercial Activities* published in 1995. This stated that 'those enterprises that are retained will operate as efficiently as any well-run Private Sector organisation', while the sale and/or restructuring of the remainder would provide revenue 'to enable meaningful investment expenditure by the Government' and 'attract foreign capital by demonstrating fiscal and monetary responsibility'.[41] In all, between November 1992 and December 1995, eighteen government enterprises were sold, twelve on the local market for US$64 million and six to various international investors for US$395 million.[42]

The second was an intensification of the drive for foreign direct investment (FDI). Again, the basic groundwork had been prepared by the NAR and from 1989 levels of FDI began to exceed US$100 million per annum as major US oil companies once more began to invest in Trinidad's oil and gas. However, what was significant for the PNM was a deliberate decision to reverse the economic nationalism of the 1970s and 1980s. One of the clearest statements of the new policy was made by Prime Minister Patrick Manning to potential US investors early in 1993. In contrast to the earlier period he stated:

We note today that the State should have a very restricted role in the economic life of the country. Current PNM policies therefore call for a role for the State as that of facilitator in the first instance but also as investor only to the extent that it is necessary to ensure that the pattern of economic development is balanced and to ensure that the society maximises on the opportunities for business expansion because it is business expansion that creates the jobs that the country so desperately requires.[43]

The announcement of huge new investments by companies such as Amoco, British Gas and Texaco thereafter became almost routine, and other companies not previously associated with the country or choosing to invest abroad for the first time (as in the decision of the Nucor Corporation to build an iron carbide production plant at a cost of US$60million) strengthened the trend. In 1994 FDI was reported as TT$3 billion and in 1996 TT$2.4 billion, prompting the comment by the Economist Intelligence Unit that 'the total of FDI in these two years is greater than the FDI undertaken during the whole oil boom period'.[44]

Third, the PNM sought to liberalise the economy still further. In 1993 the government abolished exchange controls and floated the Trinidad and Tobago dollar. Although it initially drifted downward from its fixed rate of TT$4.25 : US$1 it soon achieved relative stability, exchanging within a band of TT$5.92–TT$6.11 to the US dollar between 1994–7.[45] It also implemented measures to eliminate virtually all barriers to international trade as of 1995 and to promote financial liberalisation to encourage the growth of non-bank financial institutions. These measures were the culmination of conditions agreed in the IMF and World Bank loans to the NAR and further spelt out in loans raised by the PNM with the IADB for US$80 million and the World Bank for TT$27 million. The confidence in the country shown by these international financial institutions allowed the government to reschedule some of its debt and borrow on the international financial markets. Total external debt, however, still remained historically relatively high, at some 50 per cent of GNP in the early 1990s.[46]

The signs that the economy had now returned to sustainable growth, nevertheless, need qualification. In 1992 and 1993 there was negative growth in GDP and real growth did not resume until 1994 (3.8 per cent) and 1995 (2.4 per cent). Unemployment also remained high at 18.4 per cent (the same as for 1991), with the worst rates, as always, among black urban youth.[47] The government had also run into difficulties in implementing its ambitious public sector reform programme and it owed large sums (according to some estimates up to TT$2 billion) in back-pay to public sector employees. Manning's decision to spring a general election in November 1995, some eighteen months before it was constitutionally due, was therefore somewhat of a surprise and ultimately for the PNM a disastrous mistake. The main issues in the election were unemployment, poverty and crime. The latter had risen inexorably during the 1980s and in 1994 over 18,000 serious crimes were reported to the police, including 132 murders, 254 rapes and more than 15,000 break-ins, robberies and other crimes against property.[48] Worse, many cases remained unresolved and the criminal justice system was collapsing under the strain. The social costs of a prolonged period of adjustment were obviously beginning to tell, with the result that the better off (particularly among the Indians) turned to the UNC while the poor (particularly among the black sections of the community) withheld their vote from the PNM. The result was a victory for the PNM in the number of votes cast, 48.4 per cent compared to 45.3 per cent for the UNC, but a tie in the number of seats won in the House of Representatives at seventeen each, the other two being won by the NAR in Tobago.[49] Holding the balance of power, it decided to join the UNC to form the first coalition government in the post-independence history of the country.

The UNC government has continued on the path set by the NAR and PNM governments. Its economic policy was set out in its *Medium-Term Policy Framework 1997–99*. This promised pragmatic and prudent economic management within a context of macro-economic stability, sustainable economic growth and social equity.[50] In practice, this has meant the further enactment of reforms to liberalise the economy and attract foreign investment. In respect of the latter it has been particularly proactive, signing bilateral investment treaties with the United States, Britain, France and Canada and amending existing legislation in the Foreign Investment Act, Securities Industry Act, Finance Act and Intellectual Property Act. The result has been a flood of foreign investment into the petrochemical and natural gas industries. US companies alone committed some US$4 billion in 1996–9 (making Trinidad and Tobago second only to Canada in the Western hemisphere on a per capita basis as a recipient of US FDI) and huge sums also came from major European companies.[51] The concentration of a substantial proportion of this investment in building and refurbishing methanol and ammonia plants means that by 2000 Trinidad is expected to be the world's largest exporter of these products. Investments have also been made in oil and gas exploration and recovery, the construction of a liquefied natural gas plant (the largest construction project in the Caribbean in 1998) and iron and steel production.

Trinidad and Tobago would therefore appear to be well on the way to economic recovery. The investment bonanza has allowed the government to begin to reduce the foreign debt and embark on some social programmes. In 1997, for example, it doubled the resources of the public sector investment programme, designed to improve essential public services and the physical infrastructure of the country, and in 1998 it increased the state pension from TT$430 to TT$520 per month and announced that legislation would be introduced to establish a minimum wage of TT$7 per hour.[52] It was also able to use its good standing to access international funds from the IADB, World Bank,

Caribbean Development Bank and the European Union in support of social programmes, investment in public utilities and further privatisation. Unemployment also fell to 13.4 per cent in 1998, the lowest rate for fourteen years.[53] However, the return to growth has not been without some difficulties. In March 1998 the Finance Minister, Brian Kue Tung, had to announce supplementary measures to the budget he had introduced in January as a consequence of a 20 per cent fall in the price of oil in the previous two months (revenues from oil accounted for between 15–20 per cent of budget revenue). Methanol prices also fell that year (at US$100–135 per tonne compared to US$175 per tonne in 1997), as did those for iron and steel, causing the postponement of plans for a new plant and the closure of another.[54] In the first quarter of 1999 the Central Bank reported a real growth rate of only 0.9 per cent, plus the emergence of a growing fiscal deficit. Its governor, Winston Dookeran, however, maintained that the economy was not going into recession and forecast a growth rate of 3.5 per cent for 1999 (rates of growth were 3.2 per cent in 1997 and 3.7 per cent in 1998).[55] His upbeat assessment is, in itself, an indication that, current problems notwithstanding, the general mood remains optimistic, buoyed by the belief that the country, through structural adjustment, has put into place the measures that will ensure increased prosperity into the early years of the twenty-first century.

Conclusion

Trinidad and Tobago has emerged from a protracted and painful adjustment process that saw the standard of living of its people halved in per capita terms. In retrospect, it is clear that the 1970s boom was unsustainable and that policies would need to change. What is remarkable is the degree of consensus that has been built around what was required to restore the economy to growth. Since the publication of *The Imperatives of Adjustment* all governments have followed broadly similar policies, privatising state-owned enterprises and liberalising the economy. This has applied as much to the UNC in the more hospitable climate of the late 1990s as to the NAR in the darkest days of the late 1980s. A new development paradigm has emerged in which entrepreneurship is celebrated and encouraged as the motor force of the economy, supported and facilitated by state action. The 'enterprise state' of the 1990s has replaced the 'national development state' of the 1970s.

The new economic strategy has yielded some economic dividends for the country, but it has not been without its social and political costs. It has also, arguably, not really changed the fundamental economic structure of the country which, despite increased economic diversification, remains fundamentally dependent on oil and gas. Accordingly, while structural adjustment appears to have worked better in Trinidad and Tobago than elsewhere in the Commonwealth Caribbean, it is a relative and qualified success. Ramesh Ramsaran's observations on structural adjustment in the region apply just as much here as elsewhere:

> Structural adjustment programs may have restored some control over economic management and challenged ineffective policies, but the long-term problems remain. The question of developing a diversified production structure and vibrant non-traditional export sector remains the most daunting of these challenges. The approach to the poverty issue has to be forged through the transformation of the economy, rather than through government transfers for which stagnant and or declining revenues are unable to provide adequate funding ... countries have to earn their keep, and economic reality has to override emotions forged in conditions that no longer obtain.[56]

These harsh lessons have been acknowledged in Trinidad and Tobago, but much still remains to be done. The future, as much as the past, will therefore rest on the success of government and the private sector in turning dependence into advantage. The country is now better equipped to do so than before, but the goal of long-term sustainable economic growth will almost certainly require yet further adjustment in the years ahead.

Notes

1   House of Representatives, Republic of Trinidad and Tobago, *Budget Speech 1982*, mimeo, Port of Spain, p. 64. The word 'fête' in Trinidad means a party. Trinidad Carnival is famous the world over as a massive vibrant street party. In Trinidad and Tobago a party-like atmosphere was evident everywhere throughout the boom years, particularly in the late 1970s and early 1980s.

2   Figure in current TT\$ (converted at TT\$2.4 = US\$1.00) from Republic of Trinidad and Tobago, National Planning Commission, *Restructuring for Economic Independence: Medium Term Macro Planning Framework 1989–1995*, Port of Spain, September 1990, Appendix 1.

3   World Bank, Latin America and Caribbean Regional Office, *Trinidad and Tobago: Development Issues for the 1980s*, Report No. 4202–TR, 24 June 1983, para. iv.

4   Republic of Trinidad and Tobago, *The Imperatives of Adjustment – Draft Development Plan 1983–1986*, Port of Spain, 1984, paras. 1.10–1.11.
5   Republic of Trinidad and Tobago, Central Statistical Office, *Annual Statistical Digest 1985*, Port of Spain, 1987, Table 125.
6   Trinidad and Tobago, *The Imperatives of Adjustment*, para. 2.56.
7   Trinidad and Tobago, *Restructuring for Economic Independence*, Appendix 5.
8   Trinidad and Tobago, *The Imperatives of Adjustment*, paras. 1.27–1.81.
9   Trinidad and Tobago, *Budget Speech 1982*, p. 43.
10   Selwyn Ryan, *The Disillusioned Electorate*, Port of Spain, 1989, p. 28.
11   Trinidad and Tobago, *The Imperatives of Adjustment*, para. 1.13.
12   Trinidad and Tobago, *Restructuring for Economic Independence*, Table VIII.
13   See 'The state enterprise sector', in Selwyn Ryan (ed.), *Trinidad and Tobago: The Independence Experience 1962–1987*, St Augustine, 1988, pp. 593–9.
14   See Ryan, *The Disillusioned Electorate*, pp. 34–5.
15   *Ibid.*, p. 36.
16   See 'Introduction', in Republic of Trinidad and Tobago, *Review of the Economy 1986*, Port of Spain, 1986, pp. vii–x.
17   Ryan, *The Disillusioned Electorate*, p. 48.
18   The parties were the Organisation for National Reconstruction headed by Karl Hudson-Phillips, the United Labour Front led by Basdeo Panday, the Democratic Action Congress of A. N. R. Robinson, and Tapia House led by Lloyd Best. Collectively, they won 43 per cent of the vote in the 1981 General Elections.
19   Cited in Ryan, *The Disillusioned Electorate*, p. 8.
20   *Ibid.*, p. 86. Unemployment figure given in Republic of Trinidad and Tobago, *A Macro-Economic Survey of Trinidad and Tobago 1982–1986 and Projections 1987–1990*, Port of Spain, 1987, Table 2.
21   André-Vincent Henry, 'Structural adjustment and industrial relations in the public sector', in John LaGuerre (ed.), *Structural Adjustment: Public Policy and Administration in the Caribbean*, St Augustine, 1994, p. 122.
22   Figures given in Selwyn Ryan, *The Muslimeen Grab for Power: Race, Religion and Revolution in Trinidad and Tobago*, Port of Spain, 1991, pp. 18–19.
23   Ryan, *The Disillusioned Electorate*, p. 257.
24   'Budget Speech 1989' given in the House of Representatives, 16 December 1988, cited in *ibid.*, p. 321.
25   See Dennis Pantin, *Into the Valley of Debt: An Alternative Path to the IMF/World Bank Path in Trinidad and Tobago*, Port of Spain, 1989, especially pp. 90–6.
26   Ryan, *The Disillusioned Electorate*, pp. 325–6.
27   Ralph Henry in *Trinidad Express*, 22 September 1990, cited in Selwyn Ryan, 'Structural adjustment and the ethnic factor in the Caribbean', in Jorgé I. Dominguez *et al.* (ed.), *Democracy in the Caribbean: Political, Economic and Social Perspectives*, Baltimore, 1993, p. 134.
28   For an excellent overview of labour relations in the 1980s, see Ray Kiely, *The Politics of Labour and Development in Trinidad*, Kingston, 1996, ch. 6.
29   Ryan, *The Disillusioned Electorate*, pp. 261–3.
30   Republic of Trinidad and Tobago, Central Statistical Office, *Annual Statistical Digest 1990*, Port of Spain, 1992, Tables 198 and 189A.
31   Figures from Ryan, *The Disillusioned Electorate*, ch. 9.
32   *Ibid.*, pp. 336–42.
33   Ryan, *The Muslimeen Grab for Power*, pp. 30–45.

34 See, in particular, Ryan, *The Muslimeen Grab for Power*; Daily Express, *Trinidad Under Siege: The Muslimeen Uprising*, Port of Spain, 1990; and *Caribbean Quarterly* (special issue), 37, 2/3, 1991.

35 Cited in Bishnu Ragoonath, 'The failure of the Abu Bakr coup: the plural society, cultural traditions and political development in Trinidad', in Paul Sutton and Anthony Payne (eds), *Size and Survival: The Politics of Security in the Caribbean and the Pacific*, London, 1993.

36 Ryan, *The Muslimeen Grab for Power*, p. 218.

37 *Ibid.*, pp. 223–4.

38 House of Representatives, Republic of Trinidad and Tobago, *Budget Speech 1992* (17 January 1992), Port of Spain, 1992.

39 Government of the Republic of Trinidad and Tobago, Ministry of Finance, *Report on Public Sector Participation in Industrial and Commercial Activities*, Port of Spain, 1995.

40 *Ibid.*

41 *Ibid.*, pp. 27, 28, 40. Other important considerations were changes in development philosophy toward 'the emerging paradigm of open borders, free markets and the globalisation of capital' that had rendered the earlier economic nationalism of the PNM redundant and 'the new realities of small peripheral nations' which left them without leverage in a post-Cold War world and increasingly marginalised in the new global economy, pp. 25, 39.

42 Figures cited in Anthony P. Maingot, 'Global economics and local politics in Trinidad's divestment program', *The North-South Agenda Papers, 34, December 1998*, Miami, 1998, Table 9.

43 Information Division Office of the Prime Minister, Trinidad, 'Prime Minister Patrick Manning Addresses OPIC Luncheon Meeting, 11 January, 1993', mimeo, Port of Spain, p. 3.

44 The Economist Intelligence Unit, *Country Profile: Trinidad and Tobago, Suriname, Netherlands Antilles, Aruba 1997–98*, London, 1998, p. 20.

45 *Ibid.*, Table 18.

46 *Ibid.*, Table 16.

47 Figures from Maingot, 'Global economics and local politics in Trinidad's divestment program', Table 2.

48 Figures from Trinidad and Tobago Police Service, cited in Clifford E. Griffin, *Democracy and Neoliberalism in the Developing World: Lessons from the Anglophone Caribbean*, Aldershot and Brookfield, 1997, Table 9.4.

49 For a discussion of the elections as well as a dispute over whether the PNM lost support or not, see Selwyn Ryan, *Pathways to Power: Indians and the Politics of National Unity in Trinidad and Tobago*, St Augustine, 1996, especially ch. 13; and John La Guerre (ed.), *The General Elections of 1995 in Trinidad and Tobago*, St Augustine, 1997.

50 See Government of the Republic of Trinidad and Tobago, Ministry of Finance, *Medium Term Policy Framework: 1997–1999*, Port of Spain, 1996.

51 Figures given by US Embassy in Trinidad and Tobago, cited in Maingot, 'Global economics and local politics in Trinidad's divestment programme, p. 3 and Appendix.

52 See *Caribbean Insight*, January 1998.

53 *Ibid.*, November 1998.

54 *Ibid.*, October 1998; February 1999.

55 *Ibid.*, April 1999; July 1999.

56   Ramesh Ramsaran, 'Reflections on development and structural adjustment in the Commonwealth Caribbean', in John LaGuerre (ed.), *Issues in the Government and Politics of the West Indies*, St Augustine, 1997, p. 100.

7 | Caribbean regional integration

The Caribbean Community was established by the Treaty of Chaguaramas signed in Trinidad on 4 July 1973. It came into being at the beginning of August 1973 and initially comprised Jamaica, Trinidad and Tobago, Barbados and Guyana, but was expanded within the year to include all the other main territories of the Commonwealth Caribbean – Antigua and Barbuda, Belize, Dominica, Grenada, Montserrat, St Kitts-Nevis, St Lucia and St Vincent. The creation of CARICOM undoubtedly constituted the critical advance in the long history of Caribbean integration. It grew out of the Caribbean Free Trade Association, set up five years earlier in 1968, but substantially widened the remit of regional cooperation to embrace three goals ranging across the whole of the political and economic life of the region. The first was the furtherance of the existing level of economic integration by the establishment of a common market; the second was the expansion of functional cooperation in such fields as health, education, transport and meteorology; and the third, entirely new in the Caribbean, was the coordination of foreign policy amongst the fully independent states of the Community.[1] By the standards of comparative Third World regional integration, CARICOM was therefore quite an ambitious venture.

The key to the successful launch of CARICOM was that it eschewed any commitment to the political integration of the Commonwealth Caribbean and thus contained no threat to the notional sovereignty of the independent nation-state.[2] The Community Treaty was quite deliberately designed to avoid any mention, any hint even, of supra-nationality. CARICOM has been controlled over the years by a series of conferences and councils, made up of territorial politicians, and has only been serviced by its Secretariat.[3] With the exception of a few relatively unimportant items, decisions have had to be agreed unanimously by representatives of all member states of the Community and then legitimated by each state in accordance with its own constitutional procedures. In short, the Caribbean Community was designed and has been run by men and women who remain, as Stanley Hoffmann once put it, in 'the mental universe of traditional inter-state relations'[4] where the concept of national interest still reigns supreme. Indeed, strictly speaking, CARICOM is not an integration movement at all, if the term integration is considered to be a process in which countries have to be prepared to accept that the greater regional good must predominate over national concerns even to the point when, on occasion, their national interests are damaged. For good or ill, this has never been the case with CARICOM. It has simply not been concerned with integration in that sense; it is a structure created by national governments to make nationalist policies more effective by pursuing them within a regional framework.

From a theoretical point of view what best describes the way in which the values and beliefs of Commonwealth Caribbean governments have been translated into practice in respect of CARICOM is the concept of regionalisation. This has previously been defined as a 'method of international cooperation which enables the advantages of decision-making at a regional level to be reconciled with the preservation of the institution of the nation-state'.[5] What has been created in the Caribbean is a regionalised economy and polity, exemplified by the existence of a coherent and systemised web of relationships between the various national units. The term regionalisation is designed therefore to catch the essence of an international political structure which cannot be said to have secured the economic and political integration of the region but in which the constituent states clearly no longer make policy solely as national units. What we have on our hands, therefore, is neither nationalism nor regionalism but a hybrid creature consisting of elements of both.

Regionalisation is not, however, a process by which a neat halfway position has been reached between nationalism and regionalism; it is much more an artefact of the nation-state than the genuinely regionalist community. Of the two perspectives, the nationalist one has undoubtedly been uppermost, the regional connection being conceived primarily as a support that is brought into play when nationalist politics come under threat. This is the vital point, for it draws attention to both the strength and the weakness of CARICOM as a regional organisation. Its strength is that regional integration in the Commonwealth Caribbean has not been aimed at the replacement of economic and political action at the national level – which would have been extremely difficult given the determination of the region's politicians in the immediate post-independence era to be seen at least to possess the right to make policy – but rather at its reinforcement, which is something the politicians understood and were instinctively prepared to support. Its weakness, however, is that the step back from the politics of regionalisation to traditional inter-state nationalist politics is only a small one, and relatively easy to take.

The interests of the member states

The member states of CARICOM have always shared more commonalities of interest than differences. It is worth recalling that even though they were administered separately by Britain for most of their long colonial history, they have been tightly bound together by inheritance of the same broad historical legacies. Most importantly, they are all English-speaking. They also all have administrative, legal and political systems which owe a good deal to British provenance. The Westminster-Whitehall system is still widely respected, honoured as much by the discomfort experienced when it is occasionally breached as by the regularity with which it is practised.[6] As a consequence, governments have been defeated in elections and subsequently relinquished power in all of the region's states, including now even Guyana. Furthermore, the CARICOM countries share a wider culture of music, art and popular life-style which goes some way towards creating a genuine community of West Indians. Indeed, the notion of a West Indian nation has surfaced several times in the course of the evolution of Caribbean integration. As the former Secretary-General of CARICOM, William Demas, often argued, 'intuitively, one feels that the peoples of the English-speaking Caribbean are one people, be they from the North-Western part of the Caribbean, the Eastern Caribbean Islands, or from Guyana; be they of Indian or African origin; be they of white or Chinese extraction.'[7] The problem has long been that, politically, 'West Indianism' has never punched its psychological weight.

Beyond these broader questions of identity, it is undeniable that CARICOM member states also share many common predicaments and problems. As we have seen, several derive from the fact that, viewed globally, all are small states whether measured by land area or population. Considerations of size have thus consistently conditioned the psychology and the practice of political action in the region in the post-independence era. They are also islands, either literally or, as with Belize and Guyana, in enclave form ('islanded by jungle'), which is sometimes said to have created a distinctively insular perspective towards each other and the rest of the world.[8] Many other common problems reflect similar economic endowments (sun, sand, sea) and similar economic histories (sugar and slavery). They also, most importantly, share the opportunities and difficulties caused by the location of the US in what one might designate, to reverse the common analogy, the 'front-yard' of the Caribbean. The US has long regarded itself as the unquestioned leader of all the countries of the Western hemisphere and has rarely hesitated to intervene, militarily and by other means, in the politics of Caribbean and Central American states in order to secure outcomes favourable to its interests.[9] The Commonwealth Caribbean is thus not alone in having to grapple with this relationship: it is rather that the sheer starkness of the disparity between the very small size of its constituent states and the scale and range of the US presence in regional affairs makes for a greater temptation on the part of some CARICOM members to pursue bilateral, as opposed to regional, solutions to the problem. This has been one of the observable differences of perceived interest between CARICOM states over the years.

Apart from this, the other major intra-CARICOM divisions of interest have related to levels of development and matters of ideology. The first highlights the existence of an important distinction conventionally drawn within CARICOM between the four so-called More Developed Countries (Jamaica, Trinidad and Tobago, Barbados and Guyana) and the remaining eight Less Developed Countries. Notwithstanding the fact that all were, and indeed still are, developing states by proper identification, the terms 'MDC' and 'LDC' had become part of the language of Caribbean integration as early as the CARIFTA era. Relatively speaking, the division was meaningful. According to figures for 1970, the MDCs had a combined population of 4 million out of a total regional population of 4.6 million and a combined Gross Domestic Product of EC$4,800 million out of a regional total of EC$5,100 million. In other words, the former group accounted for 87 per cent of the population of the Commonwealth Caribbean and were responsible for 93 per cent of total production.[10] The initial negotiation of CARICOM was consistently dogged by this question and was only brought to a conclusion by the incorporation within the Treaty of Chaguaramas of a 'Special Regime for the LDCs'.[11] Over the course of the Community's existence the MDC/LDC dichotomy has changed character somewhat, with Trinidad and Tobago in effect becoming a 'super MDC' during the oil boom years after 1973, Jamaica collapsing into recession, Guyana into dislocation and some of the Eastern Caribbean LDCs surviving the 1980s in better economic shape than the MDCs. Nevertheless, the fundamental problem of disparate levels of development, even with a generally underdeveloped region, remains and has been at the root of many of the negotiating difficulties into which CARICOM has run.

The second issue draws attention to the difficulties posed for regional cooperation by what came to be known in the Caribbean as 'ideological pluralism'. CARIFTA prospered for as long as the development strategy which it had been created to sustain held favour with the region's governments. As we saw earlier, this sought to base economic development on import substitution and relied upon devising a range of investment incentives designed to encourage metropolitan industrialists, possessing technical skills and capital, actually to locate their plants in the region.[12] However, the international economic crisis which began in the very year in which CARICOM was established set in train a search in many regional states for some better means to development. In Guyana, Jamaica and Grenada this was accompanied by the proclamation of different forms of socialism which had the effect of openly shattering the ideological consensus hitherto prevailing in the Commonwealth Caribbean. These developments also served to draw the region into the front line of the Cold War and exposed CARICOM to all of the measures subsequently taken by the US to regain control of the 'sea of splashing dominoes' on its southern border. Many of the most bitter conflicts to have been experienced within CARICOM were caused by the ramifications of these ideological divisions.

Regional negotiations

The full history of CARICOM in fact begins in 1962 when the West Indies Federation, Britain's final and despairing attempt to graduate its Caribbean territories into the world of independent statehood as a single group, fell apart in acrimony and bickering. The process of rebuilding regional integration around economic issues started almost immediately and can be traced directly to the creation of CARICOM itself. This next section, which examines the political process of regional cooperation in the Commonwealth Caribbean since 1962, divides the period for purposes of analysis into six phases, characterised in turn by creation, stagnation, conflict, ritual, re-examination and lately widening.

Creation

The formal dissolution of the Federation in June 1962 undoubtedly marked the end of an important phase in the history of Caribbean integration, but it did not fully bring the curtain down on the play, as many feared it would. Both Jamaica and Trinidad became independent immediately, Guyana and Barbados following in 1966. Even the small Leeward and Windward Islands were granted Associated Status in 1967, an arrangement which conceded full internal self-government but kept responsibility for defence and foreign affairs in the hands of the British government. In other words, the region began for the first time to feel the cold draught of self-government. The various governments were concerned about the region's lack of economic development – as opposed to growth, which was in any case starting to come up against the limitations of small market size. They were anxious too about the future prospects of their vital exports of primary products in the light of Britain's application to join the European Economic Community (EEC) and its possible abandonment of the policy of Commonwealth preference; and they were alarmed by the way that opportunities for migration to Britain, the US and Canada were being eroded. In these circumstances, 'unity in adversity' seemed to most Commonwealth Caribbean governments to be a slogan worth supporting.

It was thus primarily as a means of economic salvation that the case for regional integration was reconsidered. The first move was made by the governments of Barbados and Guyana when they announced in July 1965 that a free trade area would be established between their territories not later than January 1966. It was stated that participation in the proleptically named 'Caribbean Free Trade Association' would be welcomed and that the ultimate objective was the creation of a viable economic community and common market for all Commonwealth Caribbean territories which desired them.[13] Reactions were mixed, and the pace of advance was slower than anticipated, but eventually it was agreed that a regional conference of officials would meet in Guyana in August 1967 with a view to preparing a plan for the implementation of regional economic integration to be put before a summit meeting of heads of government in Barbados two months later. This was the fourth in a periodic series of intergovernmental conferences that had been taking place since the middle of 1963, and was the first to be attended by the leaders of all the Commonwealth Caribbean territories. It was, in consequence, the largest and most prestigious gathering of West Indian leaders since the days of the Federation and, to their credit, the leaders seized the opportunity. A deal was clinched – the adoption of the CARIFTA agreement by the region as a whole, thereby providing the prospect of trading benefits for the MDCs; the establishment of a secretariat to preside over the agreement and to be located in Guyana, the country which had perhaps done most to drive the process forward; and concessions on free trade and industrial allocation, as well as the promise of the simultaneous creation of a regional bank to channel development finance in their direction, for the LDCs.

It quickly emerged, however, that the deal had not fully incorporated the perspective and interests of Jamaica. Jamaica's relationship with the Eastern Caribbean has been distant and aloof throughout its history. Jamaicans have been widely viewed by other West Indians as aggressive and forceful, whilst the prevailing Jamaican image of the 'small' islands of the Eastern Caribbean was of poverty, parochialism and a desire to exploit Jamaica's perceived greater prosperity. The experience of the Federation had served only to reinforce these stereo-typed attitudes and widen the psychological gulf between the two ends of the Commonwealth Caribbean. In the intervening years such dis-respectful feelings had been cloaked by the formal politeness of inter-governmental diplomacy, but they had never been extinguished, least of all within the ranks of the Jamaica Labour Party, the party that had opposed Jamaica's membership of the Federation and had formed the government since 1962. Under the JLP, Jamaica played its part in the widening embrace of regional economic integration in the mid-1960s, and it was obviously one of the countries with the most to gain from freer trade. Yet it had done so with obvious reluctance, preferring always to talk of regional economic cooperation, rather than integra-tion, the term always used by the other countries.[14] The Jamaican gov-ernment thus needed a way to demonstrate a measure of independence. It did so by angrily opposing the location of the Caribbean Development Bank (CDB) in St Vincent, a move which had been designed to symbolise its status as a pro-LDC instrument, and demand-ing that it be placed in Kingston. The compromise decision in favour of Barbados scarcely assuaged the Jamaican government, but it did not go so far as to renege on its decision to join CARIFTA.

During the first few years of its existence, CARIFTA lived con-stantly in the same politically charged atmosphere that had surrounded its birth. Fragility was always its most striking characteristic, and disintegration an ever-present possibility. Jamaica's ungracious accession to the agreement did little to bridge the gap separating it from the rest of the region, whilst the LDCs clearly felt that Jamaica was being allowed to dictate the pace and direction of the integration movement in a way detrimental to their particular interests. In the end, what contributed most to the preservation of the movement was the fact that the MDCs began to garner some of the trading benefits promised by the advent of regional free trade. While the heads of gov-ernment were engaging in crisis diplomacy about the CDB, CARIFTA itself was working quite efficiently. This is not to say that much else had been done to advance the integration process in the ways that had been planned. As part of the CARIFTA agreement, an annex had been signed envisaging various other steps such as the erection of a common external tariff, the harmonisation of fiscal incentives to indus-try and the initiation of joint industrial development projects in the area. In the jargon adopted, this was to constitute the 'deepening' of the movement. Guyana, Trinidad and Barbados were broadly in favour of embarking on this road, albeit perceiving the need to do so with differing degrees of urgency. The countries in doubt were the LDCs, which already felt excluded from the benefits of integration, and once again Jamaica, which insisted that the 'deepening' agenda went beyond its commitment to economic cooperation and favoured 'widening' the scope of the free trade area to embrace the non-English-speaking Caribbean.[15]

This immobilisation would probably not of itself have led to the demise of the regional integration movement, as some feared. What made disintegration a very real danger indeed was the simultaneous failure of the Commonwealth Caribbean governments to reach agreement on a common policy towards the European Economic Community. Despite the fact that the CARIFTA countries had agreed to seek a single form of relationship with the EEC as soon as Britain's intention to reapply for membership became apparent in 1970, the decision facing the region was an extremely awkward one because of the two stages of constitutional development represented within CARIFTA – independence and Associated Statehood. The LDCs, as Associated States of Britain, were automatically eligible for association with the EEC under Part IV of the Treaty of Rome; the MDCs, by contrast, had to choose between three different models of association.[16] This opened up the possibility that CARIFTA would in due course be undermined as a regional trading system by the differences between its members' trading relations with the EEC. In the context of the other difficulties into which the regional integration process had run, the temptation for individual Commonwealth Caribbean states, especially Jamaica and the LDCs once again, to seek to make separate bilateral deals with Europe was considerable.

In the event, disintegration was averted. The necessary reinvigoration of the integration movement came just in time, and from the most unlikely source. Although the reasons for the JLP's loss of office in Jamaica in the 1972 election had little to do with regional integration, the election of a People's National Party government under Michael Manley significantly altered the environment in which CARIFTA had to survive. Historically, the PNP's record on the question of Caribbean integration was very different from that of the JLP. It was the party which had supported the West Indies Federation and had only opposed entry into CARIFTA in 1968 on the grounds that it was a weak form of integration – 'neither fish nor fowl nor red herring', as its spokesman put it at the time.[17] On coming to power, Manley chose openly and enthusiastically to embrace the cause of regional economic development. The technocrats in the Secretariat in Guyana had long been trying to secure Jamaica's agreement to the 'deepening' programme and had become increasingly frustrated at their inability to do so. They now quickly organised the preparation of a booklet designed to give publicity to the various issues confronting the regional movement.

This booklet, which was published in July 1972, was called *From CARIFTA to Caribbean Community* and set out the further steps which the Secretariat thought were needed to achieve what it referred to as 'meaningful economic integration'.[18] The programme embraced most of the issues which the regional governments had been deliberating since 1967: a common external tariff and protection policy; the harmonisation of fiscal incentives; a common policy on foreign investment; rationalisation of regional agriculture; the development of a regional industrial policy; cooperation in tourism and in fiscal and monetary affairs; agreement on external commercial policy, especially towards the EEC; the adoption of further measures to enable the LDCs to benefit from economic integration; and the extension of functional cooperation into new areas. However, it also contained some items which were yet to be discussed, like the coordination of foreign policy.[19] The significant factor was that for the first time all these diverse ideas and proposals were brought together and conceived as a package. For, as the Secretariat admitted, what was really being proposed was more than just an injection of new life into CARIFTA; it was that the time had come

> to take the decisions necessary to convert CARIFTA into a Caribbean Common Market. At the same time, as common services and areas of functional cooperation generally are extended, a certain amount of tidying up is required. These two processes ... point to the need to give a formal juridical basis to the entire complex of regional cooperative arrangements, including the Heads of Government Conference, which is the apex of the entire regional movement.[20]

Thus was born the idea of CARICOM – the Caribbean Community and Common Market.

The actual process of negotiation of the new Community was long and difficult, preoccupying two summit meetings in October 1972 and April 1973. The LDCs – led by Montserrat, the smallest of them – battled hard for concessions in their favour, but, as before, were torn between an unwillingness to continue as makeweights in the integration process and a lack of confidence in their ability to 'go it alone', the latter in the end proving the stronger. Nevertheless, they won agreement to the establishment of a Caribbean Investment Corporation charged with the responsibility of providing equity capital for industrialisation projects in the smaller islands. The real political thrust behind the creation of CARICOM was, however, the determination of the four MDCs (Jamaica not only on board but in the driving seat) to develop regional cooperation. As one regional analyst noted at the time, 'the MDCs are going to advance their interests and so advance the cooperation or integration movement in so far as it protects themselves, and whether or not the Less Developed Countries are interested in coming along'.[21] Whereas in the days of the Federation it was the smaller islands of the region which were keenest on some form of regional integration and, by and large, the larger territories which were more cautious, the position was reversed with the advent of CARIFTA and firmly confirmed in that reversal with the negotiation of CARICOM. In the final analysis, all the LDCs signed the Treaty of Chaguaramas and joined CARICOM. 'Who don't sign, don't sign,' declared Dr Williams, the Trinidad Prime Minister, 'but I want to know where they are going to go'.[22]

Stagnation

Yet almost as soon as the Treaty was signed, CARICOM ran into problems. Its inauguration coincided with the moment – late 1973 to early 1974 – when the world economy entered into a long period of severe crisis. As the only oil-exporting country in the Commonwealth Caribbean, Trinidad was partly insulated from the problem and of course benefited to the extent that substantial sums of money accrued to its exchequer as a result of the new high price of oil. However, the other territories all suffered serious budgetary and balance of payments deficits and experienced significant increases in the cost of living, to which they responded with a variety of stern measures, including higher levels of taxation, the intensification of import restrictions and exchange controls and the imposition of subsidies on vital consumer goods. Barbados was temporarily helped by the high price of sugar on the world market in 1974, and Jamaica and Guyana were able to increase the revenue yield from their bauxite and alumina industries by imposing extra levies and taking into public ownership recalcitrant foreign companies. But in all these cases only palliatives were provided. Before long, Jamaica and Guyana turned to the IMF and were forced to undertake a series of devaluations, public expenditure cuts and generally restrictive measures in vain attempts to regenerate their economies. It was, in short, an unpropitious time for the launching of a renewed programme of regional economic integration, for the effects of these difficult economic circumstances unavoidably took their toll of CARICOM's prospects. The then Secretary-General of the Community, Dr Kurleigh King, commented: 'The ink was hardly dry on the signatures of the Treaty when the full force of the international economic crisis struck the bottom out of everything we had hoped to accomplish.'[23]

The first breach in the unity achieved when the Community was established came in 1975. In a speech in April that year, Dr Williams complained that the recent advances in Caribbean integration were being prejudiced by the way in which many of the member states of CARICOM were making bilateral economic arrangements on supplicant terms with wealthy Latin American countries.[24] He was particularly concerned by the growing economic penetration of the region by Venezuelan 'petro-dollars', and in a subsequent speech he contemptuously denounced the visits of several of his regional colleagues to Venezuela as 'pilgrimages to Caracas'.[25] What angered Williams most in this connection was the economic cooperation agreement signed with Jamaica in mid-1975, whereby Jamaica agreed to supply Venezuela with considerable quantities of bauxite and alumina for a planned new aluminium smelter, and Venezuela agreed to contribute part of the cost of a new alumina processing plant to be built in Jamaica. In his view, it was 'simply not possible' to regard this treaty 'as anything but a calculated attack'[26] upon the proposal, announced a year earlier, to build two CARICOM aluminium smelters to be owned jointly by the governments of Trinidad, Jamaica and Guyana. That project had been widely regarded as a major step forward in regional integration since it was the first time that an attempt had been made within CARICOM to establish a joint production programme between member states. However, as a consequence of the row over Venezuela, the scheme was cancelled and Williams informed a special convention of his party: 'One can only take so much, and I have had enough. To smelt or not to smelt, no big thing'.[27] Manley responded by insisting that the CARICOM smelter had not been deprived of its viability by Jamaica's other deals, and he succeeded in isolating Williams within the region on this issue.

Nevertheless, the row had grave implications for the coordination of foreign policy within the Commonwealth Caribbean. By this criterion, it was unquestionably a major lapse – for two reasons. First, it showed that nearly all the countries of the region (with the exception of Trinidad) were seeking bilateral deals with Venezuela, instead of trying to formulate a common regional front on the matter. The LDCs were keen to get assistance from Caracas and several pushed themselves forward. Jamaica, however, was particularly culpable because the nature of its particular deal with Venezuela – concerned, as it was, with the bauxite-alumina industry – clearly affected CARICOM policy in the same sphere. (One can be absolutely sure from the vehemence of Williams's reaction that Manley had not consulted the Trinidad government before agreeing to the deal.) Mention should also be made of the fact that one of the other equity contributors to the new Jamaican alumina plant was to be the Mexican government, which agreed to put up no less than 29 per cent of the cost in return for Jamaica contributing 29 per cent of the equity of a new aluminium smelter to be built in Mexico. This deal did not arouse Williams's anger in the same way that the Venezuelan agreement had done, but it irritated the technocrats in the Secretariat, since the Caribbean Community states, as a group, had signed a trade and cooperation agreement with the Mexican government in July 1974. It illustrated, again, the tendency to bilateralism in Jamaican foreign policy and highlighted the diverse interests that were beginning to appear in the external trade policies of the various Community states in direct contravention of the commitment they had given in the CARICOM Treaty to seek the coordination of policy in such matters.[28]

Second, the row highlighted the existence at the heart of CARICOM of two different and conflicting concepts of the countries that comprise the Caribbean – what might be termed the 'Williams Latin American doctrine' and the 'Manley Latin American doctrine'. The main ingredients of the Williams doctrine were a deep suspicion of the motives of certain Latin American states in relation to the Commonwealth Caribbean and the consequent avoidance of relations with them. It was founded upon a definition of the Caribbean which firmly excluded the Central and Latin American states except, of course, for what had once been the three Guianas. Williams was accordingly contemptuous of a Venezuelan plan to call a conference of 'the Caribbean basin' – 'whatever that may be', as he put it[29] – and saw it as his mission to preserve 'the Caribbean personality' and not allow it to be lost in a wider Latin American identity. In May 1975, he succeeded in getting the United Nations Economic Commission for Latin America to create within its structure a Caribbean Development and Co-operation Committee, designed to perform just that function. By contrast, the hallmarks of the 'Manley Latin American doctrine' were friendship, cooperation and closer ties with Latin American states in the battle to create a 'new international economic order' in favour of developing countries. It, in turn, was obviously based upon a strong sense of the Caribbean's geopolitical affinity with Latin America. Faced with this clash, the other states of the region, especially the LDCs, tried to remain agnostic. They were manifestly prepared to look upon Venezuela as a friend for as long as resources were being proffered in their direction; on the other hand, they had all had much longer than Jamaica to become attuned to the idea of West Indian unity and remained emotionally more committed to that goal. In this respect, at least, the greater global range of the foreign policy pursued by Michael Manley in Jamaica worked against the narrower interests of Caribbean regional integration.

After the angry exchanges of mid-1975, tension within the integration movement lessened for a time, but was renewed in 1977 when Guyana and Jamaica came under attack for restricting their imports, even from CARICOM partners, as a means of alleviating their financial situation. This produced a real crisis in the Community, to the point where fears were expressed about the future of the whole integration movement. Notwithstanding the fact that the Treaty permitted the imposition of quantitative restrictions on regional goods in the face of serious balance of payments difficulties, the plight of Jamaica and Guyana aroused little sympathy and some form of retaliation seemed likely. Trinidad, in fact, announced its intention of instituting its own system of quantitative controls on the import of regional goods. Some twenty-three products were identified as requiring protection.[30] In the event no action was taken, and the immediate crisis passed when both the Jamaican and Guyanese governments signalled their intention to restore the value of their imports from the rest of the region to at least 1975 levels as soon as possible.

Nevertheless, by exposing the fragility of the free trade regime, which was as much the mainstay of CARICOM in its early days as it had been of CARIFTA, the quarrel constituted another setback in the progress of regional integration and clouded the atmosphere within the Community. For part of 1978, the Secretariat found it hard to persuade the governments even to convene CARICOM meetings. The morale of the staff began to suffer, especially since the post of Secretary-General was left vacant for fifteen months during 1977 and 1978. All these factors meant that CARICOM was not developing into the deeper form of integration to which the Treaty aspired. An attempt to reach agreement on the terms on which foreign investment could enter the region failed; virtually no regional industrial programming had been achieved; and although a Regional Food Corporation was set up in an effort to organise joint schemes of agricultural production, it took a long time to become operational.[31] Even the Community's long-standing attempt to redesign the so-called 'origin rules', which determined the products which were eligible for free trade treatment, had not been brought to completion by the end of 1979.

In short, CARICOM survived the trauma of the international economic crisis of the 1970s, but at the cost of stagnation. However, the crisis did more than just temporarily disrupt the movement. In retrospect, it can be seen to have changed the nature of the circumstances in which intra-regional negotiations had to be pursued in several crucial ways. First, the approximate balance of power which had previously existed between the CARICOM MDCs was fundamentally changed. An enormous gap opened up between Trinidad, which became unequivocally the dominant economy and pivotal state within the region, and Jamaica and Guyana, which were both experiencing severe economic and political difficulties. Second, the high degree of ideological consensus in the region was shattered by Guyana's adoption of 'cooperative socialism' in 1970, Jamaica's proclamation of 'democratic socialism' in 1974 and the emergence of the revolutionary government in Grenada in 1979. The extent of the left–right split in the area, although often exaggerated by commentators, was none the less another source of real problems within CARICOM, putting paid in particular to the proposal to coordinate a regional position on inward foreign investment. Third, the rapport between the heads of government of Commonwealth Caribbean countries which had contributed so much to the transformation of CARIFTA into CARICOM disintegrated as personal relations between Williams, Manley and others cooled. Finally, there was the fact that the Caribbean was increasingly being opened up to international competition in the late 1970s as several major powers began to vie for influence in the region's affairs. This had dangerous implications for regional unity, since it contained the possibility that the region might again become, as it had been historically, a battleground for the rivalries of outside powers.

Conflict

Yet, at the time, the full impact of these changes in the political environment was not appreciated, even though it was recognised that an impasse had been reached in CARICOM affairs. With this in mind the CARICOM Council decided in March 1980 to appoint a prestigious team of regional experts, chaired by William Demas, the first CARICOM Secretary-General, to 'review the functioning of Caribbean integration' and to prepare a strategy for 'its improvement in the decade of the 1980s'.[32] The determination to inaugurate a new phase in the history of regional integration in the Commonwealth Caribbean was thus quite explicit. The group reported in January 1981 and accepted that CARICOM had lately suffered a serious loss of faith and hope amongst the regional public and the international community. Its overall assessment of the movement's record up to 1980 was blunt and is worth quoting at length.

An analysis of the performance of CARICOM in its three areas of activity shows that, although modest gains were registered in many aspects of functional cooperation and to a lesser extent with respect to intra-regional trade, inadequate progress was made in the areas of production integration and the coordination of foreign policies. Indeed, the delays encountered in moving ahead with programmes and projects for coordinated and joint efforts in production constitute the single most important factor that gives credence to some of the disappointments that have been expressed. The misunderstandings ... that also characterised certain initiatives taken by some member countries in the field of external economic relations also gave a poor public image to the Community. The fact, however, that the institutional framework of the Community remains intact, that an intergovernmental dialogue was and is being sustained and that intra-regional trade and functional cooperation continue to show resilience and in some cases growth, indicate that the foundations of the movement are still intact.[33]

Accordingly, the group did not set out new recommendations, but restated the agenda that had been before CARICOM since 1973.

In proceeding in this way, the group of experts tried in effect to sidestep the issue of the new 'ideological pluralism' of Commonwealth Caribbean politics in the 1970s. The key question had been posed by the relatively conservative government of Trinidad. In a 1979 White Paper on the future of the Caribbean Community, it had asked: 'Can mutually acceptable strategies be created to project and satisfy the conflicting demands of democratic socialism, co-operative socialism and the other numerous paths to political, economic and social development that individual member countries of CARICOM have chosen?'[34] The official answer of the Community was that ideological pluralism was not, or at least should not be, a barrier to the operation of the integration movement, a position reiterated by the group of experts in their report. Nevertheless, the experts did concede somewhat tamely that ideological pluralism 'does not mean that you can care less about CARICOM', but rather that 'you must care more'.[35] The difficulty the region faced in moving to consider the various recommendations of the experts was that their publication coincided with the accession to the US presidency of Ronald Reagan, determined *inter alia* to 'win back' the Commonwealth Caribbean for the West at the expense of whatever ideological confrontation was necessary.

The two issues came together in the politics surrounding the Caribbean Basin Initiative, the programme of special assistance for the whole Caribbean and Central American region proposed by the US in 1981. Gathering just beforehand for their first meeting since the publication of the experts' report, CARICOM's foreign ministers tried to fire a shot across Reagan's bows by officially noting their concern at the economic pressure being exerted by the US against the revolutionary government in Grenada. They were particularly irritated by US attempts to stipulate that a grant to the CDB to help the LDCs should not be disbursed to that island. The Bank's directors had voted unanimously to reject this grant on the grounds that it would contravene that aspect of the Bank's charter which prohibited it from interfering in the political affairs of any member country. Whatever they felt about the merits of Grenada's revolution, and many were very critical, the region's governments were not prepared to see one of their number isolated by an external power. As the foreign ministers put it in their communiqué, they condemned any effort 'to subvert Caribbean regional institutions built up over long years of struggle'.[36]

With the need to defend their own interests in the forefront of their minds, the ministers soon met again to formulate a set of common principles as the basis for negotiation with the US over the CBI. They insisted that the programme be open to all territories in the region, that it should respect the sovereignty and integrity of states, reflect national priorities for development and, finally, 'be directed towards strengthening ongoing regional integration and cooperation'.[37] Yet, when the details of the CBI were unveiled by Reagan in a speech to the Organisation of American States in St Lucia in February 1982, it was immediately apparent that these points had not been met. As many had feared from the outset, the CBI divided the Commonwealth Caribbean, rather than uniting it. Following Reagan's flattering reference in his speech to Jamaica as a country which, since the defeat of the Manley government in October 1980, was 'making freedom work',[38] the country's new leader, Edward Seaga, was quick to applaud the proposals. The plan, he said, was 'bold, historic and far-reaching in concept'.[39] He also indicated that he would not object to revolutionary Grenada's exclusion, since other countries would be taking care of its needs. In the rest of the region, however, the reaction varied from disappointment to bitter condemnation.

Criticism came from a variety of angles. One strand of opinion expressed concern at the emphasis placed on investment and trade, rather than on direct development aid capable of building up the region's inadequate infrastructure. Another viewpoint, held especially strongly amongst the Eastern Caribbean LDCs, felt that Jamaica had been excessively favoured in the proposed allocation of supplemental assistance under the CBI. There was also, as expected, considerable disquiet over the Reagan administration's preoccupation with the communist threat and its insistence on excluding Grenada and Nicaragua, as well as Cuba, as possible beneficiaries of the CBI. With these different positions being taken up, all CARICOM could do as a body was equivocate. The divisions could be seen clearly in the March 1982 statement of the Standing Committee of Foreign Ministers. It carefully observed that, 'while the US proposal did not adequately address all of the issues or fulfil expectations for a comprehensive plan for the development of the economies of Caribbean states, it none the less would make a positive contribution'.[40] The region's former unity could be salvaged only with respect to the governments' collective disappointment that 'there were no specific elements of supporting their own intergovernmental institutions such as CARICOM and the Caribbean Development Bank'[41] and their complaints about the information-sharing proposal which a recipient country under the CBI was required to enter into as part of a bilateral executive agreement with the US. The principle that participation in the CBI should be open to all CARICOM countries was also reaffirmed, although everyone knew that Seaga's Jamaica was not going to forgo the benefits of the programme for this cause. The whole saga was a vivid illustration of what was likely to happen when external definitions and perceptions interfered with regional aspirations. On the most important test of foreign policy coordination yet faced by CARICOM, its ranks had been split and the integration movement further weakened.

That was not all. The region's growing involvement in Cold War politics was also very nearly the cause of CARICOM's complete disintegration, with Grenada once more the main issue at stake. The heads of government conference held in Ocho Rios in Jamaica in November 1982 – which, as the first such meeting to have been held in seven years, was conceived as a 'relaunch' of Caribbean integration – was dominated by a deliberate, premeditated attempt to expel Grenada from the organisation on the grounds that its political system was no longer a parliamentary democracy. Seaga was at the centre of the attempt and, even though it did not meet with general support, he and his government remained bitterly opposed to the whole revolutionary experiment being conducted in Grenada. When the Grenadian government collapsed in bloody disarray in October 1983 and an invasion was mounted, he was quick to involve Jamaica and subsequently to reap his electoral reward. From his point of view, and that of the US, the prize was a victory in the battle against communism. For CARICOM, by contrast, the damage was enormous. It was not just that the region disagreed about what to do in Grenada once the internal coup had taken place, but that the 'invading states' (notably Jamaica and Barbados) deliberately connived to conceal their intentions from their remaining CARICOM partners – Trinidad, Guyana and Belize. As accounts of the events show, several participants in the crisis meeting of CARICOM heads of government which took place in Port of Spain during the weekend after the Grenadian implosion already knew of, and had contributed to, the decision to invade.[42] No mention was made of such a commitment during the CARICOM discussion, which focused exclusively upon the sanctions that could be brought to bear on the new military regime in Grenada.

In these circumstances, the other leaders – especially George Chambers, the Prime Minister of Trinidad, and Forbes Burnham, then President of Guyana – understandably felt that they had been made to look foolish. Bitter recrimination followed. In such an atmosphere it is hardly surprising that many commentators should have wondered whether CARICOM would finally fall apart. The critical factor was whether anyone would actually work to destroy it. Other Commonwealth Caribbean leaders had known for some time that Seaga, for one, wanted to include in CARICOM other generally pro-US countries in the wider Caribbean region, such as Haiti and the Dominican Republic. In the few weeks after the invasion of Grenada, a number of them came increasingly to suspect that his real aim was the replacement of CARICOM with a looser organisation embracing non-Commonwealth Caribbean countries and excluding any existing member state that was not willing to accept US leadership in regional affairs. He fuelled these fears by speaking of the possible creation of a CARICOM Mark II,[43] arousing the suspicion in Trinidad and Guyana that he was making a threat directed mainly at them. Yet, in the end, nothing more was heard of this idea and it is doubtful whether it would actually have been to Seaga's advantage to seek to break up CARICOM. The region was left in no doubt that during the 1980s CARICOM matters were a much lower priority in Kingston than the question of Jamaica's dealings with Washington.

These open political conflicts within CARICOM were compounded by the regional consequences of the renewed international economic difficulties caused by the further big rise in the price of oil in 1979. Inflation was attacked in the major industrial economies by the new monetarism, which had the effect of plunging the bulk of the rest of the world, including the Commonwealth Caribbean, into severe recession. Distracted by ideological divisions, CARICOM failed to develop a regional response. In fact, as was noted by Vaughan Lewis, the Director-General of the Organisation of Eastern Caribbean States, the subregional unit of the Eastern Caribbean LDCs formed in 1981, 'when the inevitable unilateral initiatives to treat the ills of the economies were made, under the guise of "structural adjustment" these policy initiatives had the effect . . . of beggar-my-neighbour policies'.[44] The most immediate and damaging result was the collapse of the CARICOM Multilateral Clearing Facility (CMCF), the mechanism which had been designed to facilitate the financing of intra-regional trade. When Guyana, whose economy had reached desperate straits, was unable to pay debts to the CMCF of US$70 million, the whole facility was pushed beyond its credit limit and was rendered effectively defunct. In truth, Lester Bird, the Deputy Prime Minister of Antigua, was not being unduly harsh when, in January 1984, he warned that, 'by our own actions, we have aided the process of external manipulation ... we have ignored resolutions, laboriously devised and painstakingly negotiated, we have sought relationships in contravention of the Treaty establishing the Community and we have fallen prey to the lure of external agencies even at the expense of our own solidarity'.[45]

Ritual

CARICOM reacted to the interlocking economic and political conflicts of the region in the early 1980s by retreating into ritual. Meetings of ministers and technocrats continued automatically in the period after the invasion of Grenada – Bird was himself addressing a CARICOM council – and, perhaps more remarkably, heads of government conferences took place on schedule each July, in 1984 in the Bahamas, in 1985 in Barbados, in 1986 in Guyana, in 1987 in St Lucia and in 1988 in Antigua. They were not disrupted by continuing personal clashes between the leaders and they managed each year to come up with a variety of declarations and commitments which promised to advance the cause of regional integration. They did not, however, find a way of overcoming the movement's fundamental problems and of thus reviving the whole CARICOM process.

The most persistent issue facing the summits was the decline in intra-regional trade, from US$577 million in 1981 to US$432.5 million in 1984. Whilst they endorsed structural adjustment as 'a conscious shift to a new development path to accelerate development'[46] in Nassau in 1984, the heads of government also agreed upon a series of measures designed both to restore the region's free trade regime and harmonise external tariffs. Yet in 1985 Trinidad imposed a new import-licensing and foreign-exchange-control system, albeit with concessions for CARICOM manufacturers, and the Barbados meeting was forced to postpone the agreed Nassau deadline for the dismantling of non-tariff trade barriers. The problem was that structural adjustment programmes inevitably restricted foreign exchange allocations for consumer goods, which were the main items in intra-CARICOM trade. The resolution of the Community's internal trading difficulties was thus contingent on the growth of foreign exchange earnings from extra-regional trade – in other words, the achievement of structural adjustment itself.[47] This remained elusive, to say the least, which meant that the postponement of deadlines for the removal of protectionist measures became a regular feature of heads of government meetings. At the same time, and for the same reasons, no more success attached to repeated efforts to revive the CMCF, or make progress with regional industrial programming, or establish an export credit facility.

During this period there were generally fewer divisions within CARICOM on political matters, although a nasty row took place in 1988 over the policy to be adopted towards Haiti during the course of its troubled transition to democracy after the eventual fall of the Duvalier regime. Broadly speaking, this reflected the old ideological divisions of the Grenada crisis. The assertively pro-US governments within CARICOM, mainly Jamaica, Dominica and Antigua, did what they could to give credibility to the elections of January 1988 and subsequently resisted attempts to suspend Haiti's observer status within CARICOM; the governments of Trinidad and Barbados (under changed party leadership since October 1983) condemned the irregularities of the Haitian election and called for the country's suspension. In the event, the communiqué of the 1988 summit did not even mention the subject, despite the fact that it had been extensively discussed, with the new Trinidadian Prime Minister, A. N. R. Robinson, lamenting CARICOM's consequent lack of 'not only political but philosophical underpinnings'[48] and Seaga countering that the organisation had admitted Haiti as an observer during the Duvalier era and in any case had maintained normal relations with Grenada after the 1979 revolution. The issue of Haiti was not of itself critical to CARICOM's well-being, but it demonstrated the ease with which the region could be divided ideologically on a matter of geopolitical concern to the US.

The argument over Haiti also spilled over into other aspects of the 1988 conference. Seaga strongly opposed Barbadian proposals for the establishment of a CARICOM parliamentary assembly and for the integration of the Community's health, customs, police and judicial services. Erskine Sandiford, the Barbadian Prime Minister, defended the idea of an assembly as a purely deliberative body without legislative functions on the grounds that, at times, CARICOM had come to resemble more a private club than a popular organisation, but conceded that the integration of services was best pursued on a bilateral basis. The latter had been condemned by Seaga as an attempt to re-establish the West Indies Federation by the back door, a worry traditionally close to the heart of Seaga's party, the JLP. Jamaica did, however, indicate some support for a Trinidadian proposal, first made the year before, to set up a Caribbean court of appeal. Decisions were taken to look further at the two ideas, which was significant in that this represented the first consideration of the institutional development of CARICOM beyond the apparatus set up at Chaguaramas in 1973. Both ideas can also be seen in their different ways as attempts to take CARICOM beyond the politics of the Grenada era.

The other main legacy of the Grenada revolution bearing upon CARICOM was the new priority attached to questions of regional security during the 1980s. Yet the point to note here is that CARICOM was not the mechanism through which governments chose to handle this problem. The new threat scenario was first enunciated in a Memorandum of Understanding concluded between Barbados and Trinidad in April 1979; it re-emerged in Article 8 of the OECS Treaty of 1981 which made explicit provision for the establishment of an inter-governmental defence and security committee, the first of its kind in the post-independence Commonwealth Caribbean. Finally, a Memorandum of Understanding was concluded between Antigua, Barbados, Dominica, St Lucia and St Vincent in October 1982 establishing a Regional Security System (RSS) which required the signatories to assist one another in the face of a variety of security threats. Following the Grenada invasion, Barbados had been keen to build up the RSS into a standing regional defence force, headquartered in its territory and substantially funded by the US. From the outset, the US reaction had been unfavourable, in part because of expense. More telling were the objections which soon began to surface in the region, notably in St Vincent, focusing on the consequences of a needless militarisation when there were many other pressing problems to resolve.[49] By the end of 1984 a consensus had been reached in the Eastern Caribbean and with the US that such a force was not required. Instead, there was a return to a focus on lower-level threats to security, such as drug trafficking, smuggling and surveillance of territorial waters, and a lower-level response, namely small para-military forces on each island with a supporting coastguard and a loose-knit RSS. The other states of the Commonwealth Caribbean showed no interest in regional defence arrangements, with the result that CARICOM acquired no status in security matters during the 1980s despite the turbulence of the times.

Re-examination

Aware of the extent to which CARICOM had marked time during the second half of the 1980s and of the accelerating pace of change in the international system as a whole, the region's leaders sought to use their 1989 summit meeting in Grenada to revitalise the integration process. They again included Michael Manley, re-elected to office in February 1989 and pledged once more to involve Jamaica more fully in the activities of the region. A new impetus was certainly evident. For the first time since the early 1970s, the heads set goals for CARICOM in a programmed way, committing themselves to fulfil all of the obligations undertaken in the founding treaty by the time its twentieth anniversary was reached four years hence in July 1993. This involved agreeing upon a new CARICOM industrial programming scheme by October 1989; enacting legislation to give effect to the CARICOM enterprise regime by February 1990; re-establishing the CMCF by December 1990; implementing the common external tariff by January 1991; removing all remaining trade barriers by July 1991; effecting regional systems of air and sea transport by July 1992; and introducing a scheme for intra-regional capital movement in 1993. Beyond these wide-ranging plans, the summit further agreed to set up an assembly of Caribbean parliamentarians and a regional judicial service commission, give further study to a proposal for a regional stock exchange, hold a major regional economic conference in the following year and eliminate the need for CARICOM nationals travelling within the region to carry a passport by the end of 1990. The last point reflected one of the commonest popular complaints made in the region about the general failure of CARICOM to address the problems of day-to-day life for ordinary Caribbean citizens.

The Grand Anse Declaration, which set out all these commitments, also included one other important decision: it announced that an independent West Indian Commission was to be established, chaired by the former Commonwealth Secretary-General Shridath Ramphal and charged with 'advancing the goals of the Treaty of Chaguaramas'.[50] It was to report to the July 1992 heads of government meeting and was to include amongst its members the CARICOM Secretary-General, Roderick Rainford, and the OECS Director-General, Vaughan Lewis, as well as other leading regional figures drawn from business, labour, the church and education. All in all, the Declaration represented a major advance for the region, at least on paper. It derived some inspiration from the fact that, from 1987 onwards, intra-regional trade had begun to grow again, albeit remaining well below its 1981 peak. But, above all, Grand Anse was a worried and slightly desperate response to what the Declaration itself described as 'the challenges and opportunities presented by the changes in the global economy'.[51] Chief amongst these from the Commonwealth Caribbean viewpoint was the approaching creation of a single market within the European Community (EC); this threatened the traditional access enjoyed by the region's agricultural products, especially bananas, to their main overseas market. More broadly, it also seemed to be characteristic of the emergence of new centres of power within the global political economy which appeared as if they might leave CARICOM marginalised.

The issue which the success of the 1989 meeting inevitably brought to the fore was an old CARICOM problem: the implementation at national level of decisions taken at regional meetings. As it happened, a review team had been appointed in early 1989 specifically to examine the administration of CARICOM programmes by the Secretariat and the other institutions of the Community. It had long been privately acknowledged that the work of the Secretariat had been damaged by its location in Guyana and the consequent pressures brought to bear on its staff by the depth of the Guyanese economic and political crisis. Chaired by Professor Gladstone Mills of the University of the West Indies, the review team made extensive criticisms of the administrative efficiency of the whole CARICOM system,[52] only to find consideration of its recommendations postponed by the 1990 heads of government conference to an informal meeting of regional leaders early in 1991. The 1990 Kingston summit did, however, address the general issue at stake when it considered, and accepted, a Trinidadian proposal to appoint a CARICOM Commissioner who could work between the Secretariat and the governments and thus help to remove obstacles to the implementation of regional agreements. This person was originally to have been in post by October 1990, but both this idea and the contents of the Mills report in general were passed to the West Indian Commission for its overall and definitive recommendation.

Other delays in the Grand Anse timetable also occurred. In particular, the long-awaited introduction of the common external tariff ran into difficulties. The January 1991 deadline was achieved only by Jamaica, Guyana and Trinidad and Tobago; the next target date of May 1991 saw Barbados and St Vincent on board; and the next, October 1991, passed with action still required from five countries – Belize, St Kitts-Nevis, Antigua and Barbuda, Montserrat and St Lucia. Moreover, little or no progress was made on revitalising the CMCF, eliminating passports, setting up a Caribbean parliament or removing non-tariff obstacles to trade, all of which were important parts of the programme set out in 1989. The criticism that CARICOM was once more moving too slowly began again to be heard, and was justified. Meeting in July 1990 in the absence of A. N. R. Robinson, who was being held hostage in his own parliament building in Port of Spain by a

Muslim group, a committee was appointed to review existing regional security arrangements at Caribbean Community level and report back urgently before the next summit. This it failed to do.

The 1991 summit did at least receive an interim report from the West Indian Commission, still boldly entitled *Towards a Vision of the Future*.[53] In an attempt to respond in the interim to the implementation difficulties experienced within CARICOM – which the Commission fully acknowledged – individual heads of government agreed to accept responsibility for convening groups to work on five areas of the Commission's immediate recommendations. The subjects and the relevant heads of government were: a common currency (A. N. R. Robinson, Trinidad and Tobago); a Caribbean investment fund (Michael Manley, Jamaica); the free movement of skills (Desmond Hoyte, Guyana); trouble-free intra-regional travel for CARICOM nationals (Nicholas Brathwaite, Grenada); and a single market and economy by 1994 (Erskine Sandiford, Barbados). Manley had also earlier been given responsibility for taking the regional lead in negotiating with the US in response to President Bush's Enterprise for the Americas Initiative of June 1990 and succeeded in persuading the summit that a framework agreement should be signed between CARICOM and the US as at least a first step towards the discussion of free trade between the two.

The Commission's various interim recommendations were carried through to its final, massive report.[54] Provocatively entitled *Time for Action*, it was considered by the CARICOM heads of government at a specially convened three-day meeting at the end of October 1992. The report's range was enormous and its quality uneven, but there was no doubt that it constituted a most thorough and serious review of the region's condition. As was expected, specific proposals were many and varied. Yet the key to them lay in the recommendation, highlighted at every opportunity by Ramphal, that a Caribbean Commission be established to oversee the simultaneous deepening and widening of the movement. An initial membership of three persons with high-level public and political experience in the region was suggested. It is not too much to say that the whole strategy of development for CARICOM outlined in the report depended on this proposal, for the new Commission was seen as the motor driving this organisation forward which it had so singularly lacked hitherto. For all that, it was rejected by the heads of government. They did not want retiring ex-leaders (possibly Manley or Robinson or Ramphal himself) interfering, as they plainly saw it, in national sovereign affairs. A weak compromise was agreed as an alternative, namely, that a so-called CARICOM Bureau composed of the past, present and next chairs of the heads of government summit be set up to fulfil something of the executive vacuum that had been detected. Although several other detailed recommendations of the report were also accepted, what manifestly was not grasped was the opportunity which the Commission proposal offered to lift CARICOM's whole operation to a new level of seriousness.

Widening

Instead CARICOM turned outwards. In part, this was a forced reaction to the pressure of external events, in part a simple reflection of the fact that agreement could be more easily reached on external initiatives. It was also the case that throughout CARICOM's existence the strategy of 'deepening' the movement had been counterposed by an alternative, less favoured strategy of 'widening' the membership of the Community beyond the English-speaking countries. Although these strategies were never mutually exclusive – indeed, by the early 1990s, they needed ever more desperately to be pursued in conjunction – the failure to deepen the movement by establishing a permanent Caribbean Commission served inevitably to focus attention on the case for widening it to other parts of the region.

Here the West Indian Commission's key proposal did generate support. This was the creation of a new body, a putative Association of Caribbean States (ACS), anchored on CARICOM but open to the wider Caribbean Basin region. This reflected a new perspective within the CARICOM sub-region, a shift towards a pro-active approach in cooperation with their non-Anglophone neighbours, based in good part on a growing awareness that a grouping of only some 5.5 million people was simply too small to meet the challenges of a fast-changing global political economy. The West Indian Commission argued in its report:

> Put simply, the peoples of CARICOM and their Governments must no longer think in narrow terms merely of 'the Commonwealth Caribbean', but in wider terms of a 'Caribbean Commonwealth' – and must work to fulfil this larger ambition. The ambition itself must encompass, besides the 13 CARICOM countries, all the countries of the Caribbean Basin. It must reach out, therefore, to all the independent island states of the Caribbean Sea and the Latin American countries of Central and South America whose shores are washed by it. And it must be open as well to the Commonwealth of Puerto Rico, the island communities of the French West Indies, the Dutch islands of Aruba and the Netherland Antilles, the US Virgin Islands and the remaining British dependencies.[55]

The ACS was envisaged as 'being functionally active in an integration sense'[56] and a wide set of possible areas of cooperation was listed, including the negotiation of special trading terms, the widening of communication links, cooperation in tourism and health matters, the management of the resources of the Caribbean Sea and the curbing of drug trafficking.

The various diplomatic responses made to this proposal were as intricate as they were slow, revealing the extent of the cultural, linguistic and political gulf which divided the English-speaking Caribbean states from their Hispanic neighbours.[57] But a convention establishing the ACS was eventually signed in July 1994 and the organisation formally came into being on 1 January 1995, with a complement of twenty-five Caribbean Basin member states (including Cuba, but excluding Puerto Rico and the US Virgin Islands). Although the ACS is still a young body and its prospects should not be written off too soon, it cannot yet be said to have achieved very much. Its secretariat is weak and it has failed to develop any profile in key aspects of the international economic and security agendas which presently face the whole of the Caribbean Basin. Nevertheless, it exists and is a potential vehicle for forging greater unity in the Basin.

Other initiatives in this period also reflected efforts to build wider forms of cooperation between CARICOM and other parts of the Caribbean. A unique summit meeting was held in Port of Spain in October 1993 between CARICOM heads of government and the leaders of Colombia, Mexico and Venezuela (and Suriname) at which an 'action plan' on economic cooperation was signed prefiguring the negotiation of one-way free trade agreements between CARICOM and Colombia and Mexico along the lines of that already agreed with Venezuela a year earlier. Despite significant US opposition, a joint CARICOM-Cuba commission was also set up in late 1993 to promote trade, technical cooperation and environmental protection, and several subsequent meetings have been held. Forging closer links with the Dominican Republic took more time, largely because of divisions and hesitancy in that country's policy-making process, and a free trade agreement between CARICOM and the Dominican Republic was not signed until August 1998. In the meantime, remarkably, CARICOM had widened not only its regional outlook but its actual membership. Suriname had for some time sought to attach itself to the grouping. Its government applied to join in 1994 and, with Commonwealth Caribbean anxieties about the recent instability of its political system at least temporarily assuaged, it was admitted into CARICOM as the fourteenth member, as of July 1995. Perhaps even more surprisingly, two years later in 1997 Haiti was provisionally accepted as the fifteenth member, welcomed into the fold as a state and society substantially converted to the democratic process, a decision which was finally confirmed in 1999. It is less likely that the Dominican Republic will actually want itself to join CARICOM since its present government openly advertises the country as the hinge that links the Caribbean with Central America. However, as a signatory of the Lomé Convention it now participates with all the other CARICOM countries in preparing for joint discussions with the European Union within a body known as CARIFORUM.

This last reference to discussions with Europe is significant. For there is no doubt that the main driving force behind this latest 'widening' phase in CARICOM's evolution has been the growing awareness amongst Commonwealth Caribbean leaders during the 1990s that the region's relations with both Europe and North America, the two traditional external sources of influence on the Caribbean, were being forcibly remade in quite fundamental ways. A sense of the growing marginalisation of the CARICOM countries in international affairs had underpinned both the Grand Anse Declaration and the work of the West Indian Commission which it established. Yet, even since that body reported, the pace of external change further accelerated, with the European Union embarking on early talks about replacing the latest Lomé Convention, due to expire in 2000, and the US, along with Canada and Mexico, creating the North American Free Trade Area, which inevitably threatened the privileged entry into the US market won by Caribbean Basin countries in the distant Cold War days of the CBI, and promising in December 1994 to negotiate into being a Free Trade Area of the Americas by 2005. The truth is that the politics of reacting to these two exogenous processes hugely outweighed in significance all of the widening moves undertaken by CARICOM from 1993 onwards. Widening was certainly a response, and generally a positive one, to these perceived pressures, but, as has already been made clear, none of the various initiatives went far enough to create a solid, coherent bloc within the wider Caribbean Basin capable of negotiating with relatively greater strength with either the European Union or the US. Within CARICOM at least it was recognised that the concept of the Bureau was inadequate to the political task of preparing for these dual sets of negotiations and it was decided in early 1997 to set up a Regional Negotiating Machinery (RNM) to undertake this work. Ironically, given the reaction to his call for a Caribbean Commission, it was eventually to be headed by none other than Shridath Ramphal. Nevertheless, its staff is both small and dispersed and genuine doubts exist as to whether the RNM can cope with the demands placed upon it.

Amidst this expansion of diplomatic activity, what one might call the further internal development of CARICOM took a back seat. But it did not totally stop. Although nothing was done to take forward plans for a single currency, one of the key recommendations of the West Indian Commission, slow progress has been made towards the creation of a single market and economy within CARICOM, due to be completed by the end of 1999. The question that arises, given the pressures towards the opening up of trade being simultaneously experienced in all the Caribbean's dealings with the EU, the US and powerful new bodies like the WTO, is whether this achievement will be worth anthing as and when it is finally achieved. Beyond this matter, the promised Assembly of Commonwealth Caribbean Parliamentarians has come into being; a Caribbean Investment Fund has been established with an initial target fund of US$50 million; agreements have been signed on multilateral air services and social security; a draft CARICOM charter of civil society has been finalised; and a new Caribbean Court of Justice should soon become operational.

Conclusion

The answer to the question of whether CARICOM has been a success or a failure is manifestly that it has been both. It has survived, but it has not developed into the articulate and capable defender of the regional interest which was the ambition of its founders. It has remained an example of regionalisation as previously defined, which has meant that its dynamic has always been the competing and common interests of its various member states mediated by intergovernmental negotiation. Its achievements and its failures have consequently been those of its constituent governments. A tension between the MDCs and the LDCs has always existed but cannot be held responsible for the periods of impasse and stagnation. It has been the Commonwealth Caribbean MDCs which have always run CARICOM.

Indeed, the main lesson which can be drawn from an examination of the record of regional negotiation is that all the four MDCs – Jamaica, Trinidad, Guyana and Barbados – need to work together smoothly and effectively for CARICOM to prosper. Hesitation, lack of interest, or opposition from even one of the four has proved problematic; from two or more it has been crippling. Too often in the years since 1973 this has been the situation. Jamaica has struggled economically under different administrations and under Seaga defined itself by reference more to US than Caribbean interests. Trinidad has ridden the undulations of an oil economy, retreating from regional leadership at a critical period in the late 1970s as Dr Williams despaired of his fellow leaders' commitment to cooperation. Guyana has suffered more than any other part of the region and its tribulations have unavoidably infected the regional process, not least by contributing to the demoralisation of the Secretariat. Barbados has generally survived better than the others, at least until recently, but has always been the weakest of the four MDCs and has been unable to move the regional process forward on its own. Indeed, it has lately focused more on the OECS as a vehicle for its ambitions.

In these various circumstances CARICOM has unfortunately languished for much of its existence as part of the furniture of Caribbean economic and political life. Nobody has really wanted to destroy it, but nobody has been able fully to rescue it either. The West Indian Commission was the latest body charged with that responsibility. Its report undoubtedly constituted a decisive moment in the history of CARICOM. It was presented to the heads of government at a time when the world order as a whole was beginning to go through a major process of transformation and required that they display a boldness and a determination in responding to its recommendations only rarely, if ever, displayed before in the Commonwealth Caribbean. As has been seen, the region's leadership did not rise to the challenge, preferring to persevere complacently with their familiar, if increasingly inadequate, format. The result of their conservatism is not that CARICOM will necessarily collapse, but, rather, that it will become increasingly marginal to the determination of the Commonwealth Caribbean's future prospects.

Notes

1 See *Treaty establishing the Caribbean Community*, Chaguaramas, 4 July 1973, Article 4.
2 For a discussion of this point, see W. G. Demas, *West Indian Nationhood and Caribbean Integration*, Bridgetown, 1974, pp. 44–5.
3 For a description of the organisational structure of the Community, see Kenneth Hall and Byron Blake, 'The Caribbean Community: administrative and institutional aspects', *Journal of Common Market Studies*, 16, 3, 1978.
4 Stanley Hoffmann, 'Discord in community: the North Atlantic Area as a partial international system', *International Organization*, 17, 3, 1963, p. 527.
5 Anthony Payne, *The Politics of the Caribbean Community 1961–79: Regional Integration amongst New States*, Manchester 1980, p. 286.
6 See Anthony Payne, 'Westminster adapted: the political order of the Commonwealth Caribbean', in Jorgé Dominguez, Robert Pastor and DeLisle Worrell (eds), *Democracy in the Caribbean: Political, Economic and Social Perspectives*, Baltimore, 1992, pp. 57–73.

7   Demas, *West Indian Nationhood*, p. 26.
8   See E. Dommen (ed.), *States, Micro-states and Islands*, London, 1985.
9   See Jenny Pearce, *Under the Eagle: US Intervention in Central America and the Caribbean*, London, 1982.
10 See Caribbean Community Secretariat, *The Caribbean Community: A Guide*, Georgetown, 1973, pp. 5–6.
11 *Treaty Establishing the Caribbean Community, Annex: The Caribbean Common Market*, Chapter VII, Articles 51–62.
12 See Norman Girvan and Owen Jefferson (eds), *Readings in the Political Economy of the Caribbean*, Kingston, 1971, Introduction, p. 1.
13 See *Agreement Establishing the Caribbean Free Trade Association*, Dickenson Bay, Antigua, 15 December 1965.
14 See Government of Jamaica, *Ministry Paper No. 57: Report on the Fourth Heads of Government Conference*, Kingston, 1967.
15 For a discussion of this impasse, see S. S. Ramphal, *West Indian Nationhood: Myth, Mirage or Mandate?*, Georgetown, 1971.
16 For this debate, see Irene Hawkins, 'The choice of agreement', *West Indies Chronicle*, January 1972.
17 *Jamaica Hansard: Proceedings of House of Representatives*, 1, 1, 1968–9, p. 251.
18 Commonwealth Caribbean Regional Secretariat, *From CARIFTA to Caribbean Community*, Georgetown, 1972, p. 5.
19 *Ibid.*, pp. 57–112.
20 *Ibid.*, p. 125.
21 Vaughan A. Lewis, *The Idea of a Caribbean Community*, New World Pamphlet No. 9, Kingston, 1974, pp. 4–5.
22 *Trinidad Guardian*, 9 July 1973.
23 Kurleigh King, 'Statement by the Secretary-General of the Caribbean Community Secretariat to the 9th Annual Meeting of the Board of Governors of the Caribbean Development Bank, Barbados, April 25–26, 1979', mimeo, p. 7.
24 See *Trinidad Guardian*, 27 April 1975.
25 *Ibid.*, 16 June 1975.
26 *Ibid.*
27 *Ibid.*
28 Andrew Axline has pointed out that an early draft of the CARICOM Treaty in fact included an article which went a long way towards a commitment to a coordinated external economic policy, but that Jamaica, among others, objected to it so strongly that a much watered-down version eventually appeared as Article 34 of the Annex of the Treaty. W. A. Axline, *Caribbean Integration: The Politics of Regionalism*, London, 1979, p. 203.
29 *Trinidad Guardian*, 16 May 1975.
30 Government of Trinidad and Tobago, *White Paper on CARICOM*, Port of Spain, 1979, p. 35.
31 See Axline, *Caribbean Integration*, pp. 136–57.
32 'Caribbean Team of Experts Appointed', Caribbean Community Secretariat, press release, April 1980.
33 A Group of Caribbean Experts, *The Caribbean Community in the 1980s*, Georgetown, 1981, pp. 20–1.
34 Government of Trinidad and Tobago, *White Paper on CARICOM*, p. 9.
35 Group of Experts, *The Caribbean Community*, p. 7.
36 'Sixth Meeting of the Standing Committee of Ministers of CARICOM Responsible for Foreign Affairs', Caribbean Community Secretariat, press release 46/1981.

37 'Memorandum by the Caribbean Community (CARICOM) Secretariat' (86/81–82/FM) in *Fifth Report of the Foreign Affairs Committee of the House of Commons: Caribbean and Central America*, together with an Appendix; part of the proceedings of the Committee relating to the report; and the minutes of evidence taken before the Committee with appendices, London, 1982, p. 304.

38 President Ronald Reagan, 'The US Caribbean Basin Initiative', speech to the Organisation of American States, Washington DC, 24 February 1982, p. 8.

39 *Latin America Regional Report: Caribbean*, RC-83–10, 9 December 1983.

40 'Seventh Meeting of the Standing Committee of Ministers of CARICOM Responsible for Foreign Affairs', Caribbean Community Secretariat, press release 16/1982.

41 *Ibid.*

42 See Anthony Payne, Paul Sutton and Tony Thorndike, *Grenada: Revolution and Invasion*, London and New York, 1984, pp. 151–3.

43 *Latin America Regional Report: Caribbean*, RC-83–10, 9 December 1983.

44 Vaughan A. Lewis, 'Then and now: future relations among the states of the Caribbean Community', *Caribbean Affairs*, 2, 2, 1989, p. 2.

45 *CARICOM Perspective*, No. 23, 1984, special supplement, p. 3.

46 *The Nassau Understanding*, a declaration issued by the heads of government of Caribbean Community countries, mimeo, Nassau, 1984.

47 See Compton Bourne, 'Trade problems and issues in the Caribbean Community', *CARICOM Perspective*, No. 23, 1984, pp. 10–11.

48 *Caribbean Insight*, August 1988, p. 2.

49 For a discussion, see Tony Thorndike, 'The Militarization of the Commonwealth Caribbean', in Peter Calvert (ed.), *The Central American Security System: North-South or East-West?*, Cambridge, 1988.

50 *The Grand Anse Declaration*, a declaration issued by the heads of government of Caribbean Community countries, mimeo, 1989.

51 *Ibid.*

52 See *Report on a Comprehensive Review of the Programmes, Institutions and Organizations of the Caribbean Community*, Bridgetown, 1990.

53 The West Indian Commission, *Towards a Vision of the Future: Progress Report on the Work of the Independent West Indian Commission*, Bridgetown, 1991.

54 The West Indian Commission, *Time for Action: Report of the West Indian Commission*, Bridgetown, 1992.

55 *Ibid.*, p. 449.

56 *Ibid.*, p. 446.

57 For a discussion, see Andrés Serbín, 'The Caribbean: myths and realities for the 1990s', *Journal of Interamerican Studies and World Affairs*, 32, 2, 1990, pp. 121–41; 'The CARICOM states and the Group of Three: a new partnership between Latin America and the non-Hispanic Caribbean', *Journal of Interamerican Studies and World Affairs*, 33, 2, 1991, pp. 53–80; and 'Towards an Association of Caribbean States: raising some awkward questions', *Journal of Interamerican Studies and World Affairs*, 39, 2, 1997, pp. 61–90.

8 | Europe and the Caribbean

Europe's presence in the Caribbean is the product of a long and eventful history. At one time or another nearly all the major European powers have identified a Caribbean interest and more than any other region of the world the Caribbean bears the impress of the era of European colonialism. It is, in consequence, not only difficult to define the exact parameters of any European involvement but also impossible to determine with any degree of precision the myriad legacies Europe has bequeathed to the region following over half a millennium of engagement with it. The European presence is rooted in the foundations and the fabric of the area and is reproduced in countless ways in nearly every aspect of the economic, social and political life of the modern Caribbean.

Europe cannot escape responsibility for making and shaping the Caribbean: as neither can the Caribbean deny the importance of Europe in the making and shaping of its own distinctive creole identity. The inter-connection is important for it serves as a reminder that the process has not all been one way. Putting to one side the important contribution the Caribbean has made (and continues to make) to Europe's development, it is abundantly clear in the Caribbean itself that adaptation, transformation and rejection of European influences are as much a part of Caribbean history as their assimilation. Caribbean interests and European interests are not identical: indeed they have been, and in some instances continue to be, antithetical. Likewise, in Europe itself, interests can conflict and, while this does not have the same dramatic import as in the eighteenth century, the effect can still be substantial, as shown in the current banana dispute.

These remarks suggest that while the Caribbean is no longer central to Europe it is not distant from it either. A long familiarity with the region has added an overlay of sentiment, which means that any inventory of tangible quantifiable interests has to be augmented by an appreciation of the historical and human dimensions of the relationship. The latter does not drive the former but it is an element in the calculus that should not be overlooked, particularly in the negotiation and implementation of the various Lomé Conventions in which the representatives of the Caribbean have regularly met their European counterparts.

The structure of this chapter reflects these considerations. It takes as read the historical dimension since space does not permit any proper investigation as to its real importance. The substance of the discussion is in consequence concentrated in three areas: the bilateral bias to the policies of European states which has prevailed historically and continues in the present; the evolving European dimension to policy which first emerged in Lomé and which has slowly gathered strength in recent years; and the place which the Caribbean now occupies in Europe's priorities as a whole, particularly as it affects Europe's relations with the developing world.

Bilateral interests

Until recently, it has been a misnomer to talk of a common fully articulated 'European' policy to the Caribbean. Instead, there has been, and continues to be, a cluster of separate foreign policies focused on distinctive parts of the region. For Britain, it is the Commonwealth Caribbean that has commanded the attention and resources of business and government and in which British interests are regularly cultivated. For France, the political status of the *Départements d'Outre Mer* (DOM) does not warrant policy being considered foreign as much as domestic, with all this entails as to the levels of support the territories receive. Dutch policy likewise remains concentrated on the Netherlands Antilles and Suriname where continuing responsibilities define a distinctive role. So also Spain, in its renewed interest in the Caribbean, has focused overwhelmingly on the old centres of its empire in Cuba, the Dominican Republic and Puerto Rico, in that order of importance.[1]

There is good reason to expect that the pattern outlined above will continue in the near future. Britain is not about to abandon its distinctive Caribbean presence. It has formal commitments to its overseas territories, which have been revised and strengthened in recent years, and a popular, symbolic and practical link with the Commonwealth Caribbean through the Queen and the Commonwealth. Neither are under any direct challenge at present, although the mystique of the monarchy is a wasting asset. Britain also has long-established commercial interests in the region which, if not substantial, provide it with a significant measure of advantage over its competitors, at least in its former colonies. Finally, it has responsibilities and understandings of a general sort, derived both from its continued territorial presence and its 'special relationship' with the US. The high-level concerns with narcotics trafficking, money laundering and security in the Eastern Caribbean are presently the main manifestation of such commitments.[2]

France also is not about to abandon its Caribbean territories. The political status of the DOM is not open to question, notwithstanding the difficulties and the costs that have attended its realisation. There is little support for independence in the DOM, buoyed by a belief in Paris that France has a right to be in the Caribbean by virtue of history and interest. Preservation of the status quo is therefore the dominant theme, the reforms of the Mitterrand governments in the 1980s being more a necessary modernisation of the policy of *départementalisation* than a fundamental challenge to it.

The Dutch similarly are not about to leave the Caribbean. Indeed, their commitments have expanded in recent years as they have had to grapple with the convoluted aftermath of a string of military coups in Suriname and the ever perplexing problem of what to do with the Netherlands Antilles. Proposals for the revision of the *Statuut* (the fundamental law governing relations between the Netherlands and the Netherlands Antilles) have been under discussion in The Hague and have resulted in closer supervision of the affairs of the Antilles than previously had been the norm. Suriname, although independent since 1975 and now returned to civilian government, nevertheless remains acutely dependent on the substantial aid programme financed and administered by the Dutch government.

In contrast to the settled presence of Britain, France and the Netherlands, that of Spain is more tenuous. There were no compelling reasons behind Spain's rediscovery of the Caribbean in the 1980s. Its interests were, and have remained, largely financial and commercial and its policies reflect this in being essentially pragmatic. As such, there is as yet no coherent policy to the region as a whole and the Caribbean is regarded in Madrid more as an area of potential than actual interest, with the parameters of involvement clearly subordinate to the wider concerns of Spain in Latin America.

In comparison to the above four countries, other states in Europe have only a limited interest in the Caribbean – Germany, Italy and Scandinavia – or none at all – those in Eastern Europe. European policies thus remain largely confined to the three states with 'traditional' ties to the region (Britain, France and the Netherlands) and to the one with a 'renewed' interest (Spain). This pattern of engagement would not be unfamiliar to anyone traversing the region at the end of the Napoleonic Wars. The European presence has been remarkably durable and comparatively stable. It has also been essentially bilateral even in the modern world. What London decides is best for its overseas territories and its interests in the Caribbean is not regularly discussed, or even followed, with any great interest in Paris or The Hague (or Madrid for that matter) and 'vice versa'. The vertical and disconnected character of European influence in the Caribbean is thus still predominant in these European capitals, although most importantly it is increasingly subject to 'multilateralism' in Brussels as the European Union has come to play an ever greater role in setting the parameters for commercial and foreign policy.

The Lomé Conventions

While the bilateral dimension has been ascendant, a 'common' policy toward the Caribbean is emerging by degrees and accelerating in pace. This arises from several considerations, the most immediately important of which is the existence of the Lomé Conventions. In so far as it is possible to talk of a 'common European approach' to the Caribbean it is encapsulated within the successive Lomé Conventions, first concluded in 1975 with the current one in force to the year 2000. It is, in consequence, important to understand the promise and possibilities, as well as the difficulties and disappointments, of Lomé in order to gauge the likely content of future multilateral relationships between Europe and the Caribbean.

The Lomé Conventions are development co-operation agreements covering trade, aid and political dialogue between the member states of the EU and the now seventy-one African, Caribbean and Pacific (ACP) countries. All independent states in the Caribbean, except Cuba, are signatory to the current Fourth Convention signed in 1990. Additionally, under a separate agreement, the Convention provides a framework for economic relations between the EU and the dependent territories of Britain and the Netherlands Antilles, collectively known as the Overseas Countries and Territories (OCT). The DOM, as integral parts of France, are considered part of the EU and are thus subject to internal EU policies, although they are accorded special trading and associated benefits with the Caribbean ACP and OCT under the Lomé Conventions.

Trade

For most countries the most important element of the Caribbean relationship with the EU is trade. In 1997 exports from the Caribbean ACP to the EU were 2.25 billion ECU, around 20 per cent of their total exports.[3] The record for individual countries, as might be expected, is rather mixed. In some there has been a steady expansion of trade; in others a decline; whilst for yet others exports have remained constant. Overall, the picture is disappointing. It is dominated by traditional commodities and highly dependent on preferential access to the EU, codified in the case of sugar, bananas and rum in separate Protocols.

The Sugar Protocol was negotiated alongside the first Lomé Convention, although ostensibly separate from it, and was to run for an indefinite period. It provides for the purchase of 1.3 million tonnes of cane sugar each year from traditional ACP sugar exporters at a price linked to the internal EU price.[4] Since these prices have nearly always been well above world market prices the Sugar Protocol has provided valuable assistance to the ACP (according to one estimate, some 14.4 billion ECU between 1975–91).[5] The Caribbean beneficiaries have been Barbados, Belize, Guyana, Jamaica, St Kitts-Nevis and Trinidad and Tobago, each of which have sugar quotas with the EU covering much, if not all, of their sugar production for export. The continued viability of the sugar industry in the region is thus extraordinarily dependent on the Sugar Protocol and subject to developments within the EU which may erode its benefits. Foremost among these is reform of the Common Agricultural Policy which will reduce prices for sugar from EU producers and hence those paid to the ACP producers.

The Banana Protocol was similarly introduced with the first Lomé Convention and has been renewed in all subsequent conventions. It operated without difficulty until the adoption of the Single European Market in 1993. This required new arrangements, which were agreed by the EU but immediately came under attack from many quarters, most importantly from the US government on behalf of major US banana transnationals and from Latin American producers. The details are set out in Chapter 10 and the dispute is yet to be finally resolved. As far as the Caribbean banana producers are concerned, the Protocol, along with a permissive banana regime, is essential for their well-being. Under the terms of the current banana regime, traditional ACP banana suppliers can supply annually up to 875,000 tonnes of bananas duty free to the EU market. This provides a crucial margin of preference over Latin American banana suppliers who pay a duty of 75 ECU per tonne on the first 2.2 million tonnes of bananas entering the EU market and higher rates thereafter. The value of the preference has been calculated as 130 million ECU for the ACP in 1995.[6] The major beneficiaries in the Caribbean have been the Windward Islands, Jamaica, Belize and Suriname, with either all or most of their export production sold on the EU market.

The Rum Protocol was also originally introduced in the first Lomé Convention to protect high cost producers in the DOM from competition from elsewhere, including the Caribbean ACP. Quotas were fixed for ACP rum imports, with the major market being the United Kingdom and the major suppliers Guyana, the Bahamas, Jamaica, Barbados and Trinidad and Tobago. Under changes in force since 1995, quotas were abolished for light rum and increased annually for dark rum with the expectation that all remaining quotas on traditional rum would be abolished in 2000. However, the prospect of the Caribbean benefiting from an expanded market in the EU has been threatened by the conclusion of an agreement between the EU and the US in March 1997 under which producers in the US offshore territories and other Third World countries will be able to export most of their rum into the EU free of tariff and quotas after 2003. This will put the producers of Caribbean rum at a commercial disadvantage, so much so that hitherto 'rival' producers in the ACP and the DOM have agreed since September 1998 to work together to preserve their position in the EU market.

Other products exported to the EU include coffee, rice, spices, bauxite and aluminium, iron compounds, and petroleum and chemical products. Although there have been some attempts to develop manufacturing exports to the EU the results have been disappointing. Instead, the emphasis in recent years has been on the expansion of services. This has sought to capitalise on 'natural advantages' to develop offshore financial services and tourism. Both these sectors engage overwhelmingly with the US. However, in both there is also a significant European dimension (the offshore financial sectors are concentrated in the OCT) and in respect of tourism the European Commission has sought to encourage it in its development assistance programmes. Tourism currently provides about 25 per cent of GDP in the Caribbean and direct and indirect employment for around 20 per cent of the population. For many Caribbean countries it is the fastest growing sector of their economies and visitors from Europe have doubled in number. They usually stay longer than US tourists and spend significantly more per day. The main destinations are the DOM (mainly French visitors); Jamaica, the Eastern Caribbean and the Bahamas (mainly British); and the Dominican Republic, which attracts visitors from all over the EU.

Aid

Financial and technical assistance to the Caribbean under the Lomé Conventions is provided under a general envelope of aid allocated for a five-year period. In Lomé I (1976–80) this amounted to 239.6 million ECU; in Lomé II (1981–5) 415 million ECU; in Lomé III (1986–90) 461 million ECU; and in the first five years of Lomé IV (1991–5) 668.7 million ECU.[7] The largest amount, 772.2 million ECU, has been allocated to development projects in individual countries according to priorities established in national programmes agreed between the EU and the country concerned, on a basis broadly reflecting the level of development in the country (i.e. the less developed countries receive proportionately more). Total national allocations to the Caribbean ACP for 1996–2000 were set at 453 million ECU, with the principal beneficiaries being Haiti (148 million ECU) and the Dominican Republic (106 million ECU).

Caribbean countries also benefit from a number of other programmes. Regional funds, designed for further integration and cooperation in the region, amounted to 262.8 million ECU from 1976 to 1995 inclusive, with a further 90 million ECU allocated for 1996–2000. In the period 1976–95, some 64.6 million ECU was provided in support of export earnings (under the STABEX system) and 48 million ECU to support mining (under the SYSMIN system). In the same period, 225 million ECU was disbursed as food aid, emergency aid and other forms of assistance and from 1991–5 approximately 37 million ECU was given in support of structural adjustment programmes. Finally, from 1976–95 the European Investment Bank loaned some 400 million ECU to various ACP and OCT countries.

The general impact of European Commission aid to the region is positive. It will be well in excess of 2 billion ECU for the twenty-five years from 1975–2000. It stands comparison with US aid and, unlike US aid, has been maintained in volume over the years. It is also additional aid, i.e. assistance over and above that given in bilateral programmes from EU states, and it has been especially welcomed in the smaller Eastern Caribbean islands where its impact has been more than marginal. This is not to deny the existence of very real problems in parts of the aid programme, especially in respect of project approval in the regional programme, slow disbursement in the case of some national programmes, and complex and cumbersome procedures in accessing funds from STABEX and SYSMIN. It is important, however, that these difficulties should be seen in perspective. Financial and technical assistance under Lomé is not perfect, but it does have the benefit of being predictable and, under the programming arrangements, of allowing a Caribbean voice to be heard. It has also been timely when the Caribbean has needed it in respect of emergencies, particularly in the wake of the many devastating hurricanes which have hit the region in recent years, or STABEX, where substantial funds have been committed in support of the banana industry.

Political dialogue

The various Lomé Conventions have provided for a structured dialogue through joint and separate institutions. The joint institutions comprise an annual ACP-EU Council of Ministers that discusses a wide range of topics, including political conditionalities, trade access and often quite technical questions relating to the Protocols or the administration of the Conventions; an ACP-EU Committee of Ambassadors, based in Brussels, that has certain powers delegated to it by the Council of Ministers and meets more frequently to ensure implementation of the Conventions; and an ACP-EU Joint Assembly, drawn from members of the European Parliament and various ACP parliamentary bodies, that meets twice a year. In recent years the Joint Assembly has become increasingly important as a forum for discussions and a stimulus to ACP-EU cooperation.

The separate institutions comprise special bodies to monitor and implement the Conventions. On the European side the most important are the meetings of the European Development Committee, comprising ministers for development cooperation from the member states, which sets out policy; the Development Committee of the European Parliament, which has growing powers to influence and make policy; and the Directorate General for Development within the European Commission (usually referred to as DG8), with responsibility for day-to-day implementation of the Conventions. To assist implementation there are various EU delegations in ACP states. These are located in all Caribbean ACP states, except some of the smaller ones in the Eastern Caribbean, which are served by the delegation in Barbados.

On the ACP side there are three institutions. The Council of Ministers defines policy, both toward the EU and within the ACP group. The Committee of Ambassadors, based in Brussels, manages day-to-day implementation of the Convention, collectively and through their various national embassies which are the counterpart to the EU delegations in ACP states. The ACP Secretariat, also located in Brussels, provides technical input and co-ordinates the activities of the ACP. The Caribbean has played an important, often leading, part in the ACP. It provided, in Edwin Carrington, a very able Secretary-General to the ACP Secretariat and has chaired a number of important committees, particularly during the periodic re-negotiations of Lomé. In the Caribbean itself, CARIFO-RUM has been established as an agency to promote development cooperation with the EU and to manage the Caribbean regional programme. Its membership comprises all the ACP Caribbean states.

This regular dialogue has enabled Lomé to acquire the characteristics of an international regime. According to one commentator, this has brought a number of benefits to all parties including stabilising mutual expectations regarding behaviour; reducing transaction costs; increasing the flow of information; and what can be called 'institutional roll-over' whereby the regime is renewed and perpetuated over time.[8] It has provided a valuable forum and source of assistance which the ACP countries, and among them those of the Caribbean, would be reluctant to forego: hence their concern over proposals to radically reform, or even abandon Lomé, which were signalled with the publication by the European Commission in November 1996 of a Green Paper on the future of EU-ACP relations.[9]

The future of Lomé

The Green Paper set in motion an unprecedented dialogue on the future of Lomé involving non-governmental organisations, states and the Commission at national, regional and international levels. In the Caribbean, a regional consultation on the Green Paper was held in the Dominican Republic in March 1997. The Caribbean expressed concern over a number of proposals including, most importantly, the end of preferential trade, revision of the Protocols, increased conditionality of aid, and the weakening of the ACP as a group through the possible regionalisation of the Convention. The strength of feeling on these and related issues was noted by Professor Pinheiro, the European Commissioner for Development, in his closing remarks to the consultation.[10]

Negotiations for a convention to succeed the fourth Convention began in Brussels in September 1998 and were due to conclude by the end of February 2000. The EU mandate, based in large part on the Green Paper, set out measures which marked significant departures from the existing Convention. The ACP, in its mandate, opted for the status quo. In introducing the ACP mandate, Billie Miller, the Deputy Prime Minister and Minister of Foreign Affairs for Barbados, quoted the words of her Prime Minister, Owen Arthur, when he welcomed delegates to the ACP-EU Ministers Meeting in Barbados in May 1998:

> In a global context, the Lomé body of relationships represents still the most effective, the most meaningful model of North-South arrangements ever conceived by man. To some that may not be saying much given the dearth of rivals but in a world which has little to be proud of in relation to sustained development cooperation between nations and across hemispheres, it is indeed saying a very great deal. In a changing world of liberalisation and globalisation, in a new world of drastic trade disciplines, Lomé too will and must change. But the soul of Lomé must not be lost, must not be cast adrift and must not be abandoned to wander on some mistaken shore.[11]

In short, the ACP saw real value in continuing close cooperation with Europe. So did the Caribbean. Indeed, given the difficulties encountered in developing relations with the US and in the Americas through the Free Trade Area of the Americas negotiations (examined in the following chapter), there were some in the region who argued for even closer association with the EU.

As expected, the Caribbean is most concerned with the EU's proposals on trade. These envision a phased end to non-reciprocal preferential trade and a review of the Protocols. On preferential trade, the EU proposed three options: (i) the status quo for least developed countries, which can continue to benefit from current Lomé preferences (in effect, available only to Haiti in the Caribbean); (ii) a move for non-LDCs to the EU's general system of preferences (GSP), something which is open to all Caribbean states, although preliminary research shows considerable loss of benefits with this option, with the Caribbean seriously affected as a group; and (iii) the negotiation of a regional free trade area (RFTA) with the EU by 2005, which would involve reciprocity and would be expected to cover substantially all trade by 2015 or thereabouts. The Commission clearly anticipated this option being taken up by the Caribbean since it exhibits the greatest cohesion and possesses the most advanced regional organisation in the ACP. A major objection from the Caribbean's point of view is that it could be trade diverting rather than trade creating and that as a consequence the Caribbean would be worse off in overall terms. This view was confirmed by an expert study initiated by the Commission and released in November 1998. It concluded that a RFTA would be a political and administrative nightmare to implement and of little or no economic benefit to the region.

The proposals to review the Protocols are also deeply worrying. On this there is a great deal of uncertainty. The World Trade Organisation (WTO) decision on the Banana Protocol has implications for the Sugar Protocol and may leave it open to challenge from other WTO members. The phasing-out of the Rum Protocol, without safeguards for the Caribbean rum industry beyond 2002, leaves it commercially exposed and subject to reduced sales in the EU market. The problem for the Caribbean is how to continue the benefits from the Protocols when there are so many competing interests at stake. The Protocols ultimately rest on a coincidence of corporate, producer and national interests in the ACP and the EU. The economic benefits they provide are the result of intense political lobbying. In this, the political acumen of the lobbyists is the main criterion, not economic logic or developmental need. In the past, Caribbean diplomats have exercised considerable skills in safeguarding these interests. In the current climate of economic liberalisation it will be more difficult to make a convincing case, to the extent that defence of the status quo, on trade or the Protocols, may be a lost cause which not even the invocation of the spirit of Lomé can restore.

There is also concern over the future of aid. Proportionately, as a region of mostly small states, the Caribbean has done well on a per capita basis within the ACP grouping and even better in relation to other developing countries. For the Caribbean the key question is: how much of this is at risk in a successor Convention? The answer is not easy to determine and depends to a considerable extent on a much wider debate on the purpose and priorities of development assistance, which is as yet incomplete. However, the omens are not good for the more developed high-income countries of the region. The EU, along with other major donors, has determined that development assistance should be targeted at the poorest. In the Caribbean, Haiti and Guyana undoubtedly qualify, but the Bahamas, Barbados and most likely Trinidad and Tobago do not. The others are in-between. This rather stark assessment is an oversimplification, but these are the examples one encounters when the question is raised with the officials charged with implementing the Caribbean programme in DG8.

All of which is to say that in any successor arrangement to Lomé, the Caribbean will have to demonstrate objective need. Current thinking has advanced the idea of vulnerability as the peg on which the special needs of the region and small states can be hung. Small states, it is argued, are more vulnerable than larger states to economic shocks, environmental risks and security threats. In particular, small developing states (those with a population of 1.5 million or below) exhibit greater volatility of output, again compared with large states, as a consequence of greater exposure to external economic forces and environmental hazards. When these are taken into account and quantified in a composite vulnerability index recently produced under the auspices of the Commonwealth Secretariat, twenty-five small ACP states out of a sample of 110 developing states of all sizes occupy the top thirty positions as the most vulnerable. Of these, nine are from the Caribbean (including Jamaica).[12]

The idea of a vulnerability index has yet to win general recognition. Its value to the Caribbean and to other small developing states, most of which are otherwise defined as middle-income states, is to provide a case for special consideration in access to official development assistance. The Commission appears open to such arguments. In its Draft Negotiating Mandate it mentioned in several places that special provision will be made for vulnerable states (landlocked and island) and proposed that the overall figure for programmable resources (those directed to specific countries and regions) 'will be calculated in the light of a country's estimated needs – size, population, income, vulnerability, geographical situation – and an assessment of its merits based on performance and sound management'.[13] If these are indeed to be the criteria, then many states in the Caribbean will be able to meet them in full.

Vulnerability can also be deployed in support of preferential trade and the Protocols. In its mandate, the ACP argued for the principle of 'positive differentiation', which 'should meet the specific and increasing development needs of the ACP LDCs and should apply in the cases of the landlocked and island countries, taking due account of their fragile and vulnerable economies'.[14] Small states are especially at risk in the global trading environment. The ACP proposal in the negotiations was to maintain existing preferences to 2005 and then enter negotiations for alternative ACP-EU trade arrangements, implementation of which would commence from 2010 and which would in themselves 'provide for the maintenance of non-reciprocal trade preferences for the least developed and other highly vulnerable ACP countries'.[15] In getting such views accepted, the ACP will have a difficult, but not impossible, task. It will need Caribbean countries to argue their case and the African countries to give support and thereby add number and weight to the case for differential treatment. Nevertheless, the expectation is that there will be a successor Convention which, if not as favourable as in the past, will continue to involve the EU in the future development of the Caribbean.

European priorities and the Caribbean

The Treaty on European Union (the Maastricht Treaty), which came into effect in November 1993, marked the most important stage in the development of the EU since its initial founding in the Treaty of Rome. Important decisions were taken to deepen the processes of integration within the EU and to take an enhanced role in external relations. For the first time member states committed themselves to introducing a common foreign and security policy (CFSP) and set out specific objectives for development policy. Member states also set out a timetable for economic and monetary union; provided for common citizenship; and agreed to increase cooperation in justice and home affairs. Finally, the European Parliament was given enhanced powers, which provided it with greater opportunities to influence development policy.

Development policy and EU foreign policy

The Caribbean is likely to feel the effect of such policies in a number of areas including monetary cooperation, immigration, rights of asylum, visa policy, and cooperation on combating drug trafficking and money laundering.[16] However, the most immediate and far-reaching will be European development policy (as distinct from the development policies of individual member states), which has become a Community policy in which decisions can be taken by qualified (weighted) majority voting rather than unanimity. This gives the European Commission opportunities to develop new policies within the general objectives of European development policy. They were set out in Title XVII of the Treaty as the sustainable economic and social development of the developing countries and, more particularly, the most disadvantaged among them; the smooth and gradual transition of the developing countries into the world economy; the campaign against poverty in developing countries; and the promotion of democracy, the rule of law and respect for human rights and fundamental freedoms.

The Commission's response, and the beginning of a 'new' direction in development policy, was set out in a document released in May 1992 entitled *Development Cooperation in the Run-Up to 2000*.[17] In it the Commission argued for a rethink of policy on several grounds. Among them were the declining interest of the major powers in the geopolitical situation of the developing world following the end of the Cold War; the development of new forms of interdependence deriving from population growth, environmental problems, drugs and major endemic diseases as distinct from traditional interdependence concerns focused on the security of supply of commodities; the failure of development policy to improve conditions in the developing countries despite the large amount of resources mobilised for this purpose; and the need for development policy to be more closely coordinated among EU states to enhance its effect and the EU's presence in international affairs. The document then went on to review the principles, objectives and instruments that would inform policy and concluded that these should be differentiated according to 'the conditions, circumstances and needs of each developing country or group of developing countries'.[18]

Following publication, the Commission quickly moved to put its ideas in practice. The most important, as far as the Caribbean was concerned, was the Mid-Term Review of the Lomé Convention, which was concluded in 1995. The Review was more wide-ranging and deeper than anticipated by the ACP, constituting in essence another set of negotiations, involving the amendment, deletion or addition of seventy-one articles (out of 369 in the existing Convention) as well as changes and an addition to the Protocols.[19] The details are too numerous to give, although the broad headings were indicative of the new thinking and new priorities.[20] They included greater emphasis on political and institutional issues and, in particular, the addition of a new article recognising the application of democratic principles and the consolidation of the rule of law as 'essential elements'. This allowed a country to be suspended if it violated such elements (the military regime in Haiti had been sanctioned in the early 1990s). There was also a shift of emphasis from trade preferences to trade promotion in recognition of the importance of developing trade competitiveness. Other measures under the trade heading included improved access to the EU market and revision of the rules of origin to enable some sourcing for production from geographically proximate non-ACP developing countries (which, for the Caribbean, meant Central and South America). Increased conditionality in the delivery of aid was emphasised, along with the adoption of a controversial policy releasing aid in two tranches. The first would amount to 70 per cent of the overall sum allocated to a country over the five-year period; the remaining 30 per cent would only be disbursed if a review could show that good use had been made of the first tranche in accordance with a programme agreed between the EU and ACP state. Such close oversight had not been a feature of previous Conventions. Finally a number of other measures were agreed to improve support for industrial development; expedite implementation of decentralised cooperation; and improve the operation of STABEX.

The Commission then moved on to define and implement new polices towards the Mediterranean, Latin America and Asia. While policy was differentiated according to each region, it was also clear that common themes were being promoted. Foremost among these was the promotion of the commercial, political and security interests of the EU. This brought into prominence its relations with the Mediterranean. It has adopted a common programme to twelve countries in the region (including Palestine) and is progressively establishing the basis for a Euro-Mediterranean Economic Area which envisages free trade between the regions, as well as increased aid and closer cooperation in the political and security fields. In Latin America, the EU has also expanded its interests, particularly with the larger countries, and in June 1999 a summit of heads of state or government of the EU and those from Latin America and the Caribbean was held for the first time in Brazil. New agreements were signed which anticipate regular dialogue, improved trade cooperation and increased European investment in the region. Finally, the EU has for the first time put a coherent policy in place in Asia, which accords Asia a higher priority. Of central concern has been the improvement of trade and investment through the promotion of economic cooperation agreements that stimulate the private sector. There is also regular dialogue in the biennial summit meetings between the heads of state or government of the EU and ten East and South-east Asian countries which cover political as well as economic topics. Elsewhere in the region, notably South Asia, the EU maintains its traditional development policy programmes, with a focus on poverty eradication. However, it is clear that South Asia is no longer perceived to be as important as it was and India has seen a substantial reduction in aid as attention in the EU has focused elsewhere.

The situation for India is mirrored for the ACP countries. They have lost their privileged position as new agendas and new interests have come to dominate EU policy. The focus has shifted from development assistance (as classically set out in the Lomé Conventions) to economic cooperation, 'aimed at improving the business and regulatory environment in partner countries in order to stimulate two-way trade and investments with the direct participation of the private sector to the benefit of both the Union and the partner country'.[21] Post-Maastricht, the favoured countries and regions have emerged as those with which the EU can do business (East and South-east Asia and South America and Mexico) or in which it has a direct security interest (the Mediterranean). This is in line with the increasing subordination of development policy to the wider goals of the CFSP, which the recently ratified Treaty of Amsterdam has further strengthened. In seeking to have its future developmental concerns met by the EU, the Caribbean will therefore have to seek ways to engage with the EU's emergence as a presence in global affairs.

Development policy and EU home policy

The Caribbean here has a distinct advantage in comparison to most other parts of the developing world, precisely because the EU has a heightened interest in security in the region through the number of its possessions there. Its borders embrace the Caribbean DOM and its overseas territories are in a close association with the EU. The policies set out in the Maastricht Treaty have the effect of binding European possessions in the region ever closer to the EU. This can be seen in a number of areas, the most important of which are related to new powers and policies encouraging and facilitating closer cooperation among the EU member states in justice and home affairs as set out in Title VI of the Treaty. These cover asylum policy, rules governing the crossing of external borders of the EU, immigration policy and policy governing nationals of third countries, combating drug addiction, combating fraud, judicial cooperation in civil and criminal matters, customs cooperation, and police cooperation to combat terrorism, drug trafficking and international crime. Although all have some resonance in the Caribbean, the main effects relate to drug trafficking and money laundering.

The Caribbean is well known as a major transit route for cocaine *en route* from the source countries of South America to the US and the EU. The United Nations International Drugs Control Programme estimates that some 400 metric tonnes of cocaine transit through the Caribbean each year, of which 180 tonnes are directed to the European market. The size of the market, and the growing incidence of drug abuse in the EU, has led to increased cooperation in the EU and in the Caribbean to tackle the problem through a variety of enforcement programmes directed particularly, but not exclusively, to the Eastern Caribbean.

Informal cooperation among the EU countries to combat drug trafficking in the Caribbean began with the establishment of the Bridgetown Group in 1990 as a regional counterpart to the EU (parent) Dublin Group. It met monthly to exchange information and develop a common approach to the drugs problem. Equivalent groups were later set up in other Caribbean countries and efforts made to involve other interested parties such as the US and the Organisation of American States. The most important initiative, however, was the agreement to send an EU experts group to visit the Caribbean in early 1996 to assess the drug problem and make recommendations. It concluded that the problems associated with drugs and drug trafficking posed the greatest single threat to the stability and economic and social development of the region and were beginning to undermine democracy there. It also urged greater cooperation between governments in the region, and with and between governments with significant interests in the region, including those in the EU.[22] In May 1996 a region-wide plan was agreed on the basis of the report. The EU pledged 35 million ECU in support of a five-year programme to combat drugs. In addition, individual initiatives were undertaken by Britain, France, the Netherlands and Spain. The close co-operation between these countries in drug enforcement activities in the Caribbean is new and unprecedented and is set to increase further with the adoption of the Treaty of Amsterdam which has provision for closer police and customs cooperation.

The problems of money laundering have also generated closer cooperation. The EU has worked closely with the US on this issue, particularly in regards to its overseas territories where major initiatives have been taken on accountability and governance.[23] It has also continued to provide funding and technical support for the Caribbean Financial Action Task Force since its establishment in 1990. The majority of the funding for a new programme (7 million ECU over five years) to improve the legal, judicial, financial and enforcement aspects of anti-money laundering measures in the region is to come from the EU. Finally, it should be noted that the adoption of a single currency in the EU is likely to have important effects on the offshore financial sector. There have been calls in the EU for tighter financial regulation and tax harmonisation which, if adopted, are likely to be extended in part to the Caribbean, thereby reducing the attractiveness of the sector not only to the money launderer but also to legitimate businesses using these facilities.

In sum, closer co-operation in the EU and processes set in train by the Maastricht Treaty and the Treaty of Amsterdam are already having significant spill-over effects on the Caribbean. In judicial and home affairs they impinge first and foremost on the overseas territories and the DOM but do not relate exclusively to them. Common rules are to be established on immigration, asylum and visa policy which will impact on the Caribbean communities resident in the EU and their families as members travel back and forth to the EU (including those, for example, who travel between neighbouring islands in the Caribbean such as Dominica or St Lucia to the DOM). The EU focus on drug trafficking in the Caribbean in response to fears about drugs in Europe (a Eurobarometer poll conducted by the European Commission in 1996 found drugs and organised crime to be the largest single fear of citizens in the EU) heightens the EU's security concerns in the region. The new concerns to establish a CFSP also have an effect on development policy as it comes increasingly to reflect the EU's external priorities. Again, the move is towards common policies, which the Treaty of Amsterdam and the appointment of a Commissioner for CFSP are designed to achieve. In this area the Caribbean may find itself less favoured than before and more marginal to the growing external portfolio of the European Commission, although for reasons of interest and security this will not result in precipitate decline.

The future of Europe and the Caribbean

To sum up, then, the EU as a whole, and several of its member states in particular, have a direct, and in some cases a major, interest in stability, security and development in the Caribbean. The bilateral dimension has shaped policy, but the various Lomé Conventions are also seen to have contributed to this end. The EU therefore has a vested interest in the success of Lomé in the Caribbean. The Caribbean ACP also views Lomé positively and seeks its continuation. Such a coincidence of interest has been a feature of EU-Caribbean policy for a number of years. It imparts an important degree of stability, even predictability, to relations between the two regions, and provides for important elements of continuity. It is therefore possible to conclude that there will be a continuing European involvement in the Caribbean.[24] In some ways this is inescapable given the fact that Europe has an important territorial presence in the region. But there is more to it than simple geopolitics. There is also a shared history and a long and intimate familiarity of each with the other. This suggests that what is at work in European-Caribbean relations is something that may be termed 'interest plus'. It is this that makes the relationship with the Caribbean different for the EU and sets it apart from those with other regions of the developing world. It is only natural to expect some dilution of the 'plus' as the pace of global change quickens. But for the moment it remains a bonus which delivers tangible developmental benefits to the region and provides it with an importance in European affairs which it would not otherwise merit.

Notes

1 For details of the individual relations between the four countries and the Caribbean, see the chapters by Anthony Payne, Helen Hintjens, Jean Grugel, Rosemarijn Hoefte and Gert Oostindie in Paul Sutton (ed.), *Europe and the Caribbean*, Basingstoke, 1991.

2 See Paul Sutton and Anthony Payne, 'The off-limits Caribbean: the United States and the European Dependent Territories', *The Annals of the American Academy of Political Science*, 533, 1994, pp. 87–99.

3 Figures calculated from European Commission, *EU-ACP Cooperation in 1997*, Brussels, September 1998. The ECU is the acronym for the European currency unit which served as the unit of account between EU member states from 1979 until its replacement by the euro in January 1999. The value of the ECU fluctuated against other currencies. On 1 October 1996 it stood at 1ECU = US$1.25 and 1ECU = £ 0.80.

4 The origins and early operation of the Sugar Protocol are set out in Paul Sutton, 'The Sugar Protocol of the Lomé Conventions and the Caribbean', in Paul Sutton (ed.), *Dual Legacies in the Contemporary Caribbean: Continuing Aspects of British and French Dominion*, London, 1986, pp. 98–119.

5 'Memorandum submitted by the Ministry of Agriculture, Fisheries and Food and the Department for International Development', International Development Committee, Fourth Report, *Renegotiation of the Lomé Convention*, House of Commons, Session 1997–8, London, 1998, Vol. 2, Appendix 13.

6 *Ibid.*

7 Figures for 1976–95 from European Commission, *The Caribbean and the European Union*, Directorate General for Development, DE 80, Brussels, June 1995.

8 See Marjorie Lister, *The European Union and the South: Relations with Developing Countries*, London, 1997, pp. 155–8.

9   See Commission of the European Communities, *Green Paper on Relations between the European Union and the ACP Countries on the Eve of the 21st Century*, COM (96) 570 final, Brussels, 20 November 1996.

10 The authors were invited to attend the consultation and took part in it.

11 ACP-EU Press Release, *Opening of EU-ACP Negotiations*, Statement by Ms Billie Miller, ACP-CE 2169/98, Presse 329, Brussels, 30 September 1998.

12 See Commonwealth Secretariat, 'Small states and development: a composite index of vulnerability', in *Small States: Economic Review and Basic Statistics*, Vol. 4, Commonwealth Secretariat, London, December 1998.

13 See European Commission, Draft Commission Communication to the Council, *Recommendations for a Council decision authorising the Commission to negotiate a development partnership agreement with the ACP countries*, Brussels, 28 January 1998.

14 See ACP Group, *Negotiating Mandate*, ACP/29/028/98Rev, Brussels, 30 September 1998.

15 *Ibid.*

16 See Paul Sutton, 'The New Europe and the Caribbean', *European Review of Latin American and Caribbean Studies*, 59, 1995, pp. 37–57.

17 Commission of the European Communities, *Development Co-operation Policy in the Run-Up to 2000*, SEC (92) 915 final, Brussels, 15 May 1992.

18 *Ibid.*, paragraph 42.

19 See European Commission, Directorate General for Development, *Lomé IV Revised: Changes and Challenges 1995–2000*, DE89, Office for Official Publications of the European Communities, Luxembourg, 1996.

20 See Paul Sutton, 'New directions in the development policy of the European Union', in D. K. Giri (ed.), *Europe and South Asia*, New Delhi, forthcoming.

21 Commission of the European Communities, *Towards a New Asia Strategy*, COM (94) 314 final, Brussels, 13 July 1994, p. 6.

22 European Commission, *The Caribbean and the Drugs Problem*, Report of EU Experts Group, April 1996, mimeo, p. 1.

23 See Sutton and Payne, 'The off-limits Caribbean' for detailed discussion of such cooperation.

24 This argument is developed at greater length in Paul Sutton, 'The future of Europe in the Caribbean', in Sutton (ed.), *Europe and the Caribbean*, pp. 250–5.

9 | North America and the Caribbean

By comparison with Europe, the issues that concern the states of North America in their relationship with the Caribbean are grounded less in the politics of history and sentiment than those of interests and power. Those former considerations can never entirely be ignored, but it is an important point of contrast in respect of North America that it has been geopolitics, rather than the colonial connection, which has been in the ascendant in the shaping of policy. This has certainly always been the case with the US. Since the days of the Monroe Doctrine, the US has regarded itself as the unquestioned leader of all of the countries of the Western hemisphere and has generally been viewed as such by other powers, including those in Europe.

On this basis, US governments have been concerned throughout the twentieth century to secure the emergence within the hemisphere of pro-American governments which could then be defended in the interests of political stability. There have been times when particular administrations have tried to encourage the growth of freedom and representative democracy in the Caribbean and elsewhere, but these have been outweighed by frequent instances of US support for oligarchic or dictatorial regimes which aligned themselves politically with US interests. On many occasions too, in situations of conflict, US governments have intervened, militarily and by other means, in the politics of Caribbean and Central American states in order to ensure the outcome that they desired. Those territories which were still colonies of the European powers were spared the direct impact of US intervention in this period but were nevertheless still embraced in the broader strategic sense by the ambit of US power. Britain's concession to the US of a number of military bases in its Caribbean territories in 1940 (in exchange for the supply of a number of destroyers) serves only to underline the overarching nature of US security interests.

These background points are important because they locate a US interest in domination of the Caribbean for its own political, strategic and economic purposes long before the period of US global hegemony began after the end of the Second World War. From this perspective, the Cold War appears as but an episode in US-Caribbean relations – a phase in which the US perceived its own standing as a hegemonic power and its associated credibility in the eyes of the Soviet Union to have been dependent, above all, on its capacity to maintain and demonstrate control of its own hemispheric community, notwithstanding the undeniable and highly visible breach of this system represented by the politics of the Castro regime in Cuba after 1959. The Caribbean thus came to matter to the US, not for the resources it commanded, nor the strategic flexibility it permitted, but because of what it represented as a proving ground both to the people of the US and to the outside world. These globalist considerations also inevitably meant the gradual ending of that measure of exceptionality accorded to some parts of the region by virtue of the European colonial connection. In the case of the Commonwealth Caribbean, US covert intervention in British Guiana in 1963–4 began a process which later saw the alleged attempt to destabilise the government of Jamaica in the mid-1970s and came to a climax with the intimidation and eventual US-led invasion of Grenada in 1983.

As with the preceding discussion on Europe, this chapter takes as read much of the history of the US-Caribbean relationship. Nevertheless, it begins by setting out the inherited bilateral interests perceived and exercised by the major North American states in Caribbean affairs during the decade of the 1980s, focusing primarily of course on the US but also incorporating the concerns of Canada and Mexico. It then considers the wider North American dimension to US policy which emerged under the auspices of the Enterprise for the Americas Initiative at the beginning of the 1990s, goes on to explore the impact on the Caribbean of the North American Free Trade Agreement ultimately brought into being by President Clinton in January 1994, and ends by endeavouring to assess the implications of the manner in which the Caribbean has now been drawn into the emerging political economy of North America.

Bilateral interests

US concern with the Caribbean has always fluctuated in relation to the degree of confidence felt in Washington about the firmness of its control of political and economic developments in the region. It was precisely the alarm felt at its faltering grip which so dramatically focused US attention upon the whole of the Caribbean Basin – the Caribbean and Central America – in the late 1970s and early 1980s. As already indicated, Grenada under the People's Revolutionary Government was the focus of aversion amongst Commonwealth

Caribbean states. The threat which it represented to US control of the region was paradoxically rendered the greater because it was so tiny in size. If Grenada could successfully pursue its chosen revolutionary course, what might be achieved by larger states in the region? Reagan could thus declare, quite without embarrassment, in March 1983 that 'it is not nutmeg that is at stake down there, it is United States' national security'.[1] The result was the initiation of a programme of US military assistance to many of the other Eastern Caribbean islands, designed to equip them with a para-military apparatus capable of preserving their security against subversive forces.

However, the main tools of the security policy applied to the Caribbean by the Reagan administration were economic. Moreover, because the context was that of security, the economic approach adopted was allowed to break with the global commitment to free trade generally pursued by the US in the Bretton Woods era. Thus the centrepiece of the strategy for the Caribbean which emerged – the so-called Caribbean Basin Initiative – was distinguished by its commitment to preferential trade for a region perceived in Washington to have become a dangerous 'sea of splashing dominoes'. Reagan himself once more revealed the underlying thinking when he introduced the plan to Congress in 1982 as a scheme specifically designed to 'help revitalise the economies of this strategically critical region by attacking the underlying causes of economic stagnation'.[2]

In practice, as is well known, the CBI was crippled from the start by the pressure of special interest lobbying within the US Congress. Shorn of the features most likely to have stimulated Caribbean production and exports, the thrust of US development policy was thus reduced to the structural adjustment packages forced upon so many states in this period by the IMF/World Bank/USAID nexus. Nevertheless, notwithstanding the many failings of the CBI (which have by now been well documented in both official and academic analyses of its impact[3]), it did at least constitute a specific US response to the particular predicament of the Caribbean Basin. Originally introduced with a finite 12-year limit on its provision, it was extended indefinitely in August 1990 as part of a series of revisions passed by Congress and known collectively as CBI 2. However, the other changes incorporated in this legislation, all of which had been circulating around the Congress for fully three years, amounted to very little, principally a small tariff reduction for certain leather-related products. They certainly did not open up the US market to any hitherto excluded items and they did not restore the sugar quotas for Caribbean countries which were so damagingly cut back during the 1980s to the point where the gains which accrued in manufacturing and other non-traditional exports as a result of the CBI were dwarfed by the losses in export revenues from sugar.[4]

Many observers have made these points and the Democrat Congressman Sam Gibbons, who was one of the people most involved in the effort to pass CBI 2, did introduce a bill – a putative CBI 3 – into the House of Representatives in March 1991 which aimed to repair both these omissions from the previous legislation. However, by that stage it had no prospect whatsoever of being passed. The Caribbean has always had a relatively small number of real 'friends' in the US Congress and the few who existed at the beginning of the 1990s were exhausted by the effort they had put into legislating CBI 2. The hard truth for the Caribbean was that the political conditions which had generated even so limited and flawed a measure as the CBI had evaporated. They came with the advent of the 'Second Cold War' and they went with its ending. By the beginning of the 1990s the salience of the old security agenda which saw the Caribbean Basin as a key battleground in the global contest with communism had been utterly superseded and the region had been returned to the place in US security perceptions which it occupied before the Cold War.

This meant that such 'threat' as the Caribbean offered to US security had to be judged solely in its own terms. That narrower agenda highlighted only two items – narcotics and migrants. The US unquestionably already had a well-advertised interest in containing the entry of the former into its domestic society. As regards narcotics production in the Caribbean, it successfully pressed crop eradication programmes on such countries as Jamaica and Belize during the 1980s. It had greater difficulty in controlling the use of Caribbean islands as key transhipment points on the route from the major South American producer countries to the US market. To this end, however, the US pushed the principle of extra-territorial jurisdiction beyond all former limits, granting authority by law to its agencies to intercept all vessels taking cargo to the US and to indict in the US foreigners allegedly conspiring to import narcotics, as well as requiring Caribbean states to sign tax information exchange agreements if they wanted to continue to enjoy some of the benefits of schemes such as CBI. US intervention was also on occasion more direct – conducting 'sting' operations in the Bahamas and the Turks and Caicos Islands, pressuring Caribbean governments to allow US agencies to select the local personnel for drugs enforcement units and exercising the right to 'hot pursuit' of suspected narcotics traffickers into non-US territorial waters. The military action taken in Panama in December 1989 also stands as evidence of the readiness and determination of the US to wield the big stick on narcotics matters, to the point where some analysts began to detect in these moves a potential post-Cold War rationale for continuing US direct intervention in the affairs of the hemisphere.[5]

Migration was the other immediate threat to the US which could be said to reside in the Caribbean. During the 1960s and 1970s more than three million people from the Caribbean islands alone permanently migrated to the US. The flow continued during the 1980s and was added to each year by an increasing number of undocumented illegal immigrants. The Haitian boat-people were thus only the most visible and tragic manifestation of a wider process which served to give an unmistakable and growing Caribbean dimension to US society. Miami and some parts of New York, for example, came to contain major concentrations of Caribbean people. These populations generally attracted more notoriety than acclaim as a result of their alleged propensity to violence, their use of drugs and involvement in crime, and they clearly added to the number of jobs which the US economy was required to generate. To that extent, continuing migration from the Caribbean, and elsewhere in the Americas, quickly became a contentious political issue in the US. On the other hand, although Caribbean groups, with the exception of exiled Cubans, have yet to organise effectively as a lobby in the US domestic political system, they have the potential still to do so in the future and thus represent to some degree the interests of their former homelands in the US policy debate.

These newer security concerns were real enough, but they did not in any way recreate for the Caribbean the attention in Washington which it experienced at the height of the 'Second Cold War' in the mid-1980s. An end had clearly been reached of a distinctive phase – in a nutshell that which gave birth to the CBI – in the bilateral dimension of US-Caribbean relations. Although it was not yet apparent, the exclusively bilateralist emphasis of these relations was also at an end.

The impact of the US on the wider geopolitics of North America as a whole has long been such that its position and politics also deeply influence the policies of the other 'middle powers' of relevance, Canada and Mexico. Both states have had interests in the Caribbean – Canada over a very long period of time – and have exercised a profile in regional affairs accordingly; yet both powers also have it in common that they have always had to treat their relationship with the US as their first priority in hemispheric diplomacy. As a result, Canadian and Mexican approaches to the Caribbean have necessarily had to be filtered through the lenses of US interests, rather than depend solely on the nature of their own bilateral concerns within the region. This needs to be kept in mind as each is now examined.

Canada has only relatively recently begun to come to terms with its location in the Americas. Long oriented more to Europe and the Commonwealth, it now seeks, in the phrase of Joe Clark, its Secretary of State for External Affairs in 1990, to make the Western hemisphere not just 'our house' but 'our home'.[6] The most striking symbol of this shift of perception was its entry into the Organisation of American States in 1990. Canada had in any case maintained trading and diplomatic links with Cuba throughout the Cold War era, although being careful never to overstep the boundaries of dissent acceptable to the US, and it had long claimed to have a 'special relationship' with the Commonwealth Caribbean. The rhetoric attached to the latter postulated the existence of a 'family feeling' between Canadians and the inhabitants of the former British Caribbean territories which was grounded in tourism, immigration and educational ties and was revealed *inter alia* in the outpouring of aid whenever a natural disaster, such as a hurricane, hit the islands.

The claim can be substantiated in political and economic terms, but only up to a point. The relationship was maintained politically by the habit of holding joint Canada-Commonwealth Caribbean heads of government conferences. At one of these gatherings, in 1985, Commonwealth Caribbean leaders put forward a series of requests for improved trade, investment and development assistance which drew a Canadian response – the announcement in 1986 of CARIBCAN, an arrangement extending preferential free trade to a number of Commonwealth Caribbean imports. Other important features of the relationship in this period included diplomatic support, the provision of development assistance (focused on education but also including airport construction and improvement and some security projects such as coastguard training) and the offer of debt relief. All of these measures were undoubtedly useful, but they tended to reflect Canadian responses to Caribbean pressure, rather than Canadian initiatives *per se*, and they cannot be said in any way to have been critical to the development prospects of the islands. Even CARIBCAN itself only increased very slightly the preferences already open to Caribbean producers in the Canadian market under the General Scheme of Preferences.

Mexico has not had the historical links with the Caribbean enjoyed by Canada. Its interests in the region derive in the main from geographical proximity: indeed, the concept was advanced in the early 1990s of Mexico's 'three borders' – the US, Central America and the Caribbean.[7] Its main concern in the region has long been Cuba, which points geographically into the Gulf of Mexico and thus sits at the entrance to Mexico's gateway to the Atlantic. Accordingly successive

Mexican governments resisted attempts to isolate the Castro regime within the hemisphere. Beyond this, the level of official attention paid to the rest of the Caribbean has fluctuated – from the active engagement promoted by President Luis Echeverria in the early 1970s, through the era of oil diplomacy which culminated in 1980 in the signing (in conjunction with Venezuela) of the San José Agreement to supply oil on concessional terms to several Caribbean Basin countries, to the retreat into economic indebtedness of the 1980s. One common theme has been co-operation, where possible, with Venezuela, an arrangement lately extended to include Colombia and duly labelled the 'Group of 3' process. However, many of the claims made for this have been rhetorical, rather than substantive. As for Mexico itself, in 1989 the government did appoint a new roving ambassador to the Caribbean, of itself an indication of a renewed interest in the common problems of the region. However, the ambassador's office was a relatively small operation and even this modest level of direct political interest in the Caribbean was not long maintained.

The EAI and NAFTA

Whilst the various bilateral interests of the US, Canada and Mexico have continued to shape aspects of their policies towards the Caribbean, these considerations have increasingly come to be subsumed within a wider policy framework which focuses not on the Caribbean, or even the old 1980s notion of the Caribbean and Central America in combination as the Caribbean Basin, but rather on the whole of the Americas. The driving force behind this reappraisal has been the new emphasis on the preservation of US economic security, and the subsequent promotion of a renewed US dynamism within the global political economy, which has emerged as perhaps the dominant component of the post-Cold War geopolitical conception in Washington.

The initiation of bilateral talks on trade liberalisation with major economic and political partners, such as Israel and Canada, was an early sign of this reorientation. As explained as early as 1985 by William E. Brock, the then US Trade Representative, 'the reasoning behind these efforts is that additional trade-creating, GATT-consistent liberalisation measures should not be postponed while some of the more inward-looking contracting parties contemplate their own economic malaise'.[8] While the primary motive for the free trade agreement with Israel could be said to be political and therefore something of a special case, the establishment of the US-Canada free trade area in

1989 – amidst not inconsiderable controversy – signalled the seriousness of purpose underpinning this new aspect of US trade policy. After all, Canada was the main single trading partner of the US, absorbing US$79 billion of US exports in 1989, some 22 per cent of the overall total and almost double the value of US shipments to Japan.

For obvious reasons, the Canadian deal attracted a lot of attention in the Americas, especially in Mexico which was itself undergoing major economic reform in the aftermath of its admission in 1982 that it could no longer keep up the interest payments on its debt. Initiated by the administration of President Miguel de la Madrid and then accelerated and deepened by his successor, Carlos Salinas de Gortari, after 1988, this involved the dismantling of Mexico's traditional statist import-substitution model of development and the full embrace of trade liberalisation. Mexico thus joined the General Agreement on Tariffs and Trade (GATT) in 1986 and thereafter unilaterally reduced its tariffs from some as high as 100 per cent to a maximum of 20 per cent, with the average on US goods only 10 per cent. In addition, the economy was comprehensively deregulated, many state-owned companies sold off, the budget deficit reduced massively and new measures put in place to attract foreign investment. Given that further foreign indebtedness was not an option, the latter was deemed to be absolutely essential to the task of meeting the demand for jobs of the million new entrants to the labour market anticipated each year during the 1990s. Salinas made a tour of the EC in January 1990 to investigate its potential for facilitating Mexican development, but returned home convinced that it was no substitute for the US and that the establishment of a free trade area with the US, as achieved by Canada, was the best means of extending investment opportunities in Mexico. The first contacts on the subject were made with Washington in March 1990, wholly, it should be noted, on the initiative of Mexico.

President George Bush's immediate reaction was one of great personal interest and enthusiasm. He had long identified himself as a Texan and the wife of one of his sons, George W. Bush, the 43rd President of the US, was Mexican. In addition, the whole idea played well against the background of a growing concern in Washington with the preservation of US economic advantage in the context of the slow progress then being made towards further multilateral trade liberalisation within the new GATT round. The Mexican government argued that, as a result of its liberalisation, US exports to Mexico had already doubled, rising from US$12.4 billion in 1986 to US$25 billion in 1989, and could be expected to increase still further in the future if the huge Mexican market (at the time some 85 million people) became still more dynamic. In general, it was claimed that Mexican prosperity would also stem the flow of immigrants across the US border and serve to 'lock into place' the Salinas reforms, a goal which was obviously appealing to the US in terms of its own ideological commitment to trade liberalisation. The argument put to Bush thus addressed political as well as economic issues, feeding cleverly on the uneasiness which has long existed in the US about relations with its nearest southern neighbour with which it shares a 2,000 mile border. When these early exploratory talks leaked to the press, Bush and Salinas met and jointly admitted their support for the initiation of US-Mexico free trade negotiations.

As already indicated, Bush himself was very much in the vanguard of his own administration on this issue. In late June 1990, shortly after the Mexican announcement, he made a speech which was given little advance publicity and was certainly not widely discussed between the various relevant government departments before delivery, but which significantly widened the policy agenda of US relations with Latin America and the Caribbean. In this speech Bush set out his Enterprise for the Americas Initiative, advancing proposals for debt reduction, investment promotion and trade liberalisation. It is quite likely that the timing of the speech reflected the President's desire to assure the rest of the hemisphere that Mexico would not be the only country with which the US was prepared to discuss closer economic ties, especially since he was committed to a trip to several leading South American countries before the end of the year. The EAI nevertheless took off politically and became the seminal statement of subsequent US economic policy towards all parts of the hemisphere, including the Caribbean.

Substantively, the EAI contained three components – the restructuring of some official debt owed to the US by hemispheric countries, the promotion of increased investment in the hemisphere via the Inter-American Development Bank (IADB), and the vision offered of a series of free trade agreements with different groups of Latin American, Central American and Caribbean countries, leading in time, as Bush himself grandly put it, to a hemispheric-wide free trade system 'stretching from the port of Anchorage to Tierra del Fuego'.[9] The first two features were useful initiatives but at the same time relatively minor in substance. The Congress was also slow to enact the necessary legislation and the investment thrust of the initiative certainly proved to be even more disappointing in impact than ambition. However, the third feature of the EAI, despite being almost casually thrown up by the US, attracted an enormous amount of interest in the rest of the Americas. Nearly all of it was favourable, reflecting the broad shift from import-substitution to export-oriented strategies of development which had taken place across the whole of Latin America and the Caribbean since the beginning of the 1980s.

Somewhat reluctantly, and for almost wholly defensive reasons, Canada expressed a wish to join the US-Mexico talks which, from February 1991 onwards, thus became trilateral, devoted to the negotiation of a North American Free Trade Agreement intended to eliminate restrictions on the flow of goods, services and investments (but not labour) between the participant countries. In the negotiations the Canadian government clung to the basic terms of the agreement it had previously signed with the US; the US government sought to open up the Mexican market as much as possible but at the same time defended its domestic producers by insisting on tough rules of origin for incoming Mexican imports; and the Mexican government succeeded in keeping its nationalised, and highly symbolic, oil industry largely outside the NAFTA framework but otherwise did what it had to do to secure the free trade accord it so badly wanted.[10] A NAFTA treaty was duly signed between the parties in August 1992 and thereafter only required domestic approval in each of the three countries before it could come into being. It promised to embrace over 360 million people and bring together a collective Gross Domestic Product of approximately US$6,239 billion.

As regards the wider hemispheric free trade proposal, the US initially limited itself to signing so-called 'framework agreements' with other South and Central American countries. Bolivia, like Mexico, had signed before the EAI announcement; Colombia and Ecuador followed in July 1990, Chile in October, Honduras and Costa Rica in November, Venezuela in April 1991, El Salvador and Peru in May, and the MERCOSUR group (Brazil, Argentina, Uruguay and Paraguay), Panama and Nicaragua all in June 1991. These bilateral framework agreements were essentially assertions of principle that reflected current US international trade concerns. They typically referred to the benefits of open trade and investment, the increased importance of services to regional economies, the need for adequate intellectual property rights protection, the importance of observing and promoting internationally-recognised workers' rights and the desirability of resolving trade and investment problems expeditiously. The parties further agreed that bilateral consultative mechanisms were useful and established accordingly Councils on Trade and Investment to meet at mutually agreed times and monitor trade and investment relations (the so-called 'immediate action agenda') in conjunction with the respective private sectors of the countries involved. In effect, the agreements served as holding operations whilst the US sought to digest free trade with Mexico.

By comparison, certainly with that of the larger Latin American states, the Caribbean's reaction to the EAI was more muted. The feeling was that Caribbean countries had less to gain and a good deal more to lose. Concern attached not so much to the debt proposals, under which Jamaica for one amongst Commonwealth Caribbean countries was expected to gain, or the new investment incentives, about which hints were dropped within the IADB that particular attention would be paid to the smaller countries within the hemisphere. The worry was the proposal for hemispheric free trade which, from the perspective of the Caribbean Basin, threatened to extend to the whole of the Americas the preferential trading advantages it enjoyed under CBI. Put starkly, the argument was, and still is, that a CBI generalised to the hemisphere was a CBI effectively eroded for the Caribbean Basin. As the president of Caribbean/Latin American Action (C/LAA) put it in a statement to a US Congressional subcommittee in February 1991, this 'would occur not because the CBI countries' access would be less, but because their Mexican competitors' access would be made greater'.[11] The NAFTA would also be mutually binding between the signatory parties, whereas CBI 2, although nominally permanent, could in theory be rescinded by Congress at any time. Moreover, Mexico would arguably gain a further psychological advantage over the Caribbean Basin in the competition for investment location by being seen in US business circles as today's, rather than yesterday's, place in the spotlight. In the light of these and other considerations, the C/LAA president concluded that, 'added to its natural advantages of size, development, and a long land border with the US', NAFTA would further 'tip the balance in favour of Mexico over the Caribbean ... [and] ... leave the countries of the Caribbean and Central America seriously vulnerable to loss of both markets and investment opportunities to their Mexican competitors'.[12]

Yet, as has been seen, the political momentum behind the notion of hemispheric free trade was such that five Central American countries had signed framework agreements with the US by the end of June 1991. In the case of the Commonwealth Caribbean, after early hesitation on the part of the region, a similar process of discussion with the US Trade Representative's Office was initiated by the Jamaican government on behalf ultimately of all the members of CARICOM. Following approval of the draft agreement by the annual conference of CARICOM heads of government, a US-Caribbean Community framework agreement was signed on 22 July 1991. The text was broadly the same as all the other agreements. It noted in the preamble that the economies of the Commonwealth Caribbean were 'small and undiversified' and agreed to look at 'measures to improve the operation of the CBI', but otherwise focused the attention of the new joint council on the following issues: 'investment liberalization including entry requirements ...; the review of investment aspects of tax treaties;

market access barriers affecting both agricultural and industrial products; liberalization of trade and investment with other regional markets; [and] trade in services'.[13] However, as in all the agreements, any topic relating to trade or investment could be raised by either party in the council.

In common with most of the Central American countries, the Commonwealth Caribbean has thus already taken a decisive step towards the wider embrace of hemispheric free trade. Yet, as was amply made clear by US officials, the conclusion of a framework agreement did not of itself mean that the US would necessarily embark on free trade talks themselves, although this was, of course, what ensued with both Canada and Mexico. The Bush administration never indicated, for example, whether it would be the US or all the NAFTA states which would be the agency which would in time negotiate with the rest of the hemisphere; whether applicants would be treated separately, collectively or in regional groupings; whether a queue would be constructed in accordance with the order in which the 'framework agreements' had been signed; or whether alternatively a threshold system would apply whereby talks were initiated first with those countries which had already most fully opened up their economies. All that was revealed by the vacuum which emerged on these matters in the last months of the Bush administration was that it would be the US which would decide whether, when, with whom and on what basis it would eventually enter free trade talks with other parts of the Americas.

Nevertheless, even in conception, the EAI and NAFTA – which need to be evaluated in conjunction – revealed a good deal about the emerging US view of its position *vis-à-vis* the rest of the Americas in the 1990s and beyond. They were designed, as we have seen, in the aftermath of a decade or more of forced structural adjustment of Latin American and Caribbean economies and they sought in effect to set out and enforce new economic and political 'rules of the game' for the 1990s, and beyond, within the hemisphere. These rules reflected the triumph of economic liberalism, of faith in export-led growth and of belief in the centrality of the private sector to the development process. They had no truck with anything beyond free trade, openly eschewing any reference to protective and/or social dimensions. The politics of the situation was therefore incontrovertible: the EAI and NAFTA required that regional countries 'sign up' for this entire ideological regime. The emerging political order of the Americas left no place for political leaders who found it difficult to endorse these nostrums. Behind all this, of course, was the threat of exclusion, of having to pursue export-led development without access to the US market – in short, the punitive consequences of crossing US economic power. In other words, the goal of the US under Bush was nothing less than to bring about the full and final integration of Latin America and the Caribbean into the new global economy of the 1990s.

Whatever advantages were or were not likely to flow to the developing parts of the hemisphere from such a project, the US itself expected to gain. Peter Hakim, staff director of the Inter-American Dialogue, explicitly emphasised this point in giving testimony to the Congress on the EAI in March 1991:

> I believe that Latin America, with its population of 400 million people, is important to the economic well-being of the United States. Even in the midst of depression, Latin America is a $50 billion a year market for US exporters – larger, for example, than the Japanese market. An economically healthy and growing Latin America could absorb $20 to $30 billion more in US exports each year, an amount equivalent to what we now export to Germany. Of every dollar Latin America spends on imports, 50 cents comes to the United States. There is nowhere else in the world where we enjoy that kind of advantage.[14]

The last comment was the telling one: in a period of intensified economic competition with the EC and Japan, the Bush administration and its corporate allies saw Latin America as a part of the world where the US had a greater natural advantage than either of its main trading rivals. It also recognised that parts of the Americas, especially North America, had become increasingly linked at the levels of production and trade over the past decade. Weintraub, for example, has referred to the process of 'silent integration' which has taken place between the US, Canadian and Mexican economies as a consequence of the spreading tentacles of multinational corporations operating across all three countries, and Maingot has shown that the same phenomenon now increasingly embraces the 'offshore Caribbean'.[15] In sum, the Bush administration conceived of the EAI and NAFTA in wholly national interest terms, as devices by which to create an increasingly integrated hemispheric economy which the US could then use as the base from which to export ever more competitively to other, more distant, markets, preferably within the ambit of an extended GATT.

The Clinton era

Bill Clinton was initially slow to see the significance of either of the trade policy initiatives passed on to him by Bush. During his presidential campaign he focused on the economy and the issue of national economic revival, but he did not clarify in any detail his position on international trade issues, seeking no doubt judiciously to distance himself from the protectionist instincts of some of his Democratic Party rivals without embracing liberalisation too enthusiastically. He thus gave support to the ongoing GATT round, implying that he could negotiate a better deal than Bush, and endorsed NAFTA, albeit expressing some reservations about it in deference to Democratic Party opposition, especially within the labour unions. In office Clinton was true to his candidacy. An early review of his policy noted the emergence of 'an *ad hoc*, even incoherent, trade approach which is characterized by a lack of philosophical underpinning'.[16] On the GATT the administration returned to the negotiating table and endeavoured to unpick some aspects of the arrangements on agriculture which had been provisionally agreed with the EC. On NAFTA it set in motion the negotiation of two so-called 'side agreements' with Mexico and Canada on environmental and labour issues. But, even when they were agreed, Clinton waited until the final stages of Congressional consideration of the whole NAFTA legislative package before committing his administration to a whole-hearted attempt to see that it was passed. He was effective and ultimately successful in this and NAFTA duly came into being on 1 January 1994.

Even at this moment of triumph, Clinton did not seize on the inauguration of NAFTA as a means to send the rest of the hemisphere a positive message (*à la* Bush) about the merits of free trade. It was not that he was opposed to this vision, for in a meeting with Salinas in late 1992 before actually taking up office he explicitly endorsed the original Bush proposal to extend free trade southwards as soon as possible. The NAFTA agreement also possessed an access clause, although it was unclear how it might be implemented in practice and interesting, to say the least, that it did not confine future membership to countries within the Americas or indeed any geographical region. Yet, once NAFTA was passed, the other governments of the region found that it was they who had to keep raising the issue with Washington, not the other way round. The US administration developed other priorities and, in general, appeared capable of only being able to focus on a tiny number of issues at any one time. In trade matters GATT naturally became the focus. It was not, therefore, until after the text of the Uruguay Round had finally, and painfully, been agreed and then approved by the Congress, and just before the opening of a meeting of the heads of government of all the states of the hemisphere (with the sole exception of Cuba) in Miami in December 1994 – a gathering which had been promised many months earlier – that there was any real sign in Washington of renewed thinking on the matter of trade policy towards the Americas.

Nevertheless, at this so-called 'Summit of the Americas', the first such Pan-American conference to have been addressed by a US president since Franklin Roosevelt went to Lima in 1936 and the first to have been held at all since 1967, Clinton did finally match Bush's EAI rhetoric. He called for the establishment of a Free Trade Area of the Americas and boldly set the year 2005 as the date of its inauguration. 'We can create a new partnership for prosperity', he intoned, 'where freedom and trade and economic opportunity become the common property of the people of the Americas' from Alaska to Argentina.[17] His underlying argument was just the same as that deployed by Bush. Global economic changes made it necessary for the US to compete and win; exports created jobs; and Latin America and the Caribbean was a growing market in which the US could sell. Again, the precise mechanism by which an FTAA was to be achieved was not spelled out, beyond the invitation to Chile to open negotiations first, which was itself merely a reiteration of a promise previously made by the Bush administration. At a minimum, though, Clinton can be said at least to have caught up with and taken on board the far-reaching economic agenda for the Americas which George Bush set out in his EAI speech in 1990 and given himself and his successors a decade in which to realise it. That period of time may well be needed. Progress towards an FTAA since Miami has been very limited. Rhetorical recommitments to the overall goal of hemispheric free trade have been made at subsequent ministerial and heads of state meetings and a series of working groups are busily 'negotiating' under different subheadings. These include – significantly from a Commonwealth Caribbean perspective – a group devoted to the special problems of smaller economies, something the US did acknowledge in the preamble to the US-CARICOM framework agreement. Nevertheless, the political reality is that, post-NAFTA, Congress will not give Clinton the fast-track negotiating authority which is needed in the US legislative system to secure any trade deal, with the result that the whole FTAA question thus awaits the next president due to be elected in 2000.

One final point is, however, worth making in this context. It has become evident beyond any doubt that Mexico has now been drawn so closely into the global economic strategy of the US that it cannot be let go, come what may. Clinton demonstrated this for all to see when, within just weeks of the Miami summit, the Mexican currency crashed and the President immediately put together a rescue package of no less that US$40 billion of loan supports. As Clinton said at the time, with studied underemphasis, 'it is in America's economic and strategic interest that Mexico succeeds'.[18]

Conclusion: The new politics of 'Caribbean America'

The same is actually true in respect of the Caribbean, even though it is not perceived in Washington to be anywhere near as important as Mexico. Yet the reality is that the changing roles forced upon the US and the various countries of the Caribbean by shifts in the structure of the world order over the past twenty to thirty years have served to entangle their respective fates in a more intense and complicated way than ever before. Expressed in more theoretical terms, the argument is that there has progressively been forged a new structural context linking the political economies of the US and the Caribbean, albeit in a fashion that is far from being symmetrical or mutually beneficial. This process is best depicted as the making of 'Caribbean America'.[19] This broad claim can be fairly easily sustained by reference to recent patterns of trade, financial flows, migration and narcotics movements and is also increasingly underpinned by the development of common cultural forms across the US and the Caribbean. The problem is that politics has not yet caught up with these deeper developments. The distinguishing feature of the current agenda of US-Caribbean relations is, paradoxically, that it lacks a single distinguishing feature. In marked contrast with the Cold War era when the objective of security, defined always as protection against the communist threat, effectively overrode every other policy consideration, the contemporary US-Caribbean relationship has been reconfigured as a series of interlocking transnational policy communities in which different actors within the US and within the Caribbean, with interests in the same economic and political issues, engage with each other in different policy arenas which do not necessarily connect easily or coherently one with the other.[20]

The main such policy arenas can be easily identified. One does clearly still concern security, but, as indicated earlier, this now relates in the main to the Caribbean's predicament as a major site of narcotics trafficking, with all the links that this business has to illegal money laundering, gun smuggling, criminal violence and other threats to the social and political order of both the US and all parts of the region.[21] Although some Caribbean governments have on occasion over the years been criticised by different parts of the US administration for the laxity of their approach to narcotics control, in recent times most have cooperated with the US to the best of their capacity. However, for a short period in the mid-1990s some aspects of US anti-narcotics policy were perceived in the Caribbean to transgress the proper limits of extra-territorial action. Notable here were the proposed US Maritime and Overflight Agreements – the so-called 'shiprider' agreements – which sought to permit US land and sea patrols and searches within the national boundaries of Caribbean countries, as well as the overflying of their air-space, in order to try to stem the intra-regional flow of narcotics. They were called 'shiprider' agreements because they involved officers of the national coastguard being placed on board US vessels. Although most Commonwealth Caribbean governments signed up to the preferred US form of the agreement fairly quickly during the early part of 1996, those of Barbados and Jamaica resisted, arguing essentially that their sovereignty over their national space had to be maintained. As a result, both countries felt that undue pressure was subsequently brought to bear on them by the US, Jamaica being verbally threatened with 'decertification' as an ally in the anti-drugs campaign by an official of the Department of State's Bureau of International Narcotics and Law Enforcement, and Barbados allegedly being alerted to a Federal Aviation Administration report that planned to reduce the safety rating of its international airport in a way that would have prevented regional airlines which used its facilities from flying to US airports.[22]

The other major policy arena concerns development, although, again as we have seen, the emphasis in that debate has moved preeminently to the question of trade. For the past few years Caribbean governments have repeatedly pressed on the US government the matter of some kind of interim 'NAFTA parity' as a stepping stone towards either admission into NAFTA or participation within the prospective FTAA. In so doing, they have come up against firm opposition from US textile and other producers and a consequent reticence on the part of the Clinton administration to put much weight behind Congressional measures that would have given the Caribbean the parity it desired. The outcome has been an impasse wherein successive legislative proposals have languished and then fallen.[23] At the same time, several Caribbean governments, especially those in the Eastern Caribbean generally still highly dependent on their protected EU markets, have been notably hesitant about their capacity to survive in the full competitive rigour of reciprocal free trade and have preferred to emphasise their need for the continuing provision of aid and other measures of support. Their case for receiving special consideration has met with little sympathy in the US, and US aid to the Caribbean has fallen dramatically from the high levels of the mid-1980s. A final and controversial subplot in the trade policy arena relates to the sale of the bananas produced by the very small Windward Island states. This is discussed extensively in the following chapter, but it should be noted that the Caribbean has universally seen the stance of the US government and its corporate supporters on this question as constituting insensitive and inimical behaviour towards its development interests.

In addition to these broad areas of policy which stretch across the whole region, albeit with different emphases and intensities, two particular Caribbean countries – Cuba and Haiti – have come to acquire policy communities within 'Caribbean America' in their own right. This reflects an important and continuing bilateralist strain in US policy towards the region. The debate about Cuban policy has long concerned the extent of the pressure which US administrations have been prepared to bring to bear on the Cuban revolutionary regime to make a transition to democracy and has lately been focused upon reactions to the Cuban Liberty and Democracy Act, passed into law in March 1996 and popularly known as the Helms-Burton Act.[24] The debate about Haiti is preoccupied with the matter of the rebuilding of that country after the overthrow of the long Duvalier dictatorship and the subsequent US intervention in September 1994. It repeatedly begs the question of how far different US state agencies and other non-state actors are prepared to go in involving themselves in that most difficult process.[25] In each case different sectional interests are aroused which make Cuba and Haiti separate and distinctive policy arenas; yet at the same time the politics they generate has often cut across the broader policy debates about economic and security matters in 'Caribbean America' as a whole in complex and sometimes confusing ways.

For the most part, then, what we have called the new politics of 'Caribbean America' is conducted via separate, connected, overlapping policy communities. That said, these communities do still on occasion find themselves brought together and their processes filtered through old-fashioned state-to-state diplomatic mechanisms. This leads finally to a brief consideration of the US-Caribbean summit meeting which took place in May 1997. Although the actual meeting, which took place in Barbados, was extraordinarily brief, it was nevertheless, as Clinton himself said in his opening remarks, 'the first time that an American President has actually held a summit with the Caribbean heads of government within the region itself'. Indeed, with that rhetorical deftness for which he is well known, he went on to observe that it was 'not a meeting between Caribbean nations and the United States, but rather a meeting among Caribbean nations *including* the United States'.[26]

Needless to say, the results of the meeting were not so striking. Discussion ranged over issues of crime and justice, narcotics, trade and bananas, as well as telecommunications, aviation, sustainable development and so on. Neither 'side' won many 'bankable' assurances from the other, although Barbados and Jamaica did secure sufficient minor concessions from the US in the run-up to the summit to sign the 'shiprider' agreements. The potential significance of the summit lies instead in the enhanced mutual understanding it *may* have generated between US and Caribbean elites. For example, the so-called Bridgetown Declaration of Principles to which the summit gave birth did contain one notable concession to Caribbean thinking in that it openly acknowledged 'the inextricable link between trade, economic development, security and prosperity in our societies'. The phrase 'inextricable link' was a Caribbean contribution to the draft which was, at least implicitly, intended to be critical of the US inclination to treat narcotics matters separately from trade matters. In similar fashion another passage expressed the conviction that 'stable and prosperous economies, buttressed by the rule of law, are bulwarks against the forces of transnational crime', although here the insertion of the reference to the rule of law reflected a US priority. Other notable features of the Declaration were a recognition of 'the significant contribution of our respective nationals as immigrant communities to the development of each other's societies' (an interesting acceptance of the social reality of 'Caribbean America') and an acknowledgement of 'the need for a new era in our partnership' (again, an acceptance that the summit had the potential to mark a break-point in US-Caribbean relations).[27] In that vein perhaps the most tangible commitment of the Declaration was that all foreign ministers of Caribbean states and the US secretary of state would henceforth meet annually to review relations, supported by the establishment of new joint committees on 'justice and security' and on 'development, finance and environmental issues' and by the continued work of the CARICOM/US Council on Trade and Investment set up in the aftermath of the EAI.

These plans were conceived, unavoidably, within the mechanisms of conventional inter-state exchanges, and they are not unimportant. But it is now a mistake to locate the contemporary US-Caribbean relationship in a context that, in the parlance of international relations theory, is too narrowly realist. By contrast, the essence of the argument of 'Caribbean America' is that the many linkages between the US and the Caribbean have reached a sufficient depth and intensity across such a range of issues that they must be seen to have created a novel structural context (itself located within the wider construct of North America) within which the politics of the relationship currently operates. From that perspective, the May 1997 summit can perhaps be interpreted as the first meeting, albeit for the moment unrecognised as such by most, if not all, of its participants, of the political directorate of an emergent 'Caribbean America'.

Notes

1   President Reagan's speech to the National Association of Manufacturers, cited in *Caribbean Contact*, April 1983.

2   President Ronald Reagan, 'The Caribbean Basin Plan', speech to Congress, mimeo, 17 March 1982, p. 2.

3   The literature here is considerable. On the official side, the US International Trade Commission has produced annual reports to Congress on *The Impact of the Caribbean Basin Recovery Act on US Industries and Consumers*, Washington DC, 1985–90. On the academic side, amongst the best discussions are Richard S. Newfarmer, 'Economic policy toward the Caribbean Basin: the balance sheet', *Journal of Interamerican Studies and World Affairs*, 27, 1, 1985, pp. 63–89; Glenn O. Phillips and Talbert O. Shaw (eds), *The Caribbean Basin Initiative: Genuine or Deceptive?*, Baltimore, 1987; Carmen Diana Deere *et al.*, *In the Shadows of the Sun: Caribbean Development Alternatives and US Policy*, Boulder, 1990; and Winston H. Griffith, 'CARICOM countries and the Caribbean Basin Initiative', *Latin American Perspectives*, 17, 1, 1990, pp. 33–54.

4   See Stuart Tucker and Maiko Chambers, *US Sugar Quotas and the Caribbean Basin*, Overseas Development Policy Council Focus No. 6, Washington DC, 1989.

5   See Waltrand Queiser Morales, 'The war on drugs: a new US national security doctrine?', *Third World Quarterly*, 11, 3, 1989, pp. 147–69.

6   Cited in George W. Schuyler, 'Perspectives on Canada and Latin America: changing context . . . changing policy?', *Journal of Interamerican Studies and World Affairs*, 33, 1, 1991, p. 19.

7   Oficina del Embajador en Mision Especial para Asuntos del Caribe, *El Caribe: Nuestra Tercera Frontera*, Memoria del I Seminario sobre el Caribe, Secretaria de Relaciones Exteriores, Mexico City, 1990.

8   William E. Brock, 'US trade policy toward developing countries', in E. H. Preeg (ed.), *Hard Bargaining Ahead: US Trade Policy and Developing Countries*, Washington DC, 1985, p. 38.

9   White House press release, 'The Enterprise for the Americas Initiative', mimeo, Washington DC, June 1990.

10 For a discussion of the competing interests of the three states, see David Leyton-Brown, 'The political economy of North American free trade', in Richard Stubbs and Geoffrey Underhill (eds), *Political Economy and the Changing Global Order*, London, 1994, pp. 352–65.

11 Statement of Frederic H. Brooks, President, Caribbean/Latin American Action and Chairman, Riddell Inc. to the Subcommittee on Trade, Committee on Ways and Means, US House of Representatives, mimeo, Washington DC, February 1991.

12 *Ibid.*

13 *Agreement between the Government of the United States of America and the Caribbean Community ('CARICOM') Concerning a United States-CARICOM Council on Trade and Investment*, US Trade Representative's Office, Washington DC, July 1991.

14 Statement of Peter Hakim, Inter-American Dialogue, to the Subcommittee on Foreign Relations, US House of Representatives Hearings on 'External Debt and Free Trade in the Americas', mimeo, Washington DC, March 1991.

15 Sydney Weintraub, 'The North American free trade debate', *Washington Quarterly*, 13, 1990, pp. 119–30; and Anthony P. Maingot, 'The offshore Caribbean', in Anthony Payne and Paul Sutton (eds), *Modern Caribbean Politics*, Baltimore, 1993, pp. 259–76.

16   Franklin L. Lavin, 'Clinton and trade', *The National Interest*, 32, 1993, p. 29.

17   White House press release, 'Clinton envisions partnership for prosperity at summit', mimeo, Washington DC, 9 December 1994.

18   *Miami Herald*, 12 January 1995.

19   The theoretical background underpinning this argument is set out in Anthony Payne, 'The new political economy of area studies', *Millennium: Journal of International Studies*, 27, 2, 1998, pp. 253–73.

20   For further elaboration of this claim, see Anthony Payne, 'Rethinking United States-Caribbean relations: towards a new mode of transterritorial governance', *Review of International Studies*, 26, 1, 2000, pp. 1–14.

21   The most informed analyses of the narcotics problem in the Caribbean have lately been found in the work of Ivelaw Griffith. See, most recently, his *Drugs and Security in the Caribbean: Sovereignty under Siege*, Pennsylvania, 1997.

22   See *Caribbean Insight*, January 1997, pp. 1, 12.

23   For an account, see Gregory K. Schopfle, 'US-Caribbean trade relations over the last decade: from CBI to ACS', in Ransford W. Palmer (ed.), *The Repositioning of US-Caribbean Relations in the New World Order*, Westport, 1997, pp. 137–9.

24   A recent review of this issue can be found in Pamela Falk, 'The US-Cuba agenda: opportunity or stalemate', *Journal of Interamerican Studies and World Affairs*, 39, 1, 1997.

25   Again, a good recent review of US Haitian policy can be found in William I. Robinson, *Promoting Polyarchy: Globalization, US Intervention, and Hegemony*, Cambridge, 1996, pp. 256–316.

26   White House press release, 'Remarks by the President during welcoming ceremony with Caribbean leaders', mimeo, Bridgetown, 10 May 1997.

27   All the quotations in this paragraph are drawn from *The Bridgetown Declaration of Principles*, mimeo, Caribbean/United States Summit, Bridgetown, 10 May 1997.

10 | The international political economy of Caribbean bananas

One of the most problematic and difficult questions that emerged in the Caribbean in the 1990s was the future of the banana trade. This was put under threat from changes introduced by the EU to its banana import regime and by the WTO in the direction of liberalised trade. Foremost at stake has been the livelihood of thousands of small-holder farmers in the Caribbean and the future prosperity of three of the Windward Islands which rely on bananas for more than half their export earnings. But beyond this immediate threat there also arose a whole range of issues which bear directly on the involvement of the Commonwealth Caribbean in the new world economic order, its relationship with the US and Latin America and the prospects for development of small vulnerable dependent economies.

This chapter seeks to make sense of a very complex, and at the time of writing still unresolved, situation by identifying the interests of the various parties directly concerned. The first part examines the background, the problem and the proposed solution to this issue as set out in the adoption of a new banana regime (NBR) in the EU. The second part then looks at the different reactions to the regime in the Caribbean, Latin America, Europe and the US and the eventual adoption of a 'Framework Agreement' (FA) through which the regime secured a workable basis in the US and Latin America. The third part then looks at the operation of the regime and the many challenges to it, not only in Latin America and the US but also in the EU, which eventually led to its reform following a ruling against it by the WTO. The final part examines the revised banana regime brought forward by the EU and the continued opposition to it by the US and Latin America in the WTO, which led to further changes to the detriment of the Caribbean.

Background

A number of competing interests and actors can be identified in Europe, the Caribbean and in Latin America.

Europe

The banana market in Europe grew from a series of national measures that sought to protect favoured companies and sources of supply. It was, as a result, immensely complex.

There were three main sources of supply: (a) EU bananas grown and marketed within the EU itself, major producers being the Canary Islands and Martinique and Guadeloupe (DOM) with the DOM having 10 per cent of market share in 1990; (b) African and Caribbean (ACP) bananas, with the Caribbean providing 11.2 per cent and Africa 6.7 per cent of the market; and (c) Latin American bananas with 57.9 per cent of the market. It is important to note that the EU market increased rapidly in the latter part of the 1980s. In 1992 it was 3.89 million tonnes, compared to 2.99 million tonnes in 1988 and 3.47 million tonnes in 1990. The main beneficiaries of growth were the Latin American producers who increased their market share from 53.6 per cent of the total in 1988 to 61.8 per cent in 1992. In 1988 the DOM accounted for 12.3 per cent and the ACP 17.2 per cent, two-thirds of which was supplied by Caribbean producers. In 1992 the figures were 9.6 per cent and 17.7 per cent respectively, with the ACP Caribbean producers again providing around two-thirds.[1]

There were three distinct banana regimes: (a) a preferential market in France, the United Kingdom, Spain, Italy, Portugal and Greece for either EU and/or ACP producers; (b) a duty-free market in Germany; and (c) a market subject to a 20 per cent tariff in Denmark, Ireland, Belgium, the Netherlands and Luxembourg. The regimes were maintained by a complex system of licences that ensured some suppliers were favoured over others. In 1990 Spain imported all its bananas from the Canary Islands; France 59 per cent of its bananas from the DOM; and Portugal 35 per cent from Madeira. The ACP provided 88 per cent of the UK market, overwhelmingly from the Caribbean; 35 per cent of the French market, mainly from Africa; and 14 per cent of the Italian market. The Latin American producers provided virtually 100 per cent of the Belgian, Danish and German markets (the latter at 1.16 million tonnes being one-third of the total for the whole EU); over 90 per cent of the Irish and Dutch markets; 85 per cent of the Italian market; as well as 12 per cent of the UK market.[2]

The above gave rise to distinctive groups of differential interests in each country, concentrated in different corporate/state alliances. In the case of France, Spain and the UK the companies thrived on preference and sought to preserve as much as possible their privileged position in the market. The UK serves as a good example. The market was dominated by two companies, Geest and Fyffes, with 60 per cent and

25 per cent of market share respectively in 1991. The companies enjoyed close relationships with the UK government and were active in shipping, ripening and wholesale distribution. By way of contrast, the companies involved in the sale of Latin American bananas in the EU favoured open markets since this would give them a price advantage. Once again, transnational corporations were dominant, in this case Standard Fruit (Chiquita) and United Fruit (Dole) with 43 per cent and 13 per cent of the EU market respectively.[3] However, given that they were US transnational corporations (TNCs) they did not enjoy the same access to government as the European companies. Their interests were therefore represented by their 'clients' in the importing, ripening, wholesale and retail trades in Europe, particularly in Belgium, Germany and the Netherlands.

The Caribbean

The banana trade from the Caribbean was governed in the case of the DOM by various national regulations in force in France, and in the case of the Windward Islands, Belize, Jamaica and Suriname largely by those in force in the UK.

Bananas are one of the principal agricultural exports from the DOM, accounting for 60 per cent of the export revenue of Guadeloupe and 49 per cent of that of Martinique.[4] Costs of production are high at some 0.555 ECU/kg,[5] and export sales were sustained only because France had a policy of reserving up to two-thirds of its market for DOM bananas and one-third for bananas from the African ACP. In 1992 France obtained 37 per cent of its bananas from Martinique and 22 per cent from Guadeloupe. Any shortfall in supply from preferential markets was filled through the purchase of Latin American bananas subject to the 20 per cent common external tariff introduced in 1963.

The principal banana exporters to the EU in the ACP Caribbean in 1992 were, in descending order, St Lucia (29 per cent of the ACP Caribbean total), Jamaica (17 per cent), St Vincent (17 per cent), Dominica (13 per cent), the Dominican Republic (9 per cent), Suriname (7 per cent), Belize (7 per cent), and Grenada (1 per cent).[6] Dependence on banana exports was and still is most acute in the Windward Islands. In the late 1980s, bananas accounted for 69 per cent of the export revenue in Dominica, 32 per cent of GDP and 50 per cent of employment; in St Lucia 59 per cent of export revenue, 37 per cent of GDP and 46 per cent of employment; and in St Vincent 42 per cent of export revenue, 25 per cent of GDP and 54 per cent of employment.[7] Costs of production were relatively high, estimated at 0.460 ECU/kg for Windward Island and Jamaican bananas.[8] Most ACP

Caribbean bananas are marketed in the UK. In 1992 the UK sourced 20 per cent of its bananas from St Lucia, 14 per cent from Jamaica, 10 per cent from St Vincent and 8 per cent from Dominica.[9] The market in the UK was controlled by a licensing system which granted duty-free entry for unrestricted quantities of ACP bananas, but imposed a quota and 20 per cent common external tariff on Latin American bananas.

Latin America

Latin America dominates the world trade in bananas, accounting for 75 per cent of world exports in 1990. The major market was the US followed by the EU and the major players in the banana trade were United Brands (Chiquita) with 35 per cent of the world market, Standard Fruit (Dole) 20 per cent and Del Monte 15 per cent in that year.[10]

The big five exporters to the EU were Ecuador with 28 per cent of the total in 1992, Colombia 22 per cent, Panama 20 per cent, Costa Rica 19 per cent and Honduras 8 per cent.[11] Bananas account for 36 per cent of export revenue in Honduras, 29 per cent in Panama, 20 per cent in Costa Rica, 14 per cent in Ecuador and 5 per cent in Colombia.[12] Costs of production are relatively low at 0.200 ECU/kg which has made Latin American bananas the most competitive in world trade.[13] This benefited Germany which, under the Treaty of Rome, enjoyed a special right to import bananas duty-free from any source. In 1992 it imported 27 per cent of its bananas from Ecuador, 17 per cent from Panama, 17 per cent from Colombia, 16 per cent from Costa Rica and 6 per cent from Honduras.[14] Other major European importers of Latin American bananas are Italy and the Benelux (Belgium, Netherlands and Luxembourg) countries. The Benelux countries are particularly important since they are major importers with an onward trade within the EU. In 1992 they imported 28 per cent of their bananas from Panama, 25 per cent from Colombia, 15 per cent from Costa Rica, 11 per cent from Ecuador and 7 per cent from Honduras.[15] All imports were subject to the 20 per cent common external tariff.

The three US banana TNCs were active in the EU market. They held 66 per cent of the EU market, divided 43 per cent to Chiquita, 13 per cent to Dole and 10 per cent to Del Monte.[16] The exploitative practices of the TNCs attracted criticism in Latin America and the US. In the EU non-governmental development organisations (NGDOs) highlighted the poor working conditions on banana plantations in Latin America and action was taken by the European Commission against United Brands (Chiquita) in 1976 for manipulation of the market. Following a complaint filed under Article 86 of the Treaty of Rome the Commission found that Chiquita had abused its dominant position (at that time 40 per cent of the market) by forbidding customers to resell green bananas; by charging different prices to customers for Chiquita bananas; by charging unfair prices to customers; and by refusing supplies to an important customer. Chiquita was fined one million ECU and required to end its abuses.[17] Further, in 1992, the European Competition Authorities found Chiquita had abused its dominant position by attempting to restrict Fyffes (in which it had recently sold its interests) from using its trademark 'Fyffes' outside of the UK and Ireland.

Problem

The situation just outlined was probably acceptable enough to most parties to have continued into the future without major revision. The problem was that it was not compatible with the aims of the Single European Market (SEM). As we have seen, this sought a European Community 'without internal frontiers' by the end of December 1992 within which there would be the free movement of goods, persons, services and capital. The various national regimes for bananas had to be replaced by a single regime applicable to all. In turn, this was bound to have major external effects on the banana producers and the various banana interests in and outside the EU as well as on wider international trading obligations, particularly within the GATT where the EU had committed itself to a policy of trade liberalisation. The difficulty the European Commission faced as the organisation charged with implementing the SEM was how to reconcile five competing sets of interests.

Article 115 and the German Protocol

Article 115 of the Treaty of Rome allowed member states to maintain national barriers to the free circulation of goods. Its provisions were the main juridical base for the preferential regimes maintained by the UK, France, Italy and Greece (those in Portugal and Spain were permitted until the end of 1995 under their treaties of accession). Article 115 was recognised as incompatible with the SEM. Equally incompatible was the protocol under the Treaty of Rome which allowed Germany its tariff-free quota, unless this was to be the new basis of the common trade regime. A 'common' regime was in operation only in Ireland, Denmark, the Netherlands, Belgium and Luxembourg where a 20 per cent external tariff was levied on all banana imports. In short, the SEM required the establishment of a new regime for bananas *common to all* in which the free circulation of bananas throughout the EU could take place.

The Banana Protocol

Article 1 of the Banana Protocol attached to the fourth Lomé Convention stated that 'in respect of its banana exports to the Community markets, no ACP state shall be placed, as regards access to its traditional markets and its advantages on those markets, in a less favourable situation than in the past or present'. Since the Lomé Convention was legally binding to the year 2000 the EU was under an obligation to maintain access for ACP bananas at current levels. The problem was that ACP bananas were not competitive with dollar bananas and only found an outlet on European markets through the various preferential licensing schemes. The same held even more so for EU-produced bananas, which were even more uncompetitive and did not benefit from inclusion in the Common Agricultural Policy. A common market for bananas (which is not the same as a free market for bananas) would therefore clearly have to maintain differential treatment of some sort for ACP and EU-produced bananas as against those from Latin America.

The GATT

At the beginning of the Uruguay Round the EU committed itself to 'the fullest possible liberalisation of trade in tropical products'. Although bananas were not included on the Tropical Product Negotiating Group's agenda, the EU was well aware of US interests on this issue. It was also acutely aware that, as the partial common market for bananas, which existed in the EU, was based on the GATT Most Favoured Nation principle, any attempt to increase the tariff or impose quotas would be resisted within and outside the EU as well as in the GATT. This was further heightened by the controversy with the US in the Uruguay Round over agricultural protection within the EU as a whole, which led to an impasse at the end of 1990. The 'solution', as advanced by Arthur Dunkel, the Secretary-General of GATT, at the end of 1991 – the conversion of all existing border restrictions on agricultural imports (quotas) into tariff equivalents (tariffication) – was not upheld by the EU, but it did have an influence on thinking within the European Commission on how best to maintain commitments to the ACP, eventually resulting in the acceptance of partial tariffication.

The consumer

The differential regimes in the EU gave rise to differing prices and levels of consumption. The highest consumption was in Germany at 14.9 kg per capita in 1992 as against 8.2 kg in the UK and 8.5 kg in France (EU average 9.3 kg).[18] The lowest prices were in Germany where in August 1991 bananas cost US$1.3 a kilo compared to US$2.07 in the UK. The free market therefore clearly benefited the consumer. The problem was, that if a free market was introduced, prices would be too low for EU and ACP producers. The market would therefore have to be 'managed', bearing in mind international obligations as well as consumer interests.

The transnationals

The dominant position of the US transnationals in the EU market was an 'unstated' but very real concern. One of the major aims of the SEM was improved efficiency through greater competitiveness. In a free market the US TNCs would dominate and prosper. By contrast, established European companies in protected markets would face difficulties and could even have been forced out of business. If that were to happen there was a fear that the US TNCs would take advantage of market dominance to increase the price of bananas to consumers. The problem was therefore one of finding appropriate mechanisms to keep the efficient EU companies in business as a means to further competition in general, while safeguarding specific European interests in particular.

These various problems were obviously not open to easy solution. The European Commission first began to consider the problem as a whole in 1988 but it did not reach any conclusion until April 1992 when it determined the general approach to be taken in drafting the regulation. The period in between was one of intense lobbying, particularly by the ACP producer countries in the Caribbean in concert with banana companies in the UK and the West India Committee. The prime ministers from ACP Caribbean countries were regular visitors to Brussels where they argued the case for a continued 'managed market' most forcefully. Within the Commission itself this found a sympathetic response from officials responsible for agriculture (DG 6) and development (DG8). The opposite case, that for free trade, was supported by those responsible for external affairs (DG1), but was not as intensively lobbied by the Latin American producers or the US TNCs. They appear to have relied on the United States within GATT, and on Germany and the 'dollar' banana importer nexus within the EU to carry their case. In the event, they were not as well co-ordinated as the 'managed market' lobby. Unsurprisingly, the Commission proposals, when they finally emerged in August 1992, leaned in favour of the ACP and EU producers. They proposed a common regime on bananas, which would give free entry to ACP and EU bananas and limit the entry of Latin American bananas by quota and tariff. They also proposed an aid package to allow EU and ACP producers to adjust to the new situation. Finally, it was specified that the regulation be subject to approval by qualified majority vote in the Agricultural Council of the Community.[19]

Solution

The new banana regime

The essential features of the NBR were adopted at the Agricultural Council meeting in Brussels in mid-December 1992. This set a basic tariff-free quota for ACP bananas at levels no less than traditional supplies; levied a tariff on banana imports from Latin America up to a fixed 2 million tonnes quota at a duty of ECU 100 per tonne and imposed a tariff of ECU 850 per tonne on imports above that level; established a 'partnership arrangement' whereby traditional importers of ACP and DOM bananas were to receive licences to import up to one-third of 'Latin American' bananas to enable them to cross-subsidise their operations; included a 'safeguard clause' to limit the entry of 'Latin American' bananas to the EU market if traditional ACP and DOM supplies were disrupted; and agreed to establish the new regime from 1 July 1993 with interim measures to be enforced up to this time. The regime was opposed by Germany, Denmark and Portugal (which voted against),[20] but was welcomed as consistent with 'the interests of ACP and of EC banana producers' by John Gummer, the British Minister of Agriculture, who noted that 'small, vulnerable democratic nations like Jamaica and St Lucia will have access to their traditional EC market whilst having a real opportunity to grow and compete'.[21]

The hostile reaction to the proposed regime in Germany, Denmark, Belgium and the Netherlands, as well as in Latin America, led to several changes being introduced when the Agricultural Council met again in February 1993 to approve the new regulations. These allowed the 2 million tonne quota to be adjusted on a monthly basis in line with demand; established that under licensing arrangements traditional importers of 'Latin American' bananas should not be disadvantaged; and agreed to regard any significant rise in price as an indication of a shortage which would require a review of the import regime.[22] These concessions, however, were still not enough for Germany, which again voted against, and Belgium and the Netherlands, which broke with precedent and reversed their previous December position of support. The regulations only passed by receiving the support of Denmark, which now occupied the rotating presidency of the EU and was obliged to defend the integrity of EU procedures by supporting measures already agreed in substance.[23]

Reactions

The immediate reactions to the NBR took a number of forms, from unqualified welcome to implacable opposition. The result was a regime that was under siege from its inception and subject to intense pressures to improve or maintain it, on the one hand, or to weaken or destroy it, on the other. The regime was finally to win a measure of acceptance from some of those most opposed, with the conclusion of a 'Framework Agreement' at the end of 1994.

The European dimension

The opposition of Germany to the new regime of a 'Europe-wide managed market' for bananas was predictable. Germany stood to lose the most, with consumers facing higher prices and banana importers facing declining markets. The initial steps were therefore for consumers, importers and the government to seek an injunction against the introduction of the regime in the European Court of Justice (ECJ). The German government did so on a number of grounds, including breach of procedure, breach of substantive rules of Community law and infringement of both the Lomé Convention (including the Banana Protocol) and GATT rules. German importers and consumers did so on the grounds that their interests were directly and adversely affected.

The ECJ ruled on the German government's application on 30 June 1993. The injunction was not approved, thereby permitting the NBR to be established from 1 July. It did, however, indicate that compensation might be due to marketing companies and others adversely affected by the regime; and did agree that the case for the German government should be heard. On 8 June 1994 an 'Opinion of the ECJ' rejected that case, stating that in making the original decision to establish the regime the Council of Ministers had not overstepped its powers. The final ruling, issued on 5 October 1994, confirmed this judgement.[24] The possibility of overturning the regime in the courts was effectively lost.

Equally as predictable was the support for the new regime from the UK and France, though qualified by a direct understanding of the national interests involved. In the French case this rested, above all, on support for banana producers in the DOM. In the British case it focused on the Windward Islands. Indeed, it was on the advice and with the encouragement of the British government that the Windward Islands first entered into commercial banana production in the 1960s. The interests of Geest, a major British agro-industrial company which provided shipping and support services in the UK for Windward bananas, were also directly involved. It was therefore in the wider interests of the UK to secure a regime that provided support to the banana industry in these islands. It is important to recognise, however, that the UK was not as directly engaged as France and that it saw the question primarily in commercial terms, i.e. the maintenance in the short-to-medium-term of a market for Caribbean ACP bananas in the UK as an aid to British companies. The question of the consequences for the islands themselves was not as dominant or as immediate as in the French case, although the British government was mindful of the importance of the industry in the Windwards and active on their behalf within the EU.

The Caribbean dimension

The ACP Caribbean welcomed the NBR. Charles Savarin, the Ambassador for Dominica to the EU and the Caribbean diplomat most directly involved in the negotiation of the regime, wrote to the Danish Presidency of the EU Council shortly after its conclusion in February 1993 thanking the EU for its 'herculean efforts ... which allows the EC to honour its many obligations under the fourth Lomé Convention'. Savarin also noted that the regime was a hard fought compromise and that it was 'possibly the only one in the circumstances'.[25]

The regulation fixed annual quotas and made provision for financial assistance. Quotas for the ACP Caribbean were set at Belize 40,000 tonnes; Dominica 71,000; Grenada 14,000; Jamaica 105,000; St Lucia 127,000; St Vincent 82,000; and Suriname 38,000. These were calculated from the size of the average volume of exports during the five years prior to 1991, after excluding the best and worst years and on this basis were deemed to be 'traditional quantities'. No provision was made for their revision. Quotas for Guadeloupe and Martinique, territories for which financial assistance was available, were established at 150,000 tonnes and 219,000 tonnes respectively.

These quotas were based on imports for the best year from each source prior to 1991 and were subject to adjustment. Provision was also made for a quota to be allocated to the Dominican Republic under arrangements covering the import of non-traditional ACP bananas.[26]

Assistance was also promised. In the case of the DOM this was very generous and took the form of compensation for loss of income from the difference between costs of production and market prices. In the first year this was set at 245 ECU per tonne. In the case of the ACP there were difficulties. The original Commission proposal was submitted on 11 November 1992, but was stalled in Council variously by the UK, Belgium, Germany and the Netherlands and was only approved in October 1994.[27] As finally agreed, this provided 180 million ECU for three years, retrospective to July 1993. The amounts ultimately made available, however, were well short of this total.

The Latin American dimension

The Latin American reaction to the NBR was hostile and took the expected form of consultation among themselves and an appeal to the GATT. Immediately following the adoption of the British proposal of December 1992 there were demonstrations in Ecuador, and Ecuador acted as host to a meeting of presidents from Colombia, Costa Rica, Guatemala, Nicaragua and Panama (with Mexico and Venezuela in attendance), which met during final negotiation of the regime in Brussels in February 1993. At the end of the meeting they issued a joint declaration stating that the EU proposals were 'protectionist, discriminatory and restrictive' and should be reconsidered. Shortly afterwards Ecuador submitted a motion to the Council of the Organisation of American States condemning the EU proposals (it and a countermotion by CARICOM were later set aside); and the matter was raised at the annual meeting of EU-Central American foreign ministers in San Salvador on 22/23 February, though without resolution of the differences. A communiqué issued by the Central American countries at the end of the meeting deplored the regime and claimed that it took no account of advances in trade liberalisation expressed in the then current Uruguay Round negotiations. The response of the EU foreign ministers was a statement maintaining that 'the EC's intention in adopting the regime was to achieve a fair and workable balance between the interests of Community producers and consumers and of ACP and Latin American suppliers as well as international obligations'.[28] Following the meeting Costa Rica and Ecuador called for a further meeting of Latin American producers, to take place in April. In the meantime, Colombia, Costa Rica, Guatemala, Nicaragua and

Venezuela had referred the matter to GATT which convened one of the two panels requested.

The GATT

The GATT was called into action immediately following the adoption of the regime. The Latin American countries which constituted the complainants sought two panels. The first was to examine the regime up to 1 July 1993 and the second from that date. The first panel was approved and began work straight away. Written and oral evidence was presented by the complainants (Colombia, Nicaragua, Costa Rica, Guatemala and Venezuela) and the defendants (the EU). The ACP, however, was unable to agree a joint position and a separate African presentation was made. Jamaica's ambassador subsequently made a Caribbean presentation with the support of interested parties in the region and outside. The panel reported at the end of May and issued two rulings. The first found that the quantitative restrictions maintained by France, Italy, Portugal, Spain and the UK in the market (i.e. the transitional arrangements in effect to 1 July) were inconsistent with both the GATT articles and existing legislation under which EU member states had become contracting parties to the GATT. The panel therefore recommended that the existing regime be brought into conformity with the GATT. The second ruling found that the tariff preference accorded by the EU to bananas originating in ACP countries was inconsistent with Article 1 of the GATT, and ruled that a legal justification for granting such preference could not arise from the Lomé Convention but only from the action of the GATT contracting parties. The EU was therefore obliged to seek approval of the GATT for any preferential arrangement entered into under Lomé.

The first ruling was largely for the record in the sense that the regime to which it referred was to end within weeks. It did, however, add force to the cause of the Latin American complainants who were seeking the establishment of a second GATT panel. The EU, having successfully resisted this in March, now found itself under intense pressure, particularly in the light of the second ruling, which had implications well beyond bananas. The EU and the ACP therefore joined forces to oppose the adoption of the first panel report at the GATT Council on 16 June. They met with mixed success. On the one hand, the Council agreed to delay decision on the report until late July; on the other hand, a second panel was convened, though it was not given fast-track approval. This provided a breathing space for the EU and the ACP and allowed other interests to be consulted. The ACP was also successful in winning the agreement of GATT to provide it with technical assistance in producing its evidence to the second panel.

The second panel reported in February 1994. It upheld the complaint that the NBR, introduced from 1 July 1993, was in contravention of the GATT. It also found against the idea of preference as enshrined in the Lomé Convention. The ruling was therefore once again vigorously contested by the EU and the ACP since, if adopted, it would have obliged the EU to seek an annual waiver from the GATT for the Lomé Convention. This likely requirement was now more of an irritation than the actual arrangements surrounding bananas, given that the outlines of a deal involving bananas had been worked out with the US as a 'Framework Agreement' and was even then under consideration by the Latin American banana-producing countries.

The United States dimension

The NBR was finalised during the transition from the Bush to the Clinton presidency. The question of whether the US would accept it or oppose it was therefore uncertain, although it was known that senior officials in both the Trade Representative's Office and the State Department believed it was counter to established US policy on free trade. The first signs that this would be the approach taken by the Clinton administration surfaced in April 1993 when a letter from the US Ambassador in London to the High Commissioner for St Lucia took the view that the ACP had gained considerably from the regime to the disadvantage of US companies selling dollar bananas to the EU. However, it was not until the discussion of the first GATT panel that US opposition was formally recorded. In the GATT Council the US pushed for immediate endorsement of the first panel and then pressed for the early establishment, under fast-track procedure, of a second panel. A week later the US Deputy Assistant Secretary of State for Latin America and the Caribbean, Donna Hrinak, issued a public statement explaining the US position:

> The European Community is proposing an unrealistic policy of preference for Caribbean bananas which is not in the best long-term interests of the Caribbean ... The EC banana regime as proposed is inconsistent with the obligation GATT members have and inconsistent with what we hope would be the outcome of the Uruguay round which when terminated will be of benefit to all trading partners ... There is no region of the world that needs to look more seriously at its role in the 21st century than the Caribbean. We have moved beyond

the age where trade preferences are the rule and any country that wants to benefit from free trade will have to look very seriously at what changes it needs to make in its economic structure to accommodate some of the needs of its trading partners.[29]

The hard line taken by the US was tempered by a recognition that a 'transition period' was needed and that funds from the United States Agency for International Development might be mobilised to promote 'diversification'.[30] Nevertheless, it was clear that the US interest in this matter was tied to the interests of US banana companies and that, inevitably, this meant qualified support for Latin American banana producers. The arena in which this could be most forcefully expressed was the GATT and the US was undoubtedly active 'behind the scenes' in support of the Latin American complainants. At the same time it was engaged in a wider discussion with the EU on concluding the Uruguay Round. The US position was therefore one that had to acknowledge wider and more important interests.

The Framework Agreement

Although the EU contained the initial challenge to the NBR via the GATT, the strength of the assault led to some modification of the regime in favour of the Latin American producer countries. This emerged in the draft 'Framework Agreement' on bananas put forward by the EU in the final stages of the GATT negotiations with the US. The agreement increased the EU's global quota in 1994 and 1995 by 100,000 tonnes in each year and divided the quota by country in the following proportions: Costa Rica 23.4 per cent; Colombia 20.2 per cent; Panama 19.7 per cent; Honduras 6.6 per cent; Nicaragua 1.8 per cent; Guatemala 1.8 per cent; and Venezuela and others, including ACP countries exporting non-traditional quantities (notably the Dominican Republic), 4.8 per cent or 80,000 tonnes whichever was lower.[31] The draft agreement also included a mechanism to allow the Commission to reallocate unused quota and provided for up to 75 per cent of quota to be supplied against export certificates from supplying countries, so enhancing the position of countries as against companies in the organisation of trade. In return for accepting the new agreement Latin American countries were to drop their complaint in GATT.

Whether by design or accident, the new proposal had the effect of beginning to sow differences between the hitherto united Latin American banana producers. Although several were thought to be inclined to accept the new offer, Guatemala, Ecuador, Honduras and Panama were forceful in opposing any new deal in advance of the second GATT panel which was expected to report within a few weeks. Guatemala, in particular, was vociferous in its objections, arguing that the overall dollar banana quota should be raised to 2.5 million tonnes. Indeed, the intransigence of Guatemala, and the failure of a meeting between the Latin American producers and the Commission to make any progress on this issue, were subsequently cited by the EU as the reason for a temporary withdrawal of its offer on 11 February 1994. At the same time the EU rejected the finding of the second GATT panel in favour of the Latin American countries. The impasse, however, was more contrived than real and in a clarification issued a few days later by René Steichen, the European Commissioner for Agriculture, the Latin American producers were informed that the offer was still on the table and that there could be an imminent increase in imports of Latin American bananas to offset recent shortages on the European market. The latter promise was given credence in late March when the Commission agreed an import ceiling of 590,120 tonnes for April to June 1994 (an increase of over 70,000 tonnes over the first quarter of 1994).

On 29 March 1994, Colombia, Costa Rica, Nicaragua and Venezuela withdrew their complaint from GATT and settled with the EU. The revised regime under the FA increased the tariff quota to 2.1 million tonnes in 1994 and 2.2 million tonnes in 1995. The in-quota tariff was also reduced to 75 ECU per tonne. Quota levels were fixed at Costa Rica 23.4 per cent, Colombia 21 per cent, Nicaragua 3 per cent and Venezuela 2 per cent. Governments were given the right to issue 70 per cent of export licences. An additional quota of 90,000 tonnes of 'non-traditional' imports was also agreed, a measure which would directly benefit the Dominican Republic. The new arrangements were to come into force from October (though they were delayed and finally implemented from 1 January 1995). In return for these concessions, the governments of Costa Rica, Colombia, Nicaragua and Venezuela agreed not to initiate GATT proceedings during the life of the regime which was to run to the end of December 2002.[32]

The important point to note about the FA is that it was negotiated and agreed between the EU and US at the end of December 1993 as part of the Uruguay Round. As such, it was tied to wider concerns and included US interests in respect of its banana companies operating in Latin America as well as its relations with Latin American countries. It also represented a compromise of sorts by the EU in respect of the improved offer it gave to the Latin American countries in exchange for them not pursuing the matter further in the GATT. Finally, in respect of divergent interests in the EU, Germany agreed the FA only on the understanding that it would not prevent it from continuing to seek redress in the ECJ and that the proposal from the Commission on legislation for the implementation of the Agreement would take German interests fully into account. In so far as the FA was the critical document in finally getting acceptance of the NBR it can be regarded as bearing the essential elements of a compromise, acceptable in some degree to most interested parties but not to all.

Practice

Although the banana regime was now established, it immediately came under challenge from a number of powerful interests which eventually were to mount a successful challenge to it in the new WTO.

The transnationals

The effects of the NBR on European companies were mixed. In the UK and France dramatic falls in prices, as a consequence of lax enforcement of the rules elsewhere in the EU, undermined the profitability of established companies such as Geest, which sold out its banana interests at the end of 1995. Germany also complained about enforcement, except that in its case it was occasioned by rising prices and cutbacks in consumption of the order of 30–40 per cent. This led to cuts in imports and the downsizing of operators.

At the same time EU companies benefited from the rules governing licences. The December 1992 proposals distributed licences on what was termed a 'partnership basis'. This favoured traditional importers of ACP and EU bananas in as much as they were eligible for licences to import up to one-third of Latin American bananas, the rationale being that this would act as a cross-subsidy improving the viability of their operations in respect of ACP/EU bananas. This discrimination was vigorously contested by the 'dollar banana' companies and in the NBR agreed in February changes were introduced which were more favourable to traditional importers of Latin American bananas. They, together with non-traditional ACP operators, were given a 66.5 per cent quota allocation on the basis of imports for the previous three years (known as the A quota); traditional ACP/EU operators were given a 30 per cent allocation with the same reference period (the B quota); and 3.5 per cent of quota was reserved for newcomers. Eligibility for licences was to be non-transferable and it was eventually decided that the share of traditional quota for Latin American bananas was to be based on a 70/30 split, with Latin

American governments issuing licences for 70 per cent of agreed quota with the remainder allocated to the companies.

The effects of the NBR on US TNCs were more uncertain. They were to some extent disadvantaged: hence their appeal to the US government for support. At the same time they remained dominant in the EU market and a study by consultants Arthur D. Little International found that, while the share of the three US transnationals in the EU market had fallen from 43.5 per cent in 1991 to 41.5 per cent in 1994, Dole and Del Monte had actually increased their market share and only Chiquita had lost out significantly, with a drop from 25 per cent of the market to 18.5 per cent. This was attributed largely to Chiquita's previous policy of oversupply designed to improve its relative position in the European market at the time the NBR was being negotiated and was regarded as a mistaken strategy which had occasioned sizeable losses for which only the company itself could be held responsible.[33]

The United States

In early September 1994 Chiquita Brands International, along with the Hawaii Banana Association, filed an application with the US government under Section 301 of the US Trade Act alleging that the EU banana regime seriously damaged their interests. This was the first application of its kind under the Clinton administration and followed a petition sent the previous month by twelve senators to Mickey Kantor, the US Trade Representative, calling for a formal inquiry into the NBR. It was also the culmination of a long lobbying campaign by Carl Lindner, head of Financial Corporation of which Chiquita is a part, against the EU's banana regime. In the course of this campaign and the pursuit of other interests, Lindner is said to have paid US$430,000 to the Republican Party and US$525,000 to the Democratic Party between January 1993-December 1994, as well as US$55,000 to Speaker of the House Newt Gingrich's GOPAC.[34] He also recruited Senator Bob Dole to his cause, persuading him to add a rider to the US Budget Bill (with the consent of Gingrich) seeking sanctions against Colombia and Costa Rica for their support for the NBR.

On 17 October Kantor announced the US would be taking up the complaint. He noted that 'American banana marketing companies should be able to compete on a fair basis in a European market, just as European firms can here'. He also indicated that the FA might also be a subject for investigation since it was 'discriminatory against US companies'.[35] One month later, this action was endorsed by several prominent US politicians, including Senator Dole and Speaker Gingrich, who, in a letter to

President Clinton, urged him to 'move with dispatch to issue an "unfairness" determination and commence retaliation against EU trade interests proportionate to the enormous US harm already caused by the EU Banana Policy'.[36]

On 9 January 1995 Kantor issued a statement indicating that a preliminary examination had concluded that the NBR was 'adversely affecting US economic interests',[37] and on 27 September he confirmed this view in a further statement indicating that the US would file a complaint against the EU at the WTO alleging discrimination against US companies in respect of the licensing system and the assignment of quotas. This was followed by another finding on 10 January 1996, announcing the results of an investigation into the banana regimes in Colombia and Costa Rica. Although this determined that the policies of both countries were unfair, Kantor lifted the threat of trade sanctions in favour of dialogue, as set within Memoranda of Understanding signed with both countries. These Memoranda committed Colombia and Costa Rica to join with the US to press for reform of the NBR as well as to alter their quotas in a way favourable to US interests, i.e. allocating a larger share to US transnationals.

Latin America

The Latin American countries opposed to the NBR sought common ground with the US. Its petition to the WTO in September 1995 was supported by Guatemala, Honduras and Mexico. A second petition (filed on 7 February 1996 and superseding the first) added Ecuador as well. The new rules governing disputes under the WTO specify that if consultations do not resolve the issue within sixty days a panel is established whose ruling is binding. On 9 April the parties to the dispute (the US, the Caribbean ACP and the Latin American producers) met in Miami to determine whether a solution could be found but failed to make headway. A letter released to US newspapers by Ecuador, Honduras and Guatemala immediately afterwards emphasised the damage done to their interests by the NBR and praised 'the commitment of the United States to dismantling the dangerous precedent-setting policies of the EU banana regime'.[38]

The Caribbean

The Caribbean ACP found itself engaged in a defence of its interest on all fronts – in the EU, in the region and in the US. The main issues in the EU were price and quota. Returns to growers in the Caribbean continued to diminish. In 1993 the average annual price to growers in the

Windward Islands was EC$0.32 compared to EC$0.41 in 1992.[39] When compounded with losses from hurricanes, such as Debbie in 1994 and Iris, Luis and Marilyn in 1995, the overall effect was to depress export earnings considerably. In 1994 for the four Windward Islands they stood at EC$216 million (their lowest level for ten years); in 1996 they were EC$224 million and in 1997 EC$148.[40] Compounding this were concerns over the operation of quotas. The total quota for the import of traditional ACP bananas in the Caribbean was set at 477,000 tonnes. In both 1993 and 1994 the quantities marketed were below quota. The Caribbean ACP requested that, when this was due to *force majeure*, as in the case of hurricanes, replacements could be sought from alternative sources, including Latin America. It also requested that unused ACP quota should be transferable to another ACP state. On these issues the Commission proved sympathetic. Counter balancing them, however, was the Commission's proposal (discussed shortly) for an additional quota for Latin American bananas following on the enlargement of the EU. This was opposed by the ACP as a threat to the maintenance of both price and quota.

The regional dimension focused on institutional reorganisation. The NBR served as a stimulus to the fundamental restructuring of banana production and marketing in the Windward Islands. In March 1994, a new banana holding company, the Windward Islands Banana Development and Export Company (WIBDECO), was established to replace the Windward Islands Banana Growers Association, and immediately entered into negotiations with Geest to ensure a better return to the growers. A new contract, which enhanced the position of WIBDECO in marketing bananas, was agreed in December 1994 and a further restructuring of the industry to improve competitiveness and management was approved in mid-1995. Finally, on 22 December 1995, WIBDECO announced that it was entering into a joint venture with Fyffes to buy Geest's banana interests for £147.5 million. This action was taken, in part, to preclude the sale of Geest to Noboa, an Ecuadorian company whose interest in acquiring Geest was seen as entirely hostile.

Lastly, the Caribbean ACP mounted a robust defence of the NBR against the US. The US, in discussions with the Caribbean ACP that began in Washington in March 1995, made a distinction between the trade preferences accorded to the region under the Lomé Convention, which it said it did not challenge, and other elements of the NBR, which it did, namely quota and licences.[41] In subsequent meetings these concerns were spelt out as (i) a larger EU quota for Latin American bananas and (ii) the abolition of the B quota, which, as noted earlier, allowed 30 per cent of Third World country import licences to be granted to traders that handled ACP and EU bananas. Neither of these proposals was acceptable to the Caribbean. A final attempt at a solution in Miami in April 1996 ended with the Caribbean claiming the US had come to the meeting with its mind already made up to refer the dispute to the WTO. Whether true or not, what is clear is that the US position had been unyielding and the Caribbean had had to fight every inch of the way to get its concerns heard. This even extended into the WTO hearings themselves where the US sought at first to exclude the Caribbean ACP from presenting its case, although it was eventually permitted to do so, after vigorous protest, as an interested third party.

The European states

The position of individual EU states on the NBR remained polarised between those in defence of the NBR and those seeking its revision. The leading state in the former camp was France. It defended the interests of the DOM in the Commission and with Germany. It opposed Commission plans to provide additional quotas for Latin American bananas, argued that additional support was needed to enable DOM producers to recover from hurricane damage, and claimed that urgent action was needed to compensate for falling prices.

The leading state in the opposition camp was Germany. It continued to contest the legality of the NBR in the ECJ by asking the Court to rule on the compatibility of the FA with WTO rules and on the regulation giving additional licences to DOM and Windward Island producers to compensate for losses caused by hurricanes. Other interests within Germany followed suit. In April 1995, Atlanta, the largest banana operator in the country, filed a complaint before the German constitutional court claiming that the NBR contravened the Maastricht Treaty;[42] and several months later German importers in Hamburg won a victory in the courts (soon overturned) when they were authorised to buy in bananas at a tariff of 75 ECU per tonne as against ECU 850. All this added weight to German pressure within the EU Council where it sought quota and licence revision in favour of Latin American producers.

The European Commission

On 11 October 1995 the new Commissioner for Agriculture, Franz Fischler, presented a report on the banana regime based on its first two years of operation. In announcing the report he noted that no other regime in the history of the Common Agricultural Policy had been as controversial nor its objectives and impact so misrepresented. He also added that, while adjustments were necessary, he was under no illusion that they would be easy to achieve or would assuage criticisms since 'experience has shown that the word "compromise" is not a word one associates with discussions on the banana regime'.[43] The Commission was manifestly faced with a difficult task. Any recommendation or action/inaction on its part was to the benefit of one party and the injury of another. This was clearly seen in arguments concerning modification of the basic regulations of the NBR to accommodate the enlargement of the EU to include Austria, Sweden and Finland as from January 1995. At issue were quotas and licences.

In April 1995 the Commission adopted proposals for an increased quota for Latin American bananas of 353,000 tonnes (determined by the average of imports for the three countries 1991–3) to take account of enlargement. It did not find favour. When it was first discussed in the Agricultural Council in July 1995, Germany, Denmark and the Benelux countries opposed it on the grounds that the quota increase was inadequate; and Britain, France and Spain on the basis that it would damage the ACP and EU producers. The Commission nevertheless went ahead and authorised it, claiming that it was doing so in order to meet expected consumer demand in the EU. The matter was next aired when the Agricultural Council discussed the report on the regime at the end of 1995. On this occasion Germany, Denmark and the Benelux countries were more supportive but France and Spain continued to object, as also did Ireland (the home base for Fyffes). The result was a decision to refer the report (with its recommendation for quota increase) to a special committee to examine it in detail and report by the end of March 1996. No agreement was reached, however, then or subsequently, leaving the Commission to act under its own market management powers to approve the increased quota.

The licensing arrangements also came under attack. The German government had long sought an increase in Category A licences and a reduction in Category B licences, arguing that it discriminated against importers of Latin American bananas. Once again enlargement brought the issue to a head. The existing distribution, Germany and others claimed, took no account of the fact that all the bananas imported into Austria, Finland and Sweden were sourced in Latin America. To take this into account the existing allocation should be changed in favour of Category A licences. The Commission took some of these arguments on board in proposals put forward in March 1996. These increased the proportion of Category A licences from 66.5 per cent to 70.5 per cent and reduced those for Category B from 30 per cent to 26 per cent. While these new figures clearly constituted a concession to the Latin American producers, the Commission nevertheless insisted that ACP interests would not be injured since the actual volume of bananas imported under Category B licences would remain the same. This was not a view shared by the ACP, importers of ACP and EU bananas, and Britain, France and Spain, all of whom mounted stiff opposition to the proposals.

The World Trade Organisation

On 8 May 1996 the WTO Disputes Settlement Body (DSB) agreed to convene a panel. Hearings were held in September and October and the report of the panel released in April 1997. It found against the NBR in several important respects although, significantly, it did not find against the EU's right to import traditional levels of bananas from the ACP countries at zero level tariff nor against binding the tariff for Latin American bananas at 2.2 million tonnes. The EU appealed against the panel's findings and a final judgement was given in September. Essentially this found that the licensing procedures – which involved the purchase of EU and/or ACP bananas in order to obtain rights to import Latin American bananas – were contrary to the non-discrimination provisions of GATT; that the tariff quota allocations to individual ACP countries were contrary to GATT; and that there were inconsistencies regarding service suppliers which were contrary to the General Agreement on Trade in Services concluded as part of the Uruguay Round. It also found against the transferability of country quotas and the allocation of hurricane licences to ACP/EU operators.

Not surprisingly, the WTO ruling was welcomed by the US and Chiquita. The latter stated it was 'extremely gratified', adding:

> This is the fourth time in four years that an independent international trade body has declared the EU banana regime to be illegal. Like the five governments that brought the case, Chiquita and many other banana trade interests look forward to full EU conformity with the ruling. Over 50 per cent of Chiquita's EU market share was illegally taken from it as a result of this EU policy.[44]

In the Caribbean, the ruling was met with anger and dismay. An emergency meeting of Windward Island banana-exporting countries held in Dominica issued a strong condemnation of the WTO:

> We feel betrayed by the WTO, because we joined the Organisation believing that its primary purpose was to bring about improved living standards and equity and fairness in international trade; that it would be the one which would ensure that the rule of the jungle, in which the powerful ride

roughshod over the smaller members of the trading community, would not be condoned. What we find is that the WTO has ended up being a system in which the legitimate interests of small countries will always be sacrificed once they conflict with those of the major players.[45]

In sum, the operation of the NBR and the interaction of the various interests concerned with it were, to say the least, complex. The NBR was neither neat nor satisfactory to all the parties. This was frankly recognised by Fischler, the Commissioner responsible for its operation. He stated that, while personally he had 'never particularly liked the banana regime', he recognised it as the only possible outcome that could be adopted. Accordingly, 'as a key element of our market organisation we cannot change it, but we may well be able to make adjustment'.[46] In pursuit of this goal some changes were mooted, though resisted, as noted above. More to the point, they were made redundant by the WTO ruling of 25 September 1997. This left the EU with little alternative but to modify the NBR to comply. It agreed to come forward with a revised regime effective from 1 January 1999.

Revision

The discussions and controversy around the formulation and implementation of the revised banana regime (RBR) echo those of the NBR. Once again, many interests were diametrically opposed and the Caribbean ACP found itself exposed to circumstances beyond its control.

The European Union

The European Commission set out its proposals for the RBR on 14 January 1998. The tariff quota was maintained at 2.2 million tonnes with a duty of 75 ECU per tonne; a further autonomous tariff quota of 353,000 tonnes was established at a duty of 300 ECU per tonne to take account of EU enlargement; with additional imports above these levels attracting a tariff of 765 ECU per tonne. The import licensing arrangements distinguishing between A and B licences were to be abolished in favour of a system that was to be WTO-compatible, most probably on the lines of distinguishing between traditional suppliers and newcomers to the EU market. The maximum quantity for traditional ACP suppliers was maintained at the current level of 857,700 tonnes at zero duty but with such a quota not being allocated to individual countries as had previously been the case; and the tariff preference for non-traditional ACP imports was raised to 200 ECU per tonne. Finally, to enable traditional ACP suppliers to continue to maintain their presence on the EU market, a special scheme of assistance was proposed over a ten-year period to enable them to improve their competitiveness.[47]

The proposals were examined in the Agricultural Council in February 1998. The principal question raised was that of WTO-compatibility. Germany, Sweden, Austria and the Netherlands were doubtful and persuaded the Council to refer the matter to the legal services division for expert opinion. They also wanted the tariff for the new autonomous quota reduced to 75 ECU per tonne. France, Spain, Greece and Portugal also had reservations, which focused on how the scheme would operate in respect of their home suppliers to the EU market. They sought additional assistance for them and a reduction in the autonomous quota. Nevertheless, no EU country opposed the scheme outright and the UK, which had the presidency, was instructed to develop the details of the regime and itself expressed confidence that it could successfully win approval of the RBR within the EU by the time it handed over the presidency in June 1998.

On 26 June the Agricultural Council agreed the RBR following a four-day meeting in which the regime was extensively discussed along with other controversial agricultural measures. The principal changes to the February proposals met the objections made then. There was a reduction on the autonomous quota rate tariff to 75 ECU per tonne and an 8 per cent increase in the amount of aid given to EU banana producers to give them a guaranteed price of 640.3 ECU per tonne. The position of the ACP remained as outlined, with traditional importers being favoured. In announcing the agreement the UK Agricultural Minister, Jack Cunningham, said: 'I personally have been very concerned to ensure that the revised arrangements secure continuing stability in the Caribbean as well as being fully defensible in the WTO. I am very pleased we have been able to reach an agreement which meets both sets of international obligations'.[48]

The final elements of the RBR were put in place with the adoption of Council Regulation 1637/98, modifying the regime on 26 July and the adoption on 28 October of Council Regulation 2362/98, setting out the new licensing arrangements. Under the latter, rights to import were given to those operators who used licences to import (as distinct from those who simply traded them) with a reference period 1994–6. Quota allocations were given to all substantial banana exporters to the EU, with 26 per cent each given to Ecuador and Costa Rica, 23 per cent to Colombia and 16 per cent to Panama. The share for 'newcomers' was increased from 3.5 per cent to 8 per cent.

The United States and the World Trade Organisation

The US response to the Commission's proposals for a RBR was immediate and hostile. In a press conference in Washington the day after they
were announced, Peter Scher, the Special Trade Ambassador, stated:
'we do not view this proposal as acceptable and our view is that the EU
needs to go back to the drawing board. ... The proposals do not give the
United States and Latin American countries enough access to sell their
bananas in the EU'.[49] This was followed by complaints from several
Latin American producers until, with the adoption of the RBR in June,
the US and the Latin American countries which had brought the
original complaint announced they would once again be taking the case
to the WTO. The matter was finally brought to a head towards the end
of 1998. On 10 October President Clinton addressed a letter to the US
House of Representatives outlining the unilateral retaliatory action his
administration was considering taking in early 1999 under Section 301
of its Trade Act. This drew an immediate and angry response from the
Commission. In a letter to Clinton, Jacques Santer, the President of the
Commission, claimed that 'unilateral action of this sort would be a clear
breach of the US's WTO commitments', adding:

> I cannot overstate the political importance of this matter for
> the Commission and the Member States. The European
> Union will therefore have to raise this matter at the
> next meeting of the WTO Dispute Settlement Body on
> 25 November and at the same time start dispute settlement in
> the WTO – unless the US has indicated before that date that
> it has decided to desist from unilateral action.[50]

Eventually, and following yet further procedural wrangling on the
involvement or otherwise of the WTO, the EU sought to force the US
hand by asking the DSB on 15 December to set up a panel to examine
the RBR 'with the mandate to find that (its regime) must be presumed
to conform to WTO rules unless their conformity has been duly challenged under the appropriate DSB procedures'.[51] In January the WTO
approved such a panel (a request for a panel had also been received
from Ecuador) and the original panel which had met to decide the
earlier complaints was reconvened.

The panel delivered its rulings on 6 April and 12 April 1999. The
first found that aspects of the RBR were inconsistent with the EU's
obligations under the GATT and upheld the right of the US to impose
retaliatory action on US$185 million worth of EU goods to compen-
sate for lost trade (the US had claimed losses of US$520 million).[52]
The second found that the quota and licensing system discriminated
against US marketing companies and Latin American suppliers and

suggested four ways under which the RBR could conform to rules: a tariff system including duty-free ACP imports; a tariff system with a quota for ACP bananas; a global quota regime without specific country quotas, together with duty-free ACP imports; or a quota regime in which country shares were negotiated with suppliers.[53] On 21 April the EU decided not to appeal against the rulings and to amend its regime accordingly (only three EU states favoured a further appeal). The US had won, although the EU could take comfort from the fact that the principle of giving preferential treatment to ACP bananas under Lomé remained intact.

The Caribbean

The main criticisms and concerns of the Caribbean ACP came to focus on three aspects of the RBR. The first was the proposal to grant an overall quota for ACP bananas instead of individual country quotas. This was likely to put ACP banana producers in the Windward Islands at a disadvantage compared to other ACP producers, particularly in West Africa, where Dole and Del Monte owned plantations and from where increased exports had led to an expanded European market share. The second was the proposed dismantling of the B licence system that provided an incentive to operators to import ACP and EU bananas in spite of their higher costs (approximately double those of Latin American producers). The cross subsidy from the sale of licences under this system was worth around 80 million ECU per year to the ACP producers.[54] The third was additional financial and technical assistance from the EU to help the ACP adapt to the new market conditions and increase competitiveness. The sum proposed was 367 million ECU to the twelve traditional ACP banana producers over a ten-year period. While the promise of aid was welcome, the amount offered was seen as inadequate and unlikely to meet the investment levels needed to ensure future competitiveness or provide for diversification away from bananas.

The Caribbean continued to lobby on all three points, winning support from the European Parliament and from major NGDOs like Oxfam which produced a widely circulated briefing on the subject.[55] The matter was also the subject of resolutions in the ACP-EU Joint Assembly and of deliberation and recommendation by the International Development Committee of the House of Commons in the UK in its report on the future of the Lomé Convention. The sum effect was to heighten public awareness of the issue, but at best only marginal changes favourable to the ACP were admitted into the regulation governing the trading aspect of the regime whilst the aid to be given to the

ACP still awaits final approval, being the subject of dispute between the European Parliament and the European Council.

As regards the dispute between the WTO and the EU, the Caribbean remained marginalised and dependent on access to the EU to defend its interests. The nearest it was able to come to direct action was the refusal by Dominica and St Lucia at the end of January 1999 to approve the agenda of the WTO DSB as long as it contained the request for punitive action against the EU. This held up proceedings for two days.[56] The final rulings, when given by the WTO, brought immediate condemnation. At a meeting on 16 April, immediately prior to the Association of Caribbean States summit in Santo Domingo, the heads of government of CARICOM concluded that the rulings represented the single most dangerous threat to the economies of the Caribbean exporting countries and that their implementation, without consideration of the vulnerability of the Caribbean banana industry, would lead to severe social and economic dislocations throughout the region.[57] They agreed to visit EU member states and the US as a matter of priority to discuss the outcome and try to influence the shape of a yet further revised regime. In so doing, P. J. Patterson, the Prime Minister of Jamaica, stated that the Caribbean was prepared to work with the EU 'in finding solutions that are acceptable to the WTO and the contending parties'.[58]

Beyond that, the only other immediate course of action was against the US. The possibility of 'issue linkage' between bananas and drugs had been mooted by Billie Miller, the Foreign Minister of Barbados, in November 1998 when she urged CARICOM governments not to renew their 'shiprider' drug surveillance agreements with the US unless there was a satisfactory resolution of the banana dispute.[59] The CARICOM heads of government subsequently agreed to review their co-operation with the US, particularly understandings reached at the special meeting with Clinton held in Barbados in May 1997. It is readily apparent that any withdrawal of co-operation on combating the illegal drugs trade would be troubling to the US. But it would also be opposed by the EU which has a substantial drugs programme in the region. The likelihood of any such action being seriously pursued is therefore slight.

Conclusion

The outcome in the example of the banana regime points to a difficult future for most countries in the Commonwealth Caribbean. Many have relied on preferential trading arrangements and adroit economic diplomacy to shore up increasingly uncompetitive exports. There has been, and there continues to be, good developmental reasons for such policies, notably the social benefits they bring through employment and related political stability. But these arguments no longer enjoy primacy among the most influential players shaping the new global economy. They demand instead macro-economic adjustment and export efficiency. The Caribbean, especially the smaller countries of the region, here find themselves particularly disadvantaged: marginalised in the development policy debate, side-lined in the corridors of power and handicapped by small size and economic dependence. Their acute vulnerability is easily overlooked or brushed aside in the search for the supposedly greater good of global free trade.

In reality, there is not a great deal the Caribbean can do on its own to combat such trends. It will need to make common cause with other small states and other less developed countries to persuade the international system to recognise its particular difficulties. This will not be easy. The banana regime points to the US as the most inflexible and the EU as the most sympathetic to the plight of the Caribbean. But this can mask as much as it reveals, particularly the way in which both the US and the EU have acted in defence of commercial interest, the matter which has lain at the heart of their dispute. The position of the Latin American banana-producing countries also shows the difficulty the Caribbean will face in finding partners when rival economic interests are at stake. This leaves the Caribbean banana-producing countries in the immediate future with little option but to save as much of their banana industry as best they can through programmes to increase international competitiveness. Fortunately, projects are already in hand to improve farming methods and deliver better product quality. There is a belief that the industry can be made viable on a smaller scale and some evidence that this can be achieved. But it will never match the competitiveness of the Latin American producers and will increasingly be subject to the commercial pre-eminence of the US banana TNCs. Its long-term future is thus questionable, which means that the imperative to find development alternatives is the central issue facing the Windward Islands and, by analogy, other parts of the Caribbean with similar situations of domestically desirable, but internationally uncompetitive, agricultural, extractive, industrial and service sectors.

Notes

1   Figures calculated from Commission of the European Communities, *Report on the Operation of the Banana Regime*, SEC (95) 1565 final, Brussels 11/10/1995, Annex 1.

2   Figures calculated from K. Nurse and W. Sandiford, *Windward Island Bananas: Challenges and Options under the Single European Market*, Kingston, 1995, Table 5.3.

3   Figures given in R. H. Pedler, 'The fruit companies and the banana trade regime', in R. H. Pedler and M. P. C. M. Van Schendelen (eds), *Lobbying the European Union: Companies, Trade Associations and Issue Groups*, Aldershot, 1995, pp. 67–91.

4   Nurse and Sandiford, *Windward Island Bananas*, Table 1.3.

5   Pedler, 'The fruit companies and the banana trade regime', Figure 8.

6   Figures calculated from European Commission, *Report on the Operation of the Banana Regime*, Annex 1.

7   Nurse and Sandiford, *Windward Island Bananas*, Table 1.3.

8   Pedler, 'The fruit companies and the banana trade regime', Figure 8.

9   Figures given in Christopher Stevens, 'EU policy for the banana market: the external impact of internal policies', in Helen Wallace and William Wallace (eds), *Policy-Making in the European Union*, Third Edition, Oxford, 1996, pp. 325–51.

10   Nurse and Sandiford, *Windward Island Bananas*, p. 85.

11   Figures calculated from European Commission, *Report on the Operation of the Banana Regime*, Annex 1.

12   Nurse and Sandiford, *Windward Island Bananas*, Table 1.3.

13   Pedler, 'The fruit companies and the banana trade regime', Figure 8.

14   Figures from Stevens, 'EU policy for the banana market'.

15   *Ibid.*

16   Nurse and Sandiford, *Windward Island Bananas*, p. 85.

17   *Ibid.*, p. 88.

18   *Ibid.*, p. 84.

19   Commission of the European Communities, *Proposal for a Council Regulation on the common organization of the market in bananas*, COM (92) 359 final, Brussels, 7 August 1992.

20   For details of the vote, see Pedler, 'The fruit companies and the banana trade regime', pp. 77–86.

21   Caribbean Council for Europe, *Europe/Caribbean Confidential*, London, 17 December 1995.

22   Council Regulation No. 404/93 of 13 February 1993 on the common organisation of the market in bananas, *Official Journal of the European Communities*, No. L 47/1, 25.2.93.

23   See Pedler, 'The fruit companies and the banana trade regime', pp. 84–5.

24   European Court of Justice, *Case C-280/93: Federal Republic of Germany v Commission of the European Communities* (Full Court 5/10/1994).

25   *Europe/Caribbean Confidential*, 17 March 1993.

26   Council Regulation 404/93.

27   Council Regulation No. 2686/94 of 31 October 1994 establishing a special system of assistance to traditional ACP suppliers of bananas, *Official Journal of the European Communities*, No. L 286/1, 5 November 1994.

28   *Europe/Caribbean Confidential*, 17 March 1993.

29   *Ibid.*, 2 July 1993.

30   *Ibid.*

31   *Ibid.*, 20 December 1993.

32   *Ibid.*, 19 April 1994.

33   European Information Service, Brussels, *European Report*, No. 2071, 30 September 1995.

34   *Caribbean Insight*, April 1995.

35   *Europe/Caribbean Confidential*, 21 October 1994.
36   Letter in 'Banana File', Caribbean Council for Europe, London.
37   *Caribbean Insight*, February 1995.
38   *Europe/Caribbean Confidential*, 13 April 1996.
39   Prices given in Overseas Development Administration, *Proposals for Restructuring the Windward Islands Banana Industry*, Report prepared by Cargill Technical Services Ltd, United Kingdom, February 1995, p. 15.
40   *Caribbean Insight*, February 1998.
41   Nurse and Sandiford, *Windward Island Bananas*, p. 125.
42   *Caribbean Insight*, May 1995.
43   European Commission, Spokesman's Service, *Report on the Operation of the Banana Regime*, IP/95/1105, Brussels, 11 October 1995.
44   *Europe/Caribbean Confidential*, 15 September 1997.
45   European Communities, *Courier*, No. 166, November/December 1997, p. 60.
46   *European Report*, No. 2046, 10 June 1995.
47   European Commission, Spokesman's Service, *Press Release IP/98/28*, Brussels, 14 January 1998.
48   *Ibid., Press Release IP/98/575*, Brussels, 26 June 1998.
49   Washington DC, *Inside US Trade*, 16, 2, 16 January 1988.
50   Letter in 'Banana File', Caribbean Council for Europe, London.
51   The International Centre for Trade and Sustainable Development, *BRIDGES Weekly Trade News Digest*, 3, 1 and 2, 18 January 1999.
52   *Caribbean Insight*, April 1999.
53   *Caribbean Insight*, April 1999.
54   *Financial Times*, 13 January 1998.
55   See Claire Godfrey, *A Future for Caribbean Bananas: The Importance of Europe's Banana Market to the Caribbean*, Policy Department, Oxfam, Oxford, March 1998.
56   *Caribbean Insight*, February 1999.
57   Caribbean Council for Europe, *Inside Europe*, 29, 20 April 1999.
58   *Caribbean Insight*, May 1999.
59   *Ibid.*, January 1999.

Select bibliography

Barry, T., B. Wood, and D. Preusch, *The Other Side of Paradise: Foreign Control in the Caribbean*, New York, 1984.

Beckford, G., *Persistent Poverty: Underdevelopment in Plantation Economies of the Third World*, Oxford, 1972.

Beckford, G. (ed.), *Caribbean Economy: Dependence and Backwardness*, Kingston, 1975.

Beckford, G. and N. Girvan, *Development in Suspense*, Kingston, 1989.

Braveboy-Wagner, J. A., *The Caribbean in World Affairs: The Foreign Policies of the English-Speaking States*, Boulder, 1984.

Bryan, A. (ed.), *The Caribbean: New Dynamics in Trade and Political Economy*, New Brunswick, 1995.

Bryan, A., J. E. Greene and T. M. Shaw (eds), *Peace, Development and Security in the Caribbean*, London, 1990.

Caribbean Community Secretariat, *Caribbean Development to the Year 2000: Challenges, Prospects and Policies*, Georgetown, 1988.

Chernick, S., *The Commonwealth Caribbean: The Integration Experience*, Baltimore, 1978.

Clarke, C. (ed.), *Society and Politics in the Caribbean*, London, 1991.

Deere, C. D. *et al.*, *In the Shadows of the Sun: Caribbean Development Alternatives and US Policy*, Boulder, 1990.

Demas, W. G., *The Economics of Development in Small Countries with Special Reference to the Caribbean*, Montreal, 1965.

Dominguez, J. I., R. A. Pastor and R. D. Worrell (eds), *Democracy in the Caribbean*, Baltimore, 1993.

Dunn, H. (ed.), *Globalization, Communications, and Caribbean Identity*, Kingston, 1995.

Edie, C. J. (ed.), *Democracy in the Caribbean: Myths and Realities*, New York, 1994.

Emmanuel, P. A. M., *Governance and Democracy in the Commonwealth Caribbean: An Introduction*, Cave Hill, 1993.

Erisman, M., *Pursuing Postdependency politics: South-South Relations in the Caribbean*, Boulder, Colo., 1992.

Girvan, N. (ed.), *Poverty, Empowerment and Social Development in the Caribbean*, Kingston, 1997.

Girvan, N. and O. Jefferson (eds), *Readings in the Political Economy of the Caribbean*, Kingston, 1971.

Griffin, C. E., *Democracy and Neoliberalism in the Developing World: Lessons from the Anglophone Caribbean*, Aldershot, 1997.

Griffith, I. L., *The Quest for Security in the Caribbean: Problems and Promises in Subordinate States*, New York, 1993.

——, *The Political Economy of Drugs in the Caribbean*, London, 1998.

Griffith, I. L. and B. N. Sedoc-Dahlberg (eds), *Democracy and Human Rights in the Caribbean*, Boulder, 1997.

Grugel, J., *Politics and Development in the Caribbean Basin*, London, 1995.

Henry, P. and C. Stone (eds), *The Newer Caribbean: Decolonisation, Democracy and Development*, Philadelphia, 1983.

Klak, T. (ed.), *Globalization and Neoliberalism: The Caribbean Context*, Lanham, 1998.

Knight. F. and C. Palmer (eds), *The Modern Caribbean*, Chapel Hill, 1989.

LaGuerre, J. G. (ed.), *Structural Adjustment: Public Policy and Administration in the Caribbean*, St Augustine, 1994.

——, *Issues in the Government and Politics of the West Indies: A Reader*, St Augustine, 1997.

Lalta, S. and M. Freckleton (eds), *Caribbean Economic Development: The First Generation*, Kingston, 1993.

Levitt, K. and M. Witter (eds), *The Critical Tradition of Caribbean Political Economy: The Legacy of George Beckford*, Kingston, 1996.

Lewis, G., *The Growth of the Modern West Indies*, London, 1968.

Lowenthal, D., *West Indian Societies*, New York, 1972.

McAfee, K., *Storm Signals: Structural Adjustment and Development Alternatives in the Caribbean*, London, 1991.

Meeks, B., *Radical Caribbean: From Black Power to Abu Bakr*, Kingston, 1996.

Mintz, S. and S. Price (eds), *Caribbean Contours*, Baltimore, 1985.

Maingot, A., *The United States and the Caribbean*, London, 1994.

Mandle, J., *Patterns of Caribbean Development: An Interpretative Essay on Economic Change*, New York, 1982.

Mohammed, P. and C. Shepherd, *Gender in Caribbean Development*, St Augustine, 1988.

Momsen, J. (ed.), *Women and Change in the Caribbean*, Kingston, 1993.

Pastor, R. (ed.), *Migration and Development in the Caribbean: The Unexplored Connection*, Boulder, 1985.

Pattullo, P., *Last Resorts: The Cost of Tourism in the Caribbean*, New York, 1996.

Payne, A. J., *The Politics of the Caribbean Community 1961–79: Regional Integration amongst New States*, Manchester, 1980.

——, *The International Crisis in the Caribbean*, Baltimore, 1984.

Payne, A. J. and P. K. Sutton (eds), *Dependency under Challenge: The Political Economy of the Commonwealth Caribbean*, Manchester, 1984.

——, *Modern Caribbean Politics*, Baltimore, 1993.

Phillips, F., *West Indian Constitutions: Post Independence Reform*, New York, 1985.

Ramsaran, R., *The Commonwealth Caribbean in the World Economy*, London, 1989.

——, *The Challenge of Structural Adjustment in the Commonwealth Caribbean*, New York, 1992.

Richardson, B. C., *The Caribbean in the Wider World, 1492–1992*, Cambridge, 1992.

Ryan, S. and D. Brown (eds), *Issues and Problems in Caribbean Public Administration*, St Augustine, 1992.

Serbin, A., *Sunset over the Islands: The Caribbean in an Age of Global and Regional Challenges*, London, 1998.

Smith, M., *Culture, Race and Class in the Commonwealth Caribbean*, Mona, Jamaica, 1984.

Stone, C., *Power in the Caribbean Basin: A Comparative Study of Political Economy*, Philadelphia, 1986.

Sunshine, C., *The Caribbean: Survival, Struggle and Sovereignty*, Washington DC, 1988.

Sutton, P. K. (ed.), *Dual Legacies in the Contemporary Caribbean: Continuing Aspects of British and French Dominion*, London, 1986.

——, *Europe in the Caribbean*, London, 1991.

Thomas, C., *The Poor and the Powerless: Economic Policy and Change in the Caribbean*, London, 1988.

Thompson, A. O., *The Haunting Past: Politics, Economics and Race in Caribbean Life*, New York, 1997.

Wallace, E., *The British Caribbean: From the Decline of Colonialism to the End of Federation*, Toronto, 1977.

Watson, H. (ed.), *The Caribbean in the Global Political Economy*, Boulder, 1994.

Wedderburn, J. (ed.), *Rethinking Development*, Kingston, 1991.

West Indian Commission, *Time for Action: Report of the West Indian Commission*, Bridgetown 1992.

Worrell, D., *Small Island Economies: Structure and Performance in the English-Speaking Caribbean since 1970*, London, 1988.

Index